—FIVE VIEWS—
ON
APOLOGETICS

Books in the Counterpoints Series

► COUNTERPOINTS ◄

— FIVE VIEWS —
ON
APOLOGETICS

Contributors:

William Lane Craig
Gary R. Habermas
Paul D. Feinberg
John M. Frame
Kelly James Clark

STEVEN B. COWAN
General Editor

STANLEY N. GUNDRY
Series Editor

ZondervanPublishingHouse
Grand Rapids, Michigan

A Division of HarperCollins*Publishers*

Five Views on Apologetics
Copyright © 2000 by Steven B. Cowan

Requests for information should be addressed to:

ZondervanPublishingHouse
Grand Rapids, Michigan 49530

Library of Congress Cataloging-in-Publication Data

Five views on apologetics / Steven B. Cowan, general editor ; William Lane
Craig ... [et al.]
    p. cm. — (Counterpoints)
    Includes bibliographical references and index.
    ISBN 0-310-22476-4 (softcover)
    1. Apologetics. I. Cowan, Steven B., 1962- . II. Craig, William Lane.
III. Counterpoints (Grand Rapids, Mich.)
BT1102.F465   2000
239—dc21   99-053551
                                         CIP

Printed in the United States of America

99 00 01 02 03 04 05 /❖ DC/ 10 9 8 7 6 5 4 3 2 1

CONTENTS

98209

INTRODUCTION

Steven B. Cowan

Fairly early in my life as a Christian—somewhere in my late teens, I think—I discovered apologetics. This discovery was very timely because I had also discovered that the faith I had in Christ was not shared by everyone. In fact, I discovered that some people outright rejected, even ridiculed, my faith. What's more, I found out that skeptics had raised arguments against my faith. And being the inquisitive fellow that I am (I hate unanswered questions!), I wondered myself, quite apart from all of these skeptical challenges, what reason or reasons there might be for believing the religious beliefs that I embraced. Thus, Paul Little's little book, *Know Why You Believe,* and Josh McDowell's *Evidence That Demands a Verdict* came at an appropriate time in my life, introducing me to apologetics. And from Little and McDowell, I jumped right into Sproul, Gerstner, and Lindsley's *Classical Apologetics*—the book that sparked an insatiable thirst in me for apologetics, philosophy, and theology.

No sooner had I discovered apologetics, however, than I also uncovered the fact that not every apologist did apologetics the same way. It was Sproul, Gerstner, and Lindsley's fault, if the truth be known. They distinguished between something they called "classical apologetics" and this bogeyman called "presuppositionalism." And I soon discovered that there were other varieties of apologetic methods as well, and that the disagreements between them could sometimes be sharp. As a young college student, I had a hard time trying to figure out who was right and who was wrong in this debate. I distinctly remember (this was in the early 1980s) wishing that someone would publish one of those "multiple views" books on apologetic methodology so that I could see all the different views side by side and have an easier time making up my own mind. I waited and waited for well over a decade, and no such book appeared. Then I decided to do it myself! And Zondervan has been gracious enough to assist me.

THE NATURE OF APOLOGETICS

This is a book about apologetic *methodology*, not a book of apologetics per se. That is, it is not a book that seeks to do apologetics as much as a book that discusses *how* one ought to do apologetics. But for the sake of some of our readers, it may help at this point to spell out what apologetics is. Apologetics is concerned with the defense of the Christian faith against charges of falsehood, inconsistency, or credulity. Indeed, the very word *apologetics* is derived from the Greek *apologia*, which means "defense." It was a term used in the courts of law in the ancient world. Socrates, for example, gave his famous "apology," or defense, before the court of Athens. And the apostle Paul defended himself *(apologeomai)* before the Roman officials (Acts 24:10; 25:8). As it concerns the Christian faith, then, apologetics has to do with defending, or making a case for, the truth of the Christian faith. It is an intellectual discipline that is usually said to serve at least two purposes: (1) to bolster the faith of Christian believers, and (2) to aid in the task of evangelism. Apologists seek to accomplish these goals in two distinct ways. One is by refuting objections to the Christian faith, such as the problem of evil or the charge that key Christian doctrines (e.g., the Trinity, incarnation, etc.) are incoherent. This apologetic task can be called *negative* or *defensive apologetics*. The second, perhaps complementary, way apologists fulfill their purposes is by offering positive reasons for Christian faith. The latter, called *positive* or *offensive apologetics*, often takes the form of arguments for God's existence or for the resurrection and deity of Christ but are by no means limited to these. Of course, some apologists, as we will see, contend that such arguments are unnecessary or perhaps even detrimental to Christian faith. These apologists focus primarily on the negative task and downplay the role of positive apologetics. Nevertheless, most, if not all, would agree that the apologetic task includes the giving of some positive reasons for faith.

THE QUESTION OF TAXONOMY

Although apologists agree on the basic definition and goals of apologetics, they can differ significantly on the proper *methodology* of apologetics. That is, they disagree about how the apologist goes about his task—about the kinds of arguments that can and should be employed and about the way the apologist should engage the unbeliever in apologetic discourse. To use a military analogy, differences of opinion exist regarding the best *strategy* to use in defending the faith. These differences in apologetic strategy usually turn upon more basic disagreements with regard to important philosophical and theological issues. This leads me to the question of *taxonomy*.

How do we delineate the different approaches to apologetics? Of all the other books on apologetic methodology, no two classify the various methods in exactly the same way. For example, Gordon Lewis classifies apologetic methods according to their respective *religious epistemologies*.[1] He distinguishes them by what each one takes to be the correct approach to acquiring knowledge of religious truths. On this basis, he differentiates six apologetic methods.[2]

Religious epistemology can be the decisive factor in distinguishing one apologetic method from another. For example, two of the methods Lewis distinguishes are *pure empiricism*, defended by J. Oliver Buswell Jr.,[3] and *rationalism*, defended by Gordon H. Clark.[4] Buswell's methodology requires us to make observations of the world and draw causal inferences from those observations, which, he believes, will lead the objective observer to belief in God and in the truth of the Christian faith. He uses the classical theistic arguments and appeals to historical evidences for

---

[1]Gordon R. Lewis, *Testing Christianity's Truth Claims* (Chicago: Moody Press, 1976).

[2]The six methods/epistemologies are (1) *pure empiricism*, exemplified in the twentieth century by J. Oliver Buswell Jr; (2) *rational empiricism*, which Lewis attributes to Stuart C. Hackett; (3) *rationalism*, which, according to Lewis, is the epistemology and method of Gordon H. Clark; (4) *biblical authoritarianism*, advocated by Cornelius Van Til; (5) *mysticism*, exemplified by the work of Earl E. Barrett; and (6) *verificationism*, which is what Lewis calls the method of E. J. Carnell.

[3]See Buswell's *A Christian View of Being and Knowing* (Grand Rapids: Zondervan, 1960).

[4]Some of Clark's works include *A Christian View of Men and Things* (Grand Rapids: Eerdmans, 1952); and *Three Types of Religious Philosophy* (Nutley, N.J.: Craig, 1973).

the resurrection of Jesus. Clark, on the other hand, repudiates the use of such arguments and evidences, largely on epistemological grounds. Instead, he argues that the apologist must begin with Scripture as a first principle. That is, Scripture serves as a rational axiom by which all other truth claims are tested. Clark then argues that Christianity is the only coherent system, all other worldviews being logically inconsistent. Thus, the religious epistemologies of these two apologists lead them to very different apologetic approaches.

There is no doubt that religious epistemology can function to demarcate different apologetic methods. But it is equally evident that religious epistemology cannot always distinguish apologetic methods. Let's again take Buswell's pure empiricism, but this time let's compare it with what Lewis calls *rational empiricism*, which he attributes to Stuart C. Hackett.[5] Buswell's epistemology follows in the vein of Locke and Hume, who believed that all knowledge arises from experience. Hackett is a Kantian who synthesizes rationalism and empiricism. Like Kant, he believes that knowledge begins with the raw data of experience, but that this data is organized and structured by *a priori* categories of the mind.

Students of epistemology know that these approaches to knowledge are significantly different, yet the apologetic approaches that derive from these epistemologies, for all practical purposes, do not differ.[6] If we compare what Buswell actually does by way of making apologetic arguments with what Hackett does, we will discern little if any variance. Hackett uses theistic arguments to establish the truth of the theistic worldview. He then, like Buswell, appeals to historical evidences to establish the resurrection and deity of Christ.

So, again, while religious epistemology is certainly important and may play a significant role in distinguishing one apologetic method from another, it is not sufficient (in every case) for distinguishing one method from another. This sentiment is strongly echoed by more than one of the contributors to this volume. Gary Habermas, for example, argues that his evidentialist

---

[5]Hackett's method and epistemology can be found in *The Reconstruction of the Christian Revelation Claim: A Philosophical and Critical Apologetic* (Grand Rapids: Baker, 1984).

[6]This point, of course, is based on the assumption that apologetic *methodology* has something to do with how one *does* apologetics.

approach to apologetics "can be accommodated by any of several epistemic viewpoints" (p. 93).

Bernard Ramm, another author who has written a book on apologetic methodology, has a more promising approach to apologetic taxonomy.[7] He distinguishes three families of apologetic systems:

1. *Systems that stress the uniqueness of the Christian experience of grace.* Ramm outlines several distinguishing traits of this apologetic approach but points out the emphasis placed on subjective religious experience. Stress is laid here because of correlative emphases on both the transcendence of God and the noetic effects of sin. Since sin blinds the human mind, and since God is so different from human beings, God can be known only through some suprarational, perhaps even paradoxical, experience or "existential encounter." Consequently, this approach has little use for natural theology or Christian evidences. The individual's "experience of religion is so profound or so unique or self-validating that the experience itself is its own proof."[8] Ramm lists Pascal, Kierkegaard, and Brunner as members of this family.

2. *Systems that stress natural theology as the point at which apologetics begins.* Those who follow this school put great trust in human reason to discover religious knowledge. Accordingly, there is less emphasis on the noetic effects of sin and the transcendence of God. Religious truths can be known and verified much the same way scientific propositions can be known and verified. Among those following this method, one will find extensive use of theistic arguments and historical evidences to demonstrate the truth of Christianity. Aquinas, Butler, and Tennant are Ramm's paradigm proponents of this apologetic approach.

3. *Systems that stress revelation as the foundation upon which apologetics must be built.* Ramm portrays this approach as falling somewhat in the middle of the first two. As he puts it, "The revelational school believes that the first school is too subjectivistic...[and] criticizes the second school for not seriously evaluating man's depravity."[9] Rather than beginning with the subjectivism of religious experience or the rationalism of natural theology, this third school begins with the objective truth of

---

[7]Bernard Ramm, *Varieties of Christian Apologetics* (Grand Rapids: Baker, 1961), 14–17.

[8]Ibid., 15.

[9]Ibid., 16.

the revealed Word of God. Reason has a role in this approach, but reason is based on faith in God's revelation and seeks to understand God's revelation. Reason cannot stand in judgment of God's revelation. This approach puts great stress on the noetic effects of sin but perhaps not so much on God's transcendence. God is able to reveal himself in propositional form to human beings through a written revelation (i.e., the Bible) and by the work of the Holy Spirit is able to lessen the blinding effects of sin in the mind of the believer. This school focuses on negative apologetics, though there is some limited use of theistic arguments and historical evidences. Ramm points to Augustine, Calvin, and Kuyper as advocates of this apologetic school.[10]

Though Ramm does not say this in so many words, it seems clear that his taxonomy is built broadly around different approaches to *the relationship between faith and reason*. The first school, which stresses religious experience, places its emphasis on faith and disregards the use of reason in acquiring religious knowledge. The "natural theology" school lies at the opposite pole, giving priority to reason over faith. And the "revelational" school tries to capture the middle ground, utilizing both faith and reason, though giving definite priority to faith.

I said above that Ramm's taxonomy is more promising than Lewis's. And, indeed, I do find much that is appealing in his approach. Yet it still falls short of providing an adequate criterion for distinguishing apologetic methods. Whereas Lewis's criterion for distinguishing apologetic methods is too narrow, I find Ramm's criterion a bit too broad. As he himself admits, these three schools of thought are *families* of apologetic systems. That means that there are, within each family, subordinate schools of thought that can be delineated. And, in my opinion, some of these subordinate schools deserve to be treated separately in any serious discussion of apologetic methodology. Ramm, however, would seem to disagree. For example, he says that

> we do not need to treat the *evidential school*. The *evidential* school would say that the Christian faith is verified apart from sophisticated philosophical considerations, but rests solidly on fulfilled prophecies, miracles, and the resurrection of Christ. But many apologists absorb evidences

---

[10]In an earlier edition of his book (*Types of Apologetic Systems* [Wheaton: Van Kampen, 1953]), Ramm lists Cornelius Van Til and E. J. Carnell as followers of this approach.

into their apologetic system at some point, and if we understand how and why they do this, we can readily understand the structure of the argument in the evidential school.[11]

I do not wish to deny all of what Ramm affirms here. It may very well be that understanding how other schools of apologetics use evidences will enable us to understand the argument of the evidentialist approach. But that does not mean that the evidentialist school is not a distinct apologetic method in its own right. And even if it is part of a larger family of approaches that all utilize evidences, the very structure of the argument constructed by evidentialists may be reason enough to discuss it separately. For instance, evidentialist apologetics may be said to belong to the same family as what I earlier called "classical apologetics" and what Ramm refers to as the "natural theology" school. Though natural theologians almost always utilize Christian evidences after they have established God's existence, some evidentialists *never* use natural theology (i.e., theistic arguments)[12] in making a positive case for Christianity. This seems to me to be a significant difference in apologetic strategy that calls for independent treatment despite any "family resemblances" that may exist between classical and evidential apologetics.

Another problem I see with Ramm's criterion is that it could have a tendency (though I am sure Ramm would not intend this) to caricature or stereotype apologetic systems in a way that may be unfair to their practitioners. For example, many of those who stress religious experience over, say, natural theology need not be pure subjectivists. Pascal, after all, put forth his famous "wager" in an attempt to show the rationality of choosing to believe in God.[13] Likewise, a natural theologian like Thomas Aquinas, while certainly having more confidence in reason than, say, Kierkegaard, would nevertheless avoid saying that philosophical argumentation can produce faith in an unbeliever.[14] So

---

[11]Ramm, *Varieties*, 15.

[12]William Lane Craig, in this book, seems to contend (contra Habermas) that it is a hallmark of evidential apologetics to eschew natural theology (p. 122).

[13]See his *Pensées*, trans. A. J. Krailsheimer (New York: Penguin, 1966), 149–53.

[14]E.g., Aquinas asserts, "Faith is called a consent without inquiry in so far as the consent of faith, or assent, is not caused by an investigation of the understanding," and "free will is inadequate for the act of faith since the contents of faith are above reason. . . . That a man should believe, therefore, cannot occur from himself

he and other natural theologians would not appreciate being characterized as downplaying the importance of faith or of the noetic effects of sin. Yet someone might incautiously take Ramm's criterion to suggest that they do.

Where does this leave us? How do we distinguish apologetic methods? There is no hard and fast rule. Issues like religious epistemology, the relationship between faith and reason, the noetic effects of sin, and so on, will no doubt play important roles, and sometimes, as I suggested earlier, any one of these areas may be decisive in demarcating one particular apologetic method from others. But what distinguishes one method from another might also be none of these. At the beginning of this section, I said that an apologetic method is a *strategy* for defending the faith. It is a way of putting together a case for the Christian faith using either positive or negative apologetics or a combination of the two. How a particular apologists goes about doing this will be influenced by many of the theoretical issues I have mentioned, as well as others. We cannot, however, establish a clear-cut set of theoretical criteria by which to distinguish apologetic methods as Lewis and Ramm tried to do. Rather, we will have to delineate apologetic methods more practically, by looking for distinctive ways of presenting the case for Christianity; distinctive types or structures of argument. This criterion for demarcating apologetic methods I will call the criterion of *argumentative strategy.*[15]

Not all the contributors to this volume will agree with me that argumentative strategy is the best criterion for establishing a taxonomy. And some of the debate that ensues in the following pages will turn on disagreements over how to distinguish apologetic methods. Nevertheless, I offer in the next section a brief out-

---

unless God gives it" (*Commentary on Saint Paul's Epistle to the Ephesians,* as quoted in Norman Geisler, *Thomas Aquinas: An Evangelical Appraisal* [Grand Rapids: Baker, 1991], 57).

[15]One author who seems to recognize this fact is David K. Clark. In his *Dialogical Apologetics: A Person-Centered Approach to Christian Defense* (Grand Rapids: Baker, 1993), 103–9, he outlines an apologetic taxonomy similar to the one used in this book and appears to distinguish them by their respective argumentative strategies. It is also gratifying to note that Norman Geisler, who has also written on apologetic methodology, has recently expressed his own dissatisfaction with attempts to rigidly classify apologetic systems. He also seems to settle for a loose taxonomy of methods very similar to my own (see his *Baker Encyclopedia of Christian Apologetics* [Grand Rapids: Baker, 1999], s.v. "Apologetics, Types of").

line of the major apologetic methods included in this volume and delineated (tentatively) according to argumentative strategy.

A TENTATIVE TAXONOMY
OF APOLOGETIC METHODS

It appears, then, that the place to begin in outlining a taxonomy of apologetic methods is to look at where the debate has raged in recent years over apologetic methodology. What approaches in apologetic literature have caused clashes between apologists over how to make a case for Christianity? I will not give any lengthy survey of these clashes, nor will I pretend that what follows represents an exhaustive list of apologetic methods. Nevertheless, given recent history, any taxonomy based on argumentative strategy has to begin with what I will call the "Big Four."

Classical Method

The *classical method* is an approach that begins by employing natural theology to establish theism as the correct worldview. After God's existence has thus been shown, the classical method moves to a presentation of the historical evidences for the deity of Christ, the trustworthiness of Scripture, et cetera, to show that Christianity is the best version of theism, as opposed to, say, Judaism and Islam. This school is called the "classical" method because it is assumed that this is the method used by the most prominent apologists of earlier centuries. William Lane Craig contributes this volume's defense of classical apologetics. Other contemporary apologists who may be classified as classical apologists include R. C. Sproul,[16] Norman Geisler,[17] Stephen T. Davis,[18] and Richard Swinburne.[19]

---

[16]Sproul's major apologetic work was mentioned earlier: *Classical Apologetics: A Rational Defense of the Christian Faith and a Critique of Presuppositional Apologetics* (Grand Rapids: Zondervan, 1984), coauthored with John Gerstner and Arthur Lindsley.

[17]Geisler has written a plethora of apologetic works, but the two that most clearly set out his methodology are *Christian Apologetics* (Grand Rapids: Baker, 1976); and, with Winfried Corduan, *Philosophy of Religion*, 2d ed. (Grand Rapids: Baker, 1988).

[18]Two of Davis's major apologetic works are his *God, Reason and Theistic Proofs* (Grand Rapids: Eerdmans, 1997); and *Risen Indeed: Making Sense of the Resurrection* (Grand Rapids: Eerdmans, 1993).

[19]See Swinburne's trilogy of works *The Existence of God* (New York: Oxford University Press, 1979); *The Concept of Miracle* (New York: Macmillan, 1970); and *Revelation: From Metaphor to Analogy* (Oxford: Clarendon, 1992).

It is usually argued that the order of the two phases in classical apologetics is essential. That is, before one can meaningfully discuss historical evidences, one has to have established God's existence because one's worldview is a framework through which miracles, historical facts, and other empirical data are interpreted.[20] Without a theistic context, no historical event could ever be shown to be a divine miracle. The flipside of this claim is that one cannot appeal to alleged miracles in order to prove God's existence. As Sproul, Gerstner, and Lindsley argue, "Miracles cannot prove God. God, as a matter of fact, alone can prove miracles. That is, only on the prior evidence that God exists is a miracle even possible."[21] However, not everyone who considers himself or herself a classical apologist will insist on this point, as William Lane Craig makes clear in this volume (see pp. 316–17). Craig argues that the classical methodology need not insist on a theoretical necessity in the order of these two steps, but only, given the nature of probability arguments, that this order is the best *argumentative strategy*.

The Evidential Method

The *evidential method* has much in common with the classical method except in solving the issue concerning the value of miracles as evidence. Evidentialism as an apologetic method may be characterized as the "one-step" approach. Miracles do not presuppose God's existence (as most contemporary classical apologists assert) but can serve as one sort of evidence for God. This method is fairly eclectic in its use of various positive evidences and negative critiques, utilizing both philosophical and historical arguments. Yet it tends to focus chiefly on the legitimacy of accumulating various historical and other inductive arguments for the truth of Christianity.

---

[20]Norman Geisler, e.g., is adamant in his claim that this is *the* distinguishing mark of classical apologetics and what sets it off from its sister, evidential apologetics. He says, "The difference between the classical apologists and the evidentialists on the use of historical evidences is that the classical see the need to first establish that this is a theistic universe.... The basic argument of the classical apologists is that it makes no sense to speak about the resurrection as an act of God unless, as a logical prerequisite, it is first established that there is a God who can act" (*Baker Encyclopedia of Christian Apologetics*, s.v. "Apologetics, Types of"). Gary Habermas agrees, pointing out that "[s]everal classical apologists have firmly asserted that a historical argument from miracles to God is an illegitimate move" (p. 58).

[21]Sproul, Gerstner, and Lindsley, *Classical Apologetics*, 146.

Given this focus, evidentialists may and will argue both for theism and *Christian* theism at the same time without recourse to an elaborate natural theology. They might begin, for instance, by arguing for the historical factuality of Jesus' resurrection and then argue that such an unusual event is explicable only if a being very much like the Christian God exists. Having then established God's existence via Christ's miraculous resurrection, the evidentialist would then go on to contend that Jesus' resurrection also authenticates his claims to be God incarnate and his teaching on the divine authority of Scripture. Besides Gary Habermas, one of the contributors to this book, advocates of evidentialism include John W. Montgomery,[22] Clark Pinnock,[23] and Wolfhart Pannenberg[24] (and see Habermas's article for a host of others that he classifies under this method[25]).

The Cumulative Case Method

The third of the Big Four is the *cumulative case method*. The term "cumulative case" is used by apologists in ways different than we are using it in this context, but Basil Mitchell, an early proponent of this view, gave this method that name, and so we will use it here.[26] The careful reader will no doubt note that this

---

[22]See his *Christianity and History* (Downers Grove, Ill.: InterVarsity Press, 1964), and *The Shape of the Past: A Christian Response to Secular Philosophies of History* (Minneapolis: Bethany Fellowship, 1975).

[23]See Pinnock's *Set Forth Your Case: An Examination of Christianity's Credentials* (Chicago: Moody Press, 1971).

[24]See Pannenberg's *Jesus—God and Man,* trans. L. L. Wilkins and D. A. Priebe (London: SCM, 1968); "Dogmatic Theses on the Doctrine of Revelation" in *Revelation as History*, ed. Wolfhart Pannenberg, trans. David Granskou (London: Macmillan, 1968), 123–58.

[25]Given Habermas's (and many classicalists') contention against Craig (see n. 20 above) that what distinguishes evidential apologetics from classical is that the former admits the legitimacy of a miracles-to-God argument, he feels comfortable including many apologists in his camp that Craig might very well have included in his (e.g., Richard Swinburne, J. P. Moreland, and R. Douglas Geivett). So, for Habermas, anyone who grants that miracles can be used to prove God's existence is an evidentialist. The reader will discover that this makes for a rather lively exchange between Habermas and Craig.

[26]See Mitchell's *The Justification of Religious Belief* (New York: Oxford University Press, 1981), 39–57. Gordon Lewis calls this approach "Verificationism" (*Testing Christianity's Truth Claims*, chaps. 7–11). Norman Geisler has referred to this approach as "Combinationalism" (*Christian Apologetics*, 117–32), but in his more recent taxonomy, it would probably be a subcategory of evidentialism (see *Baker Encyclopedia of Christian Apologetics*, s.v. "Apologetics, Types of").

method belongs in the same broad family of methods as does the evidential (and perhaps classical) method. However, it will also be apparent that as an argumentative strategy, the cumulative case method has something distinctive to offer. Indeed, this approach to apologetics arose because of the dissatisfaction that some philosophers had with these other evidential-type methods (i.e., the first two of the Big Four).

According to advocates of cumulative case apologetics, the nature of the case for Christianity is not in any strict sense a formal argument like a proof or an argument from probability. In the words of Mitchell, the cumulative case method does "not conform to the ordinary pattern of deductive or inductive reasoning."[27] The case is more like the brief that a lawyer makes in a court of law or that a literary critic makes for a particular interpretation of a book. It is an informal argument that pieces together several lines or types of data into a sort of hypothesis or theory that comprehensively explains that data and does so better than any alternative hypothesis. Paul Feinberg, this volume's cumulative case methodologist, says that "Christian theists are urging that [Christianity] makes better sense of all the evidence available than does any other alternative worldview on offer, whether that alternative is some other theistic view or atheism" (p. 152). The data that the cumulative case seeks to explain include the existence and nature of the cosmos, the reality of religious experience, the objectivity of morality, and certain other historical facts, such as the resurrection of Jesus. Besides Feinberg and Mitchell, the cumulative case school would likely include C. S. Lewis[28] and C. Stephen Evans.[29]

The Presuppositional Method

Due to the noetic effects of sin, presuppositionalists usually hold that there is not enough common ground between believers and unbelievers that would allow followers of the prior three methods to accomplish their goals. The apologist must simply presuppose the truth of Christianity as the proper starting point

---

[27]Mitchell, *Justification*, 35.

[28]See Lewis's *Mere Christianity* (London: Fontana, 1952).

[29]See Evans' *Philosophy of Religion: Thinking About Faith* (Downers Grove, Ill.: InterVarsity Press, 1982); *The Quest for Faith: Reason and Mystery as Pointers to God* (Downers Grove, Ill.: InterVarsity Press, 1986); and *The Historical Christ and the Jesus of Faith* (Oxford: Clarendon, 1996).

in apologetics. Here the Christian revelation in the Scriptures is the framework through which all experience is interpreted and all truth is known. Various evidences and arguments can be advanced for the truth of Christianity, but these at least implicitly presuppose premises that can be true only if Christianity is true. Presuppositionalists attempt, then, to argue *transcendentally*. That is, they argue that all meaning and thought—indeed, every fact—logically presupposes the God of the Scriptures. John Frame represents presuppositionalism in this volume, and he puts the matter this way: "[We] should present the biblical God, not merely as the conclusion to an argument, but as the one who makes argument possible" (p. 220). By demonstrating that unbelievers cannot argue, think, or live without presupposing God, presuppositionalists try to show unbelievers that their own worldview is inadequate to explain their experience of the world and to get unbelievers to see that Christianity alone can make sense of their experience. Other presuppositionalists include Cornelius Van Til and Gordon Clark (both mentioned earlier), as well as Greg Bahnsen[30] and Francis Schaeffer.[31]

These four apologetic methods were vying for supremacy when I first discovered apologetics and the problem of methodology in the early eighties. However, a lot has happened in the last twenty or so years in philosophy and apologetics. One of the most dramatic developments has been the arrival of *Reformed epistemology*. Kelly James Clark contributes to this volume with the suggestion that this new religious epistemology has something distinctive to say with regard to apologetic methodology.

The Reformed Epistemology Method

"Since the Enlightenment," Clark says, "there has been a demand to expose all of our beliefs to the searching criticism of reason" (p. 367). We are told that if a belief is unsupported by evidence of some kind, it is irrational to believe it. *Reformed epistemology* challenges this "evidentialist" epistemological assumption. Those who advocate this view hold that it is perfectly reasonable for a person to believe many things without evidence.

---

[30]The only book-length apologetic work by Bahnsen was published posthumously under the title *Always Ready: Directions for Defending the Faith*, ed. Robert R. Booth (Atlanta: American Vision, 1996).

[31]See Schaeffer's *Escape from Reason* (Downers Grove, Ill.: InterVarsity Press, 1968); and *He Is There and He Is Not Silent* (Wheaton: Tyndale, 1972).

Most strikingly, they argue that belief in God does not require the support of evidence or argument in order for it to be rational. The Reformed epistemology apologist will not necessarily eschew making positive arguments in defense of Christianity, but will argue that such arguments are not necessary for rational faith. If Calvin is right that human beings are born with an innate *sensus divinitatis* (sense of the divine), then people may rightly and rationally come to have a belief in God immediately without the aid of evidence.

For the Reformed epistemologist, then, the focus will tend to be on negative or defensive apologetics as challenges to one's theistic belief are encountered. On the positive side, however, the Reformed epistemologist will, in the words of Clark, "encourage unbelievers to put themselves in situations where people are typically taken with belief in God" (p. 279), attempting to awaken in them their latent sense of the divine.

The list of contemporary Reformed epistmologists includes this volume's contributor, already noted, Kelly James Clark. But four other names that would head that list would be Alvin Plantinga, Nicholas Wolterstorff, George Mavrodes, and William Alston.[32]

Again, let me say that these five apologetic methodologies do not constitute an exhaustive list of apologetic approaches. They do represent, however, the most well-known and popular argumentative strategies in the scholarly apologetics community. It is my hope, as well as that of the other contributors, that this work promotes additional fruitful discussion of apologetic methodology and proves to be of service to the church universal and our Lord Jesus Christ.

---

[32]All four of these scholars contributed articles to the ground-breaking volume *Faith and Rationality: Reason and Belief in God*, ed. Alvin Plantinga and Nicholas Wolterstorff (University of Notre Dame, 1983). Alvin Plantinga has just provided the most recent and thorough discussion of Reformed epistemology in his *Warranted Christian Belief* (New York: Oxford University Press, 1999).

GLOSSARY OF KEY TERMS
AND CONCEPTS

Readers who have read very little philosophy or apologetics before picking up this book will have already come across some terms they have never seen before, and there are many more such terms in the pages that follow. Though all the authors in this book have tried to write without presupposing that the reader is well-versed in philosophical jargon, it would be impossible for us to avoid such jargon altogether and equally impossible to pause and define each term along the way.

a posteriori. Lat., after or dependent on experience. Propositions like "Some roses are red" or "Abraham Lincoln was the sixteenth president of the United States" are said to be known *a posteriori.*

a priori. Lat., prior to or independent of experience. Propositions such as "Bachelors are unmarried men," or mathematical truths like 2+2 = 4, are usually said to be known *a priori.*

Bayes' Theorem. See Probability Calculus.

contingent. A term referring to beings or states of affairs whose existence is not necessary. A contingent being is one that has the potential for nonexistence; a dependent being.

empiricism. A theory of knowledge that claims that all knowledge begins with sense experience.

epistemology. A branch of philosophy concerned with the source, scope, and limits of knowledge. Religious epistemology is a sub-branch of epistemology concerned with the knowledge and verification of religious truth claims.

evidentialism. This term and its cognates *evidential* and *evidentialist* are used in three distinct ways in this book. It may refer to (1) a broad class or family of apologetic schools that includes classical apologetics, evidential apologetics, and cumulative case apologetics—all of which are related in part because of a similar stance on the relationship between faith and reason; (2) a particular apologetic methodology that focuses primarily on historical evidences in constructing an argument for Christianity (à la Habermas in this volume); or (3) an epistemological theory that claims that it is irrational to believe any proposition without sufficient evidence (i.e., the archenemy of Reformed epistemology). Pay careful attention to which of these three senses of evidentialism is being used at any given point in this book.

externalism. A theory of epistemic justification that claims that what justifies a particular belief for a person is external to the person and not necessarily accessible to him or her. For example, an externalist might claim that a particular belief B is justified for some person S because B happened to be produced by S's reliable or properly functioning belief-forming mechanism. Externalism is the alternative to *internalism* (which see).

foundationalism. An epistemological theory that claims that knowledge is ultimately based on certain foundational beliefs that are acquired and known independently of other beliefs. That is, these foundational or "basic" beliefs are acquired directly or immediately from experience (or in some cases, reason). *Classical* foundationalism is a particular theory for distinguishing such basic beliefs from nonbasic beliefs (i.e., beliefs that are derived from other beliefs). Classical foundationalism says that a belief is basic if and only if it is either self-evident, incorrigible, or evident to the senses.

internalism. A theory of epistemic justification that claims that what justifies a particular belief for a person is internal to the person, that the person has "internal access" to the conditions that make it justifiable for him or her to believe the belief in question. Internalism is juxtaposed to *externalism* (which see).

***kalam* cosmological argument.** A theistic argument (which see). Specifically, a version of the cosmological argument that appeals to philosophical and scientific data to show that (1) the universe began to exist (i.e., it is not eternal), (2) the beginning of the universe was caused, and (3) the cause of the universe was God.

metaphysics. A branch of philosophy concerned with the nature of reality or of what exists. The term *ontology* (study of being) is often used synonymously.

naturalism. The worldview that claims that the natural, physical world is all that exists; synonymous with atheism.

natural theology. A term that primarily refers to knowledge of God acquired without the aid of special revelation but derived instead from God's self-revelation in nature. The term is also used to designate the formal process of discovering and explaining the content of natural revelation. As one can be described as "doing" theology, one can also "do" natural theology. Natural theology is closely associated with the construction of *theistic arguments* (which see).

necessary. A term that refers to beings or states of affairs whose existence is necessary. A necessary being is one that *must* exist, that cannot not exist.

noetic effects of sin. The detrimental effects of sin upon the mind. The term "noetic" comes from the Greek *nous* ("mind").

pantheism. The worldview that claims that everything is God or a part of God. Often monistic, claiming that the only thing that exists is God, and that everything else (the physical world, the individual self, etc.) is an illusion.

probability calculus. A formal method for calculating the probability of a certain hypothesis relative to given background information. *Bayes' Theorem* is a specific thesis in probability calculus that the reader will encounter at several points in this book. Though we initially wanted to avoid the kind of technicality represented by Bayes' Theorem, it became evident in the course of this project that discussion could not proceed in any fruitful way without it. The reader should not become frustrated, because Bayes' Theorem is really not that difficult. Borrowing from Craig's response to Habermas (p. 125), let R stand for "the resurrection hypothesis" (i.e., the hypothesis that God raised Jesus from the dead), let B stand for one's background knowledge (such as the existence of God), E stand for specific evidence for R (e.g., the empty tomb and resurrection appearances), and A_i stand for various alternative explanations (e.g., the disciples stole the body of Jesus or Jesus simply swooned on the cross), with $\Sigma_{i=1}^{n}$ representing the collective probability of these alternative explanations. Using these symbols, Bayes' Theorem looks like this:

$$Pr(R/B\&E) = \frac{Pr(R/B) \times Pr(E/B\&R)}{Pr(R/B) \times Pr(E/B\&R) + \Sigma_{i=1}^{n} Pr(A_i/B) \times Pr(E/B\&A_i)}$$

The main thing you need to know is how to read this formula (you'll have to work hard on your own to *understand* it!). Starting with what lies to the left of the equal sign, this theorem says that the probability of R, given the truth of B and E, equals (now moving to the right of the equal sign) the probability of R, given B, multiplied by the probability of E, given B and R; and then all of that divided by the probability of R, given B, multiplied by the probability of E, given B and R, plus the collective probability of the alternative explanations, acquired by combining the probability for each alternative A_i, given B, multiplied by the probability of E, given B and A_i. Got it?

rationalism. A theory of knowledge that holds that all knowledge is acquired or verified through reason.

solipsism. The view that only I exist.

theism. The worldview that claims that there is a transcendent and supreme personal being who is the creator of everything other than himself; synonymous with traditional Judeo-Christian monotheism.

theistic arguments. Arguments that attempt to prove (or at least make highly probable) the existence of God. There are many theistic arguments, but the three most prominent are the *ontological, cosmological,* and *teleological.*

veridical. Truthful, veracious, genuine, not illusory.

worldview. A conceptual framework for interpreting and organizing experience. This framework comprises a set of basic assumptions about the nature of reality (what is real and unreal, possible and impossible) and about the existence and nature of God, man, knowledge, and ethics. Depending on how they are classified, there may be any number of worldviews. But in the simplest taxonomy there are three: *naturalism, pantheism,* and *theism* (which see).

Chapter One

CLASSICAL APOLOGETICS

William Lane Craig

CLASSICAL APOLOGETICS

William Lane Craig

In dealing with the question of methodology in Christian apologetics, one is, in effect, raising the age-old issue of the relationship between faith and reason. This is a problem which—if I may speak personally—remained very perplexing to me for many years of my Christian life. Raised in a non-evangelical home, I became a Christian my third year of high school, not through any careful consideration of the evidence, but because those Christian students who shared the gospel with me seemed to be living on a different plane of reality than I was. Their faith in Christ imparted meaning to their lives along with a joyous peace, which I craved.

Once I became a Christian, I was eager to share the truth of my newfound faith with my family and high school friends, and thus I soon became engaged in presenting arguments for becoming a Christian. As a young believer full of enthusiasm and faith, I went off in 1967 to study at Wheaton College. During the sixties Wheaton had become a seedbed of skepticism and cynicism, and I was dismayed to see students whose intellectual abilities I admired lose their faith and renounce Christianity in the name of reason. The prevailing atmosphere was one of theological rationalism (an epistemological view often misleadingly called evidentialism). In my theology courses I learned that none of the classical arguments for the existence of God is sound, and my Bible professors never discussed evidences for the reliability of the Gospels. Among the students, doubt was touted as a virtue of the mature Christian life, and one was supposed to follow unflinchingly the demands of reason wherever it might lead. I remember well one of my theology professors commenting that if he were persuaded that Christianity were unreasonable, then he would renounce Christianity.

Now that frightened and troubled me. For me, Christ was so real and had invested my life with such significance that I could not make the confession of my professor—if somehow through my studies my reason were to turn against my faith, then so much the worse for my reason! Thus, I confided to one of my philosophy teachers, "I guess I'm not a true intellectual. If my reason turned against Christ, I'd still believe. My faith is too real."

So I went through a temporary flirtation with Kierkegaardian fideism—though my mind could not rest long in the position that I believe Christianity because it is absurd. As often happens in the lives of earnest students, the reading of certain books proved pivotal in my thinking and directed my life along a different route. The first was E. J. Carnell's *Introduction to Christian Apologetics,* which convinced me that reason might be used to show the systematic consistency of Christian faith without thereby becoming the basis of that faith. The second was Stuart Hackett's *Resurrection of Theism,* which stunned me by its demonstration that there were, after all, persuasive, cogent arguments for God's existence. Hackett's book was part of an incomplete project, however, and left one with a sort of deism rather than Christian theism. But then, third, I became acquainted on a popular level with Christian evidences, particularly for the resurrection of Jesus, compiled, for example, by Josh McDowell in *Evidence That Demands a Verdict.* It became quite evident to me that it was possible to present a sound, convincing, positive case for the truth of Christian theism.

Still I could not embrace the view that rational argument and evidence constitute the essential foundation for faith, for the fruits of that viewpoint had become forcefully clear to me at Wheaton. I put the issue on the back burner while I pursued other questions during my seminary and doctoral studies in philosophy, but it came to the fore again in 1977 when I was invited by Campus für Christus to deliver a series of lectures on apologetics to university students in Munich. My opening lecture was to be on faith and reason, and in meditating on this problem, I hit upon a scheme that has proved to be very helpful to me personally in illuminating the relationship between faith and reason—namely, the distinction between *knowing* Christianity to be true and *showing* Christianity to be true. It has been gratifying to me that what I grasped in a rough and superficial way has been confirmed by the recent work of religious epistemologists, notably Alvin Plantinga.

The methodological approach which I shall defend in this essay is that reason in the form of rational arguments and evidence plays an essential role in our showing Christianity to be true, whereas reason in this form plays a contingent and secondary role in our personally knowing Christianity to be true. The proper ground of our knowing Christianity to be true is the inner work of the Holy Spirit in our individual selves; and in our showing Christianity to be true, it is his role to open the hearts of unbelievers to assent and respond to the reasons we present.

Such a method, as it plays itself out in showing Christianity to be true, has been called "classical apologetics." This approach is comprised of natural theology and Christian evidences. Among its practitioners are such great figures as Thomas Aquinas with his famous Five Ways of demonstrating God's existence and his appeal to the signs of credibility (miracles and prophecy) to validate Christian doctrines not demonstrable by reason alone; Hugo Grotius, the father of modern apologetics, whose *De Veritate Religionis Christianae* drew upon the traditional arguments of natural theology and inaugurated the historical approach to the truth of the Gospels; and one of my heroes, William Paley, whose *Natural Theology* is one of the most brilliant defenses of the teleological argument ever written and whose *A View of the Evidences of Christianity* was so impressive that it remained compulsory reading for every applicant to Cambridge University right up to the twentieth century.

KNOWING CHRISTIANITY
TO BE TRUE

In this section I shall address the question, How does a Christian believer know that Christianity is true? In answering this question, I distinguish between the role of the Holy Spirit and the role of rational argument and evidence. I shall argue that the inner witness of the Holy Spirit gives us an immediate and veridical assurance of the truth of our Christian faith and that rational argument and evidence may properly confirm but not defeat that assurance.

Role of the Holy Spirit

I have elsewhere characterized the witness of the Holy Spirit as self-authenticating,[1] and by that notion I mean (1) that the experience of the Holy Spirit is veridical and unmistakable (though not necessarily irresistible or indubitable) for the one who has it and attends to it; (2) that such a person does not need supplementary arguments or evidence in order to know and to know with confidence that he is in fact experiencing the Spirit of God; (3) that such experience does not function in this case as a premise in any argument from religious experience to God, but rather is the immediate experiencing of God himself; (4) that in certain contexts the experience of the Holy Spirit will imply the apprehension of certain truths of the Christian religion, such as "God exists," "I am reconciled to God," "Christ lives in me," and

---

[1]William Lane Craig, *Apologetics: An Introduction* (Chicago: Moody Press, 1984), 18. In what has become a standard article on this notion, Robert Oakes defines a self-authenticating religious experience as a "veridical experience of God which is sufficient to guarantee that the person having that veridical experience could never in principle have any justification for questioning its validity" (Robert Oakes, "Religious Experience and Rational Certainty," *Religious Studies* 12, no. 3 [1976]: 311–18). I take this definition to express the idea of what Plantinga calls an intrinsic defeater-defeater (see below). Keith Yandell offers an interesting discussion and critique of the notion of a self-authenticating religious experience in his *The Epistemology of Religious Experience* (Cambridge: Cambridge University Press, 1993), 166–75. On Yandell's account, for a person *S* and a proposition *P*, *S*'s experience *E* is self-authenticating regarding *P* if and only if the following three conditions are met: (1) *S* has *E*, (2) it is logically impossible that *S* have *E* and *P* be false, and (3) *S* accepts *P* because *S* has seen both (i) that *S* has *E* and (ii) that it is logically impossible that *S* have *E* and *P* be false. This is a helpful account apart from clause (ii). I see no reason to think that a person enjoying a self-authenticating witness of God's Spirit must be aware that (ii) is true, especially if that person is theologically untutored. Some of Yandell's objections are simply inapplicable to the on-going witness of the Spirit, since they are based on the assumption that the experience in question was a once-for-all experience about which one might later have doubts or be mistaken. Again, if I understand Yandell correctly, when he objects that no religious belief is self-authenticated to anyone because one might have an experience that one mistakenly believes to be an experience of God, he seems to forget that the definition requires that *S* have *E*—that is, actually have the witness of the Spirit. It is not *P*, after all, that is self-authenticating, but *E*; hence, it does no good to consider cases in which *S* does not have *E*. Finally, as for Yandell's objection that in order to know that one's experience is self-authenticating, one must first know it is veridical, this objection is based on the false assumption that in order to have a self-authenticating experience, one must know that one has a self-authenticating experience. This is the unjustified driving principle of skepticism, that in order to know that *P* I must know that I know that *P*.

so forth; (5) that such an experience provides one not only with a subjective assurance of Christianity's truth, but with objective knowledge of that truth; and (6) that arguments and evidence incompatible with that truth are overwhelmed by the experience of the Holy Spirit for the one who attends fully to it.

By way of procedure, I shall lay out in a nontechnical way my understanding of the biblical teaching concerning our assurance of Christianity's truth and attempt to translate this into the parlance of contemporary religious epistemology. Now at first blush it might seem self-defeating or perhaps circular for me to supply scriptural proof texts concerning the witness of the Spirit, as if to say that we believe in the Spirit's witness because the Scripture says there is such a witness. But it needs to be remembered that ours is an "in-house" discussion. Since all five authors do accept Scripture as the rule of faith, it is entirely appropriate to lay out what Scripture teaches on religious epistemology. In interacting with a non-Christian, one would simply say that we Christians do in fact experience the inner testimony of God's Spirit.

As I read the New Testament, it seems to me that for both Paul and John the fundamental way in which a believer knows the truth of the Christian faith is by the inner witness of the Holy Spirit. When I say "the Christian faith" I do not mean fine points of doctrine such as infralapsarianism or amillennialism, but rather the belief that one has been reconciled to God through Jesus Christ, or some rough equivalent. Thus, Paul tells us that every Christian believer is an adopted son of God and is indwelt with the Holy Spirit of Christ (Rom. 8:9; Gal. 4:6). It is the witness of God's Spirit with our spirit that gives us the assurance that we are God's children: "For you did not receive a spirit that makes you a slave again to fear, but you received the Spirit of sonship. And by him we cry 'Abba, Father.' The Spirit himself testifies with our spirit that we are God's children" (Rom. 8:15–16). Paul does not hesitate to use the term plērophoria ("complete confidence, full assurance") to indicate the surety that the believer possesses as a result of the Spirit's work (Col. 2:2; 1 Thess. 1:5; cf. Rom. 4:21; 14:5).

In popular Christian piety, this experience is known as "assurance of salvation," and it is the right and privilege of every regenerate believer. But the assurance of one's salvation entails that one entertains other more rudimentary beliefs, for example, that God exists or that Christ is the means of one's reconciliation. If we are assured of our salvation, then we can be assured of these other truths as well. The fact that one has assurance of the truth of such fundamental Christian beliefs does not imply that such beliefs are therefore indubitable. On the contrary, Paul teaches that we may quench the Spirit by repressing his working in our lives (1 Thess. 5:19) and grieve the Spirit through sin (Eph. 4:30). Therefore, we have the responsibility to walk in the fullness of the Holy Spirit (Gal. 5:16–17, 25; Eph. 5:18). It is a safe inference that the Christian who is living under the domination of the flesh might well doubt his salvation, including its entailments, such as the existence of God or God's self-revelation in Christ; and certainly Christian experience bears this out. Only as we walk in the fullness of the Spirit can we be guaranteed the assurance of which Paul speaks. Thus, the witness of the Holy Spirit is a veridical experience that will be unmistakable for the person who attends to that witness; that is to say, the person who responds appropriately to the Spirit's witness cannot mistake that witness for anything other than what it is. It would have been inconceivable for the apostle Paul to imagine that someone crying, "Abba, Father" through the witness of the Holy Spirit might mistakenly believe that he was not experiencing God.

Similarly, John repeatedly emphasizes that it is the Holy Spirit who imparts to the believer the knowledge that his Christian beliefs are true. In John's gospel Jesus tells his disciples that the Holy Spirit will teach them all things (John 14:26), and in his first epistle John underscores this fact by rejoicing that his readers have no need that anyone should teach them, since the anointing they received from God, which abides in them, teaches them about all things (1 John 2:20, 26–27). Similarly, in John's gospel, Jesus promises to send the Spirit of truth to abide in the disciples so that they might know that they are in Christ and Christ in them (John 14:16–17, 20). And in his first epistle John again underlines the reality of this promise: "This is how we know that he lives in us: We know it by the Spirit he gave us.... We know that we live in him and he in us, because he has given us of his Spirit" (1 John 3:24; 4:13). John uses his characteristic phrase "we know" to emphasize the confidence Christian believers have that our faith is true, that we really do abide in God and he in us. In fact, in a remarkable passage, John actually appears to compare the degree of certainty generated by the inner witness of the Spirit with that furnished by the historical testimony to the ministry of Jesus. He writes:

And it is the Spirit who testifies, because the Spirit is the truth. For there are three that testify: the Spirit, the water and the blood; and the three are in agreement. We accept man's testimony, but God's testimony is greater because it is the testimony of God, which he has given about his Son. Anyone who believes in the Son of God has this testimony in his heart (1 John 5:6–10).

The "water and the blood" in this passage probably refer to the baptism and crucifixion of Jesus as marking the beginning and end of his earthly ministry, and "man's testimony" to the apostolic witness to the events of that ministry.[2] John, who in his gospel lays such weight on the apostolic testimony to the signs of Jesus' ministry in order "that you may believe that Jesus is the Christ, the Son of God" (John 20:31), now says that the testimony of the Spirit is *even greater* than the apostolic testimony. As Christian believers we have the testimony of God living within us, assuring us of the veracity of our faith. Although John is eager to present evidences for the truth of Christ's claims, it is apparent that he does not consider such evidence necessary for knowledge of those claims.

I think it is evident that Paul and John are not talking about an argument from religious experience for the conclusion that Christianity is true, but about an immediate apprehension of its truth acquired in the context of the Spirit's witness. Belief that one's Christian faith is true is what epistemologists call a "properly basic" belief—that is, a belief which is not derived inferentially from any more foundational belief but which is rationally justified by being formed in appropriate circumstances. Belief in the Christian God is properly basic when formed in the circumstances of the witness of the Holy Spirit. It is only due to sin that persons under such circumstances do not form this belief. Moreover, the New Testament makes it clear that a person whose belief in the truth of the Christian faith is grounded in the witness of the Holy Spirit is not merely rational in so believing, but that he knows that the Christian faith is true.[3]

---

[2]See James D. G. Dunn, *Baptism in the Holy Spirit* (London: SCM, 1970), 201–4.

[3]What more is needed for such a properly basic belief to become an item of knowledge for him who believes it? Alvin Plantinga calls this additional element *warrant;* it is warrant that makes the difference between mere true belief and knowledge. Providing an adequate account of warrant has been a notoriously difficult task, to which Plantinga has devoted considerable effort (Alvin Plantinga, *Warrant: The Current Debate* [New York: Oxford University Press, 1992]; idem, *Warrant and Proper*

But what if this properly basic belief conflicts with a belief supported by evidence? In most cases the circumstances that ground a properly basic belief confer only a *prima facie* justification, not an *ultima facie* justification, to that belief. Such a belief is still subject to defeaters, that is, conflicting beliefs that have more warrant for the person involved than the original belief. In such a case if the person is to remain justified in his original belief, then he must come up with a defeater of the defeater. But then one's properly basic Christian beliefs formed in the context of the witness of the Holy Spirit would seem to require rational argument or evidence to defeat their ostensible defeaters, if one is to continue rationally to believe. Since almost all intelligent adult Christians are bombarded throughout their education and adult life with multifarious defeaters for Christianity, it seems that for a great many, if not most, people, rational argument and evidence will be indispensable to the sustenance of their faith.

Yet, a little reflection will show that such an epistemology is as religiously inadequate as theological rationalism (a.k.a. evidentialism). Consider, for example, a young German student of pietistic Lutheran upbringing who, desiring to become a pastor, goes off to the University of Marburg to study theology. There he sits under various professors of Bultmannian stripe and finds his orthodox faith in Christian theism constantly under attack. He casts about for answers but finds none either in his reading or in discussions with other persons. He feels utterly defenseless before his professors' criticisms, having nothing but the reality of his own Christian experience to oppose their arguments. Now, lacking a defeater for the defeaters brought against his Christian faith, such a student seems to be irrational to continue to believe in Christ; he has an epistemic obligation to give up his faith.

But surely this is unconscionable. How can one be obligated to ignore the witness of the Holy Spirit? How can anyone

---

Function [New York: Oxford University Press, 1993]). In his analysis the core of the vague idea of warrant is that warrant is a property of a belief that is produced by cognitive faculties functioning properly in an appropriate environment according to a design plan successfully aimed at producing true beliefs. In the soon-to-be-released third volume of his trilogy on warrant, Plantinga will argue that specifically Christian beliefs are warranted because God has designed our faculties to produce such beliefs in the context of the witness of the Holy Spirit. Whether Plantinga's specific analysis of warrant proves successful or not, he is surely in line with the teaching of the New Testament that our belief in the biblical God is not merely rational, but warranted, and therefore knowledge.

responding to the call of God himself upon his life be cognitively dysfunctional in so doing? Does not this view threaten to make being a Christian a matter of historical and geographical accident? Some persons simply lack the ability, time, or resources to come up with successful defeaters of the antitheistic defeaters they encounter. Are we going to deny them, on pain of irrationality, the joy and privilege of personal faith in God? If so, will they therefore be eternally lost for not believing in God? To answer affirmatively seems unthinkable; but to answer negatively seems contrary to the biblical teaching that all men are "without excuse" if they do not believe in God. So long as we require extrinsic defeaters for the defeaters brought against Christian faith, the sting of evidentialism has not been removed.

Finally, such a requirement seems in any case to make the proper basicality of Christian belief a matter of academic interest only. Belief that one's Christian faith is true will hardly be comparable to other basic beliefs, like "I see a tree" or "I had breakfast this morning," for it will have to be surrounded by an enormous and elaborately constructed citadel, bristling with defensive armaments to ward off the enemy. In such a case, little if anything has been gained by calling such a belief properly basic. Faith unattended by evidence will still be unwarranted and irrational. Such faith is a far cry from that spoken of by the New Testament writers.

For this reason it is important to insist on the self-authenticating nature of the Spirit's witness. The claim that the Spirit's witness is self-authenticating entails that belief grounded in the witness of the Holy Spirit is an intrinsic defeater of the defeaters brought against it; that is to say, it is a belief enjoying such a high degree of warrant that it simply overwhelms any putative defeater. An intrinsic defeater-defeater does not directly refute the defeater in the sense of providing an argument to show that the alleged defeater is false or providing reasons to doubt that the alleged defeater has been proved to be true. Rather, an overwhelming defeater simply enjoys more warrant than the defeaters lodged against it. Plantinga provides an engaging illustration of someone who knows that he has not committed a crime even though all the evidence stands against him.[4] Such a person is perfectly rational to go on believing in his own inno-

---

[4] Alvin Plantinga, "The Foundations of Theism: A Reply," *Faith and Philosophy* 3, no. 3 (1986): 310.

cence even if he cannot refute the evidence. In the same way, asks Plantinga, why could not belief in God be so warranted that it constitutes an intrinsic defeater of any considerations brought against it? With this query, Plantinga moves in the same direction as the New Testament. The witness of the Spirit is available to all believers regardless of their situation or intellectual prowess. A believer who is too uninformed or ill-equipped to refute anti-Christian arguments is rational in believing on the grounds of the witness of the Spirit in his heart even in the face of such unrefuted objections. Even a person confronted with what are for him unanswerable objections to Christian theism is, because of the work of the Holy Spirit, within his epistemic rights—nay, under epistemic obligation—to believe in God.

Of course, it may be objected that many other faiths incompatible with Christianity also claim to have a self-authenticating witness of God's Spirit. Postmodernist antirealists like John Hick or radical pluralists like Joseph Runzo might see in such a situation justification for denying the exclusive truth of the Christian faith. But how is the fact that other persons claim to experience a self-authenticating witness of God's Spirit relevant to *my* knowing the truth of Christianity via the Spirit's witness? The existence of an authentic and unique witness of the Spirit does not exclude the existence of false claims to such a witness. People can have putative experiences of God which are in fact nonveridical. How, then, does the existence of false claims of the Spirit's witness to the truth of a non-Christian religion do anything logically to undermine the fact that the Christian believer does possess the genuine witness of the Spirit? Why should I be robbed of my joy and assurance of salvation simply because someone else falsely pretends, sincerely or insincerely, to the Spirit's witness? If a Mormon or Muslim falsely claims to experience the witness of God's Spirit in his heart, how does that undermine the confidence the Spirit of God does in fact inspire in me? Why cannot the Spirit-filled Christians know immediately that his claim to the Spirit's witness is true despite the false claims made by persons adhering to other religions?

Perhaps the most plausible spin to put on this objection is to say that false claims to a witness of the Holy Spirit ought to undermine my confidence in the reliability of the cognitive faculties which form religious beliefs, since those faculties so often mislead. The fact that so many people apparently sincerely, yet falsely, believe that God's Spirit is testifying to them of the truth of their religious beliefs ought therefore to make us very leery concerning our experience of God.

A couple of things may be said in response to this objection. First, as William Alston points out in an interesting discussion of this objection, the Christian need not say that all persons in non-Christian religions are simply mistaken.[5] It may well be the case that they enjoy a veridical experience of God as the Ground of Being on whom we creatures are dependent or as the Moral Absolute from whom values derive or even as the loving Father of mankind. Second, the objection assumes that the witness of the Holy Spirit is not qualitatively distinct from religious experiences enjoyed by adherents of other faiths. But why should I think that when a Mormon claims to experience a "burning in the bosom" he is having an experience qualitatively indistinguishable from the witness of the Holy Spirit that I enjoy? Why should I think that the cognitive mechanism that enables me to form the belief that I am a child of God is the same mechanism that produced the psychological experience he mistakenly identifies as the witness of the Spirit?

When it comes to knowing one's faith to be true, therefore, the Christian will not rely primarily on argument and evidence but on the gracious witness of God himself given to all his children by the indwelling Holy Spirit.

Role of Argument and Evidence

What role, then, is left for rational argument and evidence to play in knowing the Christian faith to be true? On the basis of what has been said, it is evident that the only role left for these is a subsidiary role. Here I have found Martin Luther's distinction between the magisterial and ministerial uses of reason to be quite helpful. In its magisterial use, reason stands over and above the gospel like a magistrate and judges its truth or falsity. We must weigh the evidence and arguments both for and against the truth of the gospel in order to adjudicate the issue without any reliance on the Spirit of God. It was reason in this role that inspired Luther's vitriolic attacks on it as "Aristotle's whore." But in its ministerial role, reason submits to and serves the gospel. Reason under the sovereign guidance of God's Spirit and Word is a useful tool in helping us to understand and

---

[5]William Alston, "Response to Hick," *Faith and Philosophy* 14, no. 3 (1997): 287–88.

defend our faith. Luther endorsed the ministerial use of reason, thus placing himself squarely in the Augustinian-Anselmian tradition of faith seeking understanding.

The New Testament teaching on the witness of the Holy Spirit implies that Luther was correct. Rational argument and evidence can be used to confirm in the believer's mind the truth witnessed to him by the Holy Spirit. What he knows immediately and unmistakably via the work of the Spirit, he may also know inferentially and defeasibly via argument and evidence. But the latter obviously will be of less importance to him than the former. If, due to the contingencies of one's life situation, confirmation by argument and evidence is unavailable, the basis of one's faith remains secure. Indeed, if the evidence in some situations actually turns against Christianity, the believer will not lose faith but will persevere in the hope and expectation that further evidence will once again tip the balance in favor of Christianity. In an ideal world the witness of the Spirit and the conclusions of rational argumentation would coincide in the beliefs produced, but in the real world the contingencies of history and geography may sometimes preclude this. Fortunately, God has not left us to our own devices to determine whether Christianity is true but has given us the testimony of his own Spirit.

By contrast, those who subscribe to the magisterial use of reason face severe difficulties: (1) They would deny the right to Christian faith to all who lack the ability, time, or opportunity to understand and assess the arguments and evidence. This consequence would no doubt consign untold millions of people who are Christians to unbelief. (2) Those who have been presented with more cogent arguments against Christian theism than for it would have a just excuse before God for their unbelief. But Scripture says that all men are without excuse for not responding to the degree of revelation they have (Rom. 1:21). (3) This view creates a sort of intellectual elite, a priesthood of philosophers and historians, who will dictate to the masses of humanity whether or not it is rational for them to believe in the gospel. But surely faith is available to everyone who, in response to the Spirit's drawing, calls upon the name of the Lord. (4) Faith is subjected to the vagaries of reason and the shifting sands of evidence, making Christian faith rational in one generation and irrational in the next. But the witness of the Spirit makes every generation contemporaneous with Christ and thus secures a firm basis for faith.

For such reasons, it seems to me that we must with Luther reject the magisterial role of reason in favor of its role as a minister of the Spirit of God. The proper basis of faith is the witness of the Holy Spirit, not rational argumentation and evidence, though the latter may serve to confirm the former. In times of doubt or spiritual dryness, it can be a tremendous encouragement to faith to have sound arguments for the existence of God and evidence for the credibility of the Gospels. When confronted with ostensible defeaters of one's Christian beliefs, it is an exhilarating and edifying experience to wrestle with difficult questions and come to an intellectually satisfying solution to the problem. Part of what it means to love the Lord our God with all our mind is to attempt to construct a Christian *Weltanschauung.* Such a project inevitably involves us in the task of rationally sorting through issues of apologetic significance for the Christian faith. The Christian faith is not a brain-dead, arational faith, but a faith that seeks understanding.

In summary, therefore, it seems to me that the biblical theist ought to hold that among the circumstances that rationally ground Christian belief is the witness of the Holy Spirit, and that that belief is so warranted that it is an intrinsic defeater of any potential defeater that might be brought against it. Moreover, insofar as cogent arguments and evidence for Christian theism are available, a mature believer ought to regard these, not as supplying the basis for his belief, but as a welcome and provisional confirmation of his properly basic and warranted belief in Christian theism.

SHOWING CHRISTIANITY
TO BE TRUE

When we turn to the question of showing our faith to be true, the roles of the Holy Spirit and of rational argumentation and evidence seem to be almost completely reversed. Here I shall argue that the use of argument and evidence assumes a primary and appropriate role, while the work of the Holy Spirit plays no part in the demonstration proper but consists in opening the heart of the obdurate unbeliever to attend to and be persuaded by the argumentation. Again, I shall explain my understanding of the biblical position on this issue while placing my conclusions in the context of current philosophical discussions.

Role of Argument and Evidence

Turning first to the role of rational argument and evidence in showing Christianity to be true, we confront the difficult and controverted question of the relationship between general revelation and natural theology, a question that in the end may be biblically irresolvable. One school of thought interprets passages like Romans 1:19–20 to sanction natural theology by teaching that from the created order all persons are responsible for inferring the existence of the divine Creator. But an opposing school of thought regards the created order as the context that serves to ground belief in the Creator as properly basic. I think it is clear that the arguments of natural theology are not *identical* with general revelation; general revelation is the traits of the author reflected in his product, the fingerprints of the potter in the clay, so to speak, whereas the arguments of natural theology are the human products of men's rational reflection upon general revelation. That fact does not, however, settle the question whether the created order serves as the basis for inferring the Creator's existence or constitutes the circumstances in which belief in a Creator is properly basic.

It might be thought that Paul's saying that men are "without excuse" for not believing in God favors the basic belief interpretation, since all men could not be held to be without excuse for failing to hold to an inference, whereas they could be held responsible for a belief that is properly basic for all men. But this is to confuse proper basicality with degree of belief. As Mavrodes reminds us,[6] an inferred proposition can be as deeply and irrefragably believed as a basic belief, and many properly basic beliefs may be lightly and defeasibly held. The defender of natural theology could plausibly maintain that the inference from creation to Creator is so evident at any level of inquiry, from the observations of the primitive savage to the investigations of the scientist, that the nontheist is inexcusable in failing to draw this inference.

Commentators often favor the basic belief interpretation without sufficient justification.[7] The passage itself permits either

---

[6]George Mavrodes, "Jerusalem and Athens Revisited," in *Faith and Rationality*, ed. Alvin Plantinga and Nicholas Wolterstorff (Notre Dame, Ind.: University of Notre Dame Press, 1983), 214–15.

[7]Wilckens, e.g., thinks that Paul cannot be referring to a *Rückschluss* from the works to the artisan because the perception of God in nature does not depend on

interpretation. But the interesting phrase *"aórata . . . vooúmena kathorâtai"* (1:20) could very well indicate that inferential reasoning is involved in the perception of God's invisible nature in the creation, meaning something like "God's invisible nature is perceived through reflecting on the things that have been made." (Cf. Leenhardt's rendering: "ce qui de Dieu échappe au regard, [je veux dire] sa puissance éternelle et sa divinité, peut être contemplé quand on réfléchit à ses oeuvres.")[8] This pattern of reasoning was characteristic of Greek and Hellenistic Jewish thought, and it is interesting that Paul's language bears the imprint of that influence: *aidios* is found in pagan Greek from early times and frequently in Philo, but only here and in Jude 6 in the New Testament; *theiotēs*, a Hellenistic term, is found only here in the New Testament; on God's *dynamis kai theiotēs*, cf. *vis et natura deorum* (Cicero, *De natura deorum* 1.18.44). A very close parallel to the Romans passage—so close, in fact, that some commentators have suggested that Paul had it in mind—is the Hellenistic Jewish work Wisdom of Solomon 13:1–9, where inferential reasoning is clearly in view, especially, verses 4–5, where we find *noēsatōsan ap᾽ autōn . . . analogōs*. Moreover, Acts 14:17 states that although God let the Gentiles go their own way, still he did not leave them *amartyron*, that is, without evidence or witness, which is constituted by the created order. These passages, which doubtless reflect a common approach to Gentile audiences, may be plausibly interpreted as a legitimation of natural theology.

From the pages of the New Testament it is evident that showing the Christian faith to be true was an enterprise in which

---

intellectual ability or education (Ulrich Wilckens, *Der Brief an die Römer*, 3 vols., 2d rev. ed., EKK 6 [Köln: Benziger, 1987], 1:106). But as we have seen, the natural theologian could regard this inference as so natural and elementary that anyone could draw it, and he could see his cosmological and teleological arguments as simply more sophisticated versions thereof in response to sophisticated evasions. Schleier also asserts that Paul is not arguing from effect to cause because people's hearts, were they not clouded with sin, would be immediately open to and cognizant of God (Heinrich Schleier, *Der Römerbrief*, HTKNT 6 [Herder: Freiburg, 1977], 53). But nothing in the text precludes the interpretation that were people without sin, they would naturally and spontaneously draw the inference of a Creator, but because their minds are clouded by sin, they resist the conclusion and refuse to draw the inference, thereby condemning themselves.

[8]Franz-J. Leenhardt, *L'Epitre de saint Paul aux Romains*, CNT 6 (Neuchatel, Switzerland: Delachaux et Niestlé, 1969), 36; cf. p. 37. ("The things of God that escape our view, that is to say, his eternal power and deity, can be beheld when one reflects upon his works.")

both Jesus and the apostles were engaged. As the gospel writers portray, Jesus appealed to both his miracles and fulfilled prophecy as evidence of the veracity of his message. The miracles he performed were signs to the people of the coming of God's kingdom.[9] His exorcism of demonic forces was particularly significant in this regard. He declared, "If I drive out demons by the finger of God, then the kingdom of God has come to you" (Luke 11:20). Jesus is saying that his ability to rule the spiritual forces of darkness shows that in him the kingdom of God is already present. John's use of Jesus' miracles, which he calls "signs," is particularly interesting because John places them, not in the context of the kingdom of God and its triumph over Satan (there are, for example, no exorcisms in John), but in the context of the authentication of Jesus' claims.[10] Nicodemus reasons, "Rabbi, we know you are a teacher who has come from God. For no one could perform the miraculous signs you are doing if God were not with him" (John 3:2), and John concludes his gospel, "These [signs] are written that you may believe that Jesus is the Christ, the Son of God" (20:31). The Johannine Jesus refers to these signs as "works," and goes so far as to challenge men to believe in him, if not on his word alone, then on the basis of the works (10:38; 14:11). The sign of the healing of the blind man in John 9 is especially interesting because it displays John's attitude that while Jesus' signs did not compel belief, nevertheless, those who resisted them were completely unjustified and hardened in heart for doing so (vv. 30–33).

Jesus appealed not only to his miracles as evidence of his divine mission, but, as the Gospels portray him, also to fulfilled prophecy (Luke 24:25–27). In Jesus' response to John the Baptist's question concerning his messiahship, these two types of evidence come together (Matt. 11:5–6; cf. Isa. 35:5–6; 61:1).

Similarly, the apostles, in dealing with Jewish audiences, appealed to fulfilled prophecy, Jesus' miracles, and especially Jesus' resurrection as evidence that he was the Messiah (Acts 2:22–32). This was probably also Paul's typical approach (Acts 17:2–3, 17; 19:8; 28:23–24). When they confronted Gentile

---

[9]For a discussion of the idea that miracles as signs are distinct from evidence, see William Lane Craig, review article of *Miracles and the Critical Mind* by Colin Brown, *Journal of the Evangelical Theological Society* 17D (1984): 473–85.

[10]See helpful discussion in Raymond E. Brown, *The Gospel According to John*, Anchor Bible 29–29A (Garden City, N.Y.: Doubleday, 1970), appendix 3: "Signs and Works."

audiences who did not accept the Old Testament, the apostles appealed to God's handiwork in nature as evidence of the existence of the Creator (Acts 14:17). Then appeal was made to the eyewitness testimony to the resurrection of Jesus to show specifically that God had revealed himself in Jesus Christ (Acts 17:30–31; 1 Cor. 15:3–8).

This latter passage reveals that the witnesses for the resurrection of Jesus played a special role in the earliest Christian apologetic. Pannenberg notes that in 1 Corinthians 15:3–8 Paul is following the customary method of Greek historians, such as Herodotus, in proving a historical event, namely, the listing of witnesses.[11] Dodd further observes, "There can hardly be any purpose in mentioning the fact that most of the 500 are still alive, unless Paul is saying, in effect, 'the witnesses are there to be questioned.'"[12] Even Bultmann grudgingly concurs: "I can understand the text only as an attempt to make the resurrection of Christ credible as an objective historical fact."[13] Although Bultmann characterizes such an attempt as "fatal" because it tries to adduce proof for the kerygma,[14] he acknowledges that Paul does "think he can guarantee the resurrection of Christ as an objective fact by listing the witnesses who had seen him risen."[15] Pannenberg concludes, "The intention of this enumeration is clearly to give proof by means of witnesses to the facticity of Jesus' resurrection. . . . one will hardly be able to call into question Paul's intention of giving a convincing historical proof by the standards of that time."[16]

---

[11] Wolfhart Pannenberg, "Ist Jesus wirklich auferstanden?" in *Ist Jesus wirklich auferstanden? Geistliche Woche für Südwestdeutschland der Evang. Akademie Mannheim vom 16. bis 23. Februar 1964* (Karlsruhe: Evangelische Akademie Mannheim, 1964), 24.

[12] C. H. Dodd, "The Appearances of the Risen Christ: A Study in Form-Criticism of the Gospels," *More New Testament Studies* (Manchester: University of Manchester Press, 1968), 128.

[13] Rudolf Bultmann, *Faith and Understanding I*, 6th ed., ed. R. W. Funk, trans. L. P. Smith (London: SCM, 1969), 83.

[14] Rudolf Bultmann, "Reply to the Theses of J. Schniewind," in *Kerygma and Myth*, 2 vols., ed. H.-W. Bartsch, trans. R. H. Fuller (London: SPCK, 1953), 1:112.

[15] Rudolf Bultmann, *Theology of the New Testament*, 2 vols., trans. K. Grobel (London: SCM, 1952), 1:295; cf. 1:305. Referring specifically to Acts 17.31 and 1 Cor. 15.3–8, he admits, "Yet it cannot be denied that the resurrection of Jesus is often used in the New Testament as a miraculous proof" (Bultmann, "New Testament and Mythology," in *Kerygma and Myth*, 1:39).

[16] Wolfhart Pannenberg, *Jesus—God and Man*, trans. L. L. Wilkins and D. A. Priebe (London: SCM, 1968), 89.

And, lest we miss the forest for the trees, we should remind ourselves that in addition to individual passages of apologetic intent (such as Matthew's guard at the tomb account), there are whole books of the New Testament aimed at demonstrating the gospel's truth. One thinks immediately of Luke-Acts, an apologetic treatise *par excellence* for the Christian faith based on historical and prophetic evidences.[17] The same project characterizes the Gospel of John with its repeated emphasis on witness and Jesus' miraculous signs.

Thus, against those who think that it is inappropriate to present arguments and evidence to show that the Christian faith is true stands the New Testament involvement in just such a project, both in the example of Jesus and the apostles and in entire books dedicated to this purpose. Indeed, we are actually commanded by Scripture to have ready an *apologia* to present to any unbeliever who asks us the reason for our faith (1 Peter 3:15).

Although we know our faith to be true primarily through the witness of the Spirit, we must show our faith to be true through rational argument and evidence. While we can and should tell our interlocutor that we have an assurance grounded in the witness of the Holy Spirit that our faith is true, that does nothing to show him that our faith is true. Consider again the case of the Christian confronted with an adherent of some other world religion who rejects Christ but also claims to have a self-

---

[17]In his study of the concept of witness in the New Testament, Allison Trites points out that Luke-Acts presents the claims of Christ against a background of hostility, contention, and persecution, which accounts for the large place given to juridical terminology and ideas drawn from the law court. The operative question for Luke, states Trites, is: On what grounds or evidence can people have faith?

Luke therefore wants to present the evidence, particularly that for the resurrection, which vindicates Jesus. . . . he seeks to provide evidence for the truth of the events which have transpired, thereby giving Theophilus "authentic knowledge" ([*asphaleia*], . . . the same word used by Thucydides in the preface to his historical work, 1.22) and vindicating his name as a historian. . . . He uses the historical material for the Book of Acts according to the standards of his time as they are expressed by such ancient historians as Herodotus, Polybius, Thucydides and Josephus, and certainly intends to offer evidence that will stand the test of the closest scrutiny (Allison Trites, *The New Testament Concept of Witness* [Cambridge: Cambridge University Press, 1977], 135; cf. pp. 128, 138).

Thus, we have in Luke-Acts a sophisticated, historical apologetic for the Christian faith centering on the event of the resurrection.

authenticating experience of God. Alston points out that this situation taken in isolation results in an epistemic standoff.[18] For neither person knows how to find a common procedure for demonstrating to the other that he alone has a veridical, rather than delusory, experience. This standoff does not undermine the rationality of the Christian's belief, for even if his process of forming his belief is as reliable as can be, we have no idea what a noncircular proof of this fact would be. Thus his inability to provide such a proof does not nullify the rationality of his belief.[19] But although he is rational in retaining his Christian belief, the Christian in such circumstances is at a complete loss as to how to show his opponent that he is correct and that his opponent is wrong in his respective beliefs.

How is one to break this deadlock? Alston answers that the knowledgeable and reflective Christian should do whatever seems feasible to search for common ground on which to adjudicate the crucial differences between competing views, seeking to show in a noncircular way which of the contenders is correct.[20] If, by proceeding on the basis of considerations that are common to all parties, such as sense perception, rational self-evidence, and common modes of reasoning, the Christian can show that his own beliefs are true and those of his interlocutor false, then he will have succeeded in showing that the Christian is in a superior epistemic position for discerning the truth about these matters.

---

[18]William Alston, "Religious Diversity and Perceptual Knowledge of God," *Faith and Philosophy* 5, no. 4 (1988): 442–43.

[19]Since Alston is talking about religious experience in general, rather than the self-authenticating witness of the Spirit, he assumes the Christian's interlocutor to have an experience comparable to that of the Christian and therefore to be equally rational in holding to the veridicality of his own experience even though he cannot prove to the Christian that he is in fact in an epistemically superior position to the Christian. On the view I have defended, the non-Christian, if he persists in his rejection of Christ, will be resisting the drawing of the Holy Spirit and therefore failing to form a properly basic belief in the appropriate circumstances. Since basic beliefs are among the deliverances of reason, he is therefore irrational. This difference, however, would not affect the standoff between the Christian and the non-Christian, since neither could prove to the other that the other is deluded. Once apologetics is allowed to enter the picture, the objective difference between their epistemic situations becomes crucial, for since the non-Christian only *thinks* he has a self-authenticating experience of God when in fact he does not, the power of the evidence and argument may, by God's grace, crack his false assurance of the truth of his faith and persuade him to place his faith in Christ.

[20]Alston, "Religious Diversity," 446; cf. 433–34.

In our day, of course, even the claim, much less the demonstration, that one's faith is objectively true is anathema to the politically correct mind-set. Postmodernist antirealists and radical pluralists deny that there is any objective and exclusive truth about these matters. But however fashionable such views may be in the Literature or Religious Studies departments at the university, the vast majority of philosophers have remained unconvinced. For such positions are obviously self-refuting: if they are true, then they are false. When a postmodernist like John Caputo intones, "The truth is that there is no truth," someone should have the courage to say that the emperor is running around buck-naked.

Showing Christianity to be true is, of course, precisely the task of apologetics. Showing Christianity to be true will involve both defensive (negative) apologetics and offensive (positive) apologetics. It will involve proving that our *Weltanschauung* is both logically coherent and best fits the facts of experience. We shall be engaged not only in refuting objections that our view is incoherent or implausible in light of certain facts (defensive apologetics), but also in providing arguments and evidence that show that our view best explains the data (offensive apologetics).

This is an understanding of the methodology of apologetics that seems to mesh nicely with recent developments in religious epistemology. Plantinga, for example, does not object to the use of natural theology in *showing* one's faith to be true; he only considers it improper as one's basis for *knowing* his faith to be true. But he believes that "natural theology could be useful in helping someone move from unbelief to belief."[21] Similarly, Evans says that the story of how faith is grounded in the inner witness of the Holy Spirit "is the story that the Church tells when it is attempting to understand how Christians in fact gain the knowledge they claim to have. The evidentialist story is the story the Church tells when it is attempting to convince or persuade someone of what it takes to be the truth."[22]

EXCURSUS: Plantinga and Natural Theology

Plantinga's attitude toward the arguments of natural theology is easily misunderstood. While skeptical of *proofs* of God's existence, Plantinga

---

[21]Alvin Plantinga, "Reason and Belief in God," in *Faith and Rationality*, 73.

[22]C. Stephen Evans, *The Historical Christ and the Jesus of Faith* (Oxford: Clarendon, 1996), 283–84.

is quite open to *probabilistic arguments* that show God's existence to be more likely than not (Plantinga, "Reason and Belief," 29–30, 70, 73; idem, "Self-Profile," in *Alvin Plantinga*, ed. James E. Tomberlin and Peter Van Inwagen, Profiles 5 [Dordrecht: D. Reidel, 1985], 56). Indeed, he goes so far as to say, "... the ontological argument provides as good grounds for the existence of God as does any serious philosophical argument for any important philosophical conclusion" (Alvin Plantinga, "Reason and Belief in God," typescript dated October 1981, pp. 18–19. This paragraph was inadvertently omitted in the published version of "Reason and Belief," which causes Mavrodes's reference to it [Mavrodes, "Jerusalem and Athens," 205] to refer to nothing. Fortunately, a nearly identical paragraph appears in "Self-Profile," 71).

At first blush, this constitutes an extravagant endorsement of the arguments of natural theology. Commenting on this paragraph, Mavrodes marvels, "But if natural theology can be *that* good, as good as the best arguments anywhere in serious philosophy, good enough to provide sufficient evidence for belief in God, then ... why should we not put forward these powerful arguments as *proofs* of God?" (Mavrodes, "Jerusalem and Athens," 205–6). Noting that Plantinga's criterion for what constitutes a proof is extraordinarily restrictive, Mavrodes opines, "Plantinga is almost surely right in thinking that no piece of natural theology is successful in terms of this criterion, and that no other piece of serious philosophical argumentation satisfies it either. But so what?" (ibid., 207–8). We can define "proof" in this highly restrictive way if we want to, in which case there is no theistic proof, continues Mavrodes, or else we may make our definition less restrictive, in which case there may well be a theistic proof. The quarrel is merely terminological.

This enthusiastic endorsement needs to be qualified, however. Plantinga makes it clear that just as a person is entirely rational in accepting the key premise of the ontological argument—"Possibly, a maximally great being exists"—so a person is entirely rational in rejecting it (Alvin Plantinga, *The Nature of Necessity*, Clarendon Library of Logic and Philosophy [Oxford: Clarendon, 1974], 219–20; idem, "Self-Profile," 70). If Plantinga holds that the premises and reasoning of the other theistic arguments are not significantly more perspicuous than the ontological argument's, then in saying that there is sufficient evidence for God's existence, he means sufficient merely for rationality, for being within one's intellectual rights.

It may be thought that the key premise of the ontological argument is considerably more uncertain and epistemically turbid than the premises of the other theistic arguments and that accordingly it would be irrational for a sufficiently well-informed person to reject their conclusions. But in an unpublished lecture on theistic arguments, Plantinga, while endorsing two dozen or so of these, asserts that "these arguments are not coercive in the sense that every person is obliged to accept their premises on pain of irrationality. . . . an argument can be a good one even if it is not coercive—even if its premises are not such that any reasonable person would be obliged to accept them" (Alvin Plantinga, "Two Dozen [or so] Theistic Arguments," paper delivered at the 33rd Annual Philosophy Conference, Wheaton College, 23–25 Oct. 1986, p. 1). That is why, to return to Mavrodes's question, Plantinga does not put forward these probabilistic arguments as proofs even in a broad sense, for they only serve to make belief in God *permissible*. They serve to *confirm* one's belief that God exists and to *convince* nontheists who accept the premises of one's argument. But a nontheist who rejects a premise of one's argument remains rational in doing so. On Plantinga's view, then, theistic arguments would rank among the highest of philosophical arguments, but philosophical arguments in general have a low level of epistemic force.

But even this qualified position is not altogether clear. For what are we to make of Plantinga's claim that theistic arguments make it probable, or more likely than not, that God exists? From the foregoing, we might expect him to mean that such arguments make God's existence probable *for the one who accepts the premises*, but that these premises, like the key premise in the ontological argument, do not all present themselves to us as probably true. But this is not what Plantinga says. He states, "One could then give a probabilistic or inductive argument for the existence of God, thus showing that theistic belief is rational, or epistemically proper, in that *it is more likely than not with respect to the deliverances of reason*" (Plantinga, "Reason and Belief," 70 [my italics]). But if the argument shows that the conclusion is probable with respect to the deliverances of reason, then how can a normally situated person be rational in rejecting the argument? Similarly, in his Wheaton lecture, Plantinga grants that "perhaps in at least some of these cases if our faculties are functioning properly and we consider the premises, we are inclined to accept them; and (under those conditions) the conclusion has considerable epistemic probability . . . on the premises" (Plantinga, "Two Dozen Arguments," 1). But in such cases, to reject one of the premises is to be dysfunctional, which in Plantinga's terminology is to be irrational. If a person in such a situation is to reject the argument's conclusion while accepting its premises and reasoning, it can only be because on Plantinga's understanding, it appears, it can be rational to reject conclusions one regards as probably true—and that (so far as I can see) without any independent reason for doing so.

But if my interpretation of Plantinga is correct, the Christian apologist is likely to respond with Mavrodes, "So what?" A person who rejects all theistic arguments may be said to be "rational" in this technically defined sense, but the fact remains that he rejects without justification a theistic conclusion that he knows to be probable with respect to the deliverances of reason. He thereby reveals his hardened heart and renders himself "without excuse" before God. If the Christian apologist can show Christian theism to be probable with respect to premises that are either deliverances of reason or themselves ultimately probable with respect to them, then his task is complete.

The methodology of classical apologetics was first to present arguments for theism, which aimed to show that God's existence is at least more probable than not, and then to present Christian evidences, probabilistically construed, for God's revelation in Christ.[23] This is the method I have adopted in my own work. By means of the *kalam* cosmological argument, I have endeavored to show that a Personal Creator of the universe exists.[24] By means of the historical evidence for the resurrection

---

[23]See, e.g., such classics as Philippe de Mornay, *De la vérité de la religion chrétienne* (Anvers: 1581); Hugo Grotius *De veritate religionis christianae* (1627); Jacques Abbadie, *Traité de la vérité de la religion chrétienne* (The Hague: 1684); Samuel Clarke, *A Demonstration of the Being and Attributes of God* (London: 1705) and *A Discourse Concerning the Unchangeable Obligations of Natural Religion and the Truth and Certainty of the Christian Revelation* (London: 1706); William Paley, *Natural Theology* (London: 1802) and *A View of the Evidences of Christianity*, 2 vols. (London: 1794).

[24]See William Lane Craig, *The* Kalam *Cosmological Argument*, Library of Philosophy and Religion (London: Macmillan, 1979); idem, "Whitrow and Popper on the Impossibility of an Infinite Past," *British Journal for the Philosophy of Science* 30, no. 2 (1979): 165–70; idem, "Wallace Matson and the Crude Cosmological Argument," *Australasian Journal of Philosophy* 57, no. 2 (1979): 163–70; idem, "The Finitude of the Past," *Aletheia* 2 (1981): 235–42; idem, "Professor Mackie and the *Kalam* Cosmological Argument," *Religious Studies* 20, no. 3 (1985): 367–75; idem, review article of *Time, Creation and the Continuum* by Richard Sorabji, *International Philosophical Quarterly* 25, no. 3 (1985): 319–26; idem, "God, Creation and Mr. Davies," *British Journal for the Philosophy of Science* 37, no. 3 (1986): 163–75; idem, "'What Place, Then, for a Creator?' Hawking on God and Creation," *British Journal for the Philosophy of Science* 41, no. 4 (1990): 473–91; idem, "Time and Infinity," *International Philosophical Quarterly* 31, no. 4 (1991): 387–401; idem, "The *Kalam* Cosmological Argument and the Hypothesis of a Quiescent Universe," *Faith and Philosophy* 8, no. 1 (1991): 104–8; idem, "Theism and Big Bang Cosmology," *Australasian Journal of Philosophy* 69, no. 4 (1991): 492–503; idem, "Pseudo-Dilemma?" *Nature* 354, no. 6352 (1991): 347; idem, "The Origin and Creation of the Universe: A Reply to Adolf Grunbaum," *British Journal for the Philosophy of Science* 43, no. 2 (1992): 233–40; idem, "God and the Initial Cosmological Singularity: A Reply to Quentin Smith," *Faith and Philosophy* 9, no. 2 (1992): 237–47; idem and Quentin Smith, *Theism, Atheism, and Big Bang Cosmology* (Oxford: Clarendon, 1993); idem, "The Caused Beginning of the Universe: A Response to Quentin Smith," *British Journal for the Philosophy of Science* 44, no. 4 (1993): 623–39; idem, "Graham Oppy on the *Kalam* Cosmological Argument," *Sophia* 32, no. 1 (1993): 1–11; idem, "Smith on the Finitude of the Past," *International Philosophical Quarterly* 33, no. 2 (1993): 225–31; idem, "Professor Grunbaum

of Jesus, I have tried to show that God has revealed himself in Christ.[25]

What do I consider to be the force of these arguments? A good deductive argument will be one that is formally and informally valid and whose premises are both true and more plausible

---

on Creation," *Erkenntnis* 40, no. 3 (1994): 325–41; idem, "Creation and Big Bang Cosmology," *Philosophia Naturalis* 31, no. 2 (1994): 217–24; idem, "A Response to Grunbaum on Creation and Big Bang Cosmology," *Philosophia Naturalis* 31, no. 2 (1994): 237–49; idem, "Theism and Physical Cosmology," in *A Companion to Philosophy of Religion*, ed. P. Quinn and C. Taliaferro, Blackwell Companions to Philosophy 8 (Oxford: Basil Blackwell, 1997): 419–25; idem, "In Defense of the *Kalam* Cosmological Argument," *Faith and Philosophy* 14, no. 2 (1997): 236–47; idem, "Cosmology," in *Oxford Companion to Christian Thought*, ed. A. Hastings (Oxford: Oxford University Press, forthcoming); idem, "Personal Agency and the Origin of the Universe," in *Le vide*, ed. E. Gunzig and S. Diner (Brussels: Universite de Bruxelles, forthcoming); idem, "Design and the Cosmological Argument" in *The Design Hypothesis*, ed. William Dembski (Downers Grove, Ill.: InterVarsity Press, forthcoming); idem, "Theism and Creation," *Erkenntnis* (forthcoming); idem, "A Swift and Easy Refutation of the *Kalam* Cosmological Argument?" *Religious Studies* (forthcoming).

[25]See my companion volumes, *The Historical Argument for the Resurrection of Jesus*, Texts and Studies in Religion 23 (Toronto: Edwin Mellen, 1985), and *Assessing the New Testament Evidence for the Historicity of the Resurrection of Jesus*, Toronto Studies in Theology (Toronto: Edwin Mellen, 1989). For article length treatments, see idem, "The Bodily Resurrection of Jesus," in *Gospel Perspectives I*, ed. R. T. France and D. Wenham (Sheffield, England: JSOT Press, 1980), 47–74; idem, "The Guard at the Tomb," *New Testament Studies* 30, no. 2 (1984): 273–81; idem, "The Historicity of the Empty Tomb of Jesus," *New Testament Studies* 31, no. 1 (1985): 39–67; idem, "The Problem of Miracles: A Historical and Philosophical Perspective," in *Gospel Perspectives VI*, ed. D. Wenham and Craig Blomberg (Sheffield, England: JSOT Press, 1986), 9–40; idem, "Pannenbergs Beweis für die Auferstehung Jesu," *Kerygma und Dogma* 34 (April–June 1988): 78–104; idem, "On Doubts About the Resurrection," *Modern Theology* 6 (October 1989): 53–75; idem, "The Disciples' Inspection of the Empty Tomb (Luke 24, 12. 24; John 20, 1–10)," in *John and the Synoptics*, ed. A. Denaux, BETL 101 (Louvain: University Press, 1992), 614–19; idem, "From Easter to Valentinus and the Apostles' Creed Once More: A Critical Examination of James Robinson's Proposed Resurrection Appearance Trajectories," *Journal for the Study of the New Testament* 52D (1993): 19–39; idem, *Reasonable Faith* (Wheaton, Ill.: Crossway, 1994), 255–98; idem, "Did Jesus Rise from the Dead?" in *Jesus Under Fire*, ed. M. J. Wilkins and J. P. Moreland (Grand Rapids: Zondervan, 1995), 142–76; "John Dominic Crossan on the Resurrection of Jesus," in *The Resurrection*, ed. S. Davis, D. Kendall, and G. O'Collins (Oxford: Oxford University Press, 1997), 249–71; idem and John Dominic Crossan, *Will the Real Jesus Please Stand Up?*, ed. P. Copan with responses by R. Miller, C. Blomberg, M. Borg, and B. Witherington III (Grand Rapids: Baker, 1998); idem and Gerd Lüdemann, *Visions of Jesus*, ed. P. Copan with responses by R. Gundry, M. Goulder, S. Davis, and R. Hoover (Downers Grove, Ill.: InterVarsity Press, forthcoming).

than their contradictories.[26] When judged by this standard, the *kalam* cosmological argument strikes me as a good argument. The force of the argument will depend on how much more plausible its premises are than their negations. It seems to me that the first premise of the *kalam* cosmological argument, that *whatever begins to exist has a cause,* is a metaphysically necessary truth and a properly basic belief. To deny this proposition is, therefore, for a normal adult, irrational. It is thus to be contrasted with the key premise of the ontological argument, which has for us the epistemic opacity of Goldbach's Conjecture: we know that it is necessarily true or necessarily false, but we have no noncircular way of discerning which it is. By contrast, the first premise of the *kalam* cosmological argument expresses the intuition *ex nihilo nihil fit,* which is so perspicuous that only an effete skepticism can deny it.

The second premise, that *the universe began to exist,* is much more controversial. It is supported by at least two independent philosophical arguments for the finitude of the past and enjoys confirmation in two independent lines of evidence drawn from astrophysical cosmology.

The two philosophical arguments are based on the impossibility of the existence of an actual infinite or on the impossibility of forming an actual infinite by successive addition. It is difficult to state precisely what force these arguments have or ought to have, chiefly because their cogency has a sort of ripple effect throughout one's philosophical system, which requires that the plausibility of the arguments be measured against the plausibility of the changes that they may force in the rest of one's web of beliefs.[27] But taken in themselves, the arguments seem to

---

[26]See Stephen T. Davis, *God, Reason, and Theistic Proofs,* Reason and Religion (Grand Rapids: Eerdmans, 1997), 1–14, for a discussion of these criteria.

[27]The cogency of the first argument entails, e.g., that Platonism is incorrect with regard to abstract objects. This will give some philosophers serious pause. But this consequence seems altogether acceptable to me, since (1) we have no compelling argument, to my knowledge, that abstract objects exist, and (2) we have independent reasons to doubt their existence—namely, (a) it is not at all clear what an abstract object *is* (what, e.g., is an unexemplified property or a number?); (b) the paradoxes of naive set theory, which are avoided only at the expense of our not being able to say what a set is, ought to make us skeptical of Platonism; and (c) Platonism is theologically unacceptable because it compromises the aseity of God in positing infinite realms of reality that exist necessarily and independently of God. We may seek to elude these problems by trying to wed Platonism with theism as Christopher Menzel has recently tried to do (Christopher Menzel, "Theism, Platonism, and the Metaphysics of Mathematics," *Faith and Philosophy* 4, no. 4 [1987]: 365–82). But this

me extremely plausible and should so appear to any normal adult whose intuitions have not been jaded by the common text-book assertions that actual infinites are wholly unobjectionable.

As for the scientific confirmations based on the expansion and thermodynamic properties of the universe, these serve to show that the conclusion reached by philosophical argument alone also fits remarkably the facts of experience. It seems to me that naturalistic metaphysical hypotheses aimed at explaining the origin of the universe (for example, quantum fluctuations in some background space) enjoy no preferred status over a super-naturalistic metaphysical hypothesis and that, indeed, those pro-posed thus far are less plausible than theism.

On balance, then, it seems to me that on the basis of the *kalam* cosmological argument, a person who is sufficiently informed and whose faculties are functioning properly ought to agree that it is more likely than not that a Creator of the universe exists. This argument can thus serve as one link in the natural theologian's cumulative case for theism.

As for the evidence for the resurrection of Jesus, we are here engaged in an inductive argument for a particular historical

---

attempt seems incompatible with a robust doctrine of *creatio ex nihilo* and in any case depends on breathtaking metaphysical acrobatics (a sort of divine logicism) and, even if successful, goes no further than proving the bare possibility of such a mar-riage, which does nothing to counteract the force of the *kalam* cosmological argu-ment. Or again, the argument's cogency may force us to adopt a model of divine knowledge whereby God does not cognize an actually infinite number of proposi-tions. But William Alston has independently proposed a nonpropositional model of divine cognition that seems to me altogether acceptable (William Alston, "Does God Have Beliefs?" *Religious Studies* 22, no. 314 [1986]: 287–306; cf. William E. Mann, "Necessity," in *Companion to Philosophy of Religion*, 264–70) and perhaps even helpful in avoiding certain paradoxes of omniscience (Patrick Grimm, "Truth, Omniscience, and the Knower," *Philosophical Studies* 54, no. 1 [1988]: 9–41). So although the cogency of the first argument may entail important consequences elsewhere in our system of beliefs, such changes as are necessary are neither *ad hoc* nor implausible, since there are independent reasons for adopting those positions anyway.

Similarly, the second philosophical argument implies an A-theory of time (that tense and temporal becoming are objective), and this might be a stumbling block to certain philosophers of time and space. But in my opinion the objectivity of tense and temporal becoming is so evident on the basis of intuition and argument that its denial ranks as a prime example of philosophical self-deception (see my compan-ion volumes *The Tensed Theory of Time: A Critical Examination* and *The Tenseless The-ory of Time: A Critical Evaluation* [Dordrecht: Kluwer, forthcoming]). Hence, the force of the philosophical arguments ought not to be too seriously diminished by such changes as are entailed by their acceptance.

hypothesis. One model for sound inductive reasoning is known as inference to the best explanation.[28] According to this approach, we begin with the evidence available to us and then infer what would, if true, provide the best explanation of that evidence. Out of a pool of live options determined by our background beliefs, we select the best of various competing potential explanations to give a causal account of why the evidence is as it is and not otherwise. The process of determining which historical reconstruction is the best explanation will involve the historian's craft, since various factors will have to be weighed, such as explanatory power, explanatory scope, plausibility, degree of being *ad hoc*, and so on.[29] Since the competing explanations may meet the various criteria to different degrees, the determination of which is the best explanation may be difficult and require a good deal of skill.

In my estimation the hypothesis "God raised Jesus from the dead" furnishes the best explanation of the historical data relevant to Jesus' final fate *(das Geschick Jesu)*. The inductive grounds for the inference of this explanation consist primarily in the evidence supporting three independently established facts: (1) the tomb of Jesus was found empty by a group of his women followers on the first day of the week following his crucifixion, (2) various individuals and groups thereafter experienced on different occasions and under varying circumstances appearances of Jesus alive, and (3) the first disciples came to believe in Jesus' resurrection in the absence of sufficient antecedent historical influences from either Judaism or pagan religions. If these three facts can be historically established with a reasonable degree of certainty (and it seems to me that they can, as they are recognized by the majority of New Testament critics today) and if alternative naturalistic explanations for these facts are untenable (and the consensus of scholarship is that they are), then unless the resurrection hypothesis is shown to be even more untenable than its failed competitors (and my experience in debating the comparative merits of the hypotheses convinces me that it is not), the preferred explanation ought to be the one given in the documents themselves: God raised Jesus from the dead. The sig-

---

[28]For an account see Peter Lipton, *Inference to the Best Explanation* (London: Routledge, 1981).

[29]For discussion see C. Behan McCullagh, *Justifying Historical Descriptions* (Cambridge: Cambridge University Press, 1984), 19.

nificance of this event is then to be found in the religio-historical context in which it occurred, namely, as the vindication of Jesus' own unparalleled claim to divine authority. I think that the evidence for the resurrection of Jesus is such that a well-informed investigator ought to agree that it is more likely than not to have occurred.

Thus, using the methodology of classical apologetics, one seeks to show that Christian theism is the most credible worldview one can adopt. Of course, showing Christianity to be true will involve much more than the two arguments above: they are but two links in the coat of mail, and the positive case will need to be accompanied by a defensive case against objections. The apologetic task, then, is perhaps best seen as a collective project taken on by the believing community.

Role of the Holy Spirit

Finally, what about the role of the Holy Spirit in our showing Christianity to be true? As Pannenberg has emphasized, the work of the Spirit is not to supply the deficits in weak or unsound arguments.[30] Rather, his role is existential: he preveniently moves in the hearts of unbelievers to dissolve their sinful prejudices and open their minds to an honest consideration of the arguments and evidence. In the absence of the work of the Holy Spirit, our best arguments will fall like water on a stone, for the natural man suppresses the truth in unrighteousness (Rom. 1:21). Plantinga observes that "a person might, when confronted with an arg[ument] he sees to be valid for a conclusion he deeply disbelieves from premises he know[s] to be true, give up (some of) those premises: in this way you can reduce someone from knowledge to ignorance by giving him an argument he sees to be valid from premises he knows to be true."[31] This is an apt description of natural man confronted with a Christian apologetic. Apart from the work of the Holy Spirit, he will do all he can to resist the argument, even adopting extreme and outlandish beliefs rather than yielding to the truth of Christian theism. But it is the role of

---

[30]Wolfhart Pannenberg, "Einsicht und Glauben," in *Grundfragen systematischer Theologie* (Göttingen: Vandenhoeck & Ruprecht, 1967), 223–36; for a critique of Pannenberg's theological rationalism, see Craig, "Pannenbergs Beweis für die Auferstehung Jesu," 87–95.

[31]Plantinga, "Two Dozen Arguments," 1.

the Holy Spirit to open the heart of the unbeliever and to use the arguments as a means of drawing people to himself.

CONCLUSION

In conclusion, we have seen that a proper understanding of apologetic methodology involves making a fundamental distinction between our knowing and our showing Christian theism to be true. We *know* that our Christian beliefs are true because they are properly basic, warranted beliefs grounded in our veridical experience of the witness of the Holy Spirit in our hearts. Rational argument and evidence may confirm our Christian beliefs to us but cannot defeat them if we are walking in the fullness of the Spirit. We can *show* that Christian theism is true by presenting arguments for theism and evidences for a specifically Christian theism, which go to show, when coupled with defensive apologetics, that Christian theism is the most plausible worldview a sufficiently informed, normal adult can adopt. The Holy Spirit will then use such arguments and evidence to draw unbelievers to a knowledge of God by removing their sinful resistance to the conclusion of our arguments.

I have found this to be both an intellectually and experientially satisfying account of the matter. As I look back on my Wheaton days, I see now how infected with theological rationalism our community was and how perverse a concept I had of what it meant to be a "true intellectual." It was the testimony of Christ's Spirit within me that gave me the fundamental assurance that my faith was true; and my refusal to give this up in the face of potential defeaters was not a *sacrificium intellectus* but was wholly in accord with the deliverances of reason. By understanding the proper basis for Christian belief, we are saved from all the deleterious consequences the magisterial role of reason would imply. On a very practical level, this understanding reminds us of the importance of daily yielding to the Holy Spirit, of striving to lead pure and sinless lives, and of engaging in spiritual disciplines like Bible study, prayer, meaningful worship, and personal evangelism. At the same time, we do not abandon ourselves to pure subjectivity and mysticism, for our beliefs are confirmed by, if not based on, rational arguments and objective evidence. In times of doubt, we should not only seek the face of the Lord, but also strengthen ourselves by recalling these arguments and evidences.

This account also permits us to commend our faith to unbelievers, not merely by proclamation, but also by rational persuasion. Our appeal is to the whole person, not only to the heart, but to the head as well. We can show unbelievers that the most reasonable thing they can do with their lives is to commit them to Christ. At the same time, we are not so naive as to think that we can argue people into the kingdom of God. Conversion is exclusively the role of the Spirit. But we can rationally commend our faith to others in the confidence that some, whose hearts he has opened, will respond to the apologetic we present and place their faith in Christ.

AN EVIDENTIALIST'S RESPONSE

Gary R. Habermas

As I remark in the opening sentence of chapter 2, "Evidential Apologetics," evidentialists and classical apologists have much in common, with the major distinction being the use of historical evidences. Bill Craig's essay is frank and honest, and it expresses the need for applying apologetics.

POSITIVE CONTRIBUTIONS OF CLASSICAL APOLOGETICS

Much in Craig's essay is to be commended, and many features are shared by evidentialists. Courageously, Craig begins with a story regarding his own alma mater, introducing his critique of "theological rationalism." What emerges from this personal account is the key idea in the chapter—the distinction between *knowing* and *showing* Christianity to be true. Craig has made this distinction elsewhere,[1] but as far as I know, this is his most detailed treatment of the inner witness of the Holy Spirit.

Craig will surely be criticized in this last area, perhaps most of all by those who have been trained philosophically. I will treat some of these issues below, but I will remark here that his position is defensible. We do, however, differ on some details. At the least, I think this sort of formulation answers some very difficult

---

[1]E.g., William Lane Craig, *Apologetics: An Introduction* (Chicago: Moody Press, 1984), 17–19; idem, *The Son Rises: The Historical Evidence for the Resurrection of Jesus* (Chicago: Moody Press, 1981), 8.

questions. Epistemically, we need a starting point for religious knowledge. Biblically, while God encourages the use of evidences, they are certainly secondary to truth; facts and evidences are not equated. On both fronts, radical forms of rationalism, empiricism, and skepticism that place their theories above God's truth need to be countered. But how we should proceed in this is challenging.

Beyond the subject of the Holy Spirit's witness to believers, the remainder of Craig's essay will sound more familiar to those interested in apologetic issues. Some strong areas emerge here too. Craig defends the place of evidences in the New Testament, the *kalam* argument for God's existence, and the resurrection of Jesus. He also argues that Jesus' teachings have been vindicated.

When showing the truth of Christianity, Craig argues according to probability. Interestingly, he appears to take the option of "hard" over "soft" apologetics, with his comment that "a well-informed investigator *ought* to agree that it is more likely than not" (p. 53).[2] Making the distinction between negative and positive apologetics, Craig also provides an example of the former in his critique of postmodernism (p. 45).

Craig ends with some reminders that apologetics does not exist in a vacuum. Believers cannot be defeated "if we are walking in the fullness of the Spirit" (p. 54). This involves "daily yielding," practicing the disciplines of the Christian faith (p. 54). We should not feed our intellect only, but also our experience. I agree that we need to build bridges between theory and practice. God's radical call is to both our head and our heart.

CHALLENGES TO CRAIG'S CLASSICAL APOLOGETICS

Evidentialists and classical apologists share much of the evidential task. Still there are some issues of concern that distinguish Craig's apologetic approach from my own. I will now turn to several of these.

---

[2]See Stephen T. Davis, "Is It Possible to Know That Jesus Was Raised from the Dead?" *Faith and Philosophy* 1, no. 2 (April 1984): 151–52, 157–58. The chief issue between hard and soft apologetics concerns whether one can reject the Christian position and still remain rational. The "hard" position answers negatively while the "soft" view answers positively. Craig seems to support the former (p. 45).

Distinguishing Classical Apologetics from Evidentialism

Readers of Craig's essay may be puzzled by a distinction that does not seem to be overly apparent. What are the determining characteristics of the classical apologetic method? What distinguishes it from the other methods and especially from evidentialism?

Craig says that classical apologetics is a combination of "natural theology and Christian evidences" (p. 28). Expanding this notion somewhat, he adds that this method proceeds in a twofold manner, "first to present arguments for theism ... and then to present Christian evidences, probabilistically construed, for God's revelation in Christ," adding that this is the approach "I have adopted in my own work" (p. 48).

I don't think, however, that these explanations go far enough in demarcating the nature of the classical method. *Must* theistic arguments *necessarily* precede Christian evidences? Carefully construed, can the latter stand on their own? Asked another way, can the evidentialist case that I and others have outlined exist as a separate way to get to Christian theism, or is this move doomed to failure? Several classical apologists have firmly asserted that a historical argument from miracles to God is an illegitimate move.

For example, in their volume *Classical Apologetics*, R. C. Sproul, John Gerstner, and Arthur Lindsley argue that natural theology *must* precede miracles or they are meaningless. Miracles can never prove God's existence.[3] Norman Geisler agrees with this assessment, arguing for the necessity of the two-step method.[4]

On the other hand, Craig frequently argues that the resurrection of Jesus has strong theistic implications. Upon completing his most robust treatment of the historicity of the resurrection, Craig asks what the historian may conclude concerning this event. While his discipline may not give him the right to say that God performed the event (because history has no tools to measure supernatural causation), the evidence is still such that this is the proper human inference. So the historian

---

[3]R. C. Sproul, John Gerstner, and Arthur Lindsley, *Classical Apologetics: A Rational Defense of the Christian Faith and a Critique of Presuppositional Apologetics* (Grand Rapids: Zondervan, 1984), 146–47, 276.

[4]Norman Geisler, *Christian Apologetics* (Grand Rapids: Baker, 1976), 95–96, 147.

"may indeed rightly infer from the evidence that God has acted here in history."[5] The data indicate that this is a correct decision. One reason for this determination is the context in which the resurrection happened: "the life, teachings, and claims of Jesus."[6] Craig continues, "For as long as the existence of God is even possible, an event's being caused by God cannot be ruled out."[7]

Further, the resurrection reveals Jesus' own deity: *"The resurrection vindicates the claims that Jesus made concerning himself."*[8] So then, we have a twofold indication of a theistic universe: Jesus' resurrection doubles as an indication both of his Father's activity in history and that Jesus himself is deity.[9]

Those who have followed our publications know that Craig and I generally agree at each of these points, although we sometimes differ in details.[10] I have also argued at length that the

---

[5]William Lane Craig, *Assessing the New Testament Evidence for the Historicity of the Resurrection of Jesus* (Lewiston, N.Y.: Edwin Mellen, 1989), 419. Craig goes on to disagree with "the methodological principle that prohibits any historian from adducing a supernatural cause for an event in history" (p. 419).

[6]Ibid.

[7]Ibid., 420.

[8]Craig, *Son Rises*, 141 (his emphasis); cf. 137–41.

[9]Craig has made many similar comments. In another of his works, he states: "[I]t ought to be asked whether *on the basis of the resurrection alone,* we would be justified in inferring that a miracle has truly occurred.... I know of no critic who argues that the historical evidence shows that Jesus did rise, but that this was a purely natural occurrence." Then Craig lists two reasons for this conclusion: the resurrection is "so unnatural an event that it seems best to attribute it to a supernatural cause" and the religious context of Jesus' teachings. See his volume, *The Historical Argument for the Resurrection of Jesus During the Deist Controversy* (Lewiston, N.Y.: Edwin Mellen, 1985), 499–501 (my emphasis). He also repeats his other point that even the *possibility* of God's existence indicates that miracles like the resurrection are at least possible (Craig, *Historical Argument for the Resurrection,* 490, 516). It would seem, then, that Craig regards the resurrection as an event that at least potentially breaks through the naturalistic barrier.

Again, Craig begins his popular volume *The Son Rises* by telling his readers that he is writing to those who believe in God (p. 7). Still it seems clear that the resurrection has much to say in favor of that theism: "Once it is admitted that Jesus really did rise transformed from the dead, the conclusion that God raised Him up is virtually inescapable. Only a sterile, academic skepticism resists this inevitable inference" (p. 137). (By contrast, in *Assessing the New Testament Evidence,* the existence of God is not listed in Craig's inventory of his presuppositions [p. xvii].)

[10]For some of my differences with Craig, see my essay "The Resurrection of Jesus and Contemporary Scholarship: A Review Essay," *Bulletin of the Evangelical Philosophical Society* 14, no. 2 (1991): 44–51. Further, even though it is an excellent evidence, I do not emphasize the empty tomb as much as he does because it does

resurrection provides retrospective confirmation of God's existence as well as indicating God's activity in raising Jesus, thereby confirming Jesus' message. Thus, the event indicates the actions of God plus the deity of Jesus Christ when taken in the light of Jesus' own teachings. Seen from one angle, even the possibility of God's prior existence would be a strong confirmation here.[11] I also think that the historian can examine this event without abandoning the strictures of his or her own discipline.[12]

But Craig now appears to have a dilemma. He can accept what his classical apologetic colleagues say about the nature of their method and repudiate what appears to be his clear arguments from the resurrection to God's activity and Jesus' deity, or he can continue to accept the latter, thereby disagreeing with his colleagues. While I think the latter can be defended strongly and is definitely the way to move, that's because I think that evidentialism is a viable strategy! If Craig agrees, it would appear that he has also made an evidentialist move, and at its most crucial point too.

Could Craig make the latter move but insist that he is still a classical apologist precisely because he uses the two-step approach and this is the essence of that position? If so, what would it avail? If the second step is itself one of the indications of a theistic universe, as he seems to assert regarding the historian's proper inference, then, while the initial step may be helpful, it is not mandatory.[13] He has neither conformed to recent

---

not fit the criteria of my "minimal facts" methodology. Also, Craig needs to develop a detailed account of *how* and *why* it may be determined that the resurrection is a miracle performed by God. When proceeding from the resurrection to Christian theism, I do not think that we should argue that the "unnatural" qualities of the event point to "a supernatural cause," as does Craig (*Historical Argument for the Resurrection*, 500), for this plays directly into the hand of the critics who argue that it is precisely these same qualities that show that miracles are "freak events of nature."

[11]My most detailed account is found in *The Resurrection of Jesus: An Apologetic* (Grand Rapids: Baker, 1980; Lanham, Md.: University Press of America, 1984), chaps. 2–3. A brief summary appears in my debate with Antony Flew: *Did Jesus Rise from the Dead? The Resurrection Debate*, ed. Terry L. Miethe (San Francisco: Harper and Row, 1987), 39–42. Craig also looks back from the resurrection to God's prior causation (Craig, *Assessing the New Testament Evidence*, 419).

[12]See Gary R. Habermas, *Ancient Evidence for the Life of Jesus: Historical Records of His Death and Resurrection* (Nashville: Thomas Nelson, 1984), chap. 1: "Historical Methodology and Miracle Claims," esp. pp. 23–27.

[13]I mentioned in my initial essay that evidentialists agree at this point. Typical arguments for God's existence are frequently utilized, but unlike classical apologists,

delineations of his position nor shown why the initial step is absolutely crucial.

Or Craig might argue that the classical practice of apologetics through the centuries does not support his colleagues' contentions that the second step by itself is illegitimate. In other words, he might disagree with Sproul, Gerstner, Lindsley, Geisler, and others. That, of course, is more a matter between them. It needs to be pointed out, however, that in former centuries atheism was seldom a problem. Thus, it would be difficult to sustain the argument that miracles were *regularly* used in order to establish a theistic universe.[14] Worse, by supporting a one-step, historical approach, Craig would also be arguing against his colleagues that the evidentialist methodology itself presents a strong argument.

At the very least, we must note that Craig seems clearly to accept the mainstay of the evidentialist argument—the one-step apologetic argument from history to Christian theism. If this is the case, not only is his position inadequately differentiated from evidentialism, but he would appear to support its central argument.

The Witness of the Holy Spirit

No doubt many will be critical of the portion of Craig's essay concerning the witness of the Holy Spirit. Some will observe that it is too subjective, and his use of the term *know* will be judged to be less than philosophically rigorous. Perhaps the stronger criticism will come from those who accept older formulations of knowledge as *justified* true belief, emphasizing the initial term. But even many of those who prefer more recent conceptions in light of Edmund Gettier's[15] questions may also

---

not because they are necessary. Further, evidentialists often begin their discussions of evidence with these theistic arguments. See J. P. Moreland, *Scaling the Secular City: A Defense of Christianity* (Grand Rapids: Baker, 1987), chaps. 1–4; John Warwick Montgomery, *Sensible Christianity* (Santa Ana, Calif.: Vision House, 1976), vol. 2, tapes 1–2; R. Douglas Geivett, *Evil and the Evidence for God* (Philadelphia: Temple University Press, 1993), chap. 6; Francis J. Beckwith, *David Hume's Argument Against Miracles* (Lanham, Md.: University Press of America, 1989), chap. 5; Stephen E. Parrish, *God and Necessity: A Defense of Classical Theism* (Lanham, Md.: University Press of America, 1997), chaps. 1–5. Evidentialists just want to argue the second, historical, step as well.

[14]E.g., while William Paley's *Natural Theology* (1802) argues for God's existence, Joseph Butler's *Analogy of Religion* (1736) begins by assuming it.

[15]For Edmund Gettier's challenges, see his article "Is Justified True Belief Knowledge?" *Analysis* 23 (1963).

require more justification than Craig offers. Still, positions like Craig's are defensible, even in terms of contemporary epistemic discussions.[16]

Overall, I appreciate Craig's general direction. He and I have indicated much agreement on this topic, although he seems willing to push the subject of the Holy Spirit's witness just a little further than I have done.[17] On the positive side, such a formulation has several advantages: it at least addresses the question of a starting point for religious knowledge, takes seriously the multiple biblical references to the certitude provided the believer by the Holy Spirit, accounts for the way most individuals come to the Lord, and counters the sort of zealousness that places reason above all else.[18]

I will, however, briefly offer some caveats. I agree that the witness imparts knowledge to the believer, particularly of his or her own salvation (Rom. 8:16; Gal. 4:4–7; 1 John 3:24; 4:13).[19] Yet to highlight the word *know* to the point that we characterize the witness by this rather technical term is simply confusing in light of the current epistemological scene, even if taken in externalistic terms.[20] At the least, much clarification is needed.[21] I prefer to speak of the witness primarily in terms of assurance and conviction.

---

[16]For instance, William Alston provides sophisticated defenses (in reliabilist terms) of notions like the internal testimony of the Holy Spirit. See his two essays: "Christian Experience and Christian Belief," in *Faith and Rationality: Reason and Belief in God*, ed. Alvin Plantinga and Nicholas Wolterstorff (Notre Dame: University of Notre Dame, 1983), 103–34; "On Knowing That We Know: The Application to Religious Knowledge," in *Christian Perspectives on Religious Knowledge*, ed. C. Stephen Evans and Merold Westphal (Grand Rapids: Eerdmans, 1993), 15–39.

[17]Gary R. Habermas, "The Personal Testimony of the Holy Spirit to the Believer and Christian Apologetics," *Journal of Christian Apologetics* 1, no. 1 (Summer 1997), 49–64.

[18]I recall my chagrin the first time I read Bishop Butler's comment: "Let reason be kept to; and if any part of the Scripture account of the redemption of the world by Christ, can be shown to be really contrary to it, let the Scripture, in the name of God, be given up" (Bishop Butler, *Analogy of Religion*, ed. G. R. Crooks [New York: Harper and Brothers, 1852], 254).

[19]Habermas, "Personal Testimony," 52–57.

[20]For a discussion of externalism and its counterpart internalism, see Kelly Clark's portion of chap. 5 in this volume, "Reformed Epistemology Apologetics."

[21]For instance, it is not even sufficient to say these things on an externalist account of knowledge without some refinement, whether or not one goes in the direction of reliabilism. Several times when reading Craig it was difficult for me to get my bearings with regard to his point. I felt tugged one way, only to seemingly get jerked in the opposite direction. More specific clarification is needed.

To bolster his position, Craig presents an intriguing interpretation of 1 John 5:6–10 (p. 32), arguing that John instructs believers to place the witness of the Spirit even above the apostolic witness. This interpretation is far from clear. The text requires no more than our placing the Holy Spirit's testimony above that of human beings in general. In fact, Raymond Brown goes even further in the opposite direction, stating that the human word here is from those false teachers who left John's community of believers.[22] I think it is difficult to build a subpoint on so difficult an interpretation as Craig's.

Finally, in spite of the content, I thought that the amount of time spent on this subject in a volume on apologetic methodology gave the wrong impression. Craig's major contrast is between "knowing" and "showing" the truth of Christian theism. I thought that the latter was the chief realm of apologetics. As Craig asserts: "Reason in the form of rational arguments and evidence plays an essential role ... in our showing Christianity to be true" (p. 28). In contrast, these arguments play "a contingent and secondary role in our personally knowing Christianity to be true" (p. 28).

Since this is so, why spend between one-third and one-half of the entire essay on the witness of the Holy Spirit? Since "knowing" the truth is defined as only secondarily being concerned with reason and evidences, are we not giving the wrong impression about its place in apologetic methodology? Granted, it is seldom pursued and needs to be developed, but why is it developed to this extent in an essay that addresses how we do our apologetic methodology? In brief, it is not only an overemphasis, but a misleading emphasis, as if (in spite of the clarification) it is more integral to apologetic methodology than Craig intends.

Non-Christian Religions and Other Questions

Craig's essay includes a few other problems, too, some of which are extensions of earlier comments. For example, he poses the issue of adherents to other faiths who claim to have the same internal witness of the Spirit. What if non-Christians identify their witness to a salvation that is far different in type or extent from the New Testament?

Craig offers a few responses. He even allows the possibility that these challengers' experiences could be veridical in some

---

[22]Raymond Brown, *The Epistles of John*, Anchor Bible (Garden City: Doubleday, 1982), 599–600; cf. 29, 32.

cases. But his chief rejoinder is that not all such objections need to be refuted. The existence of challenges does not keep believers from being justified in their faith even if they are unable to answer these difficulties.

I agree that individual believers can rely on the witness of the Holy Spirit and still be rational even if they cannot answer difficulties. But perhaps Craig has misdiagnosed the specific problem that he has posed. In most cases, non-Christian challengers today are probably not questioning whether the Christian has *experienced* the Holy Spirit's testimony. It is far more likely that their reservations concern the Christian claims to exclusivity surrounding this experience—or even the way Christians behave with regard to these claims. So Craig may be confusing the witness of the Holy Spirit with its content and interpretation—the accompaniments to the doctrine.

Craig prefers to assert the epistemic rights of the believer, which does not appear to address my specific question. He seems to think that the witness of the Holy Spirit is being attacked. This is where he ends the discussion.

If I am right, this subject concerns the other side of Craig's tandem—*showing* the truth of Christianity. If so, dealing with comparative religious claims is one of the places where apologetics enters the picture. As a result, believers can and should respond to the non-Christian charges in detail. Otherwise, we beg the nonwitness issues here.

Whether or not I am correct in this particular diagnosis, there is a further point where Craig and I differ. He seems to treat "knowing" and "showing" in fairly distinct terms. True, he does admit that reason is involved to some extent in both categories, although much less so in the former (p. 28).

Even when dealing with the witness of the Holy Spirit, which is self-authenticating, there is a thin line between accepting it for its own sake and employing evidences whenever needed. For instance, I see no problem for a believer who *either* stands on his or her internal testimony *or* brings evidences to bear in defending it or some other aspect of faith. While evidence is not *required* to buttress the testimony of the Spirit, answering doubts or challenges concerning it is not problematic.[23]

---

[23]In "Personal Testimony" (p. 61) I also respond to challenges from those in other religions. As just mentioned, I move to evidential pursuits more quickly than does Craig (p. 59), even though I think the witness can stand on its own.

Although Jesus was not addressing exactly the same topic, it is helpful to note that he invited his listeners to either believe his testimony from his Father for the sake of the words themselves or to believe them because of the miracles he performed (John 14·10–11). Jesus seemed to prefer that they did the former, but he allowed the latter as well. People are different, and within parameters God permits different sorts of responses. Beyond this, evidences were not only used to answer and convince unbelievers, but Jesus employed them directly when answering John the Baptist's doubts (Luke 7:18–28).

On another subject, I think Craig is correct in rejecting the magisterial use of reason—but not for most of his reasons. It does not follow that elevating rationality would "consign untold millions of people who are Christians to unbelief" (p. 37), all because they lack the ability to reason properly. Apologetics is a corporate enterprise for the entire body of Christ—all believers may benefit. Nothing depends on whether each individual can do an equally adequate job of reasoning. That some do apologetics better just shows that we have different tasks (cf. 1 Cor. 12:4–7).

Does this create an intellectual elite, as Craig asserts? God appoints church leaders—apostles, prophets, and teachers. Paul tells us to desire the greater gifts (1 Cor. 12:28–31). But intellectuals frequently require other kinds of assistance that nonintellectuals may readily possess, which are every bit as crucial, as we will see momentarily.

Then are believers subject to the future shifting sands of evidence, as Craig contends (p. 37)? This is indeed a strange objection, since Craig does not allow it when answering naturalists who respond similarly in their attempts to explain the supernatural. Since he does not allow the challenge there,[24] why propose it here?

Lastly, it was very disappointing to note that Craig seems to link the believer's doubts to sin, while the "only ... guaranteed" remedy is walking "in the fullness of the Spirit" (p. 31). I cannot explain here, but so often it is clear (as empirical studies show[25]) that psychiatric and emotional elements are the chief factors in the most common and painful types of religious uncertainty.

---

[24]Craig, *Historical Argument for the Resurrection*, 500; *Assessing the New Testament Evidence*, 420.

[25]See James R. Beck, "Treatment of Spiritual Doubt Among Obsessing Evangelicals," *Journal of Psychology and Theology* 9, no. 3 (Fall 1981): 224–31.

Often those who are most in love with God suffer the most. Even implying that doubts are such a simple matter can be exceptionally devastating to those who suffer.[26] Here is one place where more than intellectual tools are required as we meet the needs of others in the body of Christ.

While doing a notable job of establishing the Spirit's witness, Craig overdoes it at several other junctures. Clearly, a number of items still need to be worked out.

SUMMARY AND CONCLUSION

Evidentialists and classical apologists share many common methodological interests. Yet a few areas of concern also remain.

First, Craig does not distinguish his method carefully enough. On the subject of arguing from history to Christian theism, he seems to embrace evidentialism. So why should I object? He supports the evidentialist agenda at its most crucial point!

Second, Craig's treatment of the witness of the Holy Spirit was certainly helpful, but his term *know* needs clarification. It is also questionable how much his major emphasis on the Holy Spirit plays in apologetic methodology.

Third, several additional critiques were mentioned, including begging the issue on nonwitness questions concerning other religions, taking a more open approach to the use of evidences and reason, and clarifying the relation between religious doubt and sin.

In sum, Craig is certainly an accomplished apologist, as his writings indicate. I rejoice that his concern for others is so apparent. I value his friendship and hope that, as iron sharpens iron (Prov. 27:17), we will both grow from our mutual interactions.

---

[26]See Gary R. Habermas, *The Thomas Factor: Using Your Doubts to Draw Closer to God* (Nashville: Broadman and Holman, 1999), chaps. 4–10; idem, *Dealing with Doubt* (Chicago: Moody Press, 1990), chap. 4.

A CUMULATIVE CASE
APOLOGIST'S RESPONSE

Paul D. Feinberg

In William Lane Craig's discussion of "Showing Christianity to Be True," he describes the methodology of classical apologetics as first presenting arguments for theism, or God's existence, then turning to "Christian evidences, probabilistically construed, for God's revelation in Christ" (p. 48). He has adopted a similar method in his other writings, defending the existence of a personal creator of the universe by means of the *kalam* cosmological argument; and then, by means of the historical evidence for the resurrection, he has sought to establish that God has revealed himself in Christ. If one understands this as a two-step approach to the defense of Christianity, this marks an important difference between Craig's method and mine. I argue for a one-step apologetic based on arguments drawn from a variety of elements in our experience that stand in need of explanation. Moreover, it is my contention that a Christian understanding of God and reality best explain those elements. My approach would not, however, preclude Craig's view to the defense of the Christian faith. From my reading of Craig, I do not know that he would disapprove of a cumulative case approach.

At the heart of Craig's presentation is his distinction between "knowing" and "showing" that Christianity is true. I find this distinction appealing but have some misgivings with the way in which it is developed. For example, there are compelling reasons to think there are some individuals who are within their epistemic rights in believing in God's existence and the Christian faith without evidence. Among those in this class are young children, adults who are devout but theologically uneducated, and even learned theological professors.

Take my own testimony, for instance. I was raised in the church, the son of a seminary dean and professor of Old Testament. I went through an unduly long educational process so that I would be qualified to teach at the graduate level. And for more than thirty-five years I have taught theology, philosophy of religion, and apologetics. Throughout my training and professional life, I have been exposed to and taught most of the arguments for the defense of Christian theism. However, as I think of my faith, I do not see it based on the arguments or evidence that I have studied and taught. It is not as if, were I to find out that the argument from design was not as persuasive as I had at one time thought, that my faith would totter. My faith is based on a personal relationship with Jesus Christ and on the inner testimony of the Holy Spirit, convincing me of Christianity's truthfulness. Nevertheless, these statements need some qualification. I am not so sure that some supporting beliefs do not function in my belief-forming process. It is just that my faith is not based *on* that evidence. I do not infer from some evidence or argument to God's existence or the truth of Christianity.

It is unclear whether evidence might operate at a subconscious or precritical level. Take even the case of very young children. They have not heard of the ontological argument or the moral law, so their faith cannot be based on this evidence. Yet when they are taught about the Easter story, Jesus' crucifixion, death, and empty tomb, is it unreasonable to think that they might conclude that Jesus came back to life? They might not be able to explain the relationship between "the facts" and their "conclusion" in any sophisticated way, but I am not sure that there is *no* relationship between the two.

Craig's understanding of "showing" that Christianity is true convinces me of the important point that there is a significant difference between the epistemic structures of believers and unbelievers. Reformed epistemology is best at explaining the epistemic structure of believers. For many believers, belief in God is properly basic, or not held on the basis of evidence. Unbelievers, however, are quite different. They not only think that belief in God is not properly basic, but belief in God is nowhere in their epistemic structure. For this reason, I think that Reformed epistemology cannot stand alone; it is only half the story. Put another way, evangelism and apologetics are not the same, but they are related. If at least a part of the task of apologists is to show the rational acceptability of the Christian faith to those who are not believers, then an evidentialist apologetic will have an important place in the defense of Christianity. Apologetics will be an important partner in evangelism. Certain things in an unbeliever's experience may challenge his belief that there is no God and lead him to accept belief in God and Christianity. The orderliness of the created order may lead one to the belief that this could not have happened simply by chance and thus that an intelligent designer, God, is necessary. Or the fact that Jesus fulfilled so many of the Old Testament prophecies in his first coming, and the fact that there seems to be a pattern in human history that makes a Christian understanding of the future seem likely, may lead one to believe the Christian story is true.

If what I have said is anything near the truth, then Reformed and evidentialist apologetics are not incompatible with each other; rather, they compliment each other. Craig's paper surely demonstrates this point. "Knowing" and "showing" Christianity to be true constitute the whole apologetic picture. They show that there is a need for a defensive (or negative) apologetic to answer the charge that to believe in God without evidence is irrational, as well as an offensive (or positive) apologetic to try to persuade those who doubt that Christianity is the best explanation of our common human experience.

From what I say in chapter 3 in describing a cumulative case approach to apologetics, it should surprise no one that I think Craig's strong emphasis on the role of the Holy Spirit is important. This is a recurring theme from all the writers. We would not want any of our readers to get the impression that we think people can simply be argued into belief in God and the Christian faith.

It is, however, in the discussion of the role of the Holy Spirit that I have misgivings about what Craig has to say. He distinguishes sharply between "knowing" and "showing" that Christianity is true. Each of these has a differing role for the Holy Spirit. Arguments and evidence are not the basis of our knowing that our beliefs about God and Christ are true. Those beliefs are known immediately, and as Craig says, on the basis of the inner witness of the Holy Spirit. The role of the Holy Spirit explains the tenacity of a Christian's belief. For example, it explains why a righteous sufferer like Job refuses to curse God and die in the face of what seems to be undeserved pain. Up to this point I am in agreement with Craig.

Craig then goes on to discuss defeaters and the witness of the Holy Spirit. It is in this context that my misgivings arise. Epistemologists who believe that there are beliefs that are properly basic do not want to find themselves in a position where they must accept all such claims of belief as invincibly true. Therefore, basic beliefs are only *prima facie* justified. Defeaters of basic beliefs, beliefs that have greater warrant than the original belief, may exist. In such a case, to continue to be justified in the original belief, one must find a defeater of the defeater.

Craig applies this to the question of knowing God and the truth of Christianity. He says that if we require that defeaters for defeaters of belief in God be extrinsic, then we have not removed the sting of the evidentialist knowing process (p. 34). Therefore, he argues that the Holy Spirit is the defeater *par excellence.* He is able to defeat any defeater. Moreover, the Spirit's witness is *self-authenticating*. This means that the Holy Spirit is an intrinsic defeater of any defeaters brought against a believer's belief. The witness of the Holy Spirit enjoys the highest warrant, so his witness simply overwhelms any belief that would seem to call into question a believer's belief about the truth of Christianity or God. Furthermore, an intrinsic defeater "does not directly refute the defeater in the sense of providing an argument to show that the alleged defeater is false or providing reasons to doubt that the alleged defeater has been proved to be true. Rather, an overwhelming defeater simply enjoys more warrant than the defeaters lodged against it" (p. 34).

My lack of ease with Craig's comments does not have to do with the Holy Spirit's witness being a defeater. I think that this is quite in keeping with the teaching of the New Testament. Rather, it is with the claim that the witness is self-authenticating and thus has such a high warrant that it cannot be overwhelmed by any defeater. There are many Christians who believe that the Holy Spirit has led them to believe and do things that turn out to be false. I have heard Christians who are absolutely convinced that God has told them that he is going to cure them of cancer. They believe this to the very end of their lives in spite of what the doctors have to say, in spite of the progression of their disease. In the years that I have taught divinity students, I have seen many individuals enter seminary convinced that the Holy

Spirit has called them to ministry and to preparation at our seminary. Yet they have not done well academically nor demonstrated the character that would make them effective in Christian service. If the witness of the Holy Spirit is self-authenticating in the sense that Craig describes above, it overwhelms all the defeaters to the contrary. This raises a problem. We should not give up our understanding of the Holy Spirit's leading at the first sign of difficulty. However, there seems to come a point at which the witness of the Spirit may be misunderstood, which is simply to say that even believers do not have infallible knowledge of their faith.

One way in which one could answer this problem is to grant special status to the witness of the Holy Spirit when it authenticates belief in God and the truth of Christianity, but not in other matters. Why, though, should the witness of the Spirit be beyond defeat on one matter and not all? Furthermore, this does not solve the difficulty that follows.

If the role of the Holy Spirit as self-authenticating belief is troublesome with respect to the believer, it is even more problematic when dealing with unbelievers. Christianity is not the only religion that has something akin to the witness of the Holy Spirit. Many religions claim that their beliefs about God are self-authenticating. If a claim to self-authentication overwhelms all defeaters, I do not see how we will be able to convince a Muslim or Buddhist friend that he is wrong in his beliefs. That is, both beliefs, Christian and Muslim or Buddhist, would be authenticated by a defeater that overwhelms every other defeater.

In fairness to Craig, he cites an example given by Plantinga about a man who is accused of committing a crime. All the circumstantial evidence points to this individual. He knows, however, that he has not committed the crime. His belief in his own innocence makes it rational for him to believe that he did not commit the crime even if he cannot refute the evidence. In response to this example, I am not entirely sure what to say. First, there is a maxim in law that hard cases make bad laws. This is a hard case, and I wonder whether it is wise to draw any general epistemological conclusion from it.

Second, I am not sure that the believer's witness of the Holy Spirit and the accused's knowledge of his innocence are parallel cases. The accused presumably knows more than just that he did not commit the crime and that he is unable to explain the circumstantial evidence. He would know where he was at the time of the crime, what he was doing, and so forth. So it could even be that his belief was held without the ability to explain all the evidence, but his belief in his innocence was not a basic belief.

Third, I wonder whether there is not some point at which the accused would have to change his belief. Imagine a case where the accused's fingerprints and blood were found at the crime scene. DNA testing pointed to him, making the likelihood that the blood sample was not his so staggeringly improbable that it was fair to say that it was impossible. Moreover, mountains of circumstantial evidence supported the allegation that the accused was guilty of the crime. Is it rational to continue to believe that one is innocent when that belief goes contrary to so much of the evidence and one is without ability to explain any of the evidence? At some point it would seem that one would need some reasons beyond his sense of innocence for continuing to rationally deny that he had committed the crime. Again, my problem is with the self-authenticating nature of the witness of the Holy Spirit.

Craig has a response to my objection. He argues that neither the fact that other religions make similar claims nor that such claims may be false "do anything logically to undermine the fact that the Christian believer does possess the genuine witness of the Spirit" (p. 35). The fact that there are others who make competing claims has no relevance to *my* knowing the truth of Christianity. He cites favorably William Alston's response to this objection. Alston says that it may well be that what some take to be the witness of the Spirit is in fact a veridical experience of God as the Ground of Being or as the Moral Absolute or even as the Father of all humankind. Further, Alston thinks that we cannot preclude the possibility that there is a qualitative difference between the true experience of the witness of the Holy Spirit and a false belief that one has had such an experience.

Our discussion clearly points out that there is a very different epistemological status for first person claims to have experienced the Spirit's witness and third person claims to the same. Persons are in a privileged position with respect to *their own* experiences. The problem arises with this approach in apologetics because the task is not simply to defend believers' epistemological rights to believe, but to convince those who are not believers that the Christian understanding of God and reality is true. That requires the third person perspective.

At least a part of my uneasiness is related to the fact that Craig distinguishes knowing and showing the truth of Christianity more sharply than I would. The relationship I have defended in the cumulative case approach does not so sharply divide knowing and showing. I have tried to integrate what I have called the witness of the Spirit into personal and public aspects. I also have tried to set out some criteria for settling conflicting truth claims. I think that both "knowing" and "showing" that Christianity is true takes place in the context of the establishment of worldviews.

A PRESUPPOSITIONALIST'S RESPONSE

John M. Frame

William Craig tries hard in his epistemology to achieve a balance between the testimony of the Holy Spirit and the role of reason and evidences. In my view, however, an important element of biblical epistemology is almost entirely missing from his account. That is the role of the Word of God.

THE SPIRIT AND THE WORD

What is it, after all, that the Spirit testifies to? In Scripture, the Spirit testifies to the truth of the Word. In 1 Corinthians 2:4, Paul says, "My message and my preaching were not with wise and persuasive words, but with a demonstration of the Spirit's power, so that your faith might not rest on men's wisdom, but on God's power." The witness of the Spirit is to the apostolic message, the Word that God had given to Paul (Gal. 1:11–12). In 1 Corinthians 2:12, Paul teaches that the Spirit enables us to understand "what God has freely given us." What are these things that God has freely given us? "This is what we speak, not in words taught us by human wisdom but in words taught by the Spirit, expressing spiritual truths in spiritual words. The man without the Spirit does not accept the things that come from the Spirit of God, for they are foolishness to him, and he cannot understand them, because they are spiritually discerned" (vv.13–14).

The Spirit testifies to *words* that he has given to the apostles. The same is the case in 1 Thessalonians 1:5 and 2:13. Indeed,

I know of no passage in which the Spirit's witness has any object other than the Word.[1]

It may seem as though Romans 8:9–17; Galatians 4:6; 1 John 3:24; and 4:13, which speak of the Spirit's testimony to our salvation as children of God, are exceptions to this rule. Scripture does not, after all, list the names of those who are children of God. So it seems that the Spirit here reveals an extracanonical truth, namely, that John Smith, for example, is a child of God. Clearly in Romans and Galatians, however, our assurance that we are children of God comes from the gracious promise of the gospel that those who believe belong to God (see Rom. 1:16–17). It is to that promise, a promise we have in Scripture, that the Spirit bears witness. And in all these passages, the promise of the Spirit is itself a Word given by an inspired apostle (Gal. 1:11–12; 1 John 1:1–3). As for 1 John 5:6–10, on which Craig places emphasis, the Spirit's testimony is indeed "greater" than the apostolic witness would be without it. But the Spirit's testimony is not to a different content from the apostolic witness. Rather, it gives us a new level of assurance that that witness is true. Even if these passages are exceptions to our rule, however, these exceptions would not invalidate the general correlation I have noted between Spirit and Word.[2]

Since the Spirit witnesses to God's Word, to the gospel message presented definitively in the Holy Scriptures, the Spirit's testimony is not, as some suppose today, an ineffable mystical

---

[1]The correlation between Word and Spirit, so important to the Protestant Reformers, has roots in the Old Testament. God creates the world by his Word, and the Spirit hovers over the waters (Gen. 1:2). The psalmist says that God created everything by the Word and by the "breath" of his mouth (Ps. 33:6). "Breath" is *ruach*, often translated "Spirit" (cf. Isa. 34:16; 59:21). In John 6:63 the words Jesus gives to his disciples are "Spirit" and "life." In John 14:26 Jesus promises the Holy Spirit will *teach* the apostles. The Spirit is to give them the words Paul refers to in 1 Cor. 2:13 and is to "remind" them of the words Jesus spoke during his earthly ministry (cf. John 15:26; 16:13). In Acts 2:1–4 and elsewhere in Acts, the coming of the Spirit accompanies the *preaching* of the gospel. And 2 Tim. 3:16 (the word "God-breathed" includes the *pneuma* root, which connotes the world of the Spirit) and 2 Peter 1:21 speak of the work of the Spirit in inspiring the biblical writers. So in creation, inspiration, preaching, and hearing, Spirit and Word go together. The closeness of Word and Spirit exists even in the eternal fellowship of the persons of the Trinity, for "Word" and "Spirit" are biblical names for the second and third persons of the Godhead.

[2]For more discussion of the testimony of the Spirit, see my article "The Spirit and the Scriptures" in D. A. Carson and John D. Woodbridge, *Hermeneutics, Authority, and Canon*, rev. ed. (Grand Rapids: Baker, 1995), 213–35.

experience, nor does it tell us things beyond the apostolic gospel, things we couldn't find in Scripture itself.

Craig certainly understands that the Spirit testifies to a definite content. He says that the inner work of the Spirit enables us to know "Christianity to be true" (p. 28). And certainly he understands that Scripture is the definitive formulation of Christian truth. He uses Scripture to establish his view of the Spirit's testimony as well as his view of evidence and arguments. And his evidences for the resurrection of Jesus are mostly taken from the Bible. But unless I have missed it, he assigns no distinct role to Scripture in his religious epistemology. I am not saying that Craig denies the authority of Scripture; certainly he holds a strong view of it. Rather, I am observing that there is nothing in Craig's essay about the role of Scripture as the believer's presupposition, the believer's ultimate standard of truth and falsity, of right and wrong.

SUBJECT, OBJECT, AND NORM

To raise the same issue from a somewhat different angle: Craig's understanding of the knowledge of God is a balance between two factors: evidential arguments and the Spirit's testimony. These may be described as objective and subjective respectively. For Craig, the latter is primary in "knowing" God, the former in "showing" the truth to a non-Christian. But how do we decide, in either case, what arguments are worth believing? How do we judge between rival conceptions of rationality, fact, truth, and knowledge? By more evidence? But how do we rationally evaluate that additional evidence without falling into an infinite regress? And how do we distinguish between true and false subjective impressions?

It seems to me that we need a third element, in addition to the objective and the subjective, that we might call the *normative*. The normative sets the rules for thinking and knowing, for the use of evidence and reason, for discerning the spirits. It includes such things as the law of noncontradiction and the other basic laws of thought. For Christians the ultimate norm is God's Word in Scripture. But whether we regard the normative as a distinct third factor in knowledge or only as an additional kind of evidence or subjective feeling,[3] Christians dare not

---

[3]In my *Doctrine of the Knowledge of God* (Phillipsburg, N.J.: Presbyterian and Reformed, 1987), I argue that the normative is an element of knowledge distin-

neglect our divinely given norms on matters of wisdom, knowledge, truth, and certainty.

Human knowledge of God is not autonomous knowledge, in which we set the rules and determine the criteria for believing in God. We should not tell God what he must do to satisfy the demands of our rationality. Rather, if we are to believe in him, we must come to him on his terms, bowing before his Word.

ARGUMENT AND EVIDENCE

With this correction, I certainly agree with Craig that the testimony of the Spirit is a self-authenticating, immediate apprehension of the truth of the gospel, that it is not dependent on arguments, and that it "overwhelms" contrary arguments. His response to the rival claims of other religions to self-authenticating experience is the same that I would make.

Craig is also right to say that for those who know Christ through the Spirit's witness, arguments are subsidiary. The Spirit's witness is infallible, our arguments fallible. I have a slight problem, however, with Craig's equation of "argument" with "evidence." Although Craig's use of these terms is legitimate, we should make some distinction between (1) the objective data given to us in the created world and (2) our use of these data to construct arguments for the truth of Christianity. Contrary to Craig, I prefer to use the term *evidence* to refer to (1) and, of course, *argument* for (2). In this sense, evidence is required for all human knowledge; argument is not.

Now Craig contemplates the possibility of evidence "turning against Christianity" (pp. 27, 33–34). In my proposed sense, however, that can never happen, for evidence never turns against the truth. Therefore, all evidence favors Christian theism, and there is no evidence against it.[4] If evidence appears to weigh against Christian theism, we have misunderstood or misinterpreted it.

---

guishable from the objective and subjective but that it is related to them as a distinct "perspective," not as distinct subject matter. The normative aspect of knowledge, then, is not found *only* in Scripture. God speaks his Word also through natural revelation, so it is not wrong to say that the Spirit also testifies to the evidences of nature and history. But as God's covenant servants, our thinking about nature and history should be governed by God's Word in Scripture.

[4]Cf. Rom. 1:20, which says that God is "clearly seen" by all through the created world.

There may be other ways to distinguish the objective data from human interpretation, but that distinction is important, and we should find some terminology for it if we are not to use my definitions of evidence and argument.[5] On this basis, we can say that Christianity is indeed grounded in evidence,[6] which is to say, it is grounded in objective fact. It is that objective fact, interpreted according to God's norms, to which the Spirit bears witness.

KNOWING AND SHOWING

Now, what about "showing Christianity to be true"? I think there is some difference between "knowing" and "showing," but not as great a difference as Craig says. Rational argument will play a greater role in the latter case, because "showing," by word at least,[7] is a logical activity (providing grounds for a conclusion), and because appeal to the Spirit's testimony, valid as it is, is not really an argument for the truth.[8] In both knowing and showing, our witness should be based on the norms of God's Word and the objective evidence of God's revelation in nature, history, and Scripture. We should then trust the Spirit to bear witness to our message.

INFERENCE AND PROPER BASICALITY

Craig (with the Reformed epistemologists) makes too much of the question whether Romans 1 justifies natural theology or merely "constitutes the circumstances in which belief in a Cre-

---

[5]Craig does make a similar distinction in his discussion of Rom. 1, when he distinguishes between general revelation and the arguments based on it. But he does not derive from this distinction Paul's conclusion that the general revelation (my "evidence") is so clear and cogent that it leaves people without excuse.

[6]Some readers may find it interesting that a presuppositionalist has a higher view of evidence than some evidentialists do. But that is the case. In presuppositionalism, evidence is not a merely probable witness to the truth of Christianity; rather, it is sure and certain. God's normative interpretation of it is the *only* rational interpretation of it.

[7]We should not forget that we also "show" the truth of the gospel by our lives. "Watch your life and doctrine closely," says Paul to Timothy. "Persevere in them, because if you do, you will save both yourself and your hearers" (1 Tim. 4:16).

[8]The argument, of course, is based on that to which the Spirit witnesses: the objective facts interpreted by God's Word. Again, therefore, I am disappointed that Craig does not bring out and emphasize these realities as the *objects* of the Spirit's testimony.

ator is properly basic" (p. 39). I think rather that the distinction between believing something as properly basic and believing it on the basis of argument (as in natural theology) is somewhat fluid. George Mavrodes questioned the sharpness of the distinction between "basic" and "derived" beliefs when he wrote:

> Readers of this volume [*Faith and Rationality*] who are theists might usefully try the following experiment on themselves. Pause for a moment and consider your own belief that God exists, just as it stands right now.... Is that belief ... based on some other beliefs that you hold? And if so, what are those other beliefs, and *how* is the belief in God's existence based on them? (Do they entail it, for example, or render it probable, or what?)[9]

When I try Mavrodes's experiment, I do not find it easy to answer his questions. Because I am a Christian, God is certainly the foundation of all my thinking. But I don't hesitate to recommend belief in God to others, and indeed to myself in times of doubt, on the basis of other beliefs. As I indicate in chapter 4, "Presuppositional Apologetics," there is a kind of circularity here. I hold many beliefs as part of a theistic system of beliefs, and these reinforce one another. Sometimes I take the existence of God as basic and use it to prove other things, such as the rational order of the universe. At other times I take the rational order of the universe as basic and use it to prove the existence of God. Those beliefs are mutually implicatory. God's existence implies that the universe is rational, and the rationality of the universe presupposes (and therefore implies) the existence of God. So for me the existence of God can be taken as a properly basic belief, but it is also the conclusion of many good arguments.

Indeed, I think that one major function of argument is to spell out why we are justified in holding beliefs as properly basic. Since we cannot prove everything, all our arguments begin with properly basic presuppositions. But our properly basic beliefs, if they are true, are in accord with all sound reasoning.

Certainly Paul in Romans 1 does not try to resolve the question of how properly basic beliefs are related to beliefs held on the basis of argument. Nor does he teach that belief in God is in the one category rather than the other. He says only that the

---

[9]George Mavrodes, "Jerusalem and Athens Revisited," in Alvin Plantinga and Nicholas Wolterstorff, eds., *Faith and Rationality* (Notre Dame and London: University of Notre Dame Press, 1983), 203.

created order justifies, indeed requires, belief in God. For some this belief may be an immediate response to the world around them. For others it may be the result of argument. When someone believes by way of immediate response, he may well defend his belief by argument. For if the entire created order warrants immediate belief in God, then that belief will necessarily also be consistent with the conclusions of right reasoning. And when someone believes by means of argument, he should thereafter, realizing what kind of God exists, recognize God as the foundation of all argument, of all human thought. For him, thereafter, belief in God will be properly basic, and more.[10]

COMMON GROUND

At any rate, I agree with Craig that Scripture warrants the use of evidences and arguments to show the truth of Christianity. His appeals to Scripture in this regard are quite convincing. He becomes less cogent, however, when, following Alston (but without biblical support), he insists that these arguments must be based on "common ground" like "sense perception," "rational self-evidence," and "common modes of reasoning" (p. 44). Unlike some presuppositionalists, I will not deny entirely the existence of such common ground. But we must recall Paul's statements in Romans 1 that unbelievers "suppress" the truth (v. 18) and become "futile" and "darkened" in their thinking (v. 21). They have "exchanged the truth of God for a lie" (v. 25) because they "did not think it worthwhile to retain the knowledge of God" (v. 28). Thus, they are in full battle against the knowledge of God and against the modes of reasoning that lead to God. When they concede Christian theistic reasoning,[11] as, to be sure, they sometimes do, they do it involuntarily, insincerely, and/or ignorantly. Craig is, I think, somewhat naïve about this conceptual warfare. He does not seem to understand that the unbeliever, when most self-conscious, opposes the very rational

---

[10]See my reply to Clark in this volume (pp. 307–12), where I argue that our belief in God should not merely be "properly basic" as Reformed epistemologists use the phrase, but should govern all other beliefs.

[11]This is the proper way to put it. There is no such thing as "neutral" reasoning. There is only Christian-theistic reasoning and unbelieving reasoning: the wisdom of God and the wisdom of the world. When there is common ground between believer and unbeliever, that is a sign that either believer or unbeliever is inconsistent with his or her deepest commitments.

principles to which Craig appeals,[12] and he reasons in ways designed to exclude the theistic conclusion. That is why we need to reason transcendentally, as I say in chapter 4. We need to show that God is the very presupposition of rational meaning and that reasoning without this presupposition leads to meaninglessness. Again I stress the normative: unbelief is wrong because it violates the very norms of human rationality.

CRAIG'S ARGUMENTS

Having said that, I agree with Craig that the *kalam* cosmological argument is a good argument. But it is good only on the Christian presupposition that the world is a causal order and therefore a rational order. Deny God, and you deny the need for a rational structure or for a causal order reaching back to a first cause. That is an awful price to pay for denying God, but some are willing to pay it. To those, the *kalam* argument will carry little weight.

I like Craig's account of the evidences of the resurrection of Jesus. Craig's books are among the best accounts of these evidences, and the resurrection is of immense apologetic importance, as Paul himself stresses in 1 Corinthians 15.[13] I do think, however, that Craig exaggerates the degree of critical consensus on the three central facts he discusses (pp. 52–53). Thus, again, he underestimates the motivation of unbelieving scholarship to twist the evidence according to nontheistic presuppositions.

CONCLUSION

Presuppositions, too, are norms. So my main complaints against Craig can be summarized by saying that in my view he has not reflected sufficiently on the nature and importance of norms in human knowledge, especially in Christian thinking, both knowing and showing. Above all, his approach needs to be informed by an epistemology that understands the centrality of God's Word to all human reasoning.

---

[12]Recall the comment in my essay that Satan is the very paradigm of irrationality (p. 212).

[13]Note, however, that Paul's *main* argument for the resurrection in 1 Cor. 15 is not the appeal to witnesses, but the fact that the resurrection was central to the apostolic *preaching* (see vv. 1, 2, 3, 11). In other words, Paul argues that the resurrection is part of the inspired apostolic Word of God.

A REFORMED EPISTEMOLOGIST'S RESPONSE

Kelly James Clark

I could have written William Craig's essay (at least major parts of it). I don't mean me in particular but me as a Reformed epistemologist. There is very little in Craig's essay that I or any other Reformed epistemologist could disagree with, and that makes me a little disappointed, because philosophers thrive on disagreement—if no blood is spilled, we haven't really had a good debate. I'm also disappointed because there is a view out there, held by some Christian thinkers, that goes by the title "classical apologetics" but is quite different from the position held by Craig. Let us call that view "hyper-classical apologetics."[1]

Hyper-classical apologetics assumes what Craig calls the *magisterial* use of reason: "reason stands over and above the gospel like a magistrate and judges its truth or falsity" (p. 36). Craig is right to dismiss its pretensions, for it would make everyone a philosopher—constantly assessing evidence *pro et contra* and constantly adjusting one's beliefs to the variations in evidence. One's beliefs would be like a barometer, rising and falling with the whims of new evidence and counterevidence. Hyper-classical apologetics is long on promise and short on fulfillment—demanding and promising evidence for God's existence and for the truth of Christianity and then being unable to deliver.

---

[1]See R. C. Sproul, John Gerstner, and Arthur Lindsley, *Classical Apologetics* (Grand Rapids: Zondervan, 1984). For a thorough thrashing of this book, see my *Return to Reason* (Grand Rapids: Eerdmans, 1990), 46–53.

Craig does not demand evidence in order to know God, and for that I applaud him. He does, however, fall into a similar problem—promising evidence for Christian belief that is difficult to provide.

I am pleased with Craig's essay, however, because a philosopher I know and respect holds eminently sensible views that are (nearly) identical with mine! First, I will mention some crucial points on which Craig and I agree. All I can say about those is "Amen" and perhaps develop them a bit. Then I will spill some blood—raise one or two areas of contention, especially concerning his case for the existence of God. Since I discuss evidentialism's case for Christian belief in a separate essay, I will save my comments about Craig's case until then (pp. 366–68).

EMINENTLY SENSIBLE CLAIMS

The distinction between *knowing* and *showing* seems both to fit human experience and to offer a genuine insight into human cognition. We know lots of things that we cannot show—these are what Craig, following contemporary epistemologists, calls "properly basic beliefs." But we are also intellectually curious, and the fact of disagreement about significant human beliefs makes us want not merely to know but to show—for our own intellectual satisfaction and, occasionally, to persuade (or at least appease) others.

Craig recognizes the limitations of the reason-seeking enterprise because of the problems of reasons *against* our beliefs, what he calls "defeaters." Here again I find myself in agreement with Craig. How should *reasons against* affect our believings? We often find ourselves overwhelmed with reasons against what we believe. It seems like every time I turn around there is someone, often much smarter than I am, who has a new version of the argument from evil. Or, more likely, we are just overwhelmed with our own personal experience of evil or with God's silence. What should we do when we find ourselves swamped with arguments or evil?

With arguments it is often, as Craig points out, fairly easy. Suppose someone offers an argument that to all appearances looks perfectly sound and that concludes "God does not exist." Suppose there are only two premises offered in support of the conclusion. We'll call them p and q. The argument is

1. p
2. q
3. Therefore, God does not exist.

Now suppose that at first glance *p* and *q* seem obviously true and to entail (3). What should one do? Well, it depends on how firmly one accepts (3). If one accepts (3) more firmly than one accepts either *p* or *q*, then the reasonable thing to do is to say, "I can't see how or why *p* or *q* is false, but since they entail something that I believe more firmly than either *p* or *q*, one of them must be false."

Here's a logical way to look at the reasoning involved:

(a) If *p* and *q* are true, then God does not exist. P and *q* are true. Therefore God does not exist.

Or the reasoning might go as follows:

(b) If *p* and *q* are true, then God does not exist. God does exist. Therefore, either *p* or *q* is false.

Which direction you take the reasoning, (a) or (b), depends on how firmly you are committed to the respective beliefs. Just because *p* and *q* entail that God does not exist, it does not follow that God does not exist. If God does exist, then either *p* or *q* is false. As one makes one's best judgments about which conclusion to accept, one must weigh the relative strengths of *p, q,* and *God exists.* Logic alone cannot tell us what to believe in such cases.

If the Holy Spirit has both induced belief in God in a person and assured that person that God is in Christ reconciling that person to himself, then that person's Christian beliefs will have a great deal of warrant. The strength of his or her belief—measured by the firmness with which it is held—may count against any premises that entail that God does not exist. Craig's analysis of the situation is supported by the simple logic of believing (which is to say, there is no *simple,* or unidirectional, logic of believing).

An agreement of substance but not of terms exists between Craig and myself. He writes, ". . . the work of the Holy Spirit plays no part in the demonstration proper but consists in opening the heart of the obdurate unbeliever to attend to and be persuaded by the argumentation" (p. 38). I think we would roughly agree, but I state this in such a matter that it might (wrongly) sound like we substantively disagree. I believe that passions, emotions, and the will are involved in demonstration *proper.* We are, after all, trying to demonstrate something to someone. The whole person is bound up in the demonstration process. Of course our passions and emotions can both prevent us from attending to and being persuaded by the argumentation. But attending to and being persuaded by are part of demonstration proper. Demonstration, therefore, is not simply a matter of trotting out true premises and showing their relevance to a true conclusion. It also involves helping someone to see the truth of the premises and to move them in the direction of the conclusion. This process of demonstration may require moral and spiritual reorientation, which in turn may be assisted by the work of the Holy Spirit. But the process of demonstration *proper* involves the psychological elements of *attending to* and *being persuaded by*, which are, in turn, deeply affected by our will.[2] This, of course, is directly relevant to assessments of the evidence, to which we must finally turn.

DISAGREEMENTS

Craig claims that "it [is] possible to present a sound, convincing, positive case for the truth of Christian theism" (p. 27). Likewise, he contends that he can show Christianity to be true. This showing is, once again, different from knowing. This is good, because of the shortcomings of the showings.

The problem with evidence is implicit in what I have written above and in my defense of Reformed epistemology. Our believings are inextricably entwined with our passions, emotions, and will. Our fundamental commitments shape our assessment of the evidence. Sometimes our commitments and values help us to see the truth; sometimes they obscure the truth. We are, in every case, epistemically situated—historically, culturally, socially—and we lack a God's eye view of the world. What counts as evidence, the weight that should attach to it, and the inferences that follow from it are conditioned by our commitments. No method exists for rising above our conditions and seeing the world (or the evidence) without the filters of our beliefs and values. That is the long and short of our believing situation.

The evidence that Craig offers comes in two stages. The first stage attempts to prove that God exists. He has persuasively

---

[2]For an excellent defense of this view, see William Wainwright, "The Nature of Reason" in *Reason and the Christian Religion*, ed. Alan Padgett (Oxford: Clarendon, 1994), 91–118.

defended, briefly in these pages but more extensively in other pages, one of the most intriguing and powerful arguments for the existence of God—the *kalam* cosmological argument. His explication and defense of this argument are, in my estimation, one of the great achievements in contemporary philosophy of religion. I once offered a criticism of this argument that I now take to be facile and misguided. I think that his subconclusion—that the universe began to exist—follows from the (true) premises that he offers. I am also pleased to find this conclusion supported by scientific evidence. We philosophers rarely find empirical evidence for our philosophical conclusions!

But if the *kalam* cosmological argument is sound, what exactly has been proved? That an omnipotent, omniscient, wholly good creator of the universe exists? The most that can be affirmed is that a timeless being with sufficient powers to create a universe exists. We know nothing of this being's knowledge or character. We cannot conclude, based solely on this argument, that *theism* is true. Craig admits this and contends that this argument can "serve as one link in the natural theologian's cumulative case for theism" (p. 51). Maybe it can and maybe it can't. We don't really know from what has been said. We need a cumulative case before us, and then we need to assess what is established about the divine nature on the basis of this cumulative case. We also need to look at the counterevidence in our cumulative case—God's hiddenness, for example, or the abundance of evil. The point that I wish to make here is not that such a cumulative case cannot be made, but simply that it is not clear that one can, on the basis of such an argument, establish the existence of an omnipotent, omniscient creator who cares for his creatures.

My doctoral dissertation examined cumulative case arguments for and against the existence of God. Cumulative case arguments consider all of the relevant evidence for the existence of God—the existence and design of the universe, morality, miracles, religious experience, et cetera—jointly rather than singly. The question is then asked, "What is the best explanation of all of this evidence?" Partly what led me to consideration of cumulative case arguments was their intuitive appeal. I was also struck by the fact that two brilliant and (near as I could tell) rational people could look at the same body of evidence and draw exactly opposite conclusions. Richard Swinburne, perhaps the greatest rational apologist of our era, contends:

A similar pattern of argument [as I use in my discussion of the cosmological argument] from various other phenomena such as the existence of conscious beings, the providential ordering of things in certain respects, the occurrence of certain apparently miraculous events in history and the religious experiences of many millions is . . . available to establish theism (when all the arguments are taken together) as overall significantly more probable than not.[3]

On the other hand, J. L. Mackie, a modern-day Hume, argues that

all the evidence that they can muster is easily explained in natural terms, without any improbabilities worth taking into account. Consciousness and the actual phenomena of morality and valuing as a human activity are explained without further improbabilities, given that the natural world is such as to allow life to evolve, so the only improbabilities to be scored against the naturalistic kind of explanation are whatever may be involved in there being causal regularities, the fundamental laws and physical constants being as they are, and there being any world at all. . . . In the end, therefore, we can agree with what Laplace said about God: we have no need of that hypothesis. This conclusion can be reached by an examination precisely of the arguments advanced in favour of theism, without even bringing into play what have been regarded as the strongest considerations on the other side, the problem of evil and the various natural histories of religion. When these are thrown into the scales, the balance tilts still further against theism. . . . The balance of probabilities, therefore, comes out strongly against the existence of a god.[4]

The use of formulae in the probability calculus lends an aura of objectivity and precision to these sorts of arguments. But the puzzle remains: how could two reasonable people reach such dramatically different conclusions from the same set of evidence?

After three years of careful consideration of the argument, I threw in my hat. I don't know how to settle the matter of God's

---

existence to everyone's satisfaction on the basis of a cumulative argument. The probabilities involved are either inscrutable (we simply can't tell what they are) or nonexistent (there just aren't any relevant probabilities). The best we can do is make a considered judgment of the evidence. But this means that, given the conditioned nature of believing, we will make widely divergent considered judgments of the evidence.

Can we, as Craig claims, show our opponents that we are correct and that they are wrong? Can we show that theists are in an epistemically superior position?[5] Must a person whose cognitive faculties are functioning properly and who is sufficiently informed come to the conclusion that a creator of the universe exists? Here the answer is a resounding, "I don't know." We can provide reasons or evidence that, *for all we can tell*, support our beliefs. But we can't tell if *we* are sufficiently informed or if *our* cognitive faculties are working properly (or, on the other hand, if the nontheist's are working properly). All we have direct epistemic access to is the evidence that is presently available. We don't have belief-independent access to the factors that condition our acceptance or rejection of the evidence. We can't gain a godlike grasp of all of the relevant evidence. We are finite believers with limited information and limited access to the conditions that ground our believings.

"Showing" is a success term indicating the successful demonstration of something to someone. This requires someone who is the "shower" and someone who is the "showee." Since shower and the showee are situated, finite people, the success of our showings depends not only on the logic of the argument but on the will (including passions, values, and emotions) of the people involved. This vastly muddies the intellectual waters. Cognitive deficiency exists on both sides of the equation. It doesn't follow from this that everything is true or that nothing is true. I consider myself a skeptical realist—there is truth, but it is very hard for humans to grasp.

We theists must admit that we, like everyone else, are certainty seekers and that we, like everyone else, are willing to accept less than compelling evidence for our favored conclusions and to ignore evidence unfavorable to our beliefs.[6] We want to

---

[5]As Craig rightly points out, Christians may be in an epistemically superior position without being able to show it.

[6]I am not speculating about Craig here. But, insofar as he is a person, some of what I say here applies to him.

show others but are unwilling to listen to their showings. Our apologetic projects are often little more than proclamation but should, given our cognitive limitations, involve listening. We need to listen to others for two reasons: (1) we might be wrong and (2) we need to know where we share common intellectual ground on which to base our showings. Our success as apologists depends on our willingness to recognize our own shortcomings and also our willingness to listen to the other and to begin with our shared beliefs and commitments.

CONCLUSION

Not everything above is a criticism of Craig's views, and I suspect that he will agree with some of the points I have made. What I oppose is the magisterial use of reason when it comes to nonbelievers. We often wield reason as a hammer to pound others, failing to recognize our own human cognitive limitations. While reason is a tool, it is a more modest tool; it may be *a* guide to the truth, but it is not an infallible guide.

Chapter Two

EVIDENTIAL APOLOGETICS

Gary R. Habermas

EVIDENTIAL APOLOGETICS

Gary R. Habermas

The evidential method of apologetics has much in common with the classical method, with the chief difference being the way in which historical evidences are used. Evidentialism may be characterized as the "one-step" approach to this question, in that historical evidences can serve as a species of argument for God. Instead of having to prove God's existence *before* moving to specific evidences (the "two-step" method), the evidentialist treats one or more historical arguments as being able both to indicate God's existence and activity and to indicate which variety of theism is true.[1] Like the other methods, evidentialism can be rather eclectic in its use of various "positive" evidences and "negative" critiques and answers to detractors. Yet it tends to focus chiefly on the legitimacy of accumulating various historical evidences for the truth of Christianity. After a brief discussion of another matter, I will provide an overview of some other facets of the evidentialist position.

A BRIEF WORD CONCERNING EPISTEMOLOGY

Although this volume concerns apologetic methodology, I must first make some comments on a preliminary matter. The evidentialist apologetic method discussed in this chapter is not necessarily the same as an evidentialist epistemology. The epis-

---

[1]Sometimes it is difficult to determine whether a scholar is a classical apologist or an evidentialist, often because that scholar does not indicate his or her position on the question of whether historical evidences are able to show that God exists.

temic position holds that beliefs are justified only if one has conclusive evidence for them. Typically, this evidence might take
the form of internal states to which the knowing subject can
have direct access (e.g., sensory states or rational intuitions) or
propositional evidence. While the apologetic strategy says that
there are good arguments for Christian theism, its adherents seldom comment concerning the type or amount of evidence, or
how much argumentation is necessary to justify belief. Indeed,
we will see below that some evidentialists even hold that the
Holy Spirit can provide direct confirmation to the individual
concerning the truth of Christianity *apart* from any evidences.
As David Clark (a classical apologist) points out, the apologetic
method is not to be equated with its epistemic namesake.[2]

Not only does an evidential (or evidential-like) apologetic
methodology not require an evidentialist epistemology, but the
former can be accommodated by any of several epistemic viewpoints. Instances are not difficult to find. Much more obviously,
traditional foundationalists like internalists J. P. Moreland[3] and
R. Douglas Geivett[4] favor an evidential apologetic methodology.
A "weak foundationalist" such as C. Stephen Evans argues (in
fallibilist terms) from miracles to Scripture and the actions of the
God who gave it.[5] A reliabilist like William Alston (who calls his
view an "internalist externalism,"[6] described as a "bridge" or

[2]David K. Clark, *Dialogical Apologetics: A Person-Centered Approach to Christian
Defense* (Grand Rapids: Baker, 1993), 106. For Clark's own position, see pp. 108–9.

[3]J. P. Moreland, *Scaling the Secular City: A Defense of Christianity* (Grand Rapids:
Baker, 1987). Moreland has affirmed to me on several occasions that a "one-step"
argument (from historical evidence to the existence of God) is not only a viable move,
but is a potentially forceful theistic argument. Cf. J. P. Moreland and Kai Nielson, *Does
God Exist? The Great Debate* (Nashville: Thomas Nelson, 1990), 57, 73–74, 239.

[4]R. Douglas Geivett, *Evil and the Evidence for God* (Philadelphia: Temple University Press, 1993); R. Douglas Geivett, "The Evidential Value of Miracles," in *In
Defense of Miracles: A Comprehensive Case for God's Action in History*, ed. R. Douglas
Geivett and Gary R. Habermas (Downers Grove, Ill.: InterVarsity Press, 1997), 178–
95. See pp. 179–87 in particular for Geivett's argument that "ascends" "from miracles
to the existence of God" (p. 187).

[5]C. Stephen Evans, *Philosophy of Religion: Thinking About Faith* (Downers Grove,
Ill.: InterVarsity Press, 1982), chap. 5; C. Stephen Evans, *The Quest for Faith: Reason
and Mystery as Pointers to God* (Downers Grove, Ill.: InterVarsity Press, 1986), chap. 9,
cf. p. 35.

[6]See the following works by Alston: *Epistemic Justification* (Ithaca, N.Y.: Cornell University Press, 1989); *Perceiving God* (Ithaca, N.Y.: Cornell University Press,
1991); "Knowledge of God" in *Faith, Reason, and Skepticism*, ed. Marcus Hester
(Philadelphia: Temple University Press, 1992).

"halfway house" between internalism and externalism[7]), at least in principle, could also appreciate arguments from miracles, as could a Reidian foundationalist like externalist Alvin Plantinga.[8] The point here is that more than one epistemic stance could encourage the use of some form of evidential apologetic methodology, whether or not it is held that such evidence is necessary.

SOME TENETS OF AN EVIDENTIALIST METHODOLOGY

Let us turn now to some of the emphases of the evidentialist method of doing apologetics. What are its distinctives? Where is it similar to the other major apologetic systems?

First, I have said that the chief interest of this method is the postulating and developing of historical evidences (one species of propositional data) for the Christian faith. This is its single, major contribution to the issue. Not only is it thought that these evidences provide the best means of deciding between the theistic systems of belief, but also that they can be utilized as an indication of God's existence and activity.[9]

Second, however, historical occurrences are not brute facts that interpret themselves. While the event itself is objective, its meaning is also derived from the context, which involves a number of factors. Although the past is of crucial importance, evidentialists recognize that human factors always enter into historiography. Events must be chosen for study, and since there is more than one perspective on what has happened, there is almost always more than one point of view. Personal preferences and prejudices can substantially color our interpretations, not to mention the affect of our worldviews on our research.[10]

---

[7]These last two descriptions of Alston are given by Alvin Plantinga in *Warrant: The Current Debate* (New York: Oxford University Press, 1993), 184–85.

[8]In the text of Alvin Plantinga's unpublished and informal essay "Two Dozen (or So) Theistic Arguments," he lists (but does not explain) the argument from miracles (p. 13) as one of the probabilistic arguments that can "bolster" or perhaps even "convince" faith (p. 1).

[9]We will return to this subject below, providing an example of one such approach.

[10]In spite of comments to the contrary, even John Warwick Montgomery emphasizes that these subjective elements are inevitably present in evaluations of historical events. See his volume *The Shape of the Past: A Christian Response to Secular Philosophies of History* (Minneapolis: Bethany Fellowship, 1975), 13–14, 73–74. Unfortunately, Montgomery does not always seem to be this clear, such as when he appar-

It is for reasons such as these that the careful application of historical principles, tempered by various sorts of critical analyses, are necessary in order to recognize and offset as much as possible the subjective element. Although such biases can never be completely eliminated, it is still possible to reach sturdy conclusions within the canons of historical research. There is, however, no reason to succumb to a relativistic epistemology of history here. Historiography is certainly capable of determining the past. We just must be careful not to read biases into the accounts.[11]

Third, evidentialists also engage freely in "negative" apologetics, arguing against the theses of those who would seek to defeat Christian theism. This defensive apologetic strategy could perhaps deflate aspects of the opponent's argument or even rebut it entirely.[12] This could involve responding to detractors on a number of fronts, such as (but not limited to) philosophical, scientific, historical, theological, or biblical challenges.[13]

---

ently groups history with the hard sciences in a rather positivistic fashion, or insists that, properly understood, historical facts "speak for themselves" and "carry their interpretations" (John Warwick Montgomery, *Where Is History Going?* [Grand Rapids: Zondervan, 1969], 163–68, 194; cf. *The Shape of the Past*, 286–287, 293). Comments like these have drawn an outcry from scholars, possibly because Montgomery does not spell out his views carefully enough. See the following articles: Ronald H. Nash, "The Use and Abuse of History in Christian Apologetics," *Christian Scholar's Review* 1, no. 3 (Spring 1971): 217–26; Ronald VanderMolen, "The Christian Historian: Apologist or Seeker?" *Fides et Historia* 3, no. 1 (Fall 1970); Ronald VanderMolen, "'Where Is History Going?' and Historical Scholarship: A Response," *Fides et Historia* 5, nos. 1–2 (Spring 1973): 109–12; Earl William Kennedy, "John Warwick Montgomery and the Objectivist Apologetics Movement," *Fides et Historia* 5, nos. 1–2 (Spring 1973): 117–21. Montgomery's defenders have also fired back their salvos: Paul D. Feinberg, "History: Public or Private? A Defense of John Warwick Montgomery's *Philosophy of History*," *Christian Scholar's Review* 1, no. 4 (Summer 1971): 325–31; Steven A. Hein, "The Christian Historian: Apologist or Seeker? A Reply to Ronald J. VanderMolen," *Fides et Historia* 4, no. 2 (Spring 1972): 85–93.

[11]For details, see Gary R. Habermas, *The Historical Jesus: Ancient Evidence for the Life of Christ* (Joplin, Mo.: College Press, 1996), appendix 1; idem, "Philosophy of History, Historical Relativism, and History as Evidence," in *Evangelical Apologetics*, ed. Michael Bauman, David Hall, and Robert Newman (Camp Hill, Pa.: Christian Publications, 1996), 93, 104–6; Frank Beckwith, "History and Miracles," in Geivett and Habermas, eds., *In Defense of Miracles*, 87–91.

[12]Cf. John Pollock's differentiation between "undercutting defeaters" and "rebutting defeaters" in his *Contemporary Theories of Knowledge* (Totawa, N.J.: Rowman and Littlefield, 1986), 38–39, 48. For Plantinga's evaluation of Pollock's notion of defeasibility, see Plantinga, *Warrant*, 216–21.

[13]For evidentialists who employ such tactics, see Moreland, *Scaling the Secular City*, chaps. 7–8; R. Douglas Geivett, "John Hick's Approach to Religious Pluralism,"

An example taken from the previous tenet may help here, in response to certain recent trends in postmodernism. If it is held that historical research is hopelessly subjective, or that objective data cannot be attained for other reasons, an evidentialist might respond on several grounds. These postmodernist notions could be charged with self-contradictions at more than one level, as many major researchers have noted. Or it could be asserted that informal logical fallacies have been detected, or that inconsistent historiographical applications are apparent in the skeptic's own position. Further, much subjective bias can be recognized and thwarted. Finally, the historical method is capable of rendering positive historical conclusions, too, as recognized by professional historians of almost all persuasions. Just because radical relativists might continue to shake their heads and disagree, this is decidedly not the same as refuting the evidentialist's position. It is the latter, not the former, that needs to be done.[14]

On the other hand, the postmodernist might charge a lesser degree of subjectivity. Then the evidentialist may have to patiently show, perhaps in a specific case, both how bias can be counteracted and how positive historical data can be established.

Fourth, it is impossible to force anyone into the kingdom of God by our use of logic and/or evidences. The reality of sin separates persons from God and plays a monumental role in how God's truth is viewed by the unbeliever (Rom. 1:18–32; 1 Cor. 2:14). Human agency is not responsible for regeneration. Apart from God's influence, conversion will never take place.[15]

Proceedings of the Wheaton Theology Conference 1 (Spring 1992): 43–53; John Warwick Montgomery, *The Suicide of Christian Theology* (Minneapolis: Bethany Fellowship, 1970), pts. 1 and 2; *The Shape of the Past*, pt. 2; *Where Is History Going?* chaps. 4–7; Bernard Ramm, *Protestant Christian Evidences* (Chicago: Moody Press, 1953), chaps. 2, 5; Clark Pinnock, *Set Forth Your Case: An Examination of Christianity's Credentials* (Chicago: Moody Press, 1969), chaps. 2–6, 14.

[14]For details on each of these critiques, see Habermas, "Philosophy of History, Historical Relativism, and History as Evidence," esp. pp. 100–108; on the charge of self-contradictions and other problems, see James Harris, *Against Relativism: A Philosophical Defense of Method* (La Salle, Ill.: Open Court, 1992); Donald A. Crosby, *The Specter of the Absurd: Sources and Criticisms of Modern Nihilism* (Albany: State University of New York Press, 1988); Christopher Norris, *Beyond Relativism: Philosophy of Science, Deconstruction and Critical Theory* (Oxford: Blackwell Publishers, 1997).

[15]It is not difficult to find evidentialists who include substantial treatments of sin in their apologetics. An example is Bernard Ramm, who lists sin as one of the major issues for Christian apologetics and follows the subject through several

Fifth, this does not mean that there is no common ground between the believer and the unbeliever. Apologists largely agree that there is ontological commonality in areas such as general creation, God's image in humans, and the data of history, each of which is "public." They disagree, however, concerning whether there is any epistemological common ground, especially over the issue of how the unbeliever views truth.[16]

While we cannot sift through all the details here, evidentialists insist that there are a number of epistemological similarities in areas such as sensory data (perception), scientific theories, and the general rules and application of inference. Unbelievers can at least be intellectually challenged to view data that oppose their belief systems, even though they will frequently disagree with believers and even though they cannot be converted by the facts alone.[17]

Sixth, evidentialists emphasize that the Holy Spirit may work through the use of apologetics (just as he does through preaching or witnessing), not only in bringing unbelievers to himself (Acts 17:1–4), but also in providing full assurance to believers (perhaps even apart from evidences) that they are the children of God (Rom. 8:16). This ministry is not just tacked on to the end of the evidences as an expendable extra, but is simultaneous with it. Without the interceding of the Holy Spirit, no one comes to God.[18]

---

thinkers. See his *Varieties of Christian Apologetics* (Grand Rapids: Baker, 1962), 17–27. For other examples, see John McNaugher, *Jesus Christ: The Same Yesterday, Today and Forever* (New York: Revell, 1947), chap. 5; Clark H. Pinnock, *Live Now, Brother* (Chicago: Moody Press, 1972), chaps. 1–3; John Warwick Montgomery, *How Do We Know There Is a God? And Other Questions Inappropriate in Polite Society* (Minneapolis: Bethany House, 1973), 54–62; Norman Anderson, *Jesus Christ: The Witness of History* (Leicester, England: Inter-Varsity Press, 1985), 93–110; Henry M. Morris, *Many Infallible Proofs: Practical and Useful Evidences of Christianity* (San Diego: Creation-Life Publishers, 1974), chap. 11. The apologist's specific view of sin may depend more on his theological emphases than on his particular apologetic method.

[16]Ronald B. Mayers, *Both/And: A Balanced Apologetic* (Chicago: Moody Press, 1984), 215–17; Richard L. Pratt Jr., *Every Thought Captive: A Study Manual for the Defense of Christian Truth* (Phillipsburg, N.J.: Presbyterian and Reformed, 1979), 88, 92–93; Thom Notaro, *Van Til and the Use of Evidence* (Phillipsburg, N.J.: Presbyterian and Reformed, 1980), 19, 44, 46, 52, 82.

[17]Pinnock, *Set Forth Your Case,* chap. 15 and conclusion; John Warwick Montgomery, *Sensible Christianity,* 3-vol. tape set (Santa Ana, Calif.: Vision House, 1976), vol. 1, tapes 2–4.

[18]Contrary to what seems to be a common misconception, evidentialists have published widely on the relation of the Holy Spirit to apologetics. See the major

Seventh, the vast majority of evidentialists are eclectic in their approach to apologetics: while they agree that their method is a viable way, it is not the only way to argue. Most evidentialists, for example, encourage various forms of natural theology with regard to arguments for God's existence.[19] In other words, they are still separate from classical apologists in that they think that a one-step argument from historical evidences (such as miracles) to God is feasible, and they often use this as their favorite argument.[20] This does not, however, keep evidentialists from advocating the use of many other sorts of evidences and techniques, as their writings reveal.

A final word concerning the results of apologetics: I have spoken here almost as if the sole mission of this discipline is to reach unbelievers with the gospel, or at least to challenge them in a pre-evangelistic sense, all by the power of the Holy Spirit. However, not only is apologetics exceptionally useful with believers, it may even be its major value. This is an area where we need to apply theory to life in a variety of ways, and radically so. We need to be as committed to the practical, ministry task as we are to the scholarly pursuit.[21]

---

treatise by Bernard Ramm, *The Witness of the Spirit* (Grand Rapids: Eerdmans, 1959). For other examples, see Pinnock, *Set Forth Your Case*, 14–19, 65–66, 119–25; idem, *Three Keys to Spiritual Renewal: A Challenge to the Church* (Minneapolis: Bethany House, 1985), chap. 2; Gary R. Habermas, *Dealing with Doubt* (Chicago: Moody Press, 1990), chap. 8; idem, "The Personal Testimony of the Holy Spirit to the Believer and Christian Apologetics," *Journal of Christian Apologetics* 1, no. 1 (Summer 1997): 49–64.

[19]For several instances, see Moreland, *Scaling the Secular City*, chaps. 1–4; Geivett, *Evil and the Evidence for God*, chap. 6; Francis J. Beckwith, *David Hume's Argument Against Miracles: A Critical Analysis* (Lanham, Md.: University Press of America, 1989), chap. 5; Stephen E. Parrish, *God and Necessity: A Defense of Classical Theism* (Lanham, Md.: University Press of America, 1997); Montgomery, *How Do We Know There Is a God?* 9–12; idem, *Sensible Christianity*, vol. 2, tapes 1–2; Clark Pinnock, *Reason Enough: A Case for the Christian Faith* (Downers Grove, Ill.: InterVarsity Press, 1980), chap. 3. More popular accounts are found in Morris, *Many Infallible Proofs*, chap. 9; Paul E. Little, *Know Why You Believe* (Chicago: InterVarsity Press, 1968), chap. 2.

[20]Arguably the best way to distinguish between evidentialists and classical apologists is to find out whether they are willing to utilize historical evidences as a separate argument for the truth of theism. While both types of scholars generally like a variety of arguments for God's existence, only evidentialists think that miracles, for example, can successfully provide one of these arguments without first establishing a theistic universe by another means.

[21]Thankfully, this theme is also prominent among evidential writers. For a few examples, see J. P. Moreland, *Love Your God with All Your Mind: The Role of Reason in*

In sum, evidentialist methodology has a couple of distinctives, while on other issues it takes positions that are similar to those of the other methodologies. Its most characteristic feature is its specializing in propositional evidences, of which the historical variety is the most prominent, moving on to God and the truth of Christianity by what we have called the one-step approach. The emphasis on there being enough ontological and epistemological common ground to speak meaningfully to an unbeliever is also a central concern. The fact that other apologetic evidences and approaches are rather frequently welcomed separates evidentialism from at least some adherents to the other methods. On the denial of brute historical facts, the use of "negative" apologetics, the actual and pervading presence of human sin, and the active ministry of the Holy Spirit throughout the apologetic endeavor (and beyond), evidentialists are closer to emphases that are regularly found in each of the apologetic methods. In these less distinctive areas, those within each of the methodological camps could also disagree among themselves, depending on the theological distinctives involved.

I have said that the argument from historical events to Christian theism is probably the single identifying feature of an evidential apologetic methodology. I will develop below one possible example of such a position.

DIFFERENT USES OF EVIDENCE

Before outlining a possible approach, it might be helpful to comment briefly on internal differences in evidential methodology. The most common tactic is one that, after certain preliminary questions, begins the discussion of evidences by establishing the trustworthiness of Scripture, then moving on to the tenets of Christian theism.[22] While this can be very helpful, it must be done very carefully. Just because a work is generally trustworthy, it does not always follow that everything in it (and especially the supernatural) is true. In this latter step, we thus need to proceed cautiously.

---

the Life of the Soul (Colorado Springs: NavPress, 1997), esp. pt. 3; Pinnock, Reason Enough, chaps. 5–6; idem, Three Keys to Spiritual Renewal, chaps. 2–3; Habermas, Dealing with Doubt, chaps. 6, 7, 9; Gary R. Habermas and J. P. Moreland, Beyond Death: Exploring the Evidence for Immortality (Wheaton, Ill.: Crossway, 1998), pt. 3.

[22]In classical apologetic approaches, too, Scripture is often the first evidential move after preliminary questions and the establishment of a theistic universe.

I prefer a method that I call the "minimal facts" approach. The major idea is to utilize data that have two characteristics: they are well-evidenced, usually for multiple reasons, and they are generally admitted by critical scholars who research this particular area. Of the two, having well-attested grounds is certainly the more crucial. And we should remember that not only do such grounds come in many shapes and forms, but evidentialists are able to use the data basically wherever it is found, even beyond the area of history. They just insist that the historical avenue be *one* such way.

The criterion regarding critical scholarship is less significant. Not only may the critics themselves be mistaken, but the intellectual climate may change. Nevertheless, their data remains useful to a methodological approach. Positive apologetics is all about having reasons, and the chief thrust of the minimal facts approach is to argue whenever possible on more limited grounds, both to challenge a larger range of thinkers and to show that our basis is exceptionally firm.

In what follows, I will use this minimal facts strategy even though, due to space limitations, I am not always able to show here exactly how these requirements are fulfilled. The reader may consult the listed sources for details, since this is at least the explicit apologetic method in my works.

AN OUTLINED EVIDENTIALIST CASE

It is not possible in the scope of this chapter to attempt to defend even a single detailed argument for Christian theism. All I can hope to do here is to furnish a broad outline indicating one direction that might be taken in such an enterprise. Other evidentialists may have differing views, perhaps even taking another approach altogether.

Jesus' Teachings

The first step of our case is concerned with Jesus' teaching. According to the New Testament,[23] Jesus' ministry was charac-

---

[23]There is more than one way to examine the nature of Jesus' claims. I have said that one method is to begin with a defense of the trustworthiness of Scripture and then move on to the biblical proclamation of Jesus' deity. But it is simply not possible here to develop what has been done in detailed volumes in other evidential (and evidential-like) treatments. (See the texts below.) The other way I have mentioned is to utilize those New Testament texts that are both well evidenced and have

terized by a number of unique theological claims. He seemed constantly to be making pronouncements that alternately pleased, surprised, or infuriated his listeners. But whatever the response, he made various distinctive proclamations. As Stephen Neill attests in his standard study of world religions, no matter how critically we view the Gospels, we still discover the singular nature of Jesus' message:

> Jesus is not the least like anyone else who has ever lived. The things he says about God are not the same as the sayings of any other religious teacher. The claims he makes for himself are not the same as those that have been made by any other religious teacher.[24]

What are some of these distinctive items? Did Jesus, for example, claim to be deity? I will briefly address only two subjects: two of Jesus' teachings about himself and what he said concerning his role in the coming of God's kingdom.

About Himself. Perhaps the best insight we have concerning what Jesus thought about himself comes from the titles he used.[25] Two of these are especially instructive.

1. His favorite self-designation was "Son of Man."

(a) This title appears in all of the Gospel strata (Q, Mark, M [unique to Matthew], L [unique to Luke], and John), meaning that it has excellent support in the best sources.

---

gained a fair amount of critical acceptance, building on a minimalistic foundation. While I cannot provide more than a modest amount of the necessary argumentation and even less documentation to show the data in favor of the statements I will make, it will have to suffice to say that I will stick to claims that are well-defensible, providing details wherever possible. Other crucial data are provided in the texts I will list later. As far as defending the reliability of the New Testament, see the following: Craig Blomberg, *The Historical Reliability of the Gospels* (Downers Grove, Ill.: InterVarsity Press, 1987); F. F. Bruce, *The New Testament Documents: Are they Reliable?* 5th ed. (Grand Rapids: Eerdmans, 1960); Paul Barnett, *Is the New Testament Reliable? A Look at the Historical Evidence* (Downers Grove, Ill.: InterVarsity Press, 1986); idem, *Jesus and the Logic of History* (Grand Rapids: Eerdmans, 1997); Josh McDowell, *Evidence That Demands a Verdict* (Arrowhead Springs, Calif.: Campus Crusade for Christ, 1972); R. T. France, *The Evidence for Jesus* (Downers Grove, Ill.: InterVarsity Press, 1986); David A. Fiensy, *The Message and Ministry of Jesus: An Introductory Textbook* (Lanham, Md.: University Press of America, 1996).

[24]Stephen Neill, *Christian Faith and Other Faiths*, 2d ed. (Oxford: Oxford University Press, 1970), 233. See also Norman Anderson, *Christianity and World Religions: The Challenge of Pluralism* (Downers Grove, Ill.: InterVarsity Press, 1984); Stephen Neill, *The Supremacy of Jesus* (Downers Grove, Ill.: InterVarsity Press, 1984).

[25]The reader who desires more details may consult the sources that follow.

(b) It is also exceptionally difficult to explain away as a later addition. The title would not have been attributed to Jesus by the unbelieving Jews, for they had no reason to exalt him. Neither would early Christians have been responsible for it, since, paradoxically, this title is not applied to the earthly ministry of Jesus anywhere else in the New Testament! So it was presumably not a very popular designation in the mid to late first century, when the New Testament was being written. Thus, for reasons like these, Son of Man appears to be Jesus' own choice of descriptive application.

(c) Some of Jesus' usages of the title Son of Man are more generic, referring to his own ministry. In one such instance, Jesus claimed to be able to forgive sins, which was properly recognized by the Jewish leaders as a prerogative of God alone (Mark 2:1–12). Donald Guthrie says about this incident: "Jesus as Son of man was exercising authority which he himself knew was legitimate only for God."[26] Oscar Cullmann emphasizes: "This meant a conscious identification with God."[27]

(d) Two other ways in which Jesus used the title concern the suffering and rising Son of Man (Mark 8:31; 9:31), as well as his coming in judgment to set up God's kingdom (Mark 8:38; 13:26). The latter, in particular, is similar to Daniel 7:13–14, where the preexistent Son of Man is sent by the Ancient of Days to the earth.[28] Cullmann summarizes the matter: "By means of this very term Jesus spoke of his divine heavenly character."[29]

2. Another crucial title is Jesus' use of "Son of God." It provides us with insights of a different sort.

(a) In the highly respected text in Matthew 11:27, Jesus declared that he had a unique relationship to the God of the universe, being the only one who knew him intimately. Reginald Fuller concludes that Jesus "was certainly conscious of a unique Sonship to which he was privileged to admit others."[30]

---

[26]Donald Guthrie, *New Testament Theology* (Downers Grove, Ill.: InterVarsity Press, 1981), 280.

[27]Oscar Cullmann, *The Christology of the New Testament*, trans. Shirley C. Guthrie and Charles A. M. Hall (Philadelphia: Westminster Press, 1963), 282.

[28]Two other passages that perhaps date from the first century A.D. and are very helpful in understanding the Jewish significance of this title are 4 Ezra 13 and 1 Enoch 37–71. For the relevant texts and thoughtful commentary, see C. K. Barrett, ed., *The New Testament Background: Selected Documents* (New York: Harper and Brothers, 1961), 235–37, 250–55.

[29]Cullmann, *The Christology of the New Testament*, 162; cf. 142, 151.

[30]Reginald H. Fuller, *The Foundations of New Testament Christology* (New York: Scribners, 1965), 115.

(b) Further, Jesus referred to God in highly personal terms, calling him *Abba*, which means "Father" or perhaps even "Daddy" (Mark 14:36). This certainly set him apart from the Jewish teachers of his day. Joachim Jeremias summarizes his seminal study of this topic:

> Abba ... is ... an authentic and original utterance of Jesus, and ... implies the claim of a unique revelation and a unique authority.... We are confronted with something new and unheard of which breaks through the limits of Judaism.[31]

(c) One way critics determine the reliability of a text is when a particular reading introduces a pithy problem. Many critical scholars have maintained the authenticity of Mark 13:32 because it is too difficult to explain in terms of being a late addition. Why, in order to make Jesus call himself the Son, would the problem be introduced concerning whether Jesus had knowledge about the time of his return? Couldn't someone make a simple assertion of Jesus' deity if that is what he had wanted to do? As a result, Mark 13:32 is taken quite seriously. Guthrie speaks for many scholars when he says, "It is impossible to suppose that a saying so Christologically embarrassing should have been invented. There is no strong reason to question its authenticity."[32]

The title Son of God is certainly an important one. Cullmann contends that "Jesus' consciousness of being the Son of God refers both to his person and to his work: his work of salvation and revelation shows that the Father and the Son are one."[33] As a result, the Jews respond to Jesus' self-proclamations and "correctly interpret Jesus' claim to be 'Son' as identification with God."[34] I. H. Marshall testifies that the designation was both used by Jesus as a self-designation, and that it involved deity. For the early church, it was a means by which "it was not inappropriate to call Jesus 'God.'"[35]

3. One of the most intriguing passages is Mark 14:61–64, where both of these titles are combined. As Jesus stood before his

---

[31]Joachim Jeremias, *The Central Message of the New Testament* (Philadelphia: Fortress, 1965), 30.

[32]Guthrie, *New Testament Theology,* 794, n. 14; cf. p. 308.

[33]Cullmann, *The Christology of the New Testament,* 290.

[34]Ibid., 302. See also Cullmann's strong comments on p. 270.

[35]I. H. Marshall, *The Origins of New Testament Christology,* rev. ed. (Downers Grove, Ill.: InterVarsity Press, 1990), 123.

accusers, he was asked if he was "the Christ, the Son of the Blessed One." His affirmation brought the charge of blasphemy against him. At least four items in this passage are worth noting.

(a) Jesus responded to the high priest's question by uttering the staggering words, "I am" *(ego eimi)*, which may be a reference to the name by which God identified himself to Moses (Exod. 3:14).[36]

(b) Jesus then changed the emphasis of his answer from the Son of God to the Son of Man.

(c) He said further that he would return "on the clouds of heaven," a description that is similar to wording in dozens of other passages in Scripture that are almost uniformly associated only with God.

(d) Jesus' affirmations clearly brought the charge of blasphemy. In the context of first-century Jewish theology, Jesus had crossed the line of no return. Royce Gruenler concludes, "This further evidences Jesus' messianic self-awareness and is exegetically the proper intent of the passage."[37]

4. Although the titles Jesus used are probably the best indications of his messianic self-consciousness, they are not the only pointers. He had other relevant teachings, too, like placing his own authority above that of the most respected Jewish leaders (Matt. 5:20–48). We could also discuss his actions or the convictions of those around Jesus that he was sinless. The impression he made on those who were closest to him is evidence concerning his self-understanding.[38] Fuller summarizes what we can learn from some of Jesus' claims:

> An examination of Jesus' words . . . forces upon us the conclusion that underlying his word and work is an implicit Christology. In Jesus as he understood himself, there is an immediate confrontation with "God's presence and his very self," offering judgment and salvation.[39]

About His Role as Spokesman for God. Second, Jesus claimed authority unlike that of other world religion founders. Many

---

[36]In John 8:58–59 we are told that Jesus made a similar claim, which also resulted in a charge of blasphemy.

[37]Royce Gruenler, "Son of Man," *Evangelical Dictionary of Theology*, ed. Walter A. Elwell (Grand Rapids: Baker, 1984), 1035.

[38]For these and other relevant considerations, see Terry L. Miethe and Gary R. Habermas, *Why Believe? God Exists!* (Joplin, Mo.: College Press, 1993), chap. 27.

[39]Fuller, *Foundations of New Testament Christology*, 106.

have claimed to be able to show their followers the right path or to introduce them to the way of salvation. Not only did Jesus make the functional claim to be able to lead his followers to the truth, but he added a crucial ontological component: he was the truth. What people did with him determined where they would spend eternity.[40]

The critical community almost unanimously agrees that Jesus' central teaching was the kingdom of God and its entrance requirements. He repeatedly called individuals to act in light of this reality by responding to him and his message since he was God's select messenger.[41] In no area was Jesus' authority more evident. All persons would be held accountable by how they responded to this teaching. Raymond Brown is clear about this:

> *An irreducible historical minimum* in the Gospel presentation of Jesus is that he claimed to be the *unique agent* in the process of establishing God's kingship over men. He proclaimed that in his preaching and through his deeds God's kingship over men was making itself felt.[42]

Brown adds that this message of the kingdom was the singular, distinctive target of Jesus' teachings from the very beginning of his ministry.[43]

Contemporary critical scholars agree widely in recognizing this conclusion.[44] Rudolf Bultmann affirms that in the person, message, and deeds of Jesus, the kingdom was already dawning. Jesus issued the call to decision; individuals needed to choose whether to follow.[45] Reginald Fuller declares, "God is directly present in the word of Jesus, actively demanding unreserved obedience to his will from those who have accepted the eschatological message and its offer of salvation."[46] Wolfhart

---

[40]See texts like Matt. 10:32–33; 19:28–29; 25:34–36; Mark 8:34–38; 10:45; John 10:10; 14:6.

[41]On the centrality of the kingdom of God, see Matt. 6:33; 13:44–52; Mark 1:14–15; 4:3–34; 9:43–48. For Jesus' role as the central figure in this call, see Matt. 10:37–39; 25:31–46; Mark 10:28–30, 45; Luke 11:20; 14:25–35; 24:45–47; John 3:15–16; 6:47.

[42]Raymond E. Brown, *Jesus: God and Man* (Milwaukee: Bruce, 1967), 96–97 (my emphasis).

[43]Ibid., 59, 98.

[44]This is not to say that contemporary scholars agree with either each other or with orthodox theology on the subject of the deity of Christ.

[45]Rudolf Bultmann, *Theology of the New Testament*, trans. Kendrick Grobel (New York: Scribners, 1951, 1955), 1:4–11.

[46]Fuller, *Foundations of New Testament Christology*, 105–6.

Pannenberg agrees that Jesus revealed God like no one else has ever done before or since. In his person and message God disclosed himself to humankind in a unique way.[47]

The result is that persons could enter the kingdom of God if they responded properly to Jesus and his message. William Strawson points out, "Throughout our Lord's teaching there is a continual emphasis upon the urgent need to meet the conditions which God requires for entry into eternal life."[48] But what were those specific conditions? Strawson summarizes that the requirement is dependence on Jesus Christ, who is himself the way to such life. Only by such action can persons be properly related to both God and others.[49] Brown concludes similarly:

> We have indicated an area where [Jesus'] views were not at all those of his time, namely, the area of belief and behavior called for by the coming of the kingdom. And in this area, in my personal opinion, his authority is supreme for every century, because in this area he spoke for God. No age can reject the demand that one must believe in Jesus as the unique agent for establishing God's kingship over men (a uniqueness which the Church at Nicaea finally came to formulate in terms of Jesus' being "true God of true God").[50]

Although there are other indications, what Jesus taught about himself and his role as initiator of God's kingdom are unique pointers to two crucial elements of his personal theistic worldview. From a variety of angles, we learn that Jesus thought of himself as deity. Although the particulars cannot be defended here, Jesus' preaching in these areas is distinctive, even in the field of comparative religion. At this point, however, these are only his *claims*. Why did anyone believe them?

The Death and Resurrection of Jesus

Although I must necessarily be even briefer here, I will attempt to sketch a case for the historicity of Jesus' death and

[47]Wolfhart Pannenberg, *Theology and the Kingdom of God,* ed. Richard John Neuhaus (Philadelphia: Westminster, 1969), 51.

[48]William Strawson, *Jesus and the Future Life* (Philadelphia: Westminster, 1959), 226. In his second edition (1970), Strawson writes, "We assume then that there are conditions to be met if we are to obtain everlasting life" (p. 227).

[49]Ibid., 2d ed. (1970), 227–28.

[50]Brown, *Jesus: God and Man,* 101.

resurrection appearances. It must be carefully noted that it is not being assumed or asserted at this point that such an event is a miracle performed by God. We are only concerned here with whether Jesus really died and whether he appeared afterward. The interested reader who prefers more details, such as the actual data behind my summaries, or the critical methodology, interaction, and citations, can find these elsewhere.[51]

The Death of Jesus. First, we have excellent reasons for the conclusion that Jesus actually died due to the rigors of crucifixion.

1. Numerous ancient historical sources record Jesus' death. We have the testimony of (a) several primitive, highly respected traditions that actually predate the New Testament books in which they appear,[52] (b) the rest of the New Testament (and the gospel narratives, in particular), as well as (c) a dozen extrabiblical, non-Christian references to this event.[53]

2. Several crucial medical facts indicate that death by crucifixion is clearly ascertainable. (a) Crucifixion victims essentially died of asphyxiation, complicated by other medical factors. Hanging in the low position on the cross insured death, and anyone who occupied that posture for more than a few minutes began to asphyxiate. (b) Ancient sources relate that final blows were sometimes administered to crucifixion victims to speed up or guarantee their deaths. The description and nature of Jesus' spear wound reveals that the weapon punctured his heart, insuring his death. (c) Further, if the spear also pierced one of Jesus' lungs, and he were not already dead, a fairly loud sucking sound would have signaled his executors that he had not yet died.

---

[51]Details may be found in some of my publications on this topic, such as: *The Resurrection of Jesus: A Rational Inquiry* (Ann Arbor: University Microfilms, 1976); *The Resurrection of Jesus: An Apologetic* (Grand Rapids: Baker, 1980; Lanham, Md.: University Press of America, 1984); with Antony Flew, *Did Jesus Rise from the Dead? The Resurrection Debate,* ed. Terry L. Miethe (San Francisco: Harper and Row, 1987); *The Historical Jesus: Ancient Evidence for the Life of Christ* (Joplin, Mo.: College Press, 1996); "Knowing That Jesus' Resurrection Occurred: A Response to Stephen Davis," *Faith and Philosophy* 2, no. 3 (July 1985): 295–302; "Jesus' Resurrection and Contemporary Criticism: An Apologetic," *Criswell Theological Review,* 2 pts., 4, no. 1 (Fall 1989): 159–74, and 4, no. 2 (Spring 1990): 373–85.

[52]The ones that receive the most scholarly attention are Acts 2:23–24; 3:13–15; 4:10; 5:29–30; 10:39; 13:28–29; 1 Cor. 11:26; 15:3; and Phil. 2:8. Others include Rom. 4:25 and 1 Peter 3:18.

[53]Examples include Roman historian Tacitus, Jewish sources like Josephus and the Talmud, as well as other ancient writers like Thallus, Lucian, Phlegon, and Mara Bar-Serapion.

3. Since the work of David Strauss in the nineteenth century,[54] another reason has been the most influential in persuading scholars that Jesus had truly died. Critics have long accepted the fact that the earliest disciples at least *believed* that Jesus had been raised from the dead (see below). But this belief would have been defied by the sight of a Jesus who had not died on the cross. If he had shown himself to his followers a few days after the crucifixion, as the early sources indicate, he would have been in horrible physical condition: bruised, beaten, bloody, pale, limping, and in obvious need of medical assistance. But such a condition would have disallowed the view that he had been raised from the dead in a resurrected body. He would have been alive (barely) but not raised! Further, there would be no impetus for the prominent conviction that believers would someday be raised just like Jesus. Who would want a body like this sickly one! In short, the swoon theory actually contradicts the disciples' belief that Jesus had truly been raised.

For reasons such as these, very few scholars today doubt that Jesus died by crucifixion. John Dominic Crossan boldly asserts, "That he was crucified is as sure as anything historical can ever be," and resulted in his death.[55] Marcus Borg lists Jesus' execution as "the most certain fact about the historical Jesus."[56]

The Resurrection Appearances of Jesus. As strange as this claim is to many, that Jesus was seen after his death is confirmed by a large array of data. I will mention just a few of the lines of evidence for these appearances.

1. The most widely discussed New Testament text on the subject of the historical Jesus is 1 Corinthians 15:3–8.[57] (a) Virtually all scholars, whatever their theological persuasion, agree that Paul here records a primitive Jewish tradition(s) that is not his; he received it from another source. There are many literary indications of this, such as: (i) the use of "delivered" and "re-

---

[54]David Strauss, *A New Life of Jesus*, 2 vols. (Edinburgh: Williams & Norgate, 1879), 1:408–12.

[55]John Dominic Crossan, *Jesus: A Revolutionary Biography* (San Francisco: HarperSanFrancisco, 1994), 145; cf. 154, 196, 201.

[56]Marcus Borg, *Jesus: A New Vision: Spirit, Culture, and the Life of Discipleship* (San Francisco: HarperCollins, 1987), 179; cf. 178–84.

[57]For historical details, extensive critical sources, and other argumentation for the following discussion, see Gary R. Habermas, "The Resurrection Appearances of Jesus," in Geivett and Habermas, eds., *In Defense of Miracles*, 262–75. Cf. the other sources listed in n. 51 above.

ceived," which are not only technical terms for passing along tradition, but are Paul's direct comment that this is not his material. Other indications include (ii) the Jewish parallelism and stylized accounts, along with (iii) the proper names Cephas and James. Further, (iv) the triple "and that" *(hoti)* clauses, which are typical of Hebrew narration, (v) the two references to Scripture being fulfilled, as well as (vi) the possibility of an Aramaic original also point in this direction. Finally, (vii) the terminology, diction, and structure are all non-Pauline.

(b) This creedal testimony is exceptionally early. Not only is it older than 1 Corinthians, but it very likely predates even Paul's conversion. The predominant view is that Paul probably received the material from Peter and James, the brother of Jesus, when he visited Jerusalem, around A.D. 33–38 (Gal. 1:18–20). Of course, those who gave it to Paul had it before he did. (c) As a minimum, Paul received the data from someone he, an apostle, deemed to be a trustworthy source.

2. Not to miss another significant factor, Paul personally witnessed an appearance of the risen Jesus. (a) The apostle provides his own testimony in more than one place (1 Cor. 9:1; 15:8; cf. Gal. 1:16). He did not have to rely on the word of others, because the risen Jesus had also appeared to him. (b) Three times in the book of Acts (9:1–9; 22:1–11; 26:9–19) we find non-Pauline accounts of this occurrence.

3. That Paul was accurate in his report of Jesus' appearances to others is provided on more than one front. (a) Paul actually sought out the apostolic leaders for the purpose of checking out the nature of the gospel (including the resurrection, 1 Cor. 15:1–4) that he preached (Gal. 2:1–10). The apostles Peter, John, and James the brother of Jesus specifically approved Paul's proclamation (vv. 6–10). (b) Some substantiation of this last claim is also provided in Acts 15:1–31, even though it is debated whether this is the same occasion that Paul describes in Galatians 2 or another similar conference. Either way, Paul's message of the gospel was confirmed by other apostles according to more than one source.

4. Further indications confirm the resurrection reports made by the other apostles too. (a) Paul testifies that the other apostles were preaching the same message that he was preaching in regard to Jesus' appearances (1 Cor. 15:11, 14–15). (b) The pre-Pauline creed reports the crucially important information that Jesus appeared to groups that included apostles, plus over five

hundred persons at one time. Paul's statement that most of these last witnesses were still alive (1 Cor. 15:6) implies that he may have known some of them. (c) As we have already seen, Paul knew personally some of the individuals in the list. In each of these ways, Paul is tied to the mainline apostolic reports of Jesus' appearances. (d) The Gospels also describe these appearances to the Twelve and to others (Matt. 28; Luke 24; John 20–21; cf. Mark 16:6–7). Any confirmation of these separate narratives would argue for this same point from another non-Pauline perspective.

5. Jesus' brother James was an ardent unbeliever during Jesus' public ministry. This family skeptic also witnessed the risen Jesus (1 Cor. 15:7). Critics need to explain this special appearance too.

6. An additional pointer concerning the apostolic witness to the postmortem appearances of Jesus comes from a number of creedal statements in the book of Acts.[58] Many scholars think that these speeches reflect some of the earliest Christian preaching in that they are brief proclamations that are theologically unadorned. The resurrection is at the center of each of these portions. This would certainly give us one of our best insights into the apostolic message after Pentecost.

7. That Jesus' tomb was empty does not by itself prove a resurrected body, but it would strengthen the case in that direction. For one thing, it makes naturalistic theories much more difficult to formulate, whether for Jesus' appearances or for the vacant tomb itself. Here are a few of the *many* evidences that the tomb was unoccupied that first Easter morning: (a) The earliest report in 1 Corinthians 15:3–4 strongly implies an empty tomb. As part of the triple *hoti* clause, and especially in a Jewish context, the progression from Jesus' death, to his burial, to his resurrection indicates that something happened to his body. (b) The early creedal proclamation in Acts 13:29–30, 36–37 also declares that the tomb in which Jesus was buried was later empty.

(c) Not only did the Jewish leaders not disprove the witness concerning the empty tomb, but their polemic even admitted it (Matt. 28:11–15). One well-known principle of historical research generally recognizes what one's enemies admit. That the Jewish leadership could not even eliminate this physical component of the early proclamation is itself an indictment. (d) That the Gospels tell us the women were the earliest witnesses to the open

---

[58]See Acts 1:21–22; 2:22–36; 3:13–16; 4:8–10; 5:29–32; 10:39–43; 13:28–31.

sepulcher (Matt. 28:1–10; Mark 16:1–8; Luke 24:1–10; John 20:1–2) is another reason to believe the authenticity of the report. Since the testimony of women was not allowed in a law court, why would they be cited as witnesses unless that is what happened? (e) The city of Jerusalem is the last place the disciples should have preached the gospel message if Jesus' grave was still occupied. Producing the body would have quieted the message.

8. The transformation of the witnesses, even to the point of being willing to die for their faith, is an additional indicator of the strength of their convictions that they had seen their risen Lord. It is true that people are often transformed for false causes that they also believe in, but there is a qualitative difference here. Both the disciples and the others who are willing to die share a sincere belief. But very much unlike the others, the disciples were willing to suffer not just for their belief concerning who Jesus was, but precisely because they had seen him after his death. In brief, their transformation was not simply based on beliefs about Jesus, like so many others, but on the knowledge that they had seen him alive after his crucifixion.

9. That the resurrection of Jesus was the central component of early Christian belief is also a helpful indicator of its truth. The resurrection being the pivotal doctrine led to increased amounts of attention, with investigations by the earliest witnesses increasing their faith rather than revealing any obstacles. Paul knew that there was no Christian faith apart from the resurrection (1 Cor. 15:14, 17), so he visited the apostles Peter and James in Jerusalem to discuss the nature of the gospel proclamation (Gal. 1:18–20). So important was this theme that he returned fourteen years later to repeat a similar procedure before more church leaders (Gal. 2:1–10). Luke explains that the resurrection was the chief proclamation in the early church, leading to the disciples' persecution (Acts 4:1–3, 33). Peter tells us that it secures heaven for believers, allowing them to rejoice during suffering (1 Peter 1:3–5).

A number of other evidences for the resurrection appearances might be mentioned as well. But given that we are speaking here about ancient documents, it must be admitted that there is certainly a surprising amount of data, all pointing to the fact that Jesus appeared to his followers on several occasions after he died by crucifixion.

Critics typically respect such findings too. Reginald Fuller rather boldly proclaims about the early Christian belief in the resurrection: "That within a few weeks after the crucifixion Jesus' disciples came to believe this is *one of the indisputable facts of history*." Fuller notes that the traditional cause for this belief is Jesus' appearances, then he concedes: "That the experiences did occur, even if they are explained in purely natural terms, is *a fact upon which both believer and unbeliever can agree*."[59] Along the same line, James D. G. Dunn says the fact that the first believers had experiences they thought were postmortem appearances of Jesus "is almost impossible to dispute."[60] After his detailed study of the sources, Jewish scholar Pinchas Lapide concluded that Jesus actually rose from the dead, appearing to his followers soon afterward![61]

Naturalistic Explanations. The resurrection of Jesus is such that the naturalistic strategy denies it, rather than attempting to interpret it within its own natural system. If an explanation is attempted at all, naturalists sometimes suggest alternative accounts that ignore any supernatural causation. These efforts have failed for several reasons.

1. Perhaps the chief theoretical reason for rejecting miracle-claims and seeking alternative explanations is the work of David Hume (and others who have followed him). But Hume's response has been heavily criticized by many scholars.[62] To mention just a few of the more prominent issues: (a) It is improper to reject the possibility of miracles in an *a priori* manner (a critical response that comes in many forms) without viewing the possible evidence for a miracle-claim. (b) No allowance is made for a potentially supernatural exception to nature's regularity that would actually supersede the normal lawful explanation at that moment, due to the exercise of a greater power. The most highly evidenced miracles may have certain recognizable characteristics, such as being one-time events, without meaningful

---

[59]Both quotations are from Fuller, *Foundations of New Testament Christology*, 142 (my emphasis).

[60]James D. G. Dunn, *The Evidence for Jesus* (Louisville: Westminster, 1985), 75.

[61]Pinchas Lapide, *The Resurrection of Jesus: A Jewish Perspective*, trans. Wilhelm C. Linss (Minneapolis: Augsburg, 1983), esp. 125–28.

[62]See esp. Richard Swinburne, *The Concept of Miracle* (London: Macmillan, 1970); idem, ed., *Miracles* (New York: Macmillan, 1989). Cf. Beckwith, *David Hume's Argument Against Miracles*, chaps. 3–4, 6–7; Habermas, *The Resurrection of Jesus: A Rational Inquiry*, 82–113; Habermas and Flew, *Did Jesus Rise from the Dead?* 16–19; Gary R. Habermas, "Skepticism: Hume," in *Biblical Errancy: An Analysis of Its Philosophical Roots*, ed. Norman L. Geisler (Grand Rapids: Zondervan, 1981), 23–49.

explanation by new expressions of the law in question. (c) An actual, heavily evidenced case for a miracle-claim would be difficult to explain, whether it came from (i) the past or (ii) the present. Each possibility would have its own advantages.

2. Each naturalistic theory concerning the resurrection falls prey to numerous rebuttals, even if one only uses data that are verifiable and admitted by virtually all critical scholars. In fact, these hypotheses are plagued by so many refutations that, in public debates, critics frequently even avoid choosing one of them because of the possibility that they will be forced into a corner.

Two intriguing trends in contemporary critical thought illustrate this. (a) In nineteenth-century theological liberalism, during the heyday of the naturalistic theories against the resurrection, the critics took turns decimating one another's hypotheses. For example, David Strauss dealt the most influential blow to the swoon theory (see above) of Friedrich Schleiermacher, Heinrich Paulus, and others. Strauss's hallucination theory, in turn, was disproved by Theodor Keim's attack. The legend theory was demolished by critical studies that isolated early New Testament texts like the creeds I addressed earlier. In this manner, the skeptics themselves revealed many of the weaknesses in these suppositions. (b) Twentieth-century critics have been even more radical, basically rejecting wholesale the naturalistic theories aimed at the resurrection. Comparatively seldom are these alternative hypotheses proposed today.[63]

3. In almost all cases, no single alternative view can answer all of the factual data for the resurrection. At least two theories are needed. But since each is opposed by many facts, the critic actually has the difficult role of having to overcome the need for more than one improbable theory.

Perhaps an example would be helpful. I have outlined above some of the persuasive data that have basically caused even a generation of critical scholars to be convinced that the original followers of Jesus at least believed they had visual experiences of the risen Jesus. We may recall that Reginald Fuller termed the early Christian belief in the resurrection an "indisputable fact," concluding that both believers and unbelievers could agree that visual experiences of some sort occurred.[64] Thus,

---

[63]For details see Habermas and Moreland, *Beyond Death*, 125–26.

[64]See the above quotations by Reginald Fuller and James D. G. Dunn for examples.

a successful natural response needs to account for this information. The most typical option is to charge that the disciples experienced hallucinations.

The rebuttals to such a charge, however, are prohibitive, as even a brief response reveals. (a) Hallucinations are private experiences, being "seen" by one person alone. But the appearances of Jesus were frequently to groups of people, as witnessed by sources such as the early creeds in 1 Corinthians 15:3–8 and the Acts passages, as well as the gospel accounts. (b) Another major problem regarding hallucinations is that while these incidents are fairly rare, Jesus appeared to a wide variety of persons: men and women, hard-headed Peter, soft-hearted John, devoted Mary Magdalene, and others. Jesus also appeared in a wide variety of circumstances: singly and in groups, in Jerusalem and in Galilee, outdoors and indoors. To conclude that all of these persons were in just the right frame of mind for this rather uncommon phenomena appears to be incredulous. Briefly, the details we have are almost the opposite of what is needed for hallucinations.

(c) Continuing, hallucinations are rooted in the preconditions of one's hopeful expectations, but the disciples despaired at the death of Jesus and did not expect him to rise. Their best friend of three years, to whom they had devoted their recent lives, had suddenly been taken from them. They had to have been distraught. This is simply good psychology, but it militates against these subjective occurrences. (d) It is also highly unlikely that hallucinations could produce the radical personal transformations of the disciples, causing them to be willing to die for their faith. Then what about (e) family skeptic James, Jesus' brother, and (f) church persecutor Paul? Could it be seriously charged, apart from any historical data whatsoever, that these two critics longed to see the risen Jesus? (g) Finally, hallucinations have nothing to say concerning an empty tomb, so the body should still be there! At several of these points, the critic needs another thesis.

Many other critiques can be leveled at the hallucination hypothesis and other similar subjective suggestions. As Pannenberg concludes, "These explanations have failed to date."[65]

Due to space confines, we are not able to look specifically at other alternative possibilities here, but it is my contention that

---

[65]Wolfhart Pannenberg, *Jesus: God and Man,* trans. Lewis L. Wilkins and Duane A. Priebe (Philadelphia: Westminster, 1968), 96.

they would suffer similar fates. We are justified in rejecting the naturalistic hypotheses that seek to explain the resurrection in nonsupernatural terms.[66] Even the majority of critical scholars agree that these attempts are seriously flawed. Raymond Brown concludes that, not only have critical scholars rejected these theories themselves, but new renditions of them are deemed to be unrespectable.[67]

The Minimal Facts. In my opinion, the strongest case for the resurrection appearances of Jesus involves the use of those data that are both well grounded and that receive the support of the critical community. As I said above, the former is most decisive.

Even most skeptical scholars admit a minimal core of facts pertaining to Jesus' death and the following events. Some of the above citations indicate a general direction. Virtually no one doubts Jesus' death by crucifixion. It is also recognized that the disciples despaired, due to losing their friend to whom they had dedicated their lives. As well recognized as any New Testament fact is that, shortly after Jesus' death, these followers had experiences that they believed were appearances of the risen Jesus. As a result, they were transformed from being in a state of fear to being willing to die for their faith. Very soon afterward, the disciples proclaimed Jesus' death and resurrection as their central message in Jerusalem and the surrounding area, and the church was born. Two skeptics, Jesus' brother James and Saul (Paul), became believers after they also believed that Jesus had appeared to them.[68]

The strength of this core is that these few facts are capable, in themselves, of both disproving the naturalistic hypotheses, as well as providing the best arguments for the resurrection. Yet they do so with a minimal amount of ascertainable data, so they cannot be rejected just because someone does not believe that the New Testament is a good source. It meets critics on their own

---

[66]For many more details, see Habermas, *The Resurrection of Jesus: A Rational Inquiry*, 119–71; Habermas and Moreland, *Beyond Death*, 113–26.

[67]Raymond Brown, "The Resurrection and Biblical Criticism," *Commonweal*, 24 November 1967, esp. 233.

[68]These minimal facts are discussed in each of the sources in n. 51 above. For a detailed defense of each one, including a listing of more than thirty critical scholars who hold them, see Habermas and Moreland, *Beyond Death*, 126–36. Even though the empty tomb is not as unanimously admitted by critical scholars, it is still both well evidenced and well respected, and also needs to be used in a defense of the resurrection.

(common) grounds, using their presuppositions and their methodology.

Confirmation of Jesus' Claims

I began by outlining a case for some of Jesus' major claims concerning himself. I did not decide whether they were true or false, but taken into consideration with the life he led, they are at least intriguing, just as they were in the first century.

I was also necessarily brief in my overview of Jesus' death and especially concerning the claim that afterward he appeared on several occasions to his followers. I discussed two issues: (1) Did Jesus die due to the rigors of crucifixion? (2) Was he seen afterward by his followers? I outlined a few reasons for the facticity of both as historical events. Like the previous topic, much more could be said that cannot be pursued here. I did not, however, pose the question concerning the cause of the resurrection, which involves the issue of miracles. I did not conclude that Jesus' resurrection was a miracle. So far, I have treated this as simply a possibility—a miracle-*claim*.

Now we come to this last question, including the issue of confirmation. How might one know whether Jesus' claims were indeed true? Was he the Son of Man, Son of God, and the one who held the key that unlocks the door to eternal life in God's kingdom? What convinced many of his listeners that he spoke the truth in these crucial areas?

The New Testament gives more than one answer. Undeniably, many hearers were moved simply because of the attraction of Jesus' words and the authority with which he spoke them.[69] Others were impressed by the miracles he appeared to perform (Matt. 9:33; Mark 1:27; 6:2–3). We are told that Jesus encouraged faith on both grounds (John 5:36; 10:38; 14:11). Still others believed because of the prophecy he both gave (John 4:16–19, 29, 39) and fulfilled (Luke 2:25–38). But it might be argued that Jesus' powerful acts had the greatest affect on early believers. Why might this be so? A few considerations show that miracles, in theory, and Jesus' mighty acts, in particular, were taken by his audience as indicators of something beyond themselves. I will mention three such suggestions without assuming that the resurrection fulfills them.

---

[69]See Matt. 22:46 (and parallels); Mark 1:22, 27; 6:2–3; 11:18; 12:17, 37.

1. Due to the very nature of their awe-inspiring character, miracles tend to point beyond themselves. Usually the attention is placed on the attendant message of religious significance, which is often considered to be confirmed in light of the miracle. As Richard Swinburne explains, this is an earmark of these events: "To be a miracle an event must contribute significantly towards a holy divine purpose for the world." On the other hand, if the event is extraordinary but without religious significance, it is "more appropriately characterised [sic] as magical or psychic phenomena rather than as miracles."[70] For instance, Swinburne argues that miracles can, in fact, provide evidence for God's existence and activity in the world.[71]

2. Jesus apparently had similar ideas in mind. He claimed that his miracles validated his message.[72] Perhaps surprisingly, that he believed this is conceded by numerous critical scholars[73] and serves as a contemporary witness to Jesus' thoughts about the truthfulness of his claims. More precisely, when answering the critics who accused him of blasphemy, Jesus proclaimed that his healing of a lame man served the purpose of letting his hearers "know that the Son of Man has authority on earth to forgive sins" (Mark 2:10). On another occasion, he reportedly told his accusers that his miracles showed that he was the Son of God (John 10:36–38). When asked for a sign, we are told that he even predicted that his resurrection would be his chief vindication (Matt. 12:38–40; 16:1–4).

3. Jesus' listeners seemed to acknowledge these concepts too. We read that many believed when they saw Jesus' miracles (John 3:2; 11:45). Then later, after Jesus' resurrection, Peter declared that this event was the chief sign of God's approval on Jesus' ministry (Acts 2:23–32). Paul says that the resurrection was God's vindication of the deity of Christ (Rom. 1:3–4). Paul also used the event as proof that God had corroborated Jesus' teachings, meaning that his listeners needed to repent and believe (Acts 17:30–31). It would seem that here we have the evi-

---

[70]Swinburne, *Concept of Miracle*, 7–10.

[71]See Swinburne's, *The Existence of God* (Oxford: Oxford University Press, 1979), chap. 12; cf. Swinburne's, "Historical Evidence" in idem, ed., *Miracles*, 151.

[72]See Matt. 11:1–6; 12:38–40; 16:1–4; Luke 11:20; John 5:36–37; 10:25; 11:41–42; 14:11; 15:24 for examples.

[73]For instance, see Bultmann, *Theology of the New Testament*, 1:7; Fuller, *Foundations of New Testament Christology*, 107; Pannenberg, *Jesus: God and Man*, 63–64; Brown, *Jesus: God and Man*, 97.

dential use of miracles in the New Testament as an argument from history to the God who raised Jesus.

According to Wolfhart Pannenberg, Jesus put himself in God's place in numerous ways. When he was raised from the dead, "this for a Jew can only mean that God himself has confirmed the pre-Easter activity of Jesus."[74] The resurrection served as God's mark of approval on Jesus.

All of this must be understood within the context of Judaism, in which a person could be exposed as a false prophet if his proclamations did not come to pass. But if a true prophet was ignored, the people would have to account for it before the Lord (Deut. 18:18–22). A speaker would naturally be understood by his target audience against such a backdrop.

I said above that the resurrection is the best explanation for the historical data. If Jesus was raised from the dead, which his listeners presumed to be an act that only God could perform, such a sign would be a confirmation of Jesus and his teachings. This would seem to be Jesus' point in offering his resurrection as his chief sign, as well as the best way to understand the apostolic proclamation that this event vindicated the Christian message.

Why should Jesus' resurrection be taken today as an indication that his messages concerning his Father's approval and concerning his own nature and mission are true? One way to examine this issue is to discuss worldview possibilities. If naturalism is the correct paradigm, there is no God, Son of God, or supernatural realm. So either the resurrection did not occur, or it must be thought of as nothing more than a random, chance event, a freak of nature. One option would involve formulating a viable alternative explanation(s), but I have already said that the known facts are so much opposed to this that critics often shy away from it themselves.[75] On the other hand, if Christian theism is true, the resurrection not only occurred, but was a planned occurrence. It was an orderly event designed by God for an eternal purpose.

---

[74]Pannenberg, *Jesus: God and Man*, 67–68.

[75]Skeptics appear to be in a serious bind at this point. To espouse one or more naturalistic theories that viably account for all the resurrection data is exceptionally difficult, and this may explain the reluctance to do so on the part of many critics. But it would appear to be at least as serious a problem to accept the historicity of the resurrection and deny that it was performed by God. As Stephen T. Davis declares: "Skeptics apparently cannot agree that it has occurred ... without abandoning religious skepticism" (see Stephen T. Davis, "Is it Possible to Know That Jesus Was Raised from the Dead?" *Faith and Philosophy* 1, no. 2 [April 1984]: 152).

Which view is correct? Given the two outlooks, which one provides the best explanation of the data? One hint might be provided by the apparent nature of the resurrection itself, which seems to give an edge to Christian theism. The resurrection was certainly contrary to the known laws of death and life. It seems, at least so far, to be nonrepeatable—the only event like this in history (see below). Neither can the laws of nature be modified to make room for it.[76] To make things even more difficult for the naturalistic account, the earliest texts say that Jesus exhibited a glorified body with heightened powers, at least in the case of Paul's appearance. In terms of a contrast between this event and the so-called laws of nature, the theistic universe seems to gain some momentum.

What happens when we move more specifically to Jesus' situation? It is reasonable to conclude, in light of Jesus' unique claims about himself and the historical likelihood of the resurrection, that he was in the best position to interpret the meaning of this event. His testimony is that, as the chief miracle, his theistic perspective was verified by an act of the God of the universe. It was not some unknown "John Doe" who had been raised. The only time in history that a resurrection can be ascertained,[77] it happened to the only person who ever made specific claims such as these: that he, personally, was deity, that he was God's chosen messenger and only agent of eternal life, and who taught that his miracles (including his resurrection) were accrediting signs of verification. Add to this other factors, such as the moral character of his life, and we get a more complete picture. Negatively, especially in a Jewish context, God would not have raised a heretic from the dead. Positively, God placed his stamp of approval on Jesus by raising him.

It would seem, then, that the Christian theistic framework both accounts better for the known data, as well as being more internally consistent. On the Christian thesis, Jesus was raised from the dead and was thereby shown to be correct concerning his theistic perspective. The God of the universe raised Jesus, approving both Jesus' personal claims to deity and the central thrust of his mission—to offer the opportunity for eternal life. This appears to be Jesus' view and also best represents the repeated emphasis of the earliest apostolic witness that we find

---

[76]On these issues, see Swinburne, *Concept of Miracle*, 26–32.

[77]For this conclusion, see Gary R. Habermas, "Resurrection Claims in Non-Christian Religions," *Religious Studies* 25 (1989): 167–77.

in the New Testament. As Marshall argues, the resurrection was the catalyst in the early recognition of Jesus' deity.[78]

On the naturalistic position, we have a fair number of unnatural hurdles that we must overcome, including formulating an alternative theory and/or making a major adjustment to the laws of nature, as well as explaining Jesus' claims, his view of miracles, his character, and any remaining evidence for the resurrection. That Jesus' major or basic teachings were thus verified seems warranted. Jesus' distinctive claims were ultimately validated by his resurrection from the dead. In short, history's unique messenger also experienced history's most unique event.[79]

Similar arguments have impressed many scholars.[80] For example, Swinburne asserts that numerous claims surrounding Jesus are unique among the world's major theistic religions and that extraordinary miraculous events are potentially a means of evidencing such teachings.[81] Pannenberg, after developing a detailed argument to back his thesis, contends that the unity between Jesus' declarations and his resurrection provides confirmation of his mission.[82] Prominent atheist Antony Flew even agrees that if the resurrection actually occurred, naturalists would have to be open to Jesus' teachings concerning Christian theism, including Jesus' own deity, even if it meant changing one's naturalistic worldview.[83]

CONCLUSION

I conclude that evidentialism is a viable apologetic methodology. Starting from any of a few potential religious epistemolo-

---

[78]Marshall, *Origins of New Testament Christology*, 128–29.

[79]Even if it is charged that others taught some similar things, believers could ask both for the corroboration of this claim, as well as the evidence to back it up. Jesus' teachings were still confirmed by his resurrection. These subjects are addressed at length in Habermas, *The Resurrection of Jesus: An Apologetic*, esp. chaps. 2–3.

[80]Interestingly, leading scholars like philosopher Richard Swinburne and theologian Wolfhart Pannenberg are examples of nonevangelical methodological evidentialists.

[81]Swinburne, *The Existence of God*, 222, 225–26, 233–34, 241–43.

[82]For Pannenberg's evidential system, see Pannenberg's "Dogmatic Theses on the Doctrine of Revelation," in *Revelation as History*, ed. Wolfhart Pannenberg, trans. David Granskou (London: Macmillan, 1968), 123–58. For his more specific application to Jesus, see Pannenberg's, *Jesus: God and Man*, 73, and Pannenberg's, "The Historicity of the Resurrection: The Identity of Christ," *The Intellectuals Speak Out about God*, ed. Roy Abraham Varghese (Chicago: Regnery Gateway, 1984), 263–64.

[83]Habermas and Flew, *Did Jesus Rise from the Dead?* 49–50; cf. 3.

gies, it presents both more- or less-distinctive forms of argumentation (especially its distinguishing mark of arguing to God from history, an angle on common ground with the unbeliever, and methodological eclecticism), as well as sharing some perspectives with the other major apologetic methods. I prefer arguing from a "minimal facts" scenario, but that is an open issue.

I have constructed a brief example of an outline from Jesus' resurrection to the truthfulness of several of his theistic distinctives. Necessarily, my framework has been sketchy (including not listing critical interaction and sources that have been included elsewhere), hitting some of the chief points from a multifaceted case that has been developed in more detail in other places.

To close, I will return to a point raised earlier concerning applying apologetics to ministry. I contend that evidential arguments can profitably be utilized in strengthening believers who have questions or even factual doubts and in laying a theological foundation on which to build (along with the application of additional, nonapologetic methods) for those who have certain emotional struggles concerning their beliefs. Such a strategy might also be useful in witnessing to unbelievers by the power of the Holy Spirit. One advantage of the evidential method is in presenting the gospel. Rather than necessarily having to make an additional, separate move by proving God's existence before moving to the claims of Jesus when time is often at a premium, evidentialism specializes in the one-step approach, arriving at a more direct presentation of the gospel by using data that are still very persuasive. After all, we should never lose sight of our goal of not only ministering in various ways to believers, but, by the mercy and grace of the Holy Spirit, allowing ourselves to be used to present the gospel to unbelievers. Outlining apologetic methodology should never be an end in itself.[84]

---

[84]I would like to thank Dave Beck, Doug Geivett, and J. P. Moreland for their thoughtful comments on portions of this material.

A CLASSICAL
APOLOGIST'S RESPONSE

William Lane Craig

The difficulty in responding to Gary Habermas is that he has so qualified evidentialism that it ceases to be an interesting alternative to other approaches to apologetics. Pity our poor editor! Ideally he would like to find a wild-eyed fideist on one end of the spectrum and a hard-nosed theological rationalist on the other. Instead, he winds up with a presuppositionalist who argues like an evidentialist and an evidentialist who endorses belief in Christian theism on the basis of the testimony of the Holy Spirit apart from evidence!

Habermas sees the distinctive in what he calls evidentialism as its emphasis on historical evidences justifying (Christian) theism. But he states that "most evidentialists ... encourage various forms of natural theology with regard to arguments for God's existence" (p. 98) and counts Richard Swinburne among the ranks of evidentialists. Well, I guess he had better include me, too. It seems to me that evidentialism so defined does not qualify as a distinct apologetic methodology or school of thought,[1] but is merely a personally preferred style of argumentation. And I certainly agree that an argument from miracles can be part of a cumulative case for theism. One wants to make things as uncomfortable for the naturalist as possible, so why

---

[1]For typical taxonomies of apologetic systems, see Bernard Ramm, *Varieties of Christian Apologetics* (Grand Rapids: Baker, 1962); Gordon R. Lewis, *Testing Christianity's Truth Claims: Approaches to Christian Apologetics* (Chicago: Moody Press, 1976).

not adduce historical evidence for events that seem to surpass the productive capacity of nature?

Indeed, a little reflection reveals that some of the arguments of natural theology are the argument from miracles writ large. For example, in arguing for the existence of a transcendent First Cause of the origin of the universe, the natural theologian may appeal to the evidence of the expansion of the universe and of thermodynamics to prove that the universe began to exist. Just as the Christian evidentialist pushes back to events for which no plausible, natural, causal antecedents exist (for example, the postmortem appearances of Jesus or the discovery of his empty tomb) and postulates God as the best explanation of those events, so also the natural theologian pushes back to an event (for example, the Big Bang singularity or a state of minimum entropy) for which no plausible, natural, causal antecedents exist and postulates God as the best explanation of those events. Resurrection on the one hand and creation on the other are equally miraculous acts of God. Thus, it is not surprising that the same sort of resistance to a miraculous explanation of the gospel evidence also arises in opposition to a miraculous explanation of the cosmological evidence. For example, P. C. W. Davies' opposition to inferring a supernatural cause of the Big Bang pretty obviously springs from a philosophical prejudice against miracles. He writes:

> The religious person ... finds nothing incongruous about miraculous events because they are simply another facet of God's action in the world. In contrast the scientist, who prefers to think of the world as operating according to natural laws, would regard a miracle as a "misbehaviour," a pathological event which mars the elegance and beauty of nature. Miracles are something that most scientists would rather do without.[2]

Davies therefore rejects the hypothesis of a supernatural creator of the universe. It is on the basis of this same sort of reasoning that Gerd Lüdemann will not even consider a supernatural explanation of the postmortem appearances of Jesus to the first disciples.[3]

---

[2]P. C. W. Davies, *God and the New Physics* (New York: Simon & Schuster, 1983), 197.

[3]Gerd Lüdemann, *The Resurrection of Jesus,* trans. John Bowden (Minneapolis: Fortress, 1994), 12.

Similarly, natural theologians who argue inductively must confront in science the same obstacle as Christian evidentialists do in history, namely, methodological naturalism. It is frequently asserted that the professional scientist or historian is methodologically committed to seeking only natural causes as explanations of their respective data, which procedure rules out inference to God as the best explanation. It is puzzling that some methodological naturalists in science, such as Howard Van Till with his doctrine of the "functional integrity" of creation, nevertheless want to dismiss methodological naturalism when it comes to history and to affirm the historicity of the gospel miracles. One cannot, it seems to me, have it both ways.

What is perhaps surprising is that Christian evidentialists are not more frequently slapped with the "God of the gaps" label, which is commonly affixed to the natural theologian. The problem is exactly parallel: what justifies us in inferring from the failure of naturalistic explanations of the data a miraculous explanation?

The problem with a miraculous explanation, as I see it, is not, as Hume thought, that it is improbable and therefore requires an extraordinary amount of evidence.[4] Christian apologists will agree wholeheartedly that hypotheses like "Jesus' body

---

[4]See the very helpful articles by S. L. Zabell, "The Probabilistic Analysis of Testimony," *Journal of Statistical Planning and Inference* 20, no. 3 (1988): 327–57; John Earman, "Bayes, Hume, and Miracles," *Faith and Philosophy* 10, no. 3 (1993): 293–310. Zabell shows that the probability of testimony to an improbable event cannot be assessed merely in terms of the event's improbability and the probability of the witness's telling the truth, for then we get into paradoxical situations; e.g., we should not believe a news report, known to be correct 99 percent of the time, that the winning number in last night's lottery drawing was 29701. Rather, we must also take into account the probability that the witness should be testifying as he is if the alleged event had not taken place. One is reminded of Paley's famous illustration in defense of the apostolic testimony to Jesus' resurrection about whether we should believe the report of a miracle on the part of twelve upright men who all go to their deaths rather than deny the truth of their testimony. Earman shows that the probability of the resurrection cannot be assessed by means of a simple-minded appeal to the frequency of resurrection-type events because such an approach would not only rule out the resurrection hypothesis but also many of the nonstatistical hypotheses of the advanced sciences, e.g., proton decay, which has never been observed but which scientists are investing millions of dollars and vast amounts of time to discover. Both Zabell and Earman think that any improbability in the resurrection hypothesis is such as can in principle be overridden by other considerations, e.g., the even greater improbability that the evidence should be such as it is if the resurrection did not take place; but what I challenge below is the assumption that we are in a position to say that the resurrection hypothesis is improbable.

spontaneously came back to life in the grave" or "The universe popped into being uncaused out of nothing" are enormously improbable, such that almost any naturalistic hypothesis will be more probable by comparison. But they should insist, I think, that there is nothing inherently improbable about the hypotheses "God raised Jesus from the dead" or "God created the universe." For as long as we are evenly agnostic about the existence of God, we must be equally agnostic about the probability of such hypotheses prior to any consideration of specific evidence.

That the issue is not the improbability of miraculous explanations is borne out by the interesting attempt of R. Gregory Cavin to analyze the evidentialist's case for the resurrection of Jesus in terms of Bayes' Theorem.[5] Let R = the resurrection hypothesis, B = the background evidence, E = the specific evidence, and A_i = various alternative hypotheses. Bayes' Theorem requires that

$$Pr(R/B\&E) = \frac{Pr(R/B) \times Pr(E/B\&R)}{Pr(R/B) \times Pr(E/B\&R) + \Sigma_{i=1}^{n} Pr(A_i/B) \times Pr(E/B\&A_i)}$$

$Pr(R/B\&E)$ represents the epistemic probability of the resurrection hypothesis given the total evidence, $Pr(R/B)$ represents the inherent plausibility of the resurrection hypothesis, and $Pr(E/B\&R)$ represents the explanatory power of the resurrection hypothesis. By the same token $\Sigma_{i=1}^{n} Pr(A_i/B)$ and $Pr(E/B\& A_i)$ represent the sum inherent plausibility and explanatory power of the all the alternative hypotheses to the resurrection taken together.

The implication of Bayes' Theorem is that the resurrection hypothesis will have a high epistemic probability, that is,

$$Pr(R/B\&E) > 0.5$$

just in case it has a greater balance of inherent plausibility and explanatory power than the sum of its alternatives, that is,

$$Pr(R/B) \times Pr(E/B\&R) > \Sigma_{i=1}^{n} Pr(A_i/B) \times Pr(E/B\&A_i)$$

---

[5]Robert Greg Cavin, "Miracles, Probability, and the Resurrection of Jesus," Ph.D. diss. (University of California, Irvine, 1993), 301. Cavin compares the probability of the resurrection hypothesis to the probability of all its alternatives collectively; but this is a mistake, since to be the best explanation the resurrection hypothesis need only be more probable than any other alternative hypothesis. See William J. Wainwright, "Skepticism, Romanticism, and Faith," in *God and the Philosophers*, ed. Thomas V. Morris (New York: Oxford University Press, 1994), 80.

One of the difficulties Cavin points out with the above is that even if the probability of each individual alternative to the resurrection hypothesis is low, still the sum of these probabilities might be high—and, moreover, how can we be sure that we have considered all the alternatives? But a little reflection reveals, paradoxically it might seem, that the successful Christian apologist need not show that the probability of the resurrection on the evidence and background information is greater than the probability of no resurrection on the same evidence and information. In other words, he need not show that the probability of the resurrection hypothesis is greater than 50 percent, or more probable than not. Rather, what he must show is that the probability of the resurrection is greater than any of its *separate* alternatives. The collective probability of all these alternatives taken together is meaningless, since they are mutually exclusive and the disjunction of all these alternatives $(A_1 \lor A_2 \lor A_3 \ldots)$ is not itself an alternative. In comparing the probability of the resurrection hypothesis to some individual hypothesis A_n, we should employ a different form of Bayes' Theorem, namely:

$$\frac{Pr(R/B\&E)}{Pr(A_n/B\&E)} \quad = \quad \frac{Pr(R/B)}{Pr(A_n/B)} \quad \times \quad \frac{Pr(E/B\&R)}{Pr(E/B\&\ A_n)}$$

If the top line comes out higher than the bottom line, then the resurrection hypothesis is more probable than that alternative and, hence, to be preferred. Thus, even if the resurrection hypothesis has a probability of, say, only 30 percent and yet none of its alternatives scores higher than, say, 10 percent, then it is far and away the best explanation.

In assessing these competing hypotheses, we find that the explanatory power of the resurrection hypothesis seems quite high, whereas the inherent plausibility and explanatory power of the respective alternatives are quite low. The difficulty arises with respect to assigning any value to the inherent plausibility of the resurrection hypothesis. Cavin thinks that that value is fantastically low and so subverts the evidentialists' argument. But that is because Cavin misconstrues the resurrection hypothesis. If the resurrection hypothesis is "God raised Jesus from the dead," then there is no reason to think that $Pr(R/B)$ is low, unless the inherent plausibility of theism is low.[6]

---

[6]Robin Collins has pointed out to me that, using the Jeffery Conditionalization Formula, the inherent plausibility of the resurrection can be calculated as follows (letting G = God's existence and ~G = God's nonexistence):

The arguments of natural theology can help to show that Pr(R/B) is not low by showing that a good and powerful Creator exists. They will not show its value is high, since even if God exists, we cannot anticipate what he will do. How do we know on the basis of background information alone what God would do or has done? The infrequency of resurrection-type events is no guide, since it may be precisely God's intent to reserve such a striking miracle solely for the vindication of his Son's radical claims and ministry. We are simply not in a position to say that it is improbable that God should raise Jesus from the dead. But if there is no reason to think that the epistemic probability of (R/B) is low, the evidentialist's argument for the resurrection can succeed. This helps us to see how the approach of the classical apologist can be helpful in the presentation of Christian evidences. By the same token, the natural theologian should do all that he can to build a cumulative case for the inherent plausibility of theism in order to undergird his own inductive arguments for the creation hypothesis.

Thus, the problem with an appeal to a supernatural explanation is not that miracles are improbable. Rather, the problem with miraculous hypotheses is that they seem to be *ad hoc*. They postulate what appears to be a *deus ex machina* in order to explain some event. The challenge for the Christian evidentialist will be to reduce this *ad hoc*-ness of his explanation. The difficulty of Habermas's "one-step" approach is that historical evidences alone must bear the responsibility of repulsing the objection that the Christian's explanation of the appearances and empty tomb is *ad hoc*. His task will be easier if we have a number of independent lines of evidence all pointing beyond the natural world to a supernatural being. Thus, Christian evidences will

$$\frac{Pr(R/B\&G) \times Pr(G/B) + Pr(R/B\&\sim G) \times Pr(\sim G/B)}{Pr(R/B)}$$

Now since the probability of the resurrection hypothesis relative to God's nonexistence is zero, the second line of the equation comes to zero, so that Pr(R/B) is a function solely of the first line. Natural theology will demonstrate that $Pr(G/B) \gg 0.5$. We still will not know what Pr(R/B\&G) is; but if a good and powerful Creator has been shown to exist, then we can surmise that it is not the case that $Pr(R/B\&G) \ll 0.5$. The higher Pr(G/B) is demonstrated to be, the higher the inherent plausibility of the resurrection hypothesis. For that reason the evidentialist would be imprudent to ignore the important contribution of natural theology to the success of his case.

be most effective when combined with arguments of natural theology. And, by the same token, natural theology will be most effective when several arguments for theism are adduced, not all of which are inductive.

Thus, arguments from miracles can certainly be part of a cumulative case for theism. But if the arguments of natural theology alone suffice to warrant belief in theism, then the natural role for Christian evidences to play is not to reinforce the case for theism, but to narrow the focus to warranting a Christian form of theism.

A CUMULATIVE CASE APOLOGIST'S RESPONSE

Paul D. Feinberg

Because Gary Habermas's approach to apologetics is evidentialist and one-step and uses Christ's claim to be deity on the basis of his death, burial, and resurrection, I am in substantial agreement with what he has to say. As a matter of fact, the cumulative case approach that I have advocated could be seen as an extension or modification of what is called the evidentialist approach. From what Habermas has said, it is not clear that he would object to the modification that I am suggesting, for he points out that historical evidences constitute only one kind of evidence for the Christian faith.

I will begin by commenting on methodological issues on which I find myself in agreement with Habermas. First, I think he is right in claiming that a one-step approach to apologetics is possible. This means that one does not have to establish first that God exists before moving to evidences of his activities that establish the Christian faith. Rather, it is possible through specific evidences to establish in a single step both that there is a God and that Christianity is the true religion. In this claim I do not mean that other approaches, even those advocated in this book, do not appeal to evidences in their case for Christianity. Habermas and I, however, see them as both confirmatory for the believer and as possible grounds for belief for unbelievers. Another way of putting this is that both positive and negative apologetics are important.

Second, I agree that commitment to an evidentialist apologetic approach does not predetermine one's epistemological stance. A variety of epistemologies will be represented in an evidentialist apologetic.

Third, I think that it is important to realize that there are no brute facts. Facts come to us through theories about the world, and those theories interpret our perceptions of the world. We have preunderstandings of a variety of sorts. This does not, however, mean that an objective understanding of history is impossible unless we define "objective history" in such a way that it is impossible to achieve. It is impossible for anyone to view the world from a neutral standpoint, but we can be self-reflective about our biases and seek to prevent them from obscuring the truth. There are also principles of historiography that seek to minimize the function of these biases.

Fourth, I agree that there is common ground between believers and unbelievers. We agree about many areas related to our understanding of the world. Epistemological similarities can be found in our understanding of sense perception, scientific theories that explain the function of our world, and rules of logic, to name a few. As Habermas says, this makes it possible to challenge unbelievers to face data that are contrary to their belief system.

Fifth, there are a variety of ways to defend God's existence and the Christian faith. This idea is at the very heart of the cumulative case approach to apologetics. Many elements in our common human experience require explanation and point to the truth of Christianity. For this reason, evidence and argument are person relative. That is, what one finds to be convincing may not move another. While I think that the case for Christianity is an informal rather than formal one, I agree that this does not preclude appeal to various types of natural theology or deductive or inductive arguments.

Sixth, I appreciate Habermas's development of an evidentialist argument for Christian theism. He is right in cautioning the apologist on the use of scriptural evidence. In the kind of case that he is developing, apologists often begin by trying to establish the trustworthiness of Scripture, then move to the deity of Christ verified by his resurrection, and finally try to defend the tenets of Christianity. He says, "Just because a work is generally trustworthy, it does not always follow that everything in it (and especially the supernatural) is true" (p. 99). There is no question that this is true. If, however, I understand the approach of someone like John Warwick Montgomery, he only argues that the general historical trustworthiness of a document establishes a *prima facie* case for what it says.[1] Too often critics of the Scripture dismiss a miracle story, not because there is something in the story itself that makes it unlikely, but because of a general rejection of the supernatural. What complicates matters for a Christian apologist is that the power to perform miracles is not simply limited to Christ and his agents; Satan and his agents are able to do *lying* signs and wonders. This means that one must have criteria to distinguish miracles that are from God and those that are from Satan.[2]

The "minimal facts" approach is quite helpful, though miracles will still be problematic. Contemporary thought is so thoroughly antisupernatural that it would be difficult for many to accept a miracle story as "well-evidenced." Further, it would be difficult to imagine critical scholarship accepting it as historical.[3]

Let me now turn to the extension or modification of Habermas's approach. As I said above, it is not clear that he would object to a cumulative case approach. The approach to apologetics I have advocated, however, would include all the historical evidence for Christianity that he offers but would see other elements in human experience that need explanation and point to the truth of Christian theism. These elements function as a one-step argument for Christianity. To Habermas's argument I have added characteristics of the universe in which we live; its contingency and orderliness; the experience of God's presence and a relationship with him, which many claim to have had; the existence of a moral law; a revelation that claims to come from God; and prophecies that are contained in this revelation that are fulfilled. If the argument Habermas gives is good, and I think it is, then each of these other elements can be developed into similar arguments. This seems only to strengthen the case for God's existence and Christian theism. It gives apologists a variety of places where they can start in defending the faith, depending on what arguments would be accepted by the one seeking confirmation.

---

[1]John Warwick Montgomery, *Where Is History Going? A Christian Response to Secular Philosophies of History* (Minneapolis: Bethany Fellowship, 1969). See particularly chaps. 1–3 and appendix A.

[2]See Norman L. Geisler, *Christian Apologetics* (Grand Rapids: Baker, 1976), 280–82, for a helpful discussion of criteria for determining which wonders are from God and which from Satan.

[3]For a good discussion of critical historiography see Van A. Harvey, *The Historian and the Believer* (New York: Macmillan, 1969).

A PRESUPPOSITIONALIST'S RESPONSE

John M. Frame

In my view, not a great deal of difference exists between the methods of William Craig, Gary Habermas, and Paul Feinberg. So my replies to Craig and Feinberg will, to a large extent, also apply to Habermas. For example, Habermas's presentation of the witness of the Holy Spirit, in my view, has the same weakness as Craig's. And I think that, like Craig, Habermas overestimates the agreement among Bible critics as to the "minimal facts of Christianity" and the general reliability of the resurrection accounts in Scripture. But Habermas does also raise some issues more pointedly than the others do, to which I will respond here.

ONE STEP, OR TWO, OR THREE?

Habermas defines evidential apologetics by saying that it prefers a "one-step" rather than a "two-step" approach. The latter requires first a proof of God's existence by the traditional methods of natural theology and then the establishment of the specific teachings of Christianity by the use of historical evidences. Habermas's "one-step" approach focuses on the historical evidences, believing that these alone give sufficient evidence both for theism in general and for Christianity in particular.

I can't get very excited, however, about this distinction. If this issue differentiates the "classical" from the "evidential" position, it doesn't differentiate between them very much. I did not notice in Craig's defense of classical apologetics any emphasis on the number of steps,[1] and Habermas admits that the classical theistic proofs can sometimes be of service. All in all, the essays of Habermas and Craig seem to me to differ in emphasis rather than in method.

As a presuppositionalist, I can find something good in both approaches. Apologetics may be done in one step, because every fact of creation reveals God. The facts are the product of his eternal plan, creation, and providence. Everything reveals him (Rom. 1:20; Ps. 19:1). Therefore, the apologist can begin anywhere. Both the causal order of the universe and the resurrection of Jesus prove God's existence; for no fact makes sense apart from God. Of course, this defense of one-step apologetics is rather different from that of Habermas.

On the other hand, I have some sympathy also for the two-step approach. For the two-step apologists stress that the historical evidences won't work except in the context of a theistic worldview. Unless we know that the biblical God exists, they tell us, we cannot know that Jesus is his Son, or that the resurrection (granted that it happened) bears witness to him and is therefore not a mere chance happening.

The two-steppers respond to this problem before getting to the historical evidences by providing traditional theistic proofs to establish the theistic worldview. I agree with their observation that historical evidences presuppose God's existence. But I believe the theistic worldview must come at an even earlier stage of our reasoning. For theistic proofs will not, any more than historical evidences, accomplish their purpose without the presupposition of a biblical worldview. As I mentioned in my reply to Craig, without the biblical God there is no reason to suppose that there is a rational, causal order leading to a first cause. So even a proof of God must presuppose him.[2] Counters of steps, therefore, are invited to see my position either as three steps or

---

[1]The number of steps is emphasized, however, in *Classical Apologetics* by R. C. Sproul, John Gerstner, and Arthur Lindsley (Grand Rapids: Zondervan, 1984). See my review in *Westminster Theological Journal* 47, no. 2 (Fall 1995): 279–99, reprinted in my *Apologetics to the Glory of God* (Phillipsburg, N.J.: Presbyterian and Reformed, 1994) and in my *Cornelius Van Til* (Phillipsburg, N.J.: Presbyterian and Reformed, 1995).

[2]See my main essay on the kind of circularity involved here and my response to it. The circularity need not be explicit in the argument. I might myself find occasion to use an argument like Craig's *kalam* cosmological argument. But if my inquirer insisted on discussing epistemology, eventually I would have to get around to saying that mine is governed by Scripture.

as one:[3] either as presupposition ➔ theistic proof ➔ historical argument, or as a single transcendental argument from any fact in the universe, based on revealed presuppositions.

HISTORICAL METHOD

I agree with Habermas that "historical occurrences are not brute facts that interpret themselves" (p. 94). He rightly emphasizes the need to read the facts in their contexts and to give attention to whatever personal biases may enter into our interpretations. He recognizes that such biases "can never be completely eliminated," but he says it is "still possible to reach sturdy conclusions within the canons of historical research" (p. 95).

Habermas, however, has little more to say about those "canons of historical research," except to say that "we just must be careful not to read biases into the accounts" (p. 95). But we should not, I think, be biased against bias in some general way. Some biases are good. Doubtless Habermas would agree that we should be biased in favor of evidence and logic, intellectual honesty, reliable testimony, and so on. Surely those are among the "canons of historical research." So our goal as historians should not be to eliminate bias altogether (which Habermas admits we can never do completely), nor simply to "recognize and thwart" it, or "counteract" it, as he says later, but to substitute good biases for bad ones.

There is, therefore, such a thing as an ethic of historical knowledge. For the Christian, that means that Scripture has important things to say about the way we study history. It tells us what biases are good. Besides commending honesty and truth, Scripture requires us to assume that miracles are not impossible, that divine inspiration can give us absolutely normative interpretations of events, that Scripture is not subject to the types of criticism appropriate to other historical witnesses, that God directs history toward a goal, and so on. Christians must certainly accept these among the "canons of historical research." Like Craig, Habermas does not draw sufficiently on the biblical data relevant to the questions he investigates.

Our reply to the postmodern relativist, therefore, is not ultimately that "positive historical conclusions" are "recognized by professional historians of almost all persuasions" (p. 96). It is

---

[3]Not, I think, a *vestigium trinitatis*.

possible for this scholarly spectrum to be wrong, and in any case our faith is not grounded in scholarly consensus. The more relevant point is that postmodernism has rejected fundamental norms for historical study. It is right, as Habermas suggests, to point out inconsistencies in postmodernist attitudes toward history. But the discussion of postmodernism has made clear that even the commitment to consistency is not religiously or even culturally neutral. Is logic in the tradition of Aristotle and Russell, after all, a necessity for human thought, or is it merely a form of Western, linear thinking, by which wealthy cultures oppress those who think in paradox?

COMMON GROUND

In Habermas's summary of the distinctives of evidential apologetics, he strongly emphasizes that there is "enough ontological and epistemological common ground to speak meaningfully to an unbeliever" (p. 99). I agree with him entirely about ontological common ground. Believer and unbeliever both live in God's world. In that sense, they have everything in common.

Epistemological common ground, however, requires a more careful analysis. I find it odd that although Habermas cites Romans 1:18–32 and 1 Corinthians 2:14 to show that "the reality of sin . . . plays a monumental role in how God's truth is viewed by the unbeliever" (p. 96), he never brings this fact into his discussion of epistemological common ground. Rather, in a somewhat commonsense way, he merely points out that believers and unbelievers can agree on "sensory data," "scientific theories," "general rules and application of inference" (p. 97).

Habermas is right to point out that there can be agreements on these matters and that those agreements can be apologetically useful. Sometimes unbelievers can even agree on large amounts of biblical theology, granted Jesus' critique of the Pharisees (see esp. Matt. 23:1–3). But alongside these agreements, there is a "monumental" bias toward disagreement. Romans 1 tells us that the unbeliever wants to "suppress" the truth, to "exchange it for a lie." Even when the unbeliever agrees with the Christian, he does so in the interest of fighting the truth, as when the evil spirits cried out that Jesus was "the Holy One of God" (Mark 1:24). For that reason, agreements between believers and unbelievers in apologetic discussions tend to be short-lived and to focus on matters of less than central importance to the gospel.

Further, agreements between believers and unbelievers indicate inconsistency in one or the other party. For example, when a Christian and an atheist agree on a scientific theory (assuming that theory is true), the atheist is inconsistently relying on a worldview in which the universe is a rational order, matching the rational order of the human mind. At that point, the atheist is thinking as a theist. He is assuming a structure of rationality in the world that he has no right to assume. Under intellectual and spiritual pressure, he may very well abandon that assumption and become, following Satan, more consistently irrationalist.[4]

I am not saying it is unhelpful to follow out the implications of scientific theories and other matters that believer and unbeliever *tentatively* agree upon. I am saying that the believer should be prepared for some startling shifts in the unbeliever's position, shifts not necessarily in the direction of Christian theism, and should be able to interpret such shifts in biblical terms. We should not proceed casually on the assumption that "everybody will agree" on this or that. This is one reason why I have warned against assuming too much agreement between Christians and critical biblical scholars. As the Jesus Seminar and other movements in biblical criticism have shown, there is virtually nothing in Scripture that hasn't been questioned by somebody.

THE CASE FOR CHRISTIANITY

In general, I think Habermas has done a masterful job of summarizing our Lord's claims and the evidences of his death and resurrection. I find it entirely persuasive. However, I am not the one who needs to be persuaded.

Habermas does respond to people like David Hume, who reject all supernatural explanations in principle.[5] But he does not respond to Hume's most persuasive argument (in my opinion), which is that extraordinary reports require extraordinary levels of evidence if they are to be credible. In our experience, when somebody claims to have observed a miracle (e.g., a green elephant flying two hundred feet above a seminary chapel build-

---

[4]I know that "consistent irrationalism" is an oxymoron. That's the whole point. The situation is logically hopeless.

[5]His replies to Hume designated (b) and (c) seem rather unclear to me (pp. 112–13).

ing), we usually believe that the witness is deceived or deceiving, rather than that his report is true. Even Christians, I suspect, when we turn away from the specific question of the truth of Scripture, find it hard to imagine how we might find ourselves believing the report of a miracle that we did not experience ourselves. And such verification is all the more difficult when all the reports come from ancient documents.

The attitude of many people today is that, whatever Habermas and other apologists may say, there must be some explanation of the data other than the traditional Christian explanation. We may be able to refute some naturalistic explanations of the biblical reports, but we have not refuted all possible explanations. And, for many people, the biblical claims seem too incredible and we are too far from the events in question to be sure one way or another. To such people, the issue is not whether naturalism or Christianity best explains the facts; it is rather whether the data warrant either of these explanations, indeed, whether they warrant any explanation at all.

I don't know how traditional evidential apologetics can deal with this kind of skepticism.[6] In my view, the only way to answer it is to present Christian theism as the presupposition without which no other reasoning (either about miracles or non-miracles) makes sense.

Certainly, however, there are many non-Christians who are unwilling to be so skeptical. For them, Habermas's argument may be entirely sufficient. Indeed, it is a strong argument, because, despite his emphasis on common ground, Habermas in the end presupposes a Christian view of evidence and probability rather than the view of philosophical skepticism.

---

[6]We are, of course, used to refuting skepticisms of a global kind, like Greek sophism and postmodernism, by saying that they refute themselves: they claim as a truth that there are no truths. But the skepticism to which I refer here is more modest and therefore more difficult to respond to.

A REFORMED EPISTEMOLOGIST'S RESPONSE

Kelly James Clark

Gary Habermas has offered an outline of a defense of the Christian faith along the lines of what he calls "evidential apologetics." He contends that the historical evidences supporting the deity of Christ are sufficient both to prove God's existence and the truth of Christianity. Thus, he omits the first step of William Craig's classical approach. This is, I believe, a fatal misstep: the historical evidence alone proves, I shall argue, little or nothing. But let me first tell a story.

AN ANCIENT ET STORY

Suppose someone comes knocking on your door and tells you an exciting but far-fetched story. This person tells you that over three thousand years ago an extraterrestrial, looking exactly like Albert Einstein, visited the earth in an obscure town in Africa. The alien, called (remarkably) Al E., brought with him good news of great joy—he promised that those who trusted in and followed him could tell the future and that they would receive a utopian, nonearthly life. Al E., we learn, spoke of the flush toilet and McDonald's restaurants, but most people, mystified by his predictions, simply dismissed him. Nonetheless, a few people believed and, likewise, saw into a future of flying machines and disposable diapers. A small remnant of believers in Al E. have persisted throughout history, encouraging successive generations to believe and follow.

Why should I believe in Al E., you ask? You are told that five of his followers wrote biographies of Al E. that record some of his prophecies, many of which were fulfilled shortly after his return to his planet, Hevenia. It is written that just as the local gambling commissioners were about to stone him to death, five hundred people watched him board a flying saucer and fly off. "Five of his *followers* wrote this?" you ask incredulously. Are there any independent sources that record his prophecies *before* the events occurred? "Well, no, not really," your visitor admits. "But he did some amazing things, which his followers also wrote about. He changed wine into imported beer and calculated everyone's taxes." Impressed, you still wonder if anyone—not his followers—provided any independent evidence of these wonders.

The person at your door excitedly tells you that if you believe in Al E., you, too, can tell the future (noting that, right now, the lottery is at an all-time high). What's more, since humans are fouling this planet at an alarming rate, he has foreseen that Al E. will soon return to take his faithful to Hevenia, where everyone will live forever in bliss.

You are intrigued but find it difficult to believe in Al E. How do we really know he existed, came to earth from another planet, worked wonders and delivered prophecies, returned to his planet, and will return to earth once again to reclaim his faithful and transport them to Hevenia? But there's that lottery idea enticing you...

You recognize that there are some possible significant benefits that could result from believing. But you also recognize that people don't have direct control of their beliefs; people can't turn belief on and off like water from a tap.[1] How can you get yourself into a position where you find yourself believing in Al E.?

There is some evidence—sacred Scriptures in which Al E. proclaims himself a prophet and is alleged to live an exemplary life, the apparently fulfilled prophecies, his exemplary earthly life, a few extrascriptural attestations that he suddenly appeared in a tiny village in Africa and then suddenly disappeared, and the five hundred people who claimed to witness Al E.'s dramatic

---

[1]Thought experiment #1 for the reader: Try believing that you are at the Super Bowl cheering wildly as the Detroit Lions, led by superb running back Barry Sanders, are on the verge of their first World Championship. Okay, now believe that you are back wherever you started, reading this book. Thought experiment #2: If you believe in God, stop believing in God for a few seconds. Now believe in him again. Now stop, now start. We don't just decide what to believe. Belief is, typically, something that happens to us. End of thought experiment.

exit. You examine the evidence but still find it difficult to believe that the earth was visited by a benevolent and foresighted extraterrestrial who looked like Albert Einstein and promised bliss. But suppose you still want to believe.

Against the evidence are your prior convictions. First and foremost, you are seriously skeptical about the very possibility of extraterrestrial life. You have read that the probability of life arising anywhere in the universe is $1/10^{187}$ (or some such similarly small chance), so the probability of it happening twice is (by the multiplication axiom)[2] $1/10^{187} \times 1/10^{187}$ or $1/10^{374}$. Recalling that there are only about 10^{36} electrons in the entire universe, you are rightly amazed at your own existence, but now you are more skeptical than ever that we had ever been visited by extraterrestrials! You add the additional improbability of the extraterrestrial looking just like Albert Einstein and you find that, the sincerity of this Al E.vangelist notwithstanding, you simply cannot believe in Al E. (and you spend the rest of your life in regret—could you have won the lottery *and* attained eternal bliss?).

Here's the problem with the evidence: Even if the best (available) explanation of Al E.'s remarkable but short earthly existence is that we were once visited by extraterrestrials, it doesn't follow that we are required by reason to accept it. Accepting a hypothesis on the basis of the evidence requires not only that the hypothesis in question explain the data (better than any competitors), it must also be *plausible;* it must have some significant likelihood independent of the evidence. Sometimes, even when we don't have a better explanation of the evidence, it is more rational to reject the best explanation on grounds of implausibility. Indeed, most of us regularly dismiss claims that we find wildly implausible, not due to careful consideration of the evidence, but simply because we judge them antecedently improbable. We do this with reports of UFO sightings, many reports of miracles and magic, and with tales of ghosts and dragons.

What we would need to believe first, in order to believe in Al E., is some conviction that extraterrestrials could exist. Sec-

---

[2]The multiplication axiom states that the probability of A *and* B given some body of evidence is the product of the probability of A given that same body of evidence multiplied by the probability of B given that same body of evidence or, in formal terms: $P(A\&B/E) = P(A/E) \times P(B/E)$. Probabilities are in the integer between 0 and 1, so, when multiplied, $P(A\&B/E)$ will be smaller than either $P(A/E) \times P(B/E)$. If one wishes to increase the probability of a conjunction, more evidence is required than for probability of each conjunct.

ond, we would also need some reasonable expectation that they might appear to us looking like Albert Einstein. Lacking such beliefs, it would surely be reasonable for us to reject the Al E. story (in all of its glory) even if we can't account for his sudden appearance and disappearance. Inference to wildly implausible best explanations requires *a lot* of evidence.[3] Indeed, the evidence must preponderate sufficiently to swamp our initial skepticism of the implausible hypothesis in question. And the more information included in the hypothesis in question (you must believe this and that and this other thing and, while we're at it, let's add a few more things), the more evidence is required to make it rationally acceptable.[4]

Let me illustrate the point that reason does not require us to come up with an alternative explanation when an implausible hypothesis fully explains the evidence in question. Suppose you are eating a late dinner at someone's house and you hear a loud, inexplicable sound coming from one of the bedrooms. Your host tells you not to worry—the noise is just from a ghost. Not thinking that the existence of ghosts has much *a priori* probability, you scoff.

"No, really," your host insists, "it is a ghost. We sealed off the room with caulk, so we know it's not the wind. We had a plumber fix the pipes, so we know it's not the plumbing. We had an exterminator chase out all the animals, so we know it's not rodents."

By the time your host is done, he has eliminated all of the hypotheses you had considered as more likely explanations. Are you, therefore, required by reason to accept the ghost hypothesis? I think not. Even if the evidence is unique and startling— the noise always occurs at 9:11 P.M. on Tuesdays, just the time a little girl was tragically murdered in that very room in 1893— and even if you can't think of a plausible, alternative nonphantomy explanation. I'm not sure what kind of or how much evidence is required to overcome your antecedent dismissal of ghosts, but I'm sure that it would take a lot.[5]

---

[3] Experiential evidence may prove sufficiently powerful to swamp the judgment of antecedent implausibility. Suppose you observe the landing of a UFO out of which Al E. emerges and you watch him come to your door. If that were to happen, you might be in a position to update your prior convictions.

[4] This is, again, an application of the multiplication axiom of probability calculus.

[5] I think the evidential situation would be made even worse if you were forced to rely on testimonial evidence—that someone (not you) heard this sound and then was presented with all of the data.

EVIDENCE FOR THE TRUTH OF CHRISTIANITY

It should not be difficult to see the relevance of my ET story to Habermas's case for Christianity. Before you dismiss my story's relevance because it is ludicrous, take some time and ponder the ludicrousness ("scandal" is the biblical term) of Christianity. For Christianity asserts that two thousand years ago in an obscure Palestinian village we were visited not by aliens but by *God*. God, veiled in human flesh, came to save us from our sins, redeem the world, and offer eternal bliss to all who would believe in him. It would be silly to deny what seems so obvious—this is a hard teaching. It is, as Paul writes, folly to the Greeks and a stumbling block to the Jews (1 Cor. 1:23). It is folly to the Greeks, the rational people, because it is offensive to reason. And it is a stumbling block to the Jews, God's chosen people, because it is religiously offensive as well. Christian faith demands belief in phenomena vastly more difficult to believe in than ghosts, UFOs, and magic.

What about belief in the resurrection? Isn't our uniform experience, after all, that dead people stay dead? What could make that easier to accept than ghosts and vampires? Here is where Habermas's one-step apologetic approach breaks down completely. What could make the evidence rationally support belief in a resurrection is the very thing that Habermas is trying to prove. What one needs is some initial belief that there is a God (perhaps who cares for us and makes moral demands), and that he is not unlikely to redeem us. Barring that, the initial implausibility that there is a God at all, let alone one who would appear just at that time and in just that form, sets up a believing situation that would require an enormous amount of evidence to overcome. Additionally, the evidence would have to be of higher quality than that offered by Habermas. The advantage of Craig's apologetic approach is that the first step of his two-step approach would provide such a context by establishing the existence of a divine being who might do whatever is possible to save creatures that he cares about. Habermas offers (indeed eschews) any initial reason to believe that there is a God who might redeem us in extraordinary ways. In so doing, he creates an evidential burden that he has not and, I think, cannot overcome. His evidence might be sufficient to prove something to someone who is already a theist of the, roughly, Judeo-Christian-Muslim variety; but on its own, it proves nothing.

Even if a naturalist (or Buddhist or Taoist or Native American, etc.) has no alternative explanation of the empty tomb and the alleged postmortem appearances of Jesus, that person is not required by reason to accept the supernaturalist explanation. The absence of a plausible explanation does not require that person to accept an implausible (to him or her) explanation that just so happens to be successful (any more than the ghost skeptic is required to believe in ghosts in the circumstances described above). Explanatory power is not the only factor involved in the assessment of hypotheses; hypotheses must also be judged to have some initial likelihood of being true. And judgments of initial likelihood are conditioned by our deepest commitments.

Since I omitted discussion of Craig's second step in his two-step apologetic approach, I will comment on it here. It is not clear to me that reason can establish enough about God to permit the evidence of the resurrection to overcome the vast implausibility (the scandal) of the incarnation and the resurrection. The evidence is, after all, unusual. The best records available to the life and teachings of Jesus were passed on by his followers, who had some vested interest in keeping his teachings alive. The extrabiblical references are scanty and provide little support for any of the more difficult claims. The earliest versions of the Gospels are less redolent of references to Jesus as God in the flesh than later versions. I won't continue with the skeptical diatribe here, as there are enough non- or anti-Christian biblical critics who have done so. But some of their points are not without warrant. What follows, I think, is that both Craig's and Habermas's evidential approaches cannot show the truth of Christian belief.

SKEPTICISM AND/OR FIDEISM?

Christians who are evidentialists (for knowing or showing) often vastly underestimate the evidential demand necessary to overcome the immense initial improbability that God would be in Christ reconciling the world to himself. Incarnations and resurrections, not being as plentiful as raspberries, require a great deal of evidence to support their rational belief (on the evidentialist assumptions about reason). The evidential deficiency is not ameliorated by the Christian's credulity—we are often susceptible to accepting weak evidence where strong evidence is demanded.

If the evidence for the truth of Christianity is slim, how can it be reasonable for anyone, in this day and age, to be a Christian? Here I go along with the spirit (no pun intended) of Craig's essay. The relevant warranting circumstances of Christian belief involve the work of the Holy Spirit. The Holy Spirit can assist in the readjusting of our initial commitments, our prejudices against the supernatural and the miraculous, and our fear of the loss of autonomy. Those changes could result in a reevaluation of evidence. Or the Holy Spirit could bypass all evidential considerations and move us, through a variety of means, to trust in God. But we are, after all, intellective people, and we want to be sure of the truth. How can reason play a role in the subsequent rational development of our belief?

Here I am indebted to my colleague, C. Stephen Evans.[6] Evans has persuasively argued that the role of the evidentialist story told by the likes of Craig and Habermas is sufficient neither to establish the rationality of nor to show the truth of Christian belief. Rather, the evidence available can defeat the defeaters offered by naturalistic biblical scholarship. The evidence can be taken this way or that, depending on one's assumptions. What Evans demonstrates is that the evidence does not force everyone that way—the skeptical way of the critical biblical scholar. The critical biblical scholar poses a challenge or a threat to Christian belief, which the Christian can meet through a careful sifting of the evidence. If Evans is right, and I think he is, then Christians can remain rational in their beliefs regardless of the critical challenge. Contrary to the views of Craig and Habermas, however, Evans does not believe that he has or can make a case that all rational creatures are obliged to accept. He doesn't believe he has refuted the naturalistic biblical scholar. Nonetheless, he has made a case that preserves the rational integrity of Christian belief—no mean feat in this increasingly unbelieving generation. So reason does play a role—a defeater defeating role.

CONCLUSION

There is, of course, much left to be said here. I have not written this to glory in Christianity's evidential shortcomings or to revel in fideism. I would have preferred that Habermas's case

---

[6]C. Stephen Evans, *The Historical Christ and the Jesus of Faith* (Oxford: Clarendon, 1996).

had been universally persuasive. I have simply, to the best of my ability, tried to come to a measured and reasonable assessment of the evidence for all of the parties involved. Different people will view the evidence differently depending on what assumptions they bring to it. Nonetheless, I have defended a role for evidence—it can defeat the pretensions of the naturalistic biblical scholar. The evidence can help us grow intellectually in our faith. This makes this approach to faith and reason an excellent contemporary expression of the Augustinian model of faith seeking (and finding) understanding. This may be the best that can be done, but, if so, this is to do a lot.

Chapter Three

CUMULATIVE CASE APOLOGETICS

Paul D. Feinberg

CUMULATIVE CASE APOLOGETICS

Paul D. Feinberg

THE NATURE OF THE CASE FOR THEISM
AND CHRISTIANITY

A good place to begin the discussion of apologetic methodology is to ask about the nature of the case for theism and Christianity. Various answers have been given to this question. Some have argued that we can prove the truth of Christianity or at least theism by offering *demonstrably sound arguments*. Such arguments are logically valid and have premises that can be shown to be true. A demonstrably sound argument is coercive in the sense that anyone who wants to retain rationality must accept the argument.[1]

There are two arguments that have at some time in their history been advanced as demonstrative proofs of God's existence: the ontological and the cosmological. The strategy of the *ontological argument* is to argue that there is something in the concept of God that guarantees his existence—that is, that God's existence is necessary. Unfortunately, it is agreed by most philosophers since Kant that no version of the argument succeeds in making its case as a demonstrably sound argument. The problem is that the argument has a premise that the nontheist will not accept as true. Even an ardent defender of the ontological argument like Alvin Plantinga admits that in the end there is

---

[1]See John Hick's fine discussion of "proof" and "probability" in *Arguments for God's Existence* (New York: Seabury, 1971), vii–xiii.

a premise in the argument that one will accept if one accepts the conclusion, or will reject if one rejects the conclusion, that God exists. Therefore, what this argument shows is that there is nothing contrary to reason or irrational about accepting this argument. What he claims for the argument is not that it proves the truth of theism, but its rational acceptability.[2]

The *cosmological argument* fares no better in this regard. The strategy of this argument in its various forms is to argue from the existence of contingent states of affairs to the existence of God as the only explanation for these states of affairs. A familiar form of this argument is the causal form. We have all heard of it in its simplest formulation. If something exists, it must have an adequate cause or explanation. The causal chain must either be infinite or there must be an uncaused cause, God. An infinite regress of causes is impossible. Therefore, God must exist as the uncaused cause of what exists.

Many theists, myself included, think that this and other forms of the cosmological argument are sound. Again, the difficulty is with those who are not theists. They refuse to accept one of the essential premises to this argument. They might deny that God is the only adequate explanation for the existence of anything. Or they might argue that an infinite regress of contingent causes is not impossible. I think the theist is right, but we are trying to convince the atheist, and that is the problem. Thus, if what I have said is the case, then the cosmological argument does not constitute a proof in the sense of being a demonstrably sound argument.[3]

---

[2]Alvin Plantinga, *God, Freedom and Evil* (Grand Rapids: Eerdmans, 1974), 111. For further information on the ontological argument, see Charles Hartshorne, *The Logic of Perfection and Other Essays in Neoclassical Metaphysics* (La Salle, Ill.: Open Court, 1962), 28–117; John Hick and Arthur C. McGill, eds., *The Many-Faced Argument: Recent Studies on the Ontological Argument for the Existence of God* (New York: Macmillan, 1967); Norman Malcolm, "Anselm's Ontological Arguments," in *Readings in Philosophy of Religion: An Analytic Approach,* ed. Baruch A. Brody, 2d ed. (Englewood Cliffs, N.J.: Prentice-Hall, 1992), 100–116; and Alvin Plantinga, ed., *The Ontological Argument: From St. Anselm to Contemporary Philosophers* (New York: Anchor Books, 1965).

[3]For an overview of the statement, defense, and objections to this argument, see Brody, 121–57; Donald R. Burrill, *The Cosmological Arguments: A Spectrum of Opinion* (New York: Anchor Books, 1967); William Craig, *The Cosmological Argument from Plato to Leibnitz* (New York: Barnes & Noble, 1979); idem, *The Existence of God and the Beginning of the Universe* (San Bernardino, Calif.: Here's Life, 1979); and idem, *The Kalam Cosmological Argument* (New York: Barnes & Noble, 1979).

A second way to understand the case for theism and Christianity is to argue that we can make a *probable case*. We will relax the standard and give up the search for absolute certainty. While we cannot prove that God exists and that Christianity is true, we can at least show that it is probable, maybe even very probable. There are a variety of ways to attempt this. One of the most common is through the *teleological* or *design argument*. The argument claims that the universe exhibits design or order. According to the theist, this order or design is best explained as the work of an intelligent designer.

While this argument holds a grip on theists, it is less persuasive for nontheists. What persuades many atheists to reject this argument is that there is an entirely acceptable (and perhaps equally probable) alternative explanation for any order that we find in this universe, namely, evolutionary forces. If one accepts the evolutionary theory, then any universe that survived would have to exhibit order or it would have perished. The dynamic interactions between organisms and their environment along with the need to adapt for survival are adequate explanations for any order shown by this universe.[4]

Let me summarize the case up to this point. First, traditional arguments that have been thought to prove God's existence and provide a basis for arguing to the truth of Christianity fail if we understand "prove" in some strict sense that might require the atheist to believe that there is a God. That is, there are some premises in the argument that the nontheist will refuse to accept, causing the argument to fail. Second, if we understand probability in any meaningful sense, we run into problems as well. Not only is the standard relaxed, but alternative explanations can be offered to that of the theist. If what we have argued is true, it seems that theists can take one of two approaches. They can appeal to some form of *fideism*—that is, they can claim that God's existence and the truth of Christianity are matters that are justified by faith alone. Or they can defend the possibility of a rational case for theism and Christianity of a sort other than those just examined. The latter approach is not one that con-

---

[4]Again, the argument from design can be set out and defended in very sophisticated ways. It is subject to a variety of objections as well. For a survey of the aforementioned, see Brody, 158–212; W. Salmon, "Religion and Science: A New Look at Hume's Dialogue," *Philosophical Studies* 33 (Fall 1978): 143–76; G. Schlesinger, "Theism and Confirmation, *Pacific Philosophical Quarterly* 64 (January 1983): 46–56.

forms to the normal patterns found in deductive or inductive argumentation.[5]

In my judgment, the latter course has more promise. There is a rational approach that has been called a variety of names, the *cumulative case approach* or the *inference to the best explanation approach* being the most common. Such an argument is rational but does not take the form of a proof or argument for probability in any strict sense of these words. This approach understands Christian theism, other theistic religions, and atheism as systems of belief. Such systems are rationally supported by a variety of considerations or data. The model for defending Christianity is not to be found in the domain of philosophy or logic, but law, history, and literature. This does not mean that the apologist may ignore the deliverances of philosophy or logic, but that the nature of the case for Christianity is to be found in a different field.

The cumulative case approach to apologetics has been adopted by a number of distinguished apologists, such as F. R. Tennant, Elton Trueblood, G. K. Chesterton, and C. S. Lewis. It also has been adopted by such philosophers as Basil Mitchell, Richard Swinburne, and William Abraham.[6]

Because the term *cumulative case* is used in apologetics in ways other than the way I am using it, it will be helpful to try to explain my use in precise terms.

First, the argument for theism and Christianity is an informal one, not a formal one. There are neither premises nor derivations. It is more like the brief that a lawyer brings, or an explanation that a historian proposes, or an interpretation in literature.

Second, it is a broadly based argument that is drawn from a number of elements in our experience, which in turn either require explanation or point beyond themselves. Later in the chapter I will set out what constitutes the elements for this case.

Third, none of the elements that constitute this case has any priority over any other. In the classical approach to apologetics,

---

[5]See Basil Mitchell, *The Justification of Religious Belief* (New York: Seabury, 1973), 34–39.

[6]See, e.g., ibid.; Richard Swinburne, *The Existence of God*, 2d ed. (New York: Oxford University Press, 1991); William J. Abraham, *An Introduction to the Philosophy of Religion* (Englewood Cliffs, N.J.: Prentice-Hall, 1985); and idem, "Cumulative Case Arguments for Christian Theism," in *The Rationality of Religious Belief: Essays in Honour of Basil Mitchell*, ed. William J. Abraham and Steven W. Holtzer (Oxford University Press, 1987).

priority is given to the proof that God exists. For this reason, natural theology and its arguments usually have priority. Once it has been shown that God exists, his nature and love for the sinner are defended. Such an argument is cumulative in the sense that Christianity is defended in terms of more than a single argument. It is not, however, cumulative in the sense that I am using the term because, in the classical approach, God's existence must be proven first. In the approach I am defending, one may start with any element of the case, and depending on the response, appeal may be made to some other element to support or reinforce the claim that Christianity is true.

Traditional Christian theists are urging that their explanation makes better sense of all the evidence available than does any other alternative worldview on offer, whether that alternative is some other theistic view or atheism. The opponent is contesting that claim. The dispute is over what Gilbert Ryle calls the "plausibility of theories."[7] What Christian apologists are defending is the claim that Christian theism is the best explanation of all available evidence on offer. The opponents are required to present a more convincing cumulative case.

Fourth, unlike some approaches, the cumulative case approach is not simply a defense of God's existence or theism, it is an apologetic for Christianity. Put a bit differently, if successful, it establishes the Christian worldview, not just a theistic worldview.

Basil Mitchell gives a parable of two explorers to explain the nature of a cumulative case argument.[8] They come to a hole in the ground. One explorer finds nothing unusual about it, while the other thinks there is something odd about it. They find some other holes in the vicinity. Then they come upon a papyrus fragment in a cave that looks as if it might be a part of the plan for a building. The large hole could be for the center post, and the other holes for poles that gave support to the sides of the building. They even try to reconstruct the building. One explorer thinks that he can see how a building once sat on that spot. He theorizes that there is some order or plan in the location of the holes. Though he lacks the complete plan, he thinks that the fragment supports his view. The other explorer, by contrast, sees the placing of the holes as

---

[7]Gilbert Ryle, "Induction and Hypothesis," in *Proceedings of the Aristotelian Society*, supplementary volume (1937).

[8]Mitchell, *Justification of Religious Belief*, 43–44.

accidental and argues that there are unexplained and missing elements in the data. The first explorer, in turn, thinks it is possible to explain why certain elements are missing.

Mitchell holds this parable to be a good example of a cumulative case. There is a need for ultimate and overarching explanations, but attempts to give such explanations may conflict. The data at certain points may even be capable of a number of different interpretations. However, the theory that best accounts for the data is to be preferred.

Mitchell tries to relate the parable to the question of God's existence and the truth of Christianity. He suggests that the large hole could be the need to explain certain aspects of the universe and reality, which natural theology is an attempt to address. Some of the smaller holes represent religious experiences, the experience of God's presence, of sin, and of grace. Finally, the fragment of the plan is analogous to the concept of the Bible or Christian revelation. In this example, it is even possible to see how the various elements help to reinforce one another.

Two other examples are offered by Mitchell, one from literature and the other from history. In both disciplines scholars develop theories or hypotheses to explain the text in the first case and the facts in the second. These theories or hypotheses are themselves tested for their ability to explain the data.[9]

TESTS FOR TRUTH

To settle conflicting truth claims and determine what is the best explanation for all the data, there must be some tests for truth. The reason for this is simple: Christianity is not the only worldview that claims to be true.[10] Therefore, in this section I will outline what I take to be the appropriate criteria for testing worldviews.

The Test of Consistency

The first test that any truth claim must pass is that of *consistency*. This means that a system of belief must not lead to a

---

[9]Ibid., 45–57.

[10]For another discussion of similar tests for truth, see Ronald H. Nash, *Worldviews in Conflict: Choosing Christianity in a World of Ideas* (Grand Rapids: Zondervan, 1992). While Nash's approach to apologetics would be different from mine, it is noteworthy that the tests for truth that he suggests are quite similar to mine. This is because these tests are used generally, and they are not tailored for the religious issue alone.

contradiction. Any system of belief that is internally inconsistent is false. To show that a contradiction can be generated from a group of beliefs is the strongest type of disproof. It is called a *reductio ad absurdum*. Consistency is such a strong test that logicians teach that anything whatsoever follows from a contradiction. It is fair to say that most systems of belief can be stated in sufficiently sophisticated ways that they will avoid such a failure. Take this example from the Bible. One might argue that James says that works alone can save, while Paul teaches that faith alone saves. Is this not clearly a contradiction, and should not the Christian revelation fail the test of consistency? Christian theologians and apologists have thought not. They have claimed that James and Paul are harmonizable. Paul must be understood as teaching that the basis of salvation is faith alone. James, on the other hand, deals with the evidence for saving faith. He says that works are the evidence that one has saving faith. Thus, the evaluation of this test when applied to a system of belief will not always be agreed upon. This does not detract from the fact that consistency is an exceedingly important test.

The Test of Correspondence

The second test for truth is *correspondence* or *empirical fit*. This test requires that any belief must correspond with reality. It is related to the belief that a correspondence theory of truth is the correct theory of truth. Empirical fit is a test between a system of belief and reality. Whenever some belief does not correspond to our understanding of reality, some may continue to believe it, but since it is hard to avoid the conclusion that that belief is false, it will usually not attract many followers. For example, some religious systems of belief have taught that sickness and death are not real, but illusions. The faithful may continue to believe that this is true, but, as has been said, it is hard not to think that that belief is false and that few will accept it.

The Test of Comprehensiveness

Comprehensiveness is the third test for truth. This criterion requires that we prefer theories or systems of belief that explain more of the evidence over those that might account for less. Explanations for the existence of evil in the world are good examples of this point. An atheist may claim that evil is best explained by the fact that there is no God, or at least not one with the attributes taught in the Bible. If this was the only datum religious belief had to explain, the atheist's conclusion might be best. However, there is much more that calls for explanation, and atheism fails this test when compared with Christian theism.

The Test of Simplicity

A fourth test for truth is *simplicity*. This test instructs us not to multiply explanatory items unnecessarily. It has also been called Ockham's razor. If an explanation is both simple and adequate, it is to be preferred. The application of this test is not always easy to determine, for when is an explanation adequate? However, there certainly are cases where it is clear that elements of explanations are not needed and should not be used.

The Test of Livability

The next two tests for truth might be called the "pragmatic criteria."[11] The fifth test is *livability*. It says that for a belief to be true, it must be livable. This is not the same as our second test for truth, correspondence. That test is more theoretical, while livability is practical. For example, some belief or system of beliefs may pass the theoretical test but show itself to be false, because the advocate of that system constantly contradicts his system in living out his life.

The Test of Fruitfulness

The sixth test for truth is *fruitfulness*. Here we ask what the consequences are of holding such a view of reality. Does it produce fruitful consequences? Take two systems of belief, one that holds that reality is totally disorganized and random, while the other holds that reality is characterized by regularities. On this criterion the latter theory will be preferred, as it will make things like science possible.

The Test of Conservation

Finally, I suggest *conservation* as a test for truth. By this I mean that when we find some anomaly to our theory, we first choose solutions that require the least radical revision of our

---

[11]Ibid., 62–63. Nash calls these the test of practice.

view of the world. Put another way, we seek to modify the paradigm that we are using to understand reality rather than immediately making a radical shift to a new one. For many years Newtonian mechanics constituted the reigning paradigm. Anomalies arose to this system of belief. What occurred first were attempts to modify Newton's views. At some point the problems became so great that it was decided that a new paradigm was needed, and a major shift took place. This is what conservation requires. It is based in the belief that any system of belief that has reached the position of a reigning paradigm must have a good deal of evidence supporting it. Therefore, it is not wise to abandon it as a first move.

Before I conclude this discussion, a few observations are in order. First, it should be clear that these tests for truth are tests that would be used throughout rational discourse. There is no special pleading by theists for tests that will give their views an advantage. These are tests that scientists, historians, and others—not just theists—would use in settling conflicting truth claims.

Second, not all of these tests or criteria are of equal importance. Undoubtedly, the most important test is the first, consistency. As I said, if a system of belief cannot pass this test, then it may be dismissed. Correspondence or empirical fit is next, and comprehensiveness follows that.

Third, once one gets to the criteria that follow comprehensiveness, the order of importance becomes less clear. In some case, livability might be more important than simplicity, and in another not.

Fourth, the evaluation of any system of belief in terms of these criteria will be open to debate. This is not because truth is relative, but because our knowledge of any system of belief is fallible. This explains why it is that two individuals looking at the same evidence may come to different conclusions. Further, this shows the importance of the internal witness of the Holy Spirit in the defense of Christian theism.

THE ELEMENTS OF THE
CUMULATIVE CASE FOR CHRISTIANITY

I have spoken about elements of our common human experience that require explanation and that point beyond themselves

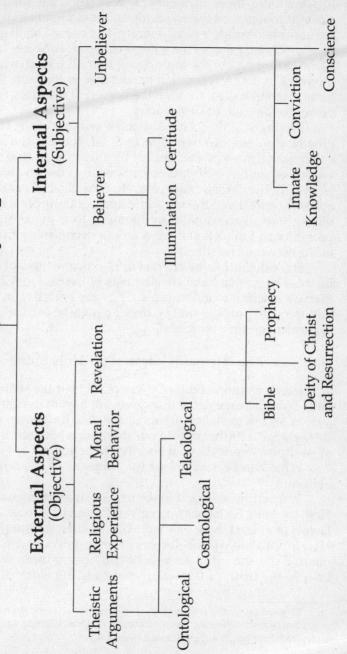

Cumulative Case for Christianity

Witness of the Holy Spirit

External Aspects
(Objective)

Internal Aspects
(Subjective)

Theistic Arguments

Religious Experience

Moral Behavior

Revelation

- Ontological
- Cosmological
- Teleological

- Bible
- Prophecy
- Deity of Christ and Resurrection

Believer

- Illumination
- Certitude

Unbeliever

- Innate Knowledge
- Conviction
- Conscience

to something more in a general way. In what follows I will attempt to describe the most important elements that make up the cumulative case for Christianity. The name I shall give to the case for Christianity is "the witness of the Holy Spirit." I take this name to emphasize the importance that all Christians place on the work of the Holy Spirit in the defense of the faith. The Scriptures teach that God, through the person of the Holy Spirit, witnesses to the truth of Christianity.

Having said that, I think that the witness of the Holy Spirit may be divided into two aspects. First, there is the *internal* or *subjective* witness of the Spirit.[12] By this I mean that the Spirit witnesses within individuals personally. I use the word "subjective" in the narrower sense of "to the subject," not in any relativistic sense. Even though some apologetic approaches would wrongly exalt the subjective element to a place of supreme prominence, I think that there is an important subjective element in the case for Christianity.

Second, there is the *external* or *objective* witness of the Spirit. By this I mean that there are elements of the case for Christianity that are external to individuals. They are objective in the sense that they are public—that is, they are available to all individuals under certain conditions.

The Internal Witness of the Holy Spirit

Let us examine each of these aspects of the witness of the Holy Spirit in some detail. First, we will turn to the internal, subjective, and personal elements of the case for Christian theism. It is helpful to further divide our discussion between the witness of the Spirit to unbelievers and that to believers.

What can be said about the ministry of the Spirit to unbelievers?

The Scriptures teach that there are at least three ministries. First, the Holy Spirit has been given to convict or convince unbelievers of at least three elements of Christian theism (John 16:8–11). He will convict unbelievers of sin, righteousness, and judgment. Thus, the ultimate task of convincing those who do not believe the truth of Christian theism is the work of the Holy

---

[12]The term *subjective* is sometimes used to refer to an entire approach to apologetics. See Norman L Geisler, *Christian Apologetics* (Grand Rapids: Baker, 1976), 65–81, where he sets out this approach and evaluates it.

Spirit; the apologist is simply an instrument in the Spirit's hand. Arguments alone, even the best of arguments, will not convince individuals of the truth of the Christian faith apart from the work of the Holy Spirit.

Second, the Spirit may appeal to the conscience, which God has placed within each individual (Rom. 2:14–16). God has written his law on the hearts of individuals so that even when they do not have the written law, their consciences either accuse or defend them. The conscience, however, is not an infallible witness, as we learn that it may be seared.

Third, God has so constituted individuals that they have a sense that there is a God (Rom. 1:19). Theologians have sometimes called this "innate" knowledge of God—that is, God has not left us in a state of neutrality about his existence. Rather, we are born with a sense that there is a God, and that we are accountable or responsible to him. Again, this is not an infallible guide, since it is possible to suppress the knowledge we have about God.

Now, the ministry of the Holy Spirit is not just to unbelievers; he witnesses to believers, too. He illuminates the minds of God's children (1 Cor. 2:9–16) and helps them to understand God's truth. He is our teacher. Because the natural man does not have the Spirit, he will not accept the things of God. They seem foolish to him, and he cannot understand them. The believer, however, knows the mind of God. Sin has affected our ability to understand and accept God's truth; thus we need the Spirit's ministry to us.

Further, the Holy Spirit is the source of certitude for believers (1 John 5:6–12). The fact that the Spirit witnesses to our spirit that we have believed the truth explains the tenacity and stubbornness of the believer's faith in God.[13] The last belief many people would give up would be belief in God's existence and his love for them. For this reason, many apologists distinguish between *certainty* and *certitude*. Certainty looks at the strength

---

[13]Ibid., 70–72. Nash makes well the point that I am trying to make here. He points out that because worldviews are about reality, we can never have logical certainty. Evidence for interpretations of reality can only have probability or plausibility as I have called it. Nash points out that some have taken this lack of logical certainty to be a sacrilege. He counters this claim that we can and often do believe matters that lack logical certainty with moral or psychological certainty. I have called this certitude to distinguish it from certainty. It is subjective, and it is the work of the Holy Spirit.

of the external evidence for a belief. Certitude looks beyond the external evidence, recognizing that there is a subjective element which can alone explain the tenacity and stubbornness of belief. This stubbornness is not the result of ignorance or stupidity; it is the work of the Holy Spirit.

So, on this view of the case for Christianity, there is an internal witness of the Holy Spirit to individuals. The unbeliever is not in a position of neutrality with regard to God's existence and moral requirements. Moreover, it is the Spirit's responsibility to convict or convince of the truth of God. The Holy Spirit helps believers to understand what God says and requires, and the Spirit also adds the subjective certitude that explains the tenacity and stubbornness of belief in God and the Scriptures.

The External Witness of the Holy Spirit

If the entire case for Christianity were subjective and personal, it might make belief simply a matter of the will. One might choose to believe whatever he wanted, claiming that he had divine assurance that he was right. That is why there is also an external witness of the Holy Spirit. That witness is objective, and it is public so that under certain conditions it is available for critical scrutiny. The elements that make up the external side of the case for Christianity are open to different interpretations. It is even possible for someone to have a cumulative case for atheism or Islam. That is why there must be tests for truth.

Again, there are many elements to the external witness of the Spirit. First, there are the *theistic arguments,* or arguments for God's existence. These arguments are now introduced as arguments, not proofs. They introduce certain aspects of our experience that appear to need explanation and seem to point to God. Take the cosmological argument, for instance. It is not claimed to "prove" that there is a transcendent creator of the universe, as before. Rather, it makes explicit one way—arguably the best way—in which the existence and nature of the universe can be explained.

The atheist is free to suggest alternative explanations or to deny that it is possible to explain the universe at all. But two things have now changed in our case. The atheist must show that the alternative explanation or theory advanced is more plausible than the one defended by the theist. And, if it is argued that the universe's existence and nature cannot be explained, the atheist must face the other elements of the theist's case. The atheist must explain why it is that people claim to have experienced God, why there is a moral law, and why there is a book that claims to be a disclosure from God. So the case for God and Christianity is now much more broadly based.

(A similar kind of claim could be made for the teleological argument in the sense that order and the fitness of means to ends need explanation.[14])

The second element of the external witness of the Holy Spirit is drawn from *religious experience*. Religious experience may be understood as functioning as an argument in two ways. The theist may argue that throughout human history a host of individuals have claimed to have known and had a personal relationship with God. This claim has been made across cultural and geographic boundaries as well as over time. For the atheist's claim that there is no God to be true, every single one of these individuals must be wrong about a matter that they themselves would characterize as the most important human concern. However, if even so much as one of these individual's claims is true, then there is a God. The atheist may respond that the belief that one has had an experience with God and has a relationship with him is explainable in a variety of ways. The theist's belief is the result of certain psychological and/or sociological factors. Both the theist's and atheist's claim can be tested for plausibility. Is there evidence that psychological and sociological factors are controlling the individual's belief? Furthermore, religious experience is only one element of the case for Christianity.

At this point the atheist might contend that such an argument cuts two ways. That is, we can make an argument of the same sort for atheism. Many people in human history have claimed that there is no God. All of them would have to be wrong for theism to be true. Since this was a matter of greatest importance to those making this claim, it would truly be incredible to think that they all were wrong.

At first it might appear that we have come to a standoff on this argument, but that is a mistake. The arguments are not on par. To know that something is true, one need only know a little of the world's knowledge. For example, to know that Deerfield is in Illinois, one only has to have a very little knowledge. I would only be required to know a bit about the geography of

---

[14]Mitchell, *Justification of Religious Belief*, 40–42.

Illinois just to the north of Chicago. But consider what one must know to know that there is no God. Would 50 percent of the world's knowledge be enough? Would even 95 percent? No. One would have to know everything, because God could be hiding in the 5 percent where one was ignorant. C. S. Lewis said that wolves are ingenious in hiding out from those who want to catch them. God is far more ingenious than wolves in his ability to hide out from those who seek him out of sheer curiosity or for the wrong reasons.

Furthermore, the theist can give an explanation for the atheist's inability to find God. It is possible that some conditions must be met for one to acquire certain types of knowledge. For instance, to know that there is a table in the next room, certain conditions must be met such as (1) one's going into the room, (2) the room having sufficient light, or (3) one's asking for and believing the testimony of someone who has met the conditions needed to have that knowledge. Thus, it is possible that the reason that the atheist has not been able to establish contact with God is that he has not met the conditions that are required for that kind of knowledge.

Now, there is a second way in which we may formulate an argument from religious experience.[15] Many have claimed that encounters with Jesus Christ changed them from sinners to saints. They lived lives that could only be characterized as evil and self-centered until they met Christ. He changed their lives radically. Now they desire to do what is right, and they seek to do acts of charity. They are altruistic and are concerned with the needs of others. Some have lived in such impressive and persuasive ways that it is difficult to doubt their claims. It is true that opponents can attribute the changed lives to psychological or sociological factors. However, it will no longer be enough to simply suggest these kinds of alternative explanations. It will be necessary to show that these explanations are more plausible than the one offered by the individual who points to the encounter with Jesus Christ.

Further, it is important to see that we are not left in a position where we must accept claims of the sort just mentioned without the ability to test them. We can think of a number of criteria for evaluating claims of influence on one's life. Think of individuals who say that an encounter with Abraham Lincoln

---

[15]Ibid. This is similar to the way Mitchell develops this element.

revolutionized their lives. How would we go about evaluating such a claim? I think that we would want to know what characterized their lives before this encounter. Suppose we were to find out that they once lived in a way that was quite contrary to the values Abraham Lincoln espoused. Then we would want to know how they came into contact with Abraham Lincoln. Did they have some personal meeting? Was their contact with Lincoln through his writings? And, finally, we would be interested in finding out how they lived their lives after their encounter. Did they change their actions and beliefs so that they reflected the principles embraced by Lincoln? If all these criteria were met and these changes were attributed to the influence of Abraham Lincoln, it would be hard to deny their claim. The same is true for those who say that Jesus Christ is the reason for their changed lives. Their claims are strengthened even further when understood in conjunction with the other elements of the case.

A third external element of the witness of the Holy Spirit, after theistic arguments and religious experience, is the *moral law*. Not only do human beings have a conscience, but they are also incurably moral.[16] Many people today deny the reality of a moral law and espouse moral relativism. They speak often about relativism, and their actions are governed by this philosophy. Moral relativism is far less believable, however, when we are reacting to someone whose actions toward us are guided by this philosophy.

A story about a college course in ethics will help to illustrate my point. The beginning philosophy teacher had a number of students in his class who were defenders of relativism, claiming that there were no universal, absolute moral laws. The teacher did his best to change students' attitudes on this issue. He talked about the impossibility of acting as a moral judge with regard to the Holocaust and slavery. Most students were not willing to defend the actions of the Nazi death camps or the actions of Southern American slaveholders as being right for some people or being right for the day in which they were practiced. The students wanted to condemn such practices as wrong. The brightest student in this class, however, would not change his mind; he continued to defend relativism. The teacher thought he would teach this student a lesson, so on the student's final exam he wrote that the student had gotten an F on the final and

---

[16]C. S. Lewis, *Mere Christianity* (New York: Macmillan, 1960), bk. 1.

an F in the course. The professor did this in spite of the fact that the student had received an A on the midterm and had written one of the best final exams. The final exams were returned to the students by university postal service, and this student was both stunned and angry when he received his grade. He went immediately to the professor's office to inquire why he had received an F. The professor told him that he had decided that anyone who did not write the final exam in purple ink had failed both the exam and the course. This explanation did not make the student any happier. He told the professor that his actions were wrong and that if the grade was not changed, he, the student, would report the professor's actions to university authorities, the campus newspaper, and local call-in radio programs. The professor listened for some time to the student's threats before saying this to him: "You really are not a relativist, are you? You do believe some things are wrong. We cannot do whatever we want. Your exam was the best in class. You got an A on it and an A in the course. Now be on your way." The point again is this: One may talk and even act like a relativist until someone treats him in terms of his own principles—then watch the relativist's reaction!

C. S. Lewis is correct in arguing that morality or the moral law is a means for showing us that there is something beyond sense experience. He says that the moral law is not simply a fact related to human behavior in the way that the law of gravity is a fact related to physical objects. The moral law is a real thing that is independent of us, not something that is made up by us. It is something beyond the ordinary facts of human behavior. Since something beyond the mere facts exists, what does this tell us about the universe? It tells us that there is something behind the universe that is more like a mind than anything else we know. This is insider's information. It is based on something other than scientific experimentation. We meet it in what we ought to do. Lewis cautions against assuming too quickly that this is the God of Christian theism. He does, however, think that we do have reasons for uneasiness when we realize that we have not always obeyed this moral law. It is at this point that we are ready for the introduction of the Christian view of reality. That is, there is a moral law, a moral lawgiver, the fall of Adam and the universality of sin, the need for a savior, the cross, and a resurrection. All of these things that are a part of the Christian story now make sense.

Finally, the external case for Christian theism includes *revelation*.[17] Christianity is one of a group of religions that claims to be based on a communication from God. While this claim is controversial today, orthodox Christianity has claimed that the Bible is a revelation from God. As such, it is authoritative where it speaks. This is drawn from what the Bible has to say about itself, as well as from external evidences that support that claim. An important element in support of the claim that the Bible is from God is the testimony of Christ himself to the Bible's authority. In both his words and actions it is clear that he thinks that the Scriptures are from God. He also authenticates the New Testament in advance by what he has to say about the gift of the Holy Spirit, who will lead his disciples into all truth (John 16:12–15).

It is also in this revelation that we come to know the central figure for Christian theism, the Lord Jesus Christ. We learn in the Scriptures that he is not simply a good man, but that he is God himself, the second person of the Christian Trinity. This was not simply something that Jesus' followers attributed to him because of his untimely death; it was something he claimed for himself (cf. John 8:58–59; 10:30–33). Jesus' claim to deity was authenticated by his resurrection from the dead. It is in the Bible that we learn of Jesus Christ's resurrection and have the primary evidence for it. The resurrection is the crucial piece of evidence in the establishment of the deity of Jesus Christ, and it was verifiable through empirical evidence, such as the empty tomb and Christ's post-resurrection appearances. What is being asserted is this: Within the Christian revelation there are claims of an empirical sort that can be tested.

While the case for the divine origin of the Scriptures is also a broadly based argument, an important aspect of that argument is the testimony of Jesus Christ, who is himself God. For those

---

[17]For a discussion of issues that make up this element of the cumulative case see Paul D. Feinberg, "The Meaning of Inerrancy," in *Inerrancy*, ed. Norman L. Geisler (Grand Rapids: Zondervan, 1980), 267–304; Paul D. Feinberg, "Bible, Inerrancy and Infallibility of," in *Evangelical Dictionary of Theology*, ed. Walter Elwell (Grand Rapids: Baker, 1984), 142–45; Gary R. Habermas, *The Verdict of History: Conclusive Evidence for the Life of Jesus* (Nashville: Thomas Nelson, 1988); Josh McDowell, *Evidence That Demands a Verdict: Historical Evidence for the Christian Faith*, rev. ed. (San Bernardino, Calif.: Here's Life, 1979); Josh McDowell, *More Than a Carpenter* (Wheaton, Ill.: Tyndale, 1977); Lee Strobel, *The Case for Christ: A Journalist's Personal Investigation of the Evidence for Jesus* (Grand Rapids: Zondervan, 1998).

who hold this view of the Bible, this is one of the most telling pieces of evidence. They cannot see how their view of Scripture can be anything less than that of their Lord.

This is not all that can be said about revelation. Apologists have thought that an argument from fulfilled prophecies supported the claims that the Bible was from God and that Christianity was true. Some have estimated that one-third of the verses in the Bible made predictions about the future. Even at this present time something like a quarter of the verses in the Bible have as yet been unfulfilled. The portion of predictive prophecy that has been fulfilled is taken to support the claim that the Bible is a revelation from God. It is in that revelation that Christianity's central truths are set forth.

The claim that there is a supernatural revelation from God, that it reveals the appearance in time and history of one who calls himself God, that that claim is validated by his resurrection from the dead, and that this God is able to control the future in such a way that he can foretell what will happen before it does, all require some explanation, and again the Christian explanation is the best on offer.

SUMMARY

This, then, is the case for Christianity. It is a broad-based argument with many subjective and objective elements. They require some explanation and in some cases can be seen as reinforcing one another to strengthen the case for Christian theism. The case is like a lawyer's brief. The claim is that Christian theism gives the most plausible explanation of all the evidence.

At this point, opponents of Christianity might make this claim: Just as the Christian theist can make a cumulative case argument, so can the apologist for other religious points of view or for atheism. Some elements of the case would undoubtedly differ from the Christian case, but others would not. For instance, Islam would defend the Koran as a revelation from God. A Muslim could formulate an argument from religious experience just like the one offered for Christianity. And he would claim his view of reality is true.

It is for this reason that there must be some tests for truth like those outlined in the previous section that can help adjudicate conflicting truth claims. It is my contention that Christianity passes these tests where other worldviews fall short.

TWO OBJECTIONS CONSIDERED

Before closing this discussion, I must address a couple of objections—one directed against cumulative case apologetics in particular, and the second against apologetics in general.

The Ten Leaky Buckets Objection

A common objection against cumulative cases arguments is that they are subject to the *ten leaky buckets objection*. It is argued against them that ten ineffective arguments, when combined, cannot make one good argument, just as ten buckets that all leak water cannot in combination hold water. This objection may be answered in two ways. First, such an objection may have force if the arguments are claimed to prove a conclusion. That is no longer the case here. These arguments point up areas in our experience that need explanation and seem to point to the existence of God. It is possible to offer explanations different from those given by the Christian theist. However, those explanations have to be as plausible and comprehensive as the one given by the Christian theist.

Second, in the kind of cumulative case that I am defending, the elements of the theist's case may tend to reinforce one another. Not all arguments may fail as proofs at just the same point. It is possible that one element reinforces an argument just at the point of its weakness. For instance, one may pose psychological explanations for someone's belief that he or she has a sense of God's presence because one thinks that God's existence is doubtful. But the theistic arguments may be advanced to show that God's existence is not contrary to reason. To use Plantinga's terms, it is rationally acceptable to believe that there is a God. Or put in terms of buckets, unless the holes in all ten buckets line up perfectly so that the water will spill out, one bucket may so reinforce another bucket so that the ten leaky buckets will indeed make a bucket that will carry water. The apologist is arguing that Christian theism is the best explanation of *all* available evidence *taken together*.

The Postmodern Objection

One objection to the task of apologetics in general grows out of the current intellectual climate. At the heart of apologetics is a belief that truth exists. Apologists may differ over how to defend that truth, but they nevertheless agree that God's existence and Christianity are true. Further, apologetics presupposes that these beliefs are true not only for me, but for everyone who has ever lived. Belief in truth of this kind is not accepted by all today. We live in what has been called "postmodern" times, and one form of postmodernism rejects the belief that there is anything that might be called objective, absolute truth. If this form of postmodernism is true, then apologetics methodology is faced with a very different problem than the one discussed in this book. Therefore I would like to describe the objection and then respond to it.

A variety of views falls under the term *postmodernism*.[18] What unites them is their dissatisfaction with the modern view of the world. Modernity is the view of reality that grows out of Enlightenment thought, in which reason is exalted and supernaturalism is denied.

While proponents of each form of postmodernism would make the point a bit differently, their assessment of modernity would be strikingly similar. They would agree that in the modern view of the world the supernatural God of the Bible has died. However, in spite of the fact that modernity celebrated the death of this supernatural God, it tried to retain the Western ideas of self, truth, history, meaning, and value, which were based on this understanding of God. Nietzsche realized this could not be done and took the radical road of rejecting these ideas, causing him to become a hero in certain forms of postmodernism.

This radical form of postmodernism is called *deconstructionism* or *eliminative postmodernism*. It is called deconstructionism because of its heavy dependence on the French movement, of which Jacques Derrida is the most important figure, and its dependence on Martin Heidegger's understanding of metaphysics. It is called eliminative because of views traceable to the American philosopher Richard Rorty. This form of postmodernism celebrates the death of the ideas mentioned above and does not seek to reinterpret them in postmodern terms.

Mark C. Taylor is certainly one of the better-known English-language advocates of deconstructionism.[19] He begins by setting

---

[18]See David Ray Griffin, William A. Beardslee, and Joe Holland, eds., *Varieties of Postmodern Theology* (Albany, N.Y.: State University of New York Press, 1989).

[19]Mark C. Taylor, *Erring: A Postmodern A/theology* (University of Chicago Press, 1984).

out the consequences of the death of the traditional idea of God. He calls deconstructionism the "hermeneutic of the death of God." In his view, the controlling, aloof deity of traditional theism is not replaced by some less repressive god, but is eliminated entirely. This means that there is no center that unifies human existence, no perspective to serve as a standard and judge for truth. What is left is only a multiplicity of perspectives, all having equal rights. No perspective is more normative than any other.

As might be seen from what has just been said, truth also dies. Taylor claims that there is no truth, not just that we cannot know what is true. With Nietzsche he declares there is no true world. When God dies, absolute relativism follows. There is no eternal truth, only never-ending flux.

The self dies, too, and no attempt is made to reconstruct it in postmodern terms. There is the elimination of any referent for language outside of itself. Linguistic signs only refer to other signs. Words do not refer to some "real," extralinguistic world beyond language. Our interpretation of these linguistic signs, on this view, are interpretations of other interpretations, not of some extralinguistic world. Moreover, if no real world exists, then truth as correspondence to that reality makes no sense. There is no intention of a writer in a text which interpretations seek to approximate. The text does not preexist its interpretations. History is no longer a directed process with some goal or *telos*. Taylor follows Nietzsche in eliminating the usual distinction between good and evil, and he encourages us to live beyond either of these. In the end, this way of thinking results in nihilism. It involves the subversion of everything that was once thought to be holy. It denies all meaning, all purpose, all ethical and aesthetical norms.

If any form of postmodernism like deconstructionism is true, then there can be no task for apologetics, and discussions about methods for defending the faith are meaningless. Therefore, every apologist must face this challenge squarely. Has truth died? Is all meaningless? Is the only way to victory to embrace such a world willingly and in so doing overcome it? I think not. Yet criticisms of views like that of Mark Taylor are difficult. Because of his radical relativism, he would reject the idea that any meaningful criticism can be made of one position from the perspective of another. While it is possible to point out inconsistencies, it is impossible to criticize a position because it does not correspond to the facts. There simply are no facts for decon-structionism. Two systems of belief are incommensurable. No neutral center of reality exists from which to judge systems of belief. Thus, it will be very difficult to criticize deconstruction-ism in terms of the two most important criteria that I have set out as tests for truth, consistency and correspondence or empir-ical fit. As long as one is careful not to describe beliefs in con-tradictory ways, one is safe from criticism, because there are no facts to fit.

The method I have set forth does, however, provide a way out.[20] One of the tests for truth was livability. I said that while some systems of belief might escape theoretical tests, they must be capable of being lived out practically. In the case of decon-structionism, theoretical tests are simply rejected as inappropri-ate because they are outside the system. But let me set out a response that Mark Taylor and deconstructionists cannot escape in terms of the test of livability. Some facts must be universally acknowledged *in practice*, irrespective of what is said in theory. These facts are *hard-core commonsense notions*. Their defining characteristic is that they cannot be denied without following them in practice.

The strategy of this critique of deconstructionism is to demonstrate that those who verbally deny things like belief in truth and good and evil continue to act in ways that presuppose them in practice. Such an approach has this important advan-tage when made against deconstructionism: its criticisms are *internal*, not *external* to the system. They do not rest on what is claimed to be a misguided understanding of facts, but rather on the demonstration of inconsistencies between explicit and implicit affirmations. Thus, there is a way beyond complete rel-ativism through hard-core commonsense notions. These notions show that there is a real world and that there are transperspec-tival facts.

Taylor repeatedly makes the claim that there is no real world beyond consciousness, yet he appeals to an "insight" that "relationships constitute all things."[21] This insight into the "nature of all things" then becomes a critical norm from which

---

[20]See David Ray Griffin, "Postmodern Theology and A/theology: A Response to Mark C. Taylor," in Griffin et al., *Varieties*, 29–61. For a thorough critique of post-modernism from an evangelical perspective, see D. A. Carson, *The Gagging of God* (Grand Rapids: Zondervan, 1996).

[21]Mark C. Taylor, *Deconstructing Theology* (New York: Crossroad, 1982), 48–49.

he is able to reject the modern view that things are independent of their relationships. In doing this, Taylor gives implicit testimony to the realist's claim that our interpretations of reality are formed by our contact with a reality that is independent of our interpretations.

Consider also what Taylor has to say about truth and what he does in practice. Taylor is quite clear that there is nothing like truth as correspondence with reality. If this is so, then his book is filled with statements that we should not take as truth claims in any traditional sense. He argues against systems of belief that try to master reality. In his arguments against such systems, he declares that reality is unmasterable. In defending a position that denies the distinction between good and evil, he asserts that "creation and destruction, life and death, are forever joined."[22] From what he says, it is clear that he believes that these ideas are true in the sense that they correspond to reality. Taylor argues that there is nothing like eternal truth, because "the play of appearances never stops and hence cannot be fixed."[23] Yet, in making this claim, one cannot escape the conclusion that Taylor thinks that this principle is an eternal truth. He claims that truth itself is an illusion, but he encourages closer inspection in examining certain matters. It would seem that this closer inspection would lead us to a better approximation of the truth. Furthermore, Taylor cannot be read without taking statement after statement in his book as a truth claim.

Taylor's treatment of other authors is another example of this kind of practical inconsistency. He refers often to figures like Hegel, Nietzsche, and Derrida. In what he says about them, it is clear that he believes that they were actual persons and that they wrote texts prior to his discussions of them. Moreover, he thinks that his interpretation of their texts is an accurate understanding of what they wrote. And unless it is possible to distinguish between what they meant and how they are interpreted, then it is impossible to know what is claimed when he talks about "a creative 'misreading' of an antecedent text."[24]

In summary, Mark Taylor and deconstructionism make claims explicitly that they cannot follow in practice. This shows that while they may deny a number of hard-core commonsense

---

[22]Taylor, *Erring*, 91, 168.

[23]Ibid., 176.

[24]Taylor, *Deconstructing Theology*, xviii.

notions, they in fact testify to their truth. Deconstructionism is not a livable system of belief. Since this is the case, truth in the sense needed to do apologetics is possible. We must take seriously Christian theism's claim that it is the best explanation of all the evidence. There is an independent reality. Good and evil do exist. Jesus Christ entered time and space. He died and rose again so that we might be forgiven of our sins. This is not just some interpretation of some interpretation. It is true regardless of how it is defended. Therefore, the discussion of methodology in this book is significant. It is not meaningless.

A CLASSICAL
APOLOGIST'S RESPONSE

William Lane Craig

I find myself largely in agreement with the conclusion of my former teacher and old friend Paul Feinberg. A successful apologetic for the Christian faith should be in an appropriate sense a cumulative case and is, therefore, I think, best thought of as a project undertaken by a community of scholars, each contributing from his area of expertise to the cumulative weight of the case for a Christian *Weltanschauung*. The arguments in which I have specialized should be seen, not as links in a single chain of reasoning, which is, after all, only as strong as its weakest link, but rather as links in a coat of chain mail, in which all the links serve to reinforce one another.

That being said, however, I think that Feinberg's supporting argumentation for his conclusion is in places confused or mistaken. Consider, for example, the question of whether one can know that the Christian faith is true in the absence of evidence and argument. I have contended that one can know that the Christian faith is true solely through the witness of the Holy Spirit. Feinberg agrees that "the Scriptures teach that God, through the person of the Holy Spirit, witnesses to the truth of Christianity" (p. 158). But he confuses the issue by claiming that the witness of the Holy Spirit is identical with "the cumulative case for Christianity" and differentiates within it the "*internal* or *subjective* witness of the Spirit" and the "*external* or *objective* witness of the Spirit" (p. 158). This is simply exegetically untenable; nowhere does Scripture identify the witness of the Holy Spirit with "arguments for God's existence" or "an argument from religious experience" (pp. 160, 162). Of course, the Holy Spirit may *use* such arguments to draw people to Christ, as he may use virtually anything, but the arguments themselves are not the witness of the Holy Spirit. By construing the witness of the Spirit so broadly, Feinberg robs this important work of God of its distinctive character and importance; it becomes almost indistinguishable from divine providence.[1] It is evident that the witness of the Spirit, properly so called, is identical with what Feinberg calls the internal witness of the Spirit.

Does Feinberg, then, think that on the basis of the Spirit's inner witness alone one is rational and warranted in believing that the biblical God exists? His answer is ambiguous: while affirming that the Spirit gives us certitude that our Christian faith is true, Feinberg seems to hold that such a subjective certitude is no indication that the tenaciously held belief is true. For he advises, "If the entire case for Christianity were subjective and personal, it might make belief simply a matter of the will. One might choose to believe whatever he wanted, claiming that he had divine assurance that he was right. That is why there is also an external witness of the Holy Spirit" (p. 160). Taken at face value, this seems to constitute an endorsement of theological rationalism, the view that Christian belief is unwarranted in the absence of supporting argumentation. As such, it faces the objections Kelly Clark and I have brought against this doctrine. Feinberg's inference that belief becomes arbitrary if the believer's entire "case" for Christianity is subjective (in the nonrelativistic sense, remember, of "to the subject" [p. 158]) and personal is a *non sequitur*. It rests on the conflation of knowing and showing one's faith to be true. Such a believer will not be able to show his faith to be true to someone else who claims divine assurance for his non-Christian beliefs, but that does nothing to rob the believer of the grounds for his knowing his faith to be true.

When it comes to Feinberg's discussion of showing Christianity to be true, he makes, in my opinion, a number of missteps. Consider first his discussion of what constitutes a theistic

---

[1]Even with respect to the internal witness of the Holy Spirit, Feinberg tends to throw everything into the mix, including the *sensus divinitatis* and the implanted dictates of conscience (p. 159). More discrimination is needed here concerning the various ministries of the Holy Spirit.

proof. He never really tells us what characteristics an argument must have in order to qualify as a proof. But he maintains that arguments for God's existence attain neither to the level of demonstratively sound arguments nor to the level of probabilistically sound arguments.

What is it to be a theistic "proof"? The best discussion I have seen of this question is by Steve Davis in his recent *God, Reason, and Theistic Proofs*.[2] On the basis of his discussion, I should say that an argument for God's existence constitutes a theistic proof if it is sound, informally valid, and its premises are more plausible than their denials.[3] This seems to be roughly what Feinberg means by a probability argument.

Are there, then, in this sense, no theistic proofs? I must confess that I find Feinberg's objections to theistic proofs to be surprisingly superficial. Take, for example, the ontological and cosmological arguments for God's existence. Granted that these are not demonstratively sound arguments, are not their premises at least more plausible than their negations? Alvin Plantinga, while admitting that the key premise in the ontological argument (*Possibly God exists*) is not demonstrable, nevertheless thinks that "the ontological argument provides as good grounds for the existence of God as does any serious philosophical argument for any important philosophical conclusion."[4] Why does Feinberg disagree?—Because "the argument has a premise that the nontheist will not accept as true" (p. 148). But so what? At best this disagreement only shows that the key premise is not demonstrable. That does nothing to show that the premise is not more plausible than its negation, *It is impossible that God exists.*

What about the cosmological argument? Feinberg says that atheists refuse to accept the premises of the argument, for example, that "an infinite regress of causes is impossible" (p. 149). But again, so what? This only shows that that premise is not demonstrably true, not that its denial is as plausible as the premise

---

[2]Stephen T. Davis, *God, Reason, and Theistic Proofs* (Grand Rapids: Eerdmans, 1997), chap. 1.

[3]Soundness means that the premises of the argument are true and that the conclusion follows from the premises by the rules of logical inference. Informal validity prevents the argument from being question-begging. If the premises are more plausible than their contradictories, then we should believe those premises.

[4]Alvin Plantinga, "Reason and Belief in God," typescript dated October 1981, pp. 18–19.

itself. One must deal with the arguments theists provide in defense of that premise. On a very practical note, I and many others have seen people come to believe in God (and even Christ) on the basis of the *kalam* cosmological argument. The fact that other nontheists resist the argument may tell us more about the psychology of atheism than about the plausibility of the premises.[5]

In short, once we agree that the ontological and cosmological arguments are not strict demonstrations (as Feinberg defines the term), no reason has been given for not regarding them as probabilistically sound theistic proofs.

What about the teleological argument? This proof has come roaring back into prominence as a result of the discovery of the fine-tuning of the universe for sentient life.[6] We now know that in order for the universe to be life-permitting, its initial conditions and constants have to be fine-tuned to an incomprehensible precision. Accordingly, we can formulate the following argument for design:[7]

1. The fine-tuning of the universe for sentient life is due to either natural law, chance, or intelligent design.
2. It is not due to natural law or chance.
3. Therefore, the fine-tuning of the universe for sentient life is due to intelligent design.

Premise (1) certainly seems true, since it posits an exhaustive disjunction of alternatives. The key premise is therefore (2).

The hypothesis of natural law as an explanation of cosmic fine-tuning seems implausible because laws must be supplemented by boundary conditions, which are contingent features

---

[5]Feinberg himself endorses the cosmological argument as "one way, *arguably the best way,* in which the existence and nature of the universe can be explained" (p. 160, my emphasis). What more could the natural theologian ask for? Notice that one does not need any argument at all merely to "make explicit" one way of explaining the universe; anyone can just propose a hypothesis. But to claim the best way one needs a good argument, for one is inferring to one's explanation as the best.

[6]See the catalogue of evidence in John D. Barrow and Frank Tipler, *The Anthropic Cosmological Principle* (Oxford: Oxford University Press, 1985). The best philosophical discussion is John Leslie, *Universes* (London: Routledge, 1989).

[7]The argument I offer conforms to the schema Dembski calls "the explanatory filter" (William Dembski, *The Design Inference*, Cambridge Studies in Probability, Induction, and Decision Theory [Cambridge: Cambridge University Press, 1998]).

of the world. Reacting to the hypothesis that there might be some unknown Theory of Everything that would explain all the apparently contingent, finely tuned features of the universe, British physicist P. C. W. Davies asserts:

> There is absolutely no evidence in favor of it.... Even if the laws of physics were unique, it doesn't follow that the physical universe itself is unique.... The laws of physics must be augmented by cosmic initial conditions.... There is nothing in present ideas about "laws of initial conditions" remotely to suggest that their consistency with the laws of physics would imply uniqueness. Far from it.... It seems, then, that the physical universe does not have to be the way it is: it could have been otherwise.[8]

So what about the alternative suggestion that the fine-tuning of the universe is due to sheer chance? Here the odds are simply too daunting to accept. Take just one cosmic quantity, for example, the entropy per baryon in the universe. Roger Penrose of Oxford University has calculated that the odds of the low entropy conditions present in the Big Bang having come about as a result of chance are around one chance in $10^{10(123)}$.[9] The number $10^{10\,(123)}$ is so huge a number that even if a zero were inscribed on every subatomic particle in the entire universe, one could not even approach writing down this number.

These unfaceable odds have compelled some theorists to embrace the hypothesis of a World Ensemble, the hypothesis that ours is but one member of an infinite collection of universes, so that the chance of sentient life's appearing somewhere must be actualized. But such a hypothesis faces formidable objections: (a) It is, in fact, a metaphysical hypothesis and as such is no better than theism. Indeed, theism is simpler than the bloated ontology of an infinite and random collection of universes and is therefore, by Ockham's razor, to be preferred. (b) There is no known mechanism for generating such a World Ensemble. Inflationary theories of the Big Bang are often suggested, but inflation itself depends on fine-tuning, so that the dilemma is not avoided. (c) The hypothesis is improbable relative to our observation of a relatively young sun. The neo-Darwinian theory of evolution through random genetic mutation and natural selection implies

---

[8] Paul Davies, *The Mind of God* (New York: Simon & Schuster, 1992), 168–69.
[9] Roger Penrose, *The Emperor's New Mind* (New York: Oxford University Press, 1989), 339–44.

that it is vastly more probable that if sentient life comparable in intelligence to *homo sapiens* were to evolve, it would do so as late in the life of the sun as possible, so as to provide sufficient time for these slow-working mechanisms. But then, given a World Ensemble, it is vastly more probable that we should observe an old sun. The fact that we do not implies that either the theory of evolution is false or else a World Ensemble does not exist. In either case, the hypothesis of chance is ruled out. (d) There is no independent evidence for the existence of a World Ensemble, but there is such evidence for God (the cosmological, teleological, and other arguments). Thus, premise (2) seems to be more plausible than its denial. It therefore follows that the fine-tuning of the universe is due to intelligent design.

What is wrong with this theistic proof? Feinberg asserts that "there is an entirely acceptable (and perhaps equally probable) alternative explanation for any order that we find in this universe, namely, evolutionary forces. If one accepts the evolutionary theory, then any universe that survived would have to exhibit order" (p. 150). This generalization is inapplicable to the fine-tuning requisite for sentient life. Perhaps Feinberg is right that, say, the proton-neutron mass ratio must have some value or other, but the fact remains that if the ratio were a hair's breadth different than what it is, then the universe would have been life-prohibiting. The truth is that our existence is balanced on a knife's edge of incredible fineness. The evolution of sentient life presupposes, rather than explains, cosmic fine-tuning. As Barrow and Tipler say, "We have no explanation for the precise numerical values taken by these . . . numbers. They are not subject to evolution or selection by any known natural or unnatural mechanism."[10] Therefore, "the fortuitous nature of many of their numerical values is a mystery that cries out for a solution."[11] Moreover, even with respect to the development of biological complexity, scientists such as Michael Denton and Michael Behe have provided very substantial reasons for thinking that, even granted the thesis of common ancestry, the irreducible complexity of organic systems cannot be explained apart from the hypothesis of intelligent design.[12]

[10]Barrow and Tipler, *Anthropic Cosmological Principle*, 31.

[11]Ibid.

[12]Michael Denton, *Evolution: A Theory in Crisis* (Bethesda, Md.: Adler and Adler, 1986); Michael J. Behe, *Darwin's Black Box* (New York: Free Press, 1996); Michael Denton, *Nature's Destiny* (New York: Free Press, 1998).

None of Feinberg's defeaters of the traditional theistic arguments serves to render their premises implausible. I do not pretend that there are not substantive and difficult questions to wrestle with here,[13] but Feinberg's objections to the arguments are far too facile.

It seems to me, therefore, that there are a number of good theistic proofs that will be part of the Christian apologist's cumulative case for theism. The ontological argument gives us a necessary being; the cosmological argument, a Creator of the universe; the teleological argument, a Cosmic Designer; the moral argument, an absolute standard and locus of value. Together these build a powerful case for theism.

Now what about Feinberg's alternative approach, his so-called cumulative case approach? In the first place, it seems to me that he incorrectly identifies this approach with inference to the best explanation. So far as I understand this latter notion, it is an analysis of inductive reasoning.[14] I use this approach in arguing for the hypothesis of the resurrection of Jesus. It is no part of inference to the best explanation that the hypothesis is rendered probable by the cumulative weight of considerations, which, taken individually, do not make the hypothesis probable. But this seems to be the essence of Feinberg's cumulative case approach. Letting G = God's existence, O = the ontological argument, C = the cosmological argument, and T = the teleological argument, the cumulative case approach seems to hold that

$$Pr(G/O) + Pr(G/C) + Pr(G/T) > 0.5$$

even though the individual probabilities are less than 0.5.

An obvious feature of such a cumulative probability is that one will get to 0.5 (or higher) much more easily if the individual probabilities are high. Indeed, unless the Christian apologist is able to make his individual probabilities high enough, there is the real danger that they may sum to less than 0.5. That is precisely what the nontheist thinks of the case for Christianity. Moreover, the Christian apologist must be concerned that his

---

[13]In the first draft of his essay, Feinberg raised further objections to the teleological argument based on the dystelogy in the universe, the uniqueness of the universe, the possible infinity of the universe, and the difficulty of discerning design. His omitting them now is unfortunate, since it makes it inappropriate for me to answer objections he has not raised, and I shall have no opportunity to answer his response to this critique if he raises them there.

[14]See Peter Lipton, *Inference to the Best Explanation* (London: Routledge, 1991).

conclusion be able to survive the subtraction due to the improbability cast on his conclusion by atheistic arguments. He will be exercised to marshal his evidence as thoroughly as he can and to defeat every defeater that is brought against his conclusions. Thus, it is evidently in the best interests of the cumulative case apologist to make sure his individual arguments establish their respective conclusions to as high a degree of probability as possible. But then he can have no in principle objection to, say, $Pr(G/C) > 0.5$, as I believe. There is no reason whatsoever to prefer arguments establishing their conclusions to a low degree of probability.

The point is, then, that the cumulative case apologist will be just as exercised as the classical apologist to present theistic arguments and Christian evidences based on premises that have as high a degree of probability as can be found. Moreover, the classical apologist will welcome the accumulation of theistic arguments and Christian evidences as a means of establishing the truth of the Christian faith.

Feinberg recognizes that proponents of non-Christian worldviews will also offer cumulative case arguments for their viewpoints, but he claims that the Christian worldview "gives the most plausible explanation of all the evidence" (p. 166) because it passes various tests for truth, such as consistency, empirical fit, and so forth, whereas other worldviews "fall short" (p. 166). Feinberg's criteria are not really tests for truth per se (a nonsimple explanation, for example, could be true), but rather are just criteria for determining the best explanation. Unfortunately, Feinberg never gets his hands dirty by actually showing us how Christianity passes these tests, in contrast to some other world religion. Therein lies the rub. For I simply do not understand how that task is to be done unless one gets down to the business of arguing, say, that the origin of the universe is best explained by a theistic worldview in contrast to a nontheistic worldview. If that is one element in your cumulative case, then you will have to argue your case; in other words, you will be doing exactly the work that classical apologists have taken it upon themselves to do. Thus, in order to show that your cumulative case for Christianity is successful, you cannot avoid engaging in natural theology and Christian evidences. If you are really going to show Christianity to be true (rather than just talk about it) you will wind up trying to present good theistic arguments and convincing evidence.

I also disagree specifically that conservation is either a test for truth or a criterion for the best explanation. As a test for truth, it leads immediately to a pluralistic, relativistic conception of truth, since proponents of two contradictory views each applying this test determine that their view is true. (Remember, we are not talking here about conservation as a principle of mere rationality, but as a test of truth.) Nor is there any reason to think that because you happen to hold a view already, that fact serves to show that your explanation is better than opposing views.

Feinberg closes his essay with some thoughts on postmodernism. But it seems to me that he (like the Zondervan editors who insisted that we address this issue) gives this faddish movement far more credit than it deserves. We do not, in fact, live in postmodern times, as Feinberg asserts. Indeed, if he is correct in his contention that postmodernism is unlivable—and I think that he is—then there can be no postmodern society. Rather we live in post-Christian times, and what has replaced Christianity is not postmodernism but rather what has been aptly called "the new absolutism." Today the absolute values of openness and tolerance are cherished and even demanded. Nor do most people, including academics, think that there is no objective truth. No one uses a postmodernist hermeneutic when reading the label of a medicine bottle. Theologians tend to think that postmodern pluralism and relativism are all the rage, when in fact such thinking is largely confined to the literature, social sciences, and religious studies departments at universities. Anglo-American philosophy has in particular sturdily resisted the sirens of postmodernity. John Searle, an eminent philosopher at Berkeley, remarks that

> Those who want to use the universities, especially the humanities, for leftist political transformation correctly perceive that the Western Rationalistic Tradition is an obstacle in their path.
> ... Historically, part of what happened is that in the late 1960s and 1970s a number of young people went into academic life because they thought that the social and political transformation could be achieved through educational and cultural transformation, and that the political ideals of the 1960s could be achieved through education. In many disciplines, for example, analytic philosophy, they found the way blocked by a solid and self-confident professorial establishment committed to traditional intellectual values.

But in some disciplines, particularly those humanities disciplines concerned with literary studies—English, French, and Comparative Literature especially—the existing academic norms were fragile, and the way was opened intellectually for a new academic agenda.[15]

Unfortunately, theologians are largely ignorant of analytic philosophy and, groping in the fog of Continental thought, mistakenly believe that postmodernism has swept the field.

In a recent review of Sokal and Bricmont's exposé of the follies of French postmodernist thinkers entitled *Fashionable Nonsense*,[16] Thomas Nagel opines that the reason relativism has been embraced by many intellectuals of the left is that it gives them "an excuse for not answering the claims of their political opponents."[17] He writes:

Postmodernism's specifically academic appeal comes from its being another in the sequence of all-purpose "unmasking" strategies that offer a way to criticize the intellectual efforts of others, not by engaging with them on the ground, but by diagnosing them from a superior vantage point and charging them with inadequate self-awareness. Logical positivism and Marxism were used by academics in this way, and postmodernist relativism is a natural successor in the role. It may now be on the way out, but I suspect there will continue to be a market in the huge American academy for a quick fix of some kind.[18]

The problem with the postmodernist quick fix is not, as Feinberg suggests, that it is unlivable, but rather that it is so obviously self-referentially incoherent. That is to say, if it is true, then it is false. Thus, one need not say a word or raise an objection to refute it; it is quite literally self-refuting. As Nagel points out, "the denial of objective truth on the ground that all systems

---

[15]John R. Searle, "Rationality and Realism, What Is at Stake?" *Daedalus: Proceedings of the American Academy of Arts and Sciences* 122, no. 4 (1993): 70–71.

[16]Alan Sokal and Jean Bricmont, *Fashionable Nonsense: Postmodern Intellectuals' Abuse of Science* (New York: Picador, 1998). Sokal achieved fame in 1996 when the journal *Social Text* published as a serious study his farcical article "Transgressing the Boundaries: Toward a Transformative Hermeneutics of Quantum Gravity," a hoax consisting of pseudoscientific nonsense and postmodernist jargon. In Nagel's opinion their new book shows the French postmodernists discussed to be either charlatans, idiots, or a combination of the two.

[17]Thomas Nagel, "The Sleep of Reason," *The New Republic*, 12 Oct. 1998, 37.

[18]Ibid., 38.

of belief are determined by social forces is self-refuting if we take it seriously, since it appeals to a sociological or historical claim that would not establish the conclusion unless it were objectively correct."[19] If postmodernist claims are objectively true, then those claims are themselves the mere products of social forces and so are not objectively true. Of course, if postmodernist claims are not objectively true, then they are just the arbitrary opinions of certain people that we are free to ignore. Postmodernism is thus an attempt to cut the feet from under one's opponents without having to engage one's opponents' arguments, a strategy that is ultimately self-refuting.

It would therefore be terribly tragic if, out of deference to this incoherent, faddish, and widely repudiated movement, the church were to conclude mistakenly that we are now living in a postmodern era and that we therefore need a new postmodern apologetic for our time. Such a realignment would be not only unnecessary, but counterproductive, for the abandonment of objective standards of truth and rationality could only undermine the Christian faith in the long run by making its call to repentance and faith in Christ but one more voice in the cacaphony of subjectively satisfying but objectively vacuous religious interpretations of the world.

---

[19]Ibid., 36. Feinberg is concerned that postmodernists reject the criterion of consistency. But notice that the problem is not just inconsistency but self-refutation. In any case, what is to prevent the postmodernist from rejecting the criterion of livability?

AN EVIDENTIALIST'S RESPONSE

Gary R. Habermas

Paul Feinberg's approach could be considered as a sub-species in the camp of evidentialist methodology. Though he says little about the place of historical evidences and does not provide many details of how the evidences would work together, he does give some hints. We have some differences, but these are rarely substantial.

POSITIVE CONTRIBUTIONS OF CUMULATIVE CASE APOLOGETICS

Feinberg's chief goal is to formulate a complete, multifaceted case for Christian theism, drawn from a variety of evidences. Then he challenges Christianity's opponents to do likewise by presenting "a more convincing cumulative case" (p. 152).

I think Feinberg makes a good move here and one that has much in common with other mainline evidentialist approaches. When outlining some of the trends in typical evidentialist methodologies, one of the chief tendencies I mentioned was embracing an eclectic approach to apologetics. The writings of evidentialists advocate the use of several different sorts of positive arguments for the truth of Christianity, as well as various delivery techniques.[1] Feinberg develops this aspect in more detail.

---

[1] I also mentioned that this separates evidentialists from some, but not necessarily all, other apologists. I think there has been a fairly widespread openness to other approaches in recent apologetic writings as a whole. See my comments in the section "Some Tenets of an Evidentialist Methodology" in chap. 2, "Evidential Apologetics" (pp. 94–99).

Feinberg's treatment of seven tests for truth, representing both theoretical and pragmatic angles, is fairly standard. But it is still a helpful discussion for those developing a methodology. Feinberg rightly points out that these tests do not represent some sort of attempt to argue a contrived case for Christianity, since they are widely used by both believers and unbelievers alike.

Like other authors in this volume, Feinberg is another example of how evangelical apologists take seriously the work of the Holy Spirit. He develops several aspects, including the Holy Spirit's ministry to unbelievers.

Like evidentialism and classical apologetics, Feinberg speaks highly of several arguments for God's existence, including varieties of the cosmological argument. Other prongs of his cumulative argument include religious experience (including the thoughtful claim that religious experience is superior to the nonreligious response), the "incurably moral" (p. 163) nature of human beings, and special revelation, including fulfilled prophecy. The chief reason to believe that God has spoken to us is that this was Jesus' testimony, and God vindicated him by raising him from the dead.

Feinberg provides a strong answer to certain postmodernists in terms of their inability to live with the results of their own teachings, since they practice some "universally acknowledged" principles, "irrespective of what is said in theory" (p. 170). In particular, Feinberg argues that the postmodernists' behavior sometimes denies their own teachings in areas like their belief in good and evil, the truth of their own position, a reality that is independent of our interpretations, and employing a notion of historical truth.

On subjects like these, I embrace many of Feinberg's points. His emphasis on the force of constructing an entire case, rather than stand-alone arguments, is the hallmark of his approach and deserves special mention. It complements the evidentialist appreciation of other arguments but encourages a more integrative approach.

SOME CHALLENGES TO FEINBERG'S CUMULATIVE CASE APOLOGETICS

Before I briefly present a few areas where I think Feinberg's approach could be strengthened, I wish to begin with a perspectival note. I offer these thoughts even though I suspect that

Paul Feinberg is also an evidentialist. Thus, I am largely in agreement with him; however, we may disagree in some details. My critique, then, is a matter of degree, rather than a difference in kind.

The Use of Scripture

In chapter 2 I differentiated between two apologetic approaches to the use of Scripture. The tactic used by the majority of evangelical scholars is to establish by various means the general trustworthiness of the Bible, afterward moving from there to other tenets of Christian theism, like inspiration, on the basis of having a good textual foundation.[2] I cautioned that such must be done very carefully, since, to name just one important issue here, even having a book that is generally reliable does not automatically insure everything between its covers. For example, our best libraries are filled with "generally trustworthy" volumes with which believers do not hesitate to take specific issue here and there. When someone uses such a basis to ensure the truth of supernatural reports in these texts, the practice becomes even more critical, since claims involving divine activity are much more difficult to check out.[3]

In contrast, I described what I call the "minimal facts" apologetic method. The most decisive data that are used in a case for Christian theism should have at least two major characteristics. They should be strongly evidenced by a variety of factors at several levels, as well as being recognized as credible by a large majority of critical scholars who study that particular area. Of the two criteria, I said that the initial one, concerning having well-grounded data, is easily the most crucial.[4]

---

[2] By "general trustworthiness" here, I am referring to attempts that employ various arguments for the reliability of an entire volume without producing much specific evidence for the particular passages in question. As applied to the New Testament, this would be to argue that the text as a whole is trustworthy, then to move on to supernatural topics like inspiration, salvation, or the deity and resurrection of Jesus Christ. The conclusion is that each of these beliefs is true because of the umbrella affirmation that has already been given, without providing specific, evidenced treatments of the texts that teach each of these doctrines.

[3] We especially find this problem in various books that make religious claims. A couple of examples from ancient history are given below.

[4] For details, including some reasons for this last distinction, see "Different Uses of Evidence" in chap. 2, "Evidential Apologetics," pp. 99–100. I develop these criteria in several other places as well; see my *The Historical Jesus: Ancient Evidence*

Therefore, the minimal facts method does not begin with a belief in the inspiration of Scripture, no matter how well this may be established. In fact, this approach does not even require that Scripture have the quality of general trustworthiness. Rather, it argues from separate texts that have the characteristics mentioned above. But it should be very carefully noted that concepts like the trustworthiness and inspiration of Scripture are still crucially important in an overall case for Christian theism, or in order to address certain issues that may arise in defending the faith. They are simply not required in order to establish the central tenets of the Christian position, since, as an apologetic *methodology*, this would hamper their effectiveness in presenting the best-evidenced case we can to those who don't recognize such foundations.[5]

How do these distinctions affect Feinberg's use of Scripture? He takes the first path just described. In his discussion of the subject, he states that the Bible is authoritative, based on more than one avenue: "This is drawn from what the Bible has to say about itself, as well as from external evidences that support that claim." An important consideration here is Jesus' testimony to Scripture. From this he moves on to Jesus' claims to be deity, made in texts like John 8:58–59 and 10:30–33. These claims are "authenticated by [Jesus'] resurrection from the dead" (p. 165).[6]

This general approach is an example of the sort of problems I pointed out. I still think this sort of case can be developed if we are exceptionally careful. However, Feinberg's hints indicate that some of these difficulties are not being avoided. For example, a generally trustworthy text does not guarantee the truth of all its details, especially when these are supernatural claims. So when an otherwise trustworthy book declares that it is inspired, scholars must be cautious. How do we know that the writer's theology

for the Life of Christ (Joplin, Mo.: College Press, 1996), 158–67; Gary R. Habermas and J. P. Moreland, *Beyond Death: Exploring the Evidence for Immortality* (Wheaton, Ill.: Crossway Books, 1998), 133–36.

[5]Still, I think we should tell those to whom we are making our case that we think there are good reasons to accept both the trustworthiness and the inspiration of Scripture, even though we are not using either in our discussion with them.

[6]It is unclear to me from Feinberg's wording here whether he is only arguing for trustworthiness at this point, moving on to the deity of Christ, or if, in between these two, he has inserted the inspiration of Scripture as well. In any case, his initial basis is the reliability (and inspiration?) of the text, hence the issues I am raising here.

wasn't added to a historical core? This is not a minor point, either. If we don't employ these distinctions, we will have some severe problems with non-Christian religious claims. Since evangelicals would agree with regard to the nonbiblical sources, mustn't we be careful about using the same methods?

Consider two examples from just a decade or so after the completion of the New Testament. Roman historian Tacitus has been called the "greatest historian" of ancient Rome, who "never consciously sacrifices historical truth," yet he made many allowances for Fate, the actions of the gods, and the divinity of some of the Caesars.[7] While another Roman, Suetonius, is described as a "trustworthy" historian, he was well known for his interplay of various omens, along with imparting other religious beliefs, including the divinizing of five of the first dozen Caesars.[8]

So even if the critic grants some general trustworthiness of the New Testament text (which few allow), do all supernatural claims to inspiration follow? Will the critic admit that, because the texts claim that Jesus taught its inspiration, that he therefore must have done so? Or might they say that the teachings were placed on his lips at some later time? So in spite of general reliability, they may argue that we don't have a sufficient basis for specific claims like Jesus' exact teachings on this subject. But then, Christians would argue similarly concerning the non-Christian sources.

Regarding the deity of Christ, what about Feinberg's argument using John 8:58–59 and 10:30–33? Does a generally reliable Bible establish the truth of such remarkable claims? Then how would believers answer Suetonius's assertions concerning the five deified Caesars or his records of supernatural events like the divine apotheosis of Julius Caesar, various prophecies, and so on?[9] Further, critics will point out that John is the latest gospel and the one with the most theological development. Of course

---

[7]For several instances, see Tacitus's *Annals* 1:11, 19, 28, 42, 55; 12:43. For the compliments on Tacitus's abilities, see Moses Hadas in his introduction to *The Complete Works of Tacitus*, trans. A. F. Church and W. J. Brodribb (New York: Random House, 1942), ix, xiv, xvii–xviii.

[8]The five deified Caesars were Julius Caesar, Augustus, Claudius, Vespasian, and Titus. For some of the supernatural reports surrounding the Roman emperors, see Gaius Suetonius Tranquillas, *The Twelve Caesars*, trans. and introduced by Robert Graves (Baltimore: Penguin Books, 1957), Tiberius, 74–75; Gaius Caligula, 57; Titus, 10; Domitian, 23. For Graves' compliment about Suetonius's reliability, see the foreword, p. 7. Other details of supernatural claims among the Romans are provided below.

[9]Suetonius, *Twelve Caesars*, Julius Caesar, 88; Augustus, 100; Claudius, 45–46; Gaius Caligula, 57, 59; Nero, 56; Vespasian, 4, 25.

there are good responses, but the battle for reliability at this point will be a long one.

Moreover, there are other texts in the New Testament that more clearly assert Jesus' deity and are also better evidenced than these in John. So why shouldn't we use our best data when arguing such central tenets of theological importance?

Concerning the resurrection, Feinberg has an even tougher task. In the same context he says, "It is in the Bible that we learn of Jesus Christ's resurrection and have the primary evidence for it" (p. 165). Of course he is right that the Bible is the chief source for this event. But on what grounds? Feinberg seems to be continuing the same sort of process—a trustworthy Scripture is the basis for gaining evidence for the resurrection. But won't critics argue that, since general reliability doesn't guarantee all the specific contents, this is simply far too insufficient a basis on which to establish the most fantastic event in history? Would believers allow a similar move in Tacitus or Suetonius, from their trustworthiness to even the less spectacular supernatural items they mention?[10] It would appear that we are in a bind here.

Then how do we dispute the supernatural claims by these Roman historians? I would suggest, again, that we should not do so by arguing from generally trustworthy texts, for there are too many ambiguities. But by constructing a minimal argument, as outlined above, we can differentiate between the New Testament data and that of the Roman histories. There is a much stronger case for Jesus' resurrection, including abundant and varied evidences that are not built on general trustworthiness.[11]

---

[10]One might suggest challenging Suetonius or Tacitus by discussing other issues, such as the time between their writing and the events they describe, or raising the question of whether they present eyewitness testimony, but the answers might be surprising. Both Roman historians were closer to many of the occurrences we just listed above than John was to Jesus' time. Tacitus consulted good sources, such as biographies, memoirs, and official Roman records, since he held administrative posts in the Roman government (Hadas, *Complete Works of Tacitus*, x, xviii), including being personally promoted by three of the Caesars I have mentioned (*Histories* 1:1). Suetonius served as chief secretary to Emperor Hadrian and had access to the official imperial and senatorial records. Further, he got much of his data on some of the Caesars directly from eyewitnesses (Graves, *Twelve Caesars*, 7). On many occasions, Suetonius makes it clear that he checked other sources as well (Julius Caesar, 87; Tiberius, 73; Gaius Caligula, 58; Galba, 21; Otho, 10).

[11]I gave a brief outline of such an approach in chap. 2. For those interested in additional details, this is also my approach in each of my nine books and other publications specifically on the resurrection.

Yet no specific information favors the supernatural accounts found in the Roman texts. Thus, there is really no comparison when we look at the individual cases, since we have no direct evidence for the latter reports. But by following the traditional approach, it would be much more difficult to critique the Roman reports, due to their general historicity.

I don't want to be misunderstood here. I am not saying that an argument for the trustworthiness of Scripture is illegitimate or useless. It could even be very helpful in certain places. And there are answers to each of the critical objections to the New Testament texts. I simply wonder why we shouldn't put our best foot forward especially on subjects of central concern to believers. That's the strength of the minimal facts argument. If we use only the best-evidenced passages, especially for the deity and resurrection of Jesus, we will have stronger arguments directly at these crucial points, plus we will encourage far more critical agreement. To me, this is preferable to the traditional approach, and that is why I use it. After all, our chief concern in this volume is apologetic methodology. Besides, there are points here where the traditional method even breaks down and fails to do the job, as I've tried to show.

Postmodernism and Other Issues

There are no other substantial issues on which Paul Feinberg and I differ. If I am correct that his method is essentially evidentialist, this is not surprising. Here I will briefly mention a few caveats that I would offer concerning his approach. Again, these come from the perspective of a fellow evidentialist.

Feinberg presented a notable critique of certain types of postmodernism,[12] concentrating on the livability of these positions. He recognizes some of the difficulties in criticizing these stances, but I think he gives up too easily on harder philosophical critiques, like those involving truth claims. Feinberg thinks that, since there is very little logical or factual common ground

---

[12]Incidentally, I do not concur that modernity since the Enlightenment always denies supernaturalism (p. 168), as indicated by an entire host of arguments for beliefs like the existence of God, objective morality, miracles, and an afterlife, which are regularly found in the relevant literature. Besides, postmodernists regularly consider Christians to be a part of modernity precisely because they profess to believe in truth and falsehood, right and wrong, and regularly apply logical and empirical standards even to their thinking about religious beliefs.

by which to judge many postmodernists, we must resort to other critiques such as their not being able to live with their position. But the instances he provides do far more than point out that Mark Taylor cannot live with his position.

For examples, Taylor's notion of "insight" takes on the sense of a norm; he holds that his view is correct; he thinks that historical figures of the past like Hegel and Nietzsche were actual persons who wrote books; and he believes that he adequately understands and interprets their views (pp. 171–72). Further, postmodernists go to the doctor when they are ill—trusting the physician's "modernist" medical training, following their "objective" testings and diagnoses, and exerting faith in the research-derived medication. All of this belies their belief in transperspectival facts. So it reaches far beyond the failure to *live* with truth; Taylor and others show, to the contrary, that they accept truth at every turn. Therefore, they also fail additional tests for truth like logical consistency, correspondence, and comprehensiveness.

That some postmodernists claim to reject logic and other truth has less force than they might wish. Just because a boxer denies that his opponent has a right cross, it doesn't follow that the punch doesn't exist! This is precisely the best time to use it!

Another matter is Feinberg's thought that, "Whenever some belief does not correspond to our understanding of reality . . . it will usually not attract many followers." His example is the belief that "sickness and death are not real, but illusions" (p. 154). But what about the several hundred million Hindus in the world? Or what about the current popularity of Mormonism in spite of Joseph Smith's "translation" of the Book of Abraham being shown to be totally inaccurate?[13] The lesson here is the influence that our own presuppositions have, frequently even outweighing what the data dictate.[14]

---

[13]The Book of Abraham is part of one of the Mormon scriptures, *The Pearl of Great Price*. It is true that comparatively few Mormons seem to have heard these details, but very few of those who know them abandon their faith after hearing the results of the research. For an overview of the problem, see Harry L. Ropp, *The Mormon Papers: Are the Mormon Scriptures Reliable?* (Downers Grove, Ill.: InterVarsity Press, 1979), chap. 5.

[14]While Feinberg recognizes that there will always be "some" faithful followers who continue to believe anyway (p. 154), I still don't think this quite does enough justice to the *majority* who don't switch even after knowing the problematic particulars, as with those who still cling to Hinduism's beliefs in the illusory nature of sickness and death. Once again, this points to the weight of our preconceptions.

The emphasis that Feinberg and others in this volume place on the role of the Holy Spirit is overdue, especially from evidentialists.[15] I did wonder about his comment that "the tenacity and stubbornness" of the Christian's belief is an example of the Spirit's internal witness (p. 160). While I agree that something like this is happening, I immediately wondered about parallels in other systems, like the claims in the Book of Mormon that the Holy Spirit will provide an internal assurance of the truth of Mormonism[16] and that anyone can try what is called "the experiment" by tasting Mormon claims and realizing that they are true.[17] I wonder about the Mormon "tenacity and stubbornness" and how Feinberg would respond when challenged by non-Christians who claim to have the same experience. Personally, I doubt that we can fully answer these sorts of rival claims without referring to more objective indications.[18]

Regarding Feinberg's response to the leaky buckets objection, I do not think that his two responses are the best ones we can make. I think the stronger response is that this is simply the nature of all inductive research, including the sciences. But although there could be a hole in the research, this is not necessarily the case. We must evaluate whether there is a problem and how it may be patched up. But this objection potentially plagues any inductive study, so the knife cuts both ways—it could refer to naturalism as easily as theism. This is precisely why we must investigate arguments to determine which ones don't have any holes that are large enough to spoil the project.

A last area of minor disagreement concerns Feinberg's assertion that "none of the elements that constitute this case has any priority over any other," meaning that "one may start with

[15]For other examples from evidentialists, see Bernard Ramm, *The Witness of the Spirit* (Grand Rapids: Eerdmans, 1959); Gary R. Habermas, "The Personal Testimony of the Holy Spirit to the Believer and Christian Apologetics," *Journal of Christian Apologetics* 1, no. 1 (Summer 1997): 49–64; Bill Craig's main essay (chap. 1) in this volume.

[16]Moroni 10:1–5.

[17]Alma 32:25–43; 34:4–5. I know of a Mormon who, after hearing the details about the problem with the Book of Abraham, admitted no known answer that could vindicate Joseph Smith but concluded that Mormonism is still true anyway because she had tried it and therefore knew unequivocally that it is so. The text in Moroni was her defense.

[18]For a discussion of rival claims in the context of how the witness of the Holy Spirit is indispensable for apologetics, see Habermas, "Personal Testimony of the Holy Spirit to the Believer," 59–61.

any element of the case" (pp. 151–52). Initially, we need some clarification here. I am not sure what kind of priority he means— ontological, epistemological, existential, or some other sort. I have said that most evidentialists are eclectic, and I think there are many potential arguments that could be used, but I also think there is some priority between them. We must adapt our methodology on a case-by-case basis. But the trademark of evidentialism is historical argumentation, because it is often considered to be both the strongest, as well as the most versatile data. Plus, it often deals directly with the Gospel.

SUMMARY AND CONCLUSION

I appreciate the general direction and details of Paul Feinberg's approach. My only major problem is the issue of how to use Scripture in our apologetic, especially for those who don't allow either the trustworthiness or inspiration of the text. The minimal facts approach has several advantages that the traditional approach does not. Further, the latter can even keep us from being able to answer some tough questions.

Unfortunately, due I'm sure to space requirements, Feinberg doesn't really develop any detailed arguments for Christianity. I would also be interested to observe how his suggestions would be worked out into a detailed apologetic system. He differentiates his approach from the best-known forms of inductive argument, but his argument is certainly still inductive.[19] Thus, the sense in which it is a separate apologetic approach is diminished. I have called his cumulative case a species of evidential argument, and I think his comments support such an identification.

---

[19]I think his discussion of induction, including how the cumulative case approach differs from other examples of induction (pp. 151–52), is somewhat confusing. It is difficult to see exactly how this separates Feinberg's system from other methods.

A PRESUPPOSITIONALIST'S RESPONSE

John M. Frame

Paul Feinberg begins his paper by defining a demonstrably sound argument as one that is both valid and sound and is also "coercive in the sense that anyone who wants to retain rationality must accept the argument" (p. 148). He then analyzes the traditional ontological, cosmological, and teleological arguments for the existence of God to show that they are not demonstrably sound in this sense. In this discussion, however, his definition of demonstrable soundness changes somewhat. He says that the problem with the ontological argument, for example, is that it "has a premise that the nontheist will not accept as true" (p. 148). But on the original definition, that should not be a barrier to saying the ontological argument is demonstrably sound. I take it that the *must* in the original definition expresses normativity: human beings have an *obligation* to accept demonstrably sound arguments.[1] But the fact that nontheists will not accept a premise in the ontological argument does not prove that they do not have an *obligation* to accept it. So Feinberg's examples, in my view, fail to prove that the traditional theistic arguments are not demonstrably sound on his definition.

Actually, I like Feinberg's original definition of demonstrative soundness. I hoped that it would move him to discuss the

---

[1]The only other interpretation of the *must* is that people are somehow forced, against their will if need be, to accept such arguments if they want to be rational. But it would be hard to show that any argument is coercive in this sense if indeed there are any such arguments.

whole question of epistemic norms: When does a person have an obligation to believe something? But like our other colleagues in this volume, Feinberg ignores the question. After the first paragraph, he drops his potentially fruitful definition and discusses apologetics in more traditional terms.

But let us overcome this initial disappointment and follow Feinberg's discussion further. The fact that nontheists usually reject premises of the traditional proofs is a genuine problem, one with which apologists must wrestle. Feinberg's proposal is that instead of trying to demonstrate the truth of Christianity or trying to show it highly probable, we should, in Feinberg's view, produce a "cumulative case" for Christianity, like a legal brief, an "inference to the best explanation."

Whatever we may think of the cumulative case approach, it should be obvious that it does not solve the specific problem Feinberg mentions with the traditional approaches. The problem is that nontheists fail to grant some premises of the theistic arguments. Certainly nontheists question the premises of cumulative case arguments as well. An atheist would be very likely to deny Feinberg's claim that prophets in Scripture foretold the future centuries in advance. And I rather think that many postmodernists would not be persuaded of Feinberg's assertion that their position is not livable. They are actually living with it, are they not? Perhaps they are being inconsistent; but might they not ask whether the demand for consistency is itself an oppressive metanarrative by which Western male linear thinkers impose their rigid systems on women and minorities?

The cumulative case approach actually worsens the problem Feinberg has noted in the other approaches. For on Feinberg's complex approach, there are many more arguments and therefore many more premises[2] to which nontheists can object.

So, in my view, Feinberg has not presented very well the need for a cumulative case approach. Nor do I think this approach is as different from classicalism and evidentialism as

---

[2]Feinberg may object to my putting it this way, because he says that in the cumulative case approach "there are neither premises nor derivations" (p. 151). But clearly there are. His case includes, for example, the traditional theistic arguments, posed in such a way as to challenge the atheist to produce better explanations for the cosmos and for data within the cosmos. But these arguments are traditional arguments with premises and conclusions. At least they claim some level of probability; if they did not, it would make little sense to ask the atheist to produce a better explanation. The atheist may well question that claim by questioning the premises.

Feinberg would have us believe. He says that the cumulative case approach "does not take the form of a proof or argument for probability in any strict sense of these words" (p. 151). I think I understand why he says the cumulative case approach is not a "proof." But why should we not think of it as an argument from probability? Certainly, if Feinberg is right, the arguments of the cumulative case come together to reinforce one another, and they outweigh rival hypotheses. But then the reinforcement and the refutation of alternative explanations certainly ought to render the theistic conclusion more probable than it would be without those arguments. If the argument does not at least render the theistic conclusion more probable than its alternatives, then what use is it? If in the end theism and atheism are rendered as equally probable, or theism as less probable than atheism, the only way we can adopt the theistic hypothesis is *fideistically*.

Nevertheless, I think the cumulative case approach does have much to recommend it. I like Feinberg's emphasis that "this approach understands Christian theism, other theistic religions, and atheism as systems of belief" (p. 151), requiring us to investigate them from a number of perspectives, looking at different kinds of evidence. Certainly it is better, when we have the time and the inquirer's attention, to present a system of mutually reinforcing arguments, rather than arguments of just one type. And looking at worldviews as systems helps us to see how one doctrine is linked to others, how the elements of a worldview often stand or fall together. I wish that Feinberg had recognized that these systems differ also in that they have different views of the place of reason and the way it should operate. But, as with his definition of demonstrative soundness, Feinberg avoids the important issue of epistemic normativity and goes on to other things.

Presuppositionalism may be understood as a cumulative case approach that recognizes the problem of epistemic normativity. It sees, as other schools of apologetics do not, that the issue between theists and nontheists is not merely about certain facts or arguments, but also about the way they look at all facts and arguments. If, however, the issue of epistemic normativity can be resolved, then the cumulative case argument will be demonstrably sound, for it will show that nontheists are utterly unable to make any case against theism. The theistic arguments will prevail by default, and their conclusion will be certain, because it will be shown to be the very foundation of certainty.

Feinberg suggests seven tests of truth that should be applied within a cumulative case argument. Significantly, the most important test of truth within a Christian worldview, *scripturality*, is omitted, although Feinberg does sometimes mention Scripture among the data of which the debate must take account. He omits this test doubtless because he doesn't want to be perceived as arguing in a circle. But circularity of a sort can be defended. As I have maintained elsewhere in this volume, argument is always circular when it is an argument for an ultimate criterion of truth. If I am right, then we lose a great deal when we omit scripturality from a list of tests for truth. God does not intend us to gain truth neutrally, but to interpret it in the light of his Word. Without that light, our sinful tendency is to repress the truth in unrighteousness (Rom. 1:18).

I am certainly not opposed to Feinberg's other tests. They too play important roles in apologetic argument and in all human knowledge. Scripturality is the major test, but consistency, correspondence, and the others can be helpful when governed by biblical presuppositions. Without those presuppositions, however, they need direction. Feinberg mentions the apparent conflict between Paul and James, which certainly shows that questions about whether two propositions are contradictory are not always easy to resolve. Christians know there is no contradiction here, because they believe that Scripture is always consistent with itself. Of course we can also defend our view by suggesting interpretations of Paul and James that are consistent with each other. But not all believers in biblical inerrancy agree as to *how* this apparent contradiction is to be resolved. And just as one Christian may take issue with another's attempt to reconcile these passages, a non-Christian may very well take issue with all these attempts. Then, not presupposing the authority and consistency of Scripture, the non-Christian will find in the inadequacy of these reconciliations evidence that Scripture contradicts itself. So the test of consistency is itself problematic, and the standards for the proper use of logical arguments are religiously problematic. Logic is not neutral. It can be used to glorify God or to resist him.

Even more obviously, Feinberg's other tests are also religiously problematic. (If any test is neutral, it would have to be the test of logical consistency; but we have seen that logical consistency is not neutral.) Christians and non-Christians simply do not agree on what constitutes empirical correspondence, comprehensiveness, simplicity, and the rest. Feinberg is right: Christian theism and nontheism are *systems;* and, contra Feinberg, these systems include their own distinctive tests of truth.

Feinberg's sketch of an actual argument for Christianity seems to me to be fine as far as it goes. I think it rather odd to refer to external evidences as a form of the Holy Spirit's witness. This is not a common theological way of putting it, and I doubt that Scripture ever refers to evidences in that way. But certainly the Spirit, who with the Father and Son made all things (Gen. 1:2; Pss. 33:6;[3] 104:30) is witnessing to us throughout his creation.

But if Feinberg is to deal with nontheists who are epistemologically self-conscious, he will need to consider the issue of presuppositions. Indeed we do need to compare the Christian case with the non-Christian's countercases. But we cannot do that adequately or persuasively unless we recognize that the non-Christian may be using logic, empirical data, comprehensiveness, and so on rather differently from the way we do.

After this sample argument, Feinberg deals with a couple of objections to his approach. He faces first the "ten leaky buckets" objection to this procedure, namely, that ten inadequate arguments cannot generate a sure conclusion. I confess I don't understand his reply on the level of the metaphor. He seems to be saying that we can compensate for the leaks by embedding the ten buckets inside one another, so that one bucket that leaks through the bottom will be protected by another that leaks only four inches above the bottom, and so on. I am not an expert in hydraulics, but it seems to me that if the buckets are full, this embedding will only slow down or reduce the leakage, not stop it entirely.[4]

Beyond the metaphor, what Feinberg seems to be saying here is that each defect in each argument is remedied by another argument. That strategy won't work for the defect Feinberg found in the cosmological argument. For that defect is not a lack of soundness, but simply that nontheists might deny its premises. How could that problem be remedied by another argument? The only argument that could remedy that particular problem would be an argument that would force the atheist

[3]"Breath" in this verse is the Hebrew *ruach,* Spirit.

[4]I observe here, for no particular purpose except verbal irony, that Van Til wrestles with a "full bucket difficulty," while Feinberg must face the difficulty of empty buckets. See my book *Cornelius Van Til: An Analysis of His Thought* (Phillipsburg, N.J.: Presbyterian and Reformed, 1995), 155–56.

to accept these premises, and of course such an argument is inconceivable.

I won't quibble further. Certainly Feinberg is right to say that an argument for God's actual existence can remedy some of the implausibilities of a report of religious experience, and this procedure of reinforcement can certainly help in other cases. My real concern here, to risk being overly repetitious, is that without a clearly developed Christian epistemology, the whole cumulative case will contain a general implausibility that cannot be remedied.

As for the objection of postmodernism against the whole apologetic enterprise: I don't object to asking the postmodernist, as Feinberg does, whether he can live with the incongruities of his approach. My problem is that the postmodernist will, I fear, answer that question in the affirmative. Yes, he can live with it, and he is living with it! People don't have to have a logically consistent intellectual system to live their lives day by day. Many are content to live with contradictions. Why shouldn't the postmodernist do the same? Because he ought not to be content with contradictions? But to say that is to bring up the question of epistemic normativity, which Feinberg prefers to avoid, and which in my view can only be answered by presuppositionalism.

One might try the approach I suggested in my paper, simply to say that those who deny objective truth in general must extend that denial to their own assertions. And if postmodernism is not objectively true, then the postmodernist has nothing to argue for against other positions. That means that the argument is over before it begins. But to approach postmodernism this way is to argue normative epistemology. One who denies the objectivity of truth has violated *rules* of thought that exist at the outset of any discussion.

Thus, the chief problem in Feinberg's paper is that he does not consider the question as to the rules of the rational game and the further question of whether these rules are religiously neutral. In apologetic methodology most everything hinges on those questions.

A REFORMED
EPISTEMOLOGIST'S RESPONSE

Kelly James Clark

Paul Feinberg makes his case for the existence of God cumulatively. That is, he takes as evidence the existence and design of the universe as well as religious experience and contends that God is the best explanation of this evidence. He makes a similar "inference to best explanation" in his cumulative case for Christian belief. I have myself defended cumulative case arguments; indeed, I believe that more often than not we have to come to a considered judgment about some issue with less than adequate or compelling evidence. Nonetheless, we can, like a jury in a criminal trial, make our best judgment of all of the available evidence. Unlike juries, however, Feinberg thinks that there is only one reasonable conclusion that a person can come to given the evidence. Here is where we depart in our judgments of the success of cumulative case arguments. Since I have already made similar points in my other critiques, I will be briefer in my response to Feinberg.

JUST WHAT IS A CUMULATIVE CASE?

Feinberg's characterization of a cumulative case argument is puzzling. He contrasts it with demonstratively strong arguments, which are sound arguments that employ premises that are agreed to be true by the disputants or can be demonstrated to be true. Feinberg rejects demonstratively strong arguments because, at least concerning arguments for the existence of God, nontheists will refuse (reasonably?) to accept one of the crucial premises. A cumulative case, in contrast to a demonstratively strong argument, "relax[es] the standard" (p. 150). But Feinberg leaves it unclear which standard is relaxed: soundness or demonstrativeness. The only thing that seems to be relaxed is the requirement that the premises be mutually agreed to be true or demonstrable (to nontheists). If this is what Feinberg means when he speaks of relaxing the standard, a "proof" need not be cumulative, for it is possible to construct a deductive argument for the existence of God with premises that nontheists are unlikely to accept. Indeed, I shall argue that cumulative arguments fall prey to exactly the same problems as Feinberg alleges of deductive arguments.

Feinberg seems to take the failure of deductive proofs—that nontheists will reject the crucial premise—as a serious defect; but of what? They cause, he says, the argument to fail; again, to fail at what? It is an apologetic defect, surely, if the goal of apologetics is to persuade someone to believe something that he or she did not initially believe. Feinberg seems to think that the failure of a compelling argument is likewise a defect in the *believer's* rationality. The failure of a compelling argument entails, according to Feinberg, that only two options are left: fideism or a cumulative case. But why should the nonbeliever's unwillingness to accept a true or reasonably held premise have any effect whatsoever on the believer's rationality? Why should the nonbeliever's ignorance make any difference at all to the believer's knowledge? Suppose the believer sees that certain premises are true (perhaps guided by the Holy Spirit) and the nontheist cannot see they are true; if these premises either deductively or probabilistically entail that God exists, then the believer is rational in his or her belief in God. When it comes to assessments of rationality, the nonbeliever be damned (not literally, of course).

Feinberg further elucidates the cumulative case approach—it is the *"inference to the best explanation"* (p. 151). But there are infinitely many logically possible explanations, so it is difficult to ensure that one has *the* best explanation. So, he clarifies that such an explanation might make better sense of the evidence than its alternatives. This reduces to inference to *the best explanation that we (as finite human beings) have come up with to this point*. A cumulative case is more like the kind of reasoning done not by philosophers but by juries (Feinberg says the model is law [p. 151], but I think it better fits our understanding of cumulative cases if we imagine a jury examining various, apparently disparate pieces of evidence to determine if they point toward a single suspect). Cumulative cases involve judgments of the "plausibility of theories" (p. 152). And, finally, cumulative cases must (1) explain a variety of otherwise unexplained data, and (2) the arguments involved must mutually reinforce one another. Aside from the leaky-bucket analogy, Feinberg does little to show how mutual reinforcement works with arguments for Christianity.

What are cumulative case arguments supposed to do? One view of apologetics is that it is supposed to persuade. Another view of apologetics is that it is to show that theistic or Christian beliefs are or can be rational. Which view is Feinberg defending here? If the former, then he falls prey to his own criticism of the demonstratively sound argument—nontheists will reject crucial premises. If the latter, then his position is probably not much different from mine. However, the manner in which Feinberg proceeds suggests that he is offering a case for Christianity that the nontheist could reject only on pain of irrationality. That is, Feinberg seems to take himself to be making a cumulative case for Christianity that is rationally compelling to theist and nontheist alike. Let us turn to Feinberg's cumulative case and see if Christianity is *the* best explanation of all the available evidence.

TESTS FOR TRUTH

Before proceeding to his cumulative case, Feinberg pauses to consider tests for truth. He claims that consistency is undoubtedly the most important test (pp. 153–54). One wonders, however, why correspondence is not the most important test. If our belief corresponds to reality, then isn't it true? All we really require, if correspondence is a test, is the test of correspondence. I don't think correspondence is or could be a *test* of truth, so I don't think that thinking of it as a test of truth is a very fruitful avenue of pursuit. But I'm not sure that any of Feinberg's other tests for truth are very fruitful either. Surely we could construct a system of beliefs that is consistent, comprehensive, simple, livable, fruitful, and conservative but which is, nonetheless, not true. I believe that idealism, the claim that matter is not real, could pass all of these tests, but I don't think it is true. Aristotelian physics passed all of the above tests (for thousands of years, although not everyone realized that his or her physics was

Aristotelian), but it is not true. I could continue, but I will simply make my logical point: Many significant and fundamental, but mutually incompatible, belief systems could pass the above tests, but they can't all be true.

THE CUMULATIVE CASE

I will consider only two of Feinberg's arguments involving the external witness of the Holy Spirit. He understands the external witness of the Holy Spirit first along the lines of the cosmological argument. The onus, Feinberg suggests, is on the atheist to provide an alternative explanation (to theism) of the existence of the world. He writes, "And, if it is argued that the universe's existence and nature cannot be explained, the atheist must face the other elements of the theist's case" (pp. 160–61). (I take it that Feinberg means "argued *successfully*.") But has Feinberg shown that theism is a better or more plausible explanation than nontheism? If so, it is not contained in these pages. Can nontheists account for the existence and nature of our universe on the basis of matter plus energy (or simply energy) and time? Again, if so, Feinberg has not done so. William Craig has offered a powerful but difficult argument suggesting that they cannot. But Craig's argument is deductive, not inference to best explanation. It is not clear, nor has Feinberg attempted to make it clear, that conceiving of the argument as inference to best explanation is at all necessary (nor does it seem necessary to invoke the witness of the Holy Spirit—surely reason alone could make this point).

Suppose we can argue successfully for a nonmaterialistic (or energistic) First Cause. Have we drawn close yet to the God of Abraham, Isaac, and Jacob? Closer than we might have been before, but not too close. Perhaps we need to move along, as Feinberg does, to the second argument, drawn this time from religious experience. The thoughtful and tolerant atheist will not deny that the theist has had a unique and powerful experience. She will deny, of course, that the theist had an experience *of God*. And why not, since she doesn't believe that divine beings exist?

Feinberg's defense of religious experience cuts deeply into his own argument. For the atheist to deny that such experiences are veridical, Feinberg notes, is to hold that across cultures, geography, and time, a multitude of individuals have been wrong about the most fundamental of human concerns (p. 161). He finds this amazing (and perhaps arrogant) and seems to take this as an argument that they ought to take such experiences as veridical. What Feinberg says is, strictly speaking, correct: If just one of those people is telling the truth, then there is a God. But this logical point is scarcely at issue; the question is what is reasonable for the nontheist to believe.[1]

Feinberg's defense of his claim that testimony of religious experience is rationally compelling (even to the nontheist) is doubly defective. First, it does not alleviate the problem of competing claims to divine reality based on religious experience. Would he claim that Buddhists, Shintoists, Taoists, and Hindus are all correct? Should we accept their claims simply on the basis of their sincere testimony? All it takes is one. Feinberg contends that his criteria of truth can adjudicate conflicting truth claims of just this sort. Unfortunately, he never makes his case in favor of Christianity over any other religion. Indeed, I suspect it would be difficult (here I speak with great understatement) to argue (with care) that Christianity is more consistent, comprehensive, livable, and so on than every other religion. All we have to go on is Feinberg's assertion that Christianity passes these tests and that other worldviews fail. He hasn't, however, given us a single reason to favor Christianity over, say, Islam.

PLAUSIBILITY

Judgments about the veracity of religious experience are always made against the background of one's other beliefs. I routinely judge reports of flying swamis or of a two-hundred-foot-tall Jesus endorsing one's fund-raising projects as deception or illusion. Likewise, I paid no heed to Joseph Smith's or David Koresh's claims to divine revelation. Perhaps I should have, but, given my beliefs, such claims seem (to me) ludicrous and are rejected at the outset. The situation that Feinberg describes of accepting reports of religious experience is not at all like accepting the belief that Deerfield is a city. Since most of us readily admit of city kinds of things, the testimony that one of them is named "Deerfield" won't seem odd. We are prepared to accept that Deerfield is a city because we have a rich background of city-beliefs against which to judge it. Likewise, it does not

---

[1]I am not claiming that truth is not important. Feinberg is discussing belief change based on testimonial evidence. The question, therefore, is this: Is testimonial evidence or religious experience sufficient to make belief in God rational for an unbeliever?

require the admission of any radically new sorts of things to our catalogue of things, nor does it require any substantial belief revision. Accepting the belief that Deerfield is a city, therefore, requires very little by way of evidence for most people.[2]

However, the nontheist is not in a similar position when it comes to accepting reports of religious experience as veridical. Not believing in gods, she is not inclined to accept such reports without, I suspect, a great deal of corroborating evidence (or personal experience). For her, acquiring a new belief about a city is quite unlike acquiring a new belief about the gods. For in the former case, she admits no new kinds of entities to her belief system; but in the latter case, concerning belief in a deity, she would be required to undergo a radical addition to and revision of the kinds of entities she is willing to countenance. A better analogy than cities would be an unbeliever in ghosts being required, on the basis of testimony alone, to change his belief in ghosts. Surely it won't do to say that if just one of those reporters is making a true claim, then there are ghosts. The change of beliefs in ghosts and gods does not have a ghost of a chance given certain background beliefs.

The second consideration Feinberg brings to bear on acceptance of the veracity of religious experience is the positive moral transformation of the persons involved. One can scarcely doubt that encounters with Jesus (veridical or illusory) can have a dramatic effect on a person's character. But the jury is out on whether Christianity, and it alone, is superior to all other belief systems regarding moral transformation. One of my former students contends that the net effect of Christian belief on the world has been in favor of evil, and given Christianity's involvement in, endorsement of, or silence concerning a tremendous variety and quantities of evils, one wonders if he might be right. But suppose that Christianity has resulted in a net gain of the good; is that grounds for accepting its claims to revelation as true? Even Feinberg must admit that it does not constitute *sufficient* grounds for a religion's claims to be true, for then he would have to admit that religions that are equally effective at moral transformation are likewise true (or, worse, if some religion were better at moral transformation, then it would be a better candidate

---

[2]Accepting city names is not always simply a matter of testimony. When someone is first told that there are cities named "Intercourse" and "Paradise," one usually demands some proof and even more so when one is told that they were given these names by the Amish.

for the truth). Since various religions make competing truth claims, not all religions can be true. Again, unless Feinberg can prove that Christianity is better on all the other counts, he has given us no reason to prefer Christian belief to any other belief.[3]

Feinberg's appeal to Abe Lincoln won't do either. Again, plausibility judgments are made against the background of one's beliefs. Plausibility, therefore, is in the mind of the beholder. The nontheist will not likely reject the sincere report that Abraham Lincoln changed a person's life, because she already believes in Honest Abe. But surely she will reject, not believing in gods, the sincere report that God changed a person's life. Believing that Lincoln changed a person's life adds no radically new categories of being to the nontheist's ontology; adding belief in God does.

If the nontheist has not made it this far down the road, I think it unlikely that she will make it all the way to Christian belief based on Feinberg's cumulative argument.

CONCLUSION

Feinberg's cumulative case fails at persuasion. Feinberg fails because he does not recognize that what seems plausible to him can reasonably seem implausible to someone else. If this is a failure of deductive theistic arguments that they are not demonstrative, then it is likewise a failure of Feinberg's cumulative case argument that it is not demonstrative.

---

[3]The problem runs still deeper, for surely many people have undergone significant moral transformation for nontheistic and nonreligious reasons.

Chapter Four

PRESUPPOSITIONAL APOLOGETICS

John M. Frame

PRESUPPOSITIONAL APOLOGETICS

John M. Frame

In apologetics, as in every aspect of the Christian life, the most important thing is to glorify God. Therefore, it is important for us to look in God's Word, the Bible,[1] to see if our Lord gives us any directives relevant to the apologetic task. It might seem strange to look in Scripture for teachings about knowledge, reasoning, proof, evidence, logic, and so on, but God often surprises us by getting involved in areas of life we would prefer to keep to ourselves. Indeed, every part of life is his domain, and thus he rules all of life, directly or indirectly, by his Word (1 Cor. 10:31; Col. 3:17; 2 Tim. 3:16–17).

BIBLICAL EPISTEMOLOGY

Scripture actually has a great deal to say about epistemology, or theory of knowledge.[2] It teaches that the fear of the Lord

---

[1]Presuppositional apologists unanimously hold strong views of Scripture, affirming that the biblical canon is God's Word, infallible and inerrant in the original manuscripts. I realize that even in evangelical circles there are many who question or limit the inerrancy of Scripture in some way. Obviously, I cannot enter into this issue here. For defense of a strong inerrantist position, I recommend Donald Carson and John Woodbridge, eds., *Scripture and Truth* (Grand Rapids: Zondervan, 1983); idem, eds., *Hermeneutics, Authority, and Canon* (Grand Rapids: Zondervan, 1986); Wayne Grudem, *Systematic Theology* (Grand Rapids: Zondervan, 1994); Carl F. H. Henry, *God, Revelation, and Authority* (Waco: Word, 1976), vols. 1–4; Meredith G. Kline, *The Structure of Biblical Authority* (Grand Rapids: Eerdmans, 1972); B. B. Warfield, *The Inspiration and Authority of the Bible* (Grand Rapids: Baker, 1948); and Edward J. Young, *The Word Is Truth* (Grand Rapids: Eerdmans, 1957).

[2]For a much more detailed account of biblical epistemology as I understand it, see my *Doctrine of the Knowledge of God* (Phillipsburg, N.J.: Presbyterian and Reformed, 1987).

is the beginning of wisdom (Ps. 111:10; Prov. 9:10; 15:33) and of knowledge (Prov. 1:7). "Fear" here is that reverent awe that yields obedience. It is based on the conviction that God is Lord, and we are his creatures and servants. He has the right to rule every aspect of our lives. When he speaks, we are to hear with the profoundest respect. What he says is more important than any other words we may hear. Indeed, his words judge all the affairs of human beings (John 12:48). The truth of his words, then, must be our most fundamental conviction, our most basic commitment. We may also describe that commitment as our most ultimate *presupposition*, for we bring that commitment into all our thought, seeking to bring all our ideas in conformity to it. That presupposition is therefore our ultimate criterion of truth. We measure and evaluate all other sources of knowledge by it. We bring every thought captive to the obedience of Christ (2 Cor. 10:5).

To say this is to say that for Christians faith governs reasoning just as it governs all other human activities. Reasoning is not in some realm that is neutral between faith and unbelief. There is no such realm, since God's standards apply to all of life. We may not lay our faith aside when we study God's world. Unfortunately, many enter institutions of higher education thinking they may honor God on Sunday, while accepting all the standards of secular scholarship in their daily studies. That is not bringing every thought captive to Christ. The Christian must have a critical perspective on scholarship, testing every hypothesis by Scripture.[3]

But if faith governs reasoning, where does faith come from? Some might think it is essentially irrational, since in one sense it precedes reason. But that conclusion would not be warranted. The question, "Where does faith come from?" may be taken in two senses. (1) It may be asking the *cause* of faith. In that sense, the answer is that God causes faith by his own free grace. This is the regenerating work of the Holy Spirit.[4] (2) Or it may be asking the *rational basis* of faith. In that sense, the answer is that faith

---

[3]See "In Defense of Something Close to Biblicism," appendix B in my *Contemporary Worship Music: A Biblical Defense* (Phillipsburg, N.J.: Presbyterian and Reformed, 1997).

[4]I don't apologize for the Calvinistic assumption here. Presuppositional apologists are Calvinists for the most part. And the Scriptures do teach that faith is a gift of God. See Ezek. 36:26; Matt. 11:25–27; John 3:3–8; 6:44, 65; Acts 13:48; 16:14; 1 Cor. 2:4–5, 14; 12:3; Eph. 2:1–10; 1 Thess. 1:5, 6; 2:13.

is based on reality, on truth. It is in accord with all the facts of God's universe and all the laws of thought that God has ordained. The Holy Spirit does not cause us to believe lies. He is the God of truth, and so he makes us believe what is true, what is in accord with all evidence and logic. The faith he gives us agrees with God's own perfect rationality.

There is a kind of circularity here, but the circularity is not vicious. It sounds circular to say that faith governs reasoning and also that it is based on rationality. It is therefore important to remember that the rationality that serves as the rational basis for faith is God's own rationality. The sequence is: God's rationality → human faith → human reasoning. The arrows may be read "is the rational basis for."[5] That sequence is linear, not circular.

If faith is in accord with God's own thought, then it will also be in accord with human reasoning at its best, which images God's. God gave us our rational equipment, not to deceive us, but so that we might gain knowledge. Apart from sin, we may trust it to lead us into the truth; and the facts of God's creation bear clear witness of him even to the minds of sinners (Rom. 1:20). Thus, it is not wrong to use evidences and human logic to confirm faith. Scripture itself frequently calls upon people to look at the evidences of the truth (Ps. 19:1; Luke 1:1–3; John 20:30–31; Acts 1:1–3; 26:26; Rom. 1:19–20). Biblical religion is unique in its appeal to history as the locus of divine revelation. God has revealed himself plainly in nature and in historical events.

The content of faith, Scripture, may transcend reason in these senses: (1) it cannot be proved by human reason alone; (2) it contains mysteries, even apparent contradictions, that cannot be fully resolved by human logic; (3) only the Spirit, not reason alone, can create belief from the heart, overcoming the sinful impulse toward unbelief. There is no conflict between faith and reason, however, when the latter functions in accord with God's norms.

THE NOETIC EFFECTS OF SIN

Of course human reasoning in the present age is never completely free from the influence of sin. Therefore, we must now discuss the nature of unbelief, of disobedience to God's words,

---

[5]For more observations on this circularity, see my *Doctrine of the Knowledge of God*, 130–33; my *Apologetics to the Glory of God* (Phillipsburg, N.J.: Presbyterian and Reformed, 1994), 9–14; and my *Cornelius Van Til: An Analysis of His Thought* (Phillipsburg, N.J.: Presbyterian and Reformed, 1995), 299–309.

and how that unbelief affects knowledge and reasoning—what theologians call the "noetic effects of sin."

Those who deny God do so, not because they lack evidence, but because their hearts are rebellious. In Romans 1:19–20, the apostle Paul says that

> what may be known about God is plain to them, because God has made it plain to them. For since the creation of the world God's invisible qualities—his eternal and divine nature—have been clearly seen, being understood from what has been made, so that men are without excuse.

Paul even says that they "knew God" (v. 21). God's revelation is clear, but fallen human beings "suppress the truth by their wickedness" (v. 18). So the unbeliever's problem is first ethical, and only secondarily intellectual. His intellectual problems stem from his ethical unwillingness to acknowledge the evidence. Unbelief distorts human thought.

From unbelief, then, comes the "wisdom of the world" that Paul contrasts so sharply with the wisdom of God (1 Cor. 1:18–2:16; 3:18–23; 8:1–3), the foolishness that the author of Proverbs sets over against true wisdom. The wisdom of the world tends to dominate human cultures as they unite in defiance of God. Those considered wise, influential, and noble (1 Cor. 1:26) according to the world's standards are experts in this false wisdom, and they are honored for it. In our day, this "conventional wisdom" dominates mainstream politics, education, arts, science, media, and religion. To such "wise" people, Christianity appears foolish and weak. But to God, the opposite is the case. It is the secular wisdom that is foolish and weak, and the worldly wise will learn that in God's time.

Though the unbeliever[6] suppresses the truth, he sometimes acknowledges it in spite of himself. He lives, after all, in God's world, and he must accept that objective world if he is to continue living at all. So Jesus taught that "the people of this world are more shrewd in dealing with their own kind than are the people of the light" (Luke 16:8). Jesus also regarded the Pharisees as people with many true ideas but devoid of real heart obedience. He urged his disciples to accept their teaching but not to follow the example of their behavior (Matt. 23:2–3). Even

---

[6]All that I say about the individual unbeliever can also be applied to the corporate conventional wisdoms, that is, to the wisdom of the world described earlier.

the demons sometimes face up to reality. In Mark 1:24 an evil spirit says truly that Jesus is the "Holy One of God." Nevertheless, like Satan and the demons, the unbeliever seeks to escape from the truth. Ultimately, he would like to see God replaced by Satan as the Lord of the universe and the truth replaced by Satan's lie.

When someone recognizes the truth but seeks to repress it, the result is irrationality. In some cases, we call such repression "wishful thinking." Sometimes there is psychological repression, in which a person relegates the truth to some subconscious level of the mind. Other times, the truth and error simply exist side by side, interacting in odd ways, creating contradictions in thought and life. For example, the unbeliever may accept historical evidences for Wellington's defeat of Napoleon, while denying equally cogent evidences for the resurrection of Jesus. This sort of inconsistency does not come from a mere lack of intelligence. It has, rather, a spiritual root.[7] It comes from living in God's world with a mind created to acknowledge God, but with a disposition of resistance and rebellion against him.

So the paradigm of irrationality is Satan himself. Satan knows more about God than any of us. He is not stupid: certainly he knows that rebels against God are doomed. Yet he persists in his rebellion anyway. So, intelligent as he may be, he is the very paradigm of foolishness.

Cornelius Van Til[8] maintained that every unbeliever is both rationalistic and irrationalistic at the same time—irrationalistic by denying the only possible source of order and meaning in the universe, rationalistic in setting himself or herself in the place of God as the ultimate determiner of truth and falsity. So it is not unusual for modern secularists to claim that all truth is relative while insisting that naturalistic evolution is a proven fact, never conscious of the contradiction into which they have fallen.

---

[7]Presuppositional apologists have found it difficult to formulate precisely how it is that truth and error coexist in the unbelieving mind. Cornelius Van Til, who rarely admitted that there were difficulties in his apologetic system, recognized that this was a "difficult point"; see his *Introduction to Systematic Theology* (Philadelphia: Presbyterian and Reformed, 1974), 26. In my view, Van Til's own formulations are somewhat inconsistent, though some are insightful. See *Cornelius Van Til*, 187–213.

[8]In *A Christian Theory of Knowledge* (Philadelphia: Presbyterian and Reformed, 1969), he traces this dualism back to the Garden of Eden: Eve was an irrationalist, denying any authoritative interpretation of the tree of knowledge; but she was also a rationalist, claiming the right to make such authoritative interpretations herself. See *Cornelius Van Til*, 231–38.

In the philosophical tradition of the West, some thinkers have been relativists and skeptics, like the Greek sophists and the contemporary postmodernists. These emphasize the irrationalism of unbelief. But they are also rationalistic, for they dogmatically affirm their skepticism, their sophism, or their postmodernism as if it were objectively true.

Other philosophers have been mainly rationalistic, like Parmenides, Spinoza, and Hegel, who believed that autonomous human reason is the ultimate standard of truth. But most students of philosophy agree that these men failed in their attempts to build up the whole fabric of human knowledge based on autonomous reason. Their defense of rationalism requires a certain amount of mythology (in the case of Parmenides), unargued assumptions (Descartes and Spinoza), or a dialectical self-negation that devours itself (Hegel).

Still other philosophers, the greater ones, like Plato, Aristotle, and Kant, have tried to be rationalistic about one sector of the world (form for the Greeks, the phenomenal for Kant) and irrationalistic about another (matter or the noumenal, respectively). But for such thinkers there is no possibility of achieving a unified vision of reality. Neither rationalism nor irrationalism can be confined; each demands total sovereignty over human thought. If part of the universe is irrational, autonomous reason cannot be the ultimate criterion of truth. If part of the universe is accessible to autonomous reason, irrationalism cannot succeed in its attempt to deny the existence of objective truth.

THE NOETIC EFFECTS OF CONVERSION

Becoming a Christian does not immediately erase all sin and its effects. For Jesus' sake, God forgives our sins; but we will not be sinlessly perfect until we enter heaven (1 John 1:8–10). In this life, we do commit sin, and we struggle to overcome it with God's help. As we have seen, reasoning is part of life, and it is subject to ethical predication: it can be done righteously or sinfully. So God deals with our sinful reasoning as he deals with all our sins. He forgives our noetic sins in Christ; but we do sin with the mind as well as with the body until we enter glory.

What is the difference, then, between believer and unbeliever? Both commit sin, and both grasp the truth in some measure. But neither is perfect, and neither is as bad as the devil. Is the difference between the two only a difference in degree?

No, the differences are too substantial to be described as mere differences in degree. The new Christian is regenerate, born again (John 3:3), a new creation, in whom all things have become new (2 Cor. 5:17). Conversion involves repentance, a decisive turning away from sin, and faith, a decisive turning to Christ. And every believer is united to Christ in Christ's death, burial, and resurrection (Rom. 6; 1 Cor. 15). The change is not a change from sin to sinlessness, but it is a radical change in *direction*. Before conversion we love sin and want to indulge in it more and more. After conversion we hate sin, and our deepest desire is to be rid of it. Another way to put it is that before conversion sin is our *master*; after conversion, our master is Christ (John 8:31–36; Rom. 6:14).

Intellectual change is part of that. Christians do sometimes engage in reasoning distorted by the ideal of autonomy. But that is not the deepest desire of their hearts. They have repented of that autonomy and have sought wisdom in Christ alone (1 Cor. 1:30). So sinful thinking does not master them. They have that fear of the Lord that is the beginning of wisdom.

We have seen how important it is to think of epistemology in ethical terms, but ethics isn't all there is to epistemology. The epistemologist must also wrestle with such matters as the relation between sense experience and reason; the precise nature of belief, of justification for belief, and of truth; and other matters that we cannot discuss in detail here. But the connection between ethics and epistemology is a biblical datum of special importance for apologetics. Reasoning is good or bad, right or wrong, in God's sight, just like other human actions. After the fall of Adam, human reason operated in defiance of God.[9] Through Christ, God forgives our proud, false wisdom and grants intellectual repentance, giving us a new heart's desire to think God's thoughts after him.

THE VALUE OF APOLOGETICS

Jesus calls his people to "make disciples of all nations" (Matt. 28:19). Apologetics is part of that discipling or teaching ministry. Scripture mentions that aspect of the teaching ministry in 1 Peter 3:15, where the apostle tells us,

---

[9] I am not saying that reason became less efficient. As I have indicated, unbelievers are often more brilliant than believers, using their reason in the service of falsehood. Van Til likens fallen reason to a buzz saw that works well except for being pointed in the wrong direction.

But in your hearts set apart Christ as Lord. Always be prepared to give an answer to everyone who asks you to give the reason for the hope that you have. But do this with gentleness and respect, keeping a clear conscience, so that those who speak maliciously against your good behavior in Christ may be ashamed of their slander.[10]

Paul also speaks of his ministry as including the defense and confirmation of the gospel (Phil. 1:7; cf. v. 16). He tells the Corinthians, "We demolish arguments and every pretension that sets itself up against the knowledge of God, and we take captive every thought to make it obedient to Christ" (2 Cor. 10:5). Indeed, all biblical writers speak rationally to their readers, offering reasons for believing the truths God has given them.

Apologetics has value for both believers and unbelievers, since even believers in this life must wrestle with their unbelief (Mark 9:24). I understand it to have three elements: (1) *proof*, rational confirmation for faith; (2) *defense*, replies to criticisms; and (3) *offense*, bringing criticisms against non-Christian ideas. Each of these contributes to the others, so the three elements cannot be sharply separated.

As "Reformed epistemologists"[11] have emphasized, we do legitimately believe most things without proof or argument. This is obviously the case with young children, but it is also the case with adults, and with some of our fundamental beliefs: the belief that there is an external world beyond our own mind, the belief that other people have minds like ours, the belief that the future will resemble the past, and so on. I also agree with the Reformed epistemologists that it is quite legitimate for someone to believe in Christ without basing that belief on some argument or other. The Spirit creates faith in the heart, as we have seen, and that faith may or may not arise through an argumentative process. I do believe that faith is always (logically, not causally) based on *evidence*. Romans 1:18–32 makes clear that the evidence of the natural world yields knowledge of God in every human being,

---

[10]Note that life as well as word plays an important role in apologetics—another confirmation of the relation between ethics and knowledge.

[11]See the discussion of Reformed epistemology elsewhere in this volume (pp. 266–84). In my view, presuppositionalism is also a "Reformed epistemology," since it is deeply influenced by the great Reformed thinkers John Calvin, Abraham Kuyper, and Cornelius Van Til. Indeed, I think presuppositionalism makes a more profound use of Reformed convictions than does the Plantinga version. But I won't try to make the historical argument here.

a knowledge that many suppress. But argument is not strictly necessary for faith.[12] The importance of apologetics, then, is not that one can't believe without it; it is rather that apologetic arguments can articulate and confirm the knowledge of God that we all have from creation.

Some have raised another question about the value of apologetics, based on the biblical teachings discussed in previous sections of this paper. One problem is this: If we are to *presuppose* the truth of Christianity in all our thinking, then how can an argument help to confirm that presupposition? If we presuppose that God's Word is true, then its truth is assured at the beginning of the argument. But if the truth of Christianity is assured already at the beginning of the argument, what can the argument add to that assurance? Here, it seems, another form of circularity vitiates the process of reasoning. But that is not the case. Recall the logical chain between God's rationality → our faith → our reasoning. The chain, as we have seen, is linear, rather than circular. But once the Spirit plants faith in our heart, our reasoning reflects God's and therefore puts into our thoughts and language the divine rationality that began the chain. The third link reflects the first and thus grants assurance. So the ground of faith becomes more evident to us, and God thereby confirms our faith to us.

Practically speaking: as we read the Bible, and as we look at God's world with biblical presuppositions (what Calvin called "the spectacles of Scripture"), the gospel becomes more reasonable to us, more cogent. After all, when we think with biblical presuppositions, we are thinking the way God designed us to think. Thus, our thinking is energized, empowered. Things that once seemed incredible now seem like obvious truth. One who thinks according to secular presuppositions, for example, may find it very difficult to believe in the biblical miracles. But once one begins to think according to the biblical worldview, in which the world is governed by a personal God rather than impersonal forces, it is not at all hard to believe in miracles. If God exists, miracles are possible.

---

[12]Argument and evidence, of course, are not the same thing. Evidence is those objective facts in the world that warrant a conclusion. Argument is our attempt to show in words how that conclusion is warranted by the facts. But in most of life's situations, we simply draw conclusions from the facts themselves without formulating arguments. It is helpful to note that animals respond to evidence, but they do not formulate arguments.

But are we not still forced to say, "God exists (presupposition), therefore God exists (conclusion)," and isn't that argument clearly circular? Yes, in a way. But that is unavoidable for any system, any worldview. For God is the ultimate standard of meaning, truth, and rationality. For a philosophical rationalist, human reason is the ultimate standard. But how can the rationalist argue that position? He must, in the final analysis, say, "Reason is the ultimate standard because reason says so." Or if a Muslim believes that Allah is the standard of rationality, he must argue that Allah is the standard because Allah says so. One cannot argue for an ultimate standard by appealing to a different standard. That would be inconsistent.

So there is a kind of circle here. But even this circle, as I indicated earlier, is linear in a sense. For it is a movement from God's truth, to the gift of faith, to the reflection of God's truth in human reasoning.

A more difficult question: Of what value is this argument to the unbeliever? How can a Christian ask a non-Christian to believe in Christ on Christian presuppositions? The unbeliever, by definition of "unbeliever," does not have those presuppositions. So how can he or she be expected to employ them in the apologetic encounter? Here, several points should be noted:

1. Faith is a demand of God. He calls us in Scripture to repent and believe in Christ (Matt. 3:2; 4:17; John 14:1; Acts 2:38; 16:31). God commands us to do many things that we cannot do in our own strength. To summarize, he calls us to please him in all we do; but apart from grace none of us can please him at all (Rom. 8:7–8). Similarly, the command to believe is one we cannot carry out in our own strength. It requires the grace of God. So in the present context we may say, yes, the unbeliever cannot think according to Christian presuppositions;[13] but that is nevertheless what God demands. And the inquirer will do so, if (and only if) in the course of the apologetic encounter God plants faith in his heart. The apologist can do no more than proclaim the truth, trusting that God will plant faith if and when he wills.

2. The apologetic argument based on biblical presuppositions conveys truth, and certainly the work of apologetics is to communicate truth. If we abandoned our biblical presuppositions,

---

[13]Again, I am referring here to the unbeliever's *dominant* presuppositions. As I said before, unbelievers often think Christianly in spite of themselves.

claiming a position of "neutrality,"[14] then at that point we would be telling a lie to the inquirer. There is no such neutrality, and the very idea of neutrality is at the heart of Satan's deception of those who are lost. To claim neutrality is to claim that *I* am the one who ultimately decides what is true or false, that *I* am on the intellectual throne. Such neutralist pretensions must be rebuked, not indulged. They are a form of pride, of which God commands the sinner to repent.

3. Whether unbelievers admit it or not, God made them to think with the Christian-theistic worldview as their presupposition. And at one level of their consciousness, they do think that way. Remember that Romans 1:21 describes them as knowing God from the created world yet suppressing that knowledge. So we may ask the unbeliever to think on Christian presuppositions, because in one sense he already does.[15] Our plea is that he drop the unbelieving presuppositions that dominate his thought and give heed to those principles that he knows but suppresses.

4. Knowledge suppressed creates contradiction in thought and life. Part of the unbeliever says that God's revelation is true; part of him says it is false. He holds contradictory beliefs simultaneously, with corresponding confusion in his decisions, actions, and feelings. The apologist should appeal to the part of the unbeliever that acknowledges God in spite of himself, to that knowledge which the unbeliever keeps trying to suppress. We can do that only by reasoning consistently on biblical presuppositions.

5. The apologist, then, may and should legitimately require the unbeliever to reason on Christian presuppositions. That is nothing less than the demand of God. But this demand may be made in subtle ways. One way, suggested by Cornelius Van Til, is to ask the unbeliever to present his own system for analysis. The apologist agrees to accept the unbeliever's presuppositions "for the sake of argument," for the purpose of showing that these provide no basis at all for meaning and truth. The Chris-

---

[14]A position of neutrality would either be a state of mind without any presuppositions at all (impossible, because everyone must enter the discussion with a criterion of truth), or a set of presuppositions acceptable either to God or Satan (impossible, because no one can serve two masters [Matt. 6:24]. He who is not with Jesus is against him [Matt. 12:30]).

[15]Indeed, there is a sense in which all of the unbeliever's *thinking* is Christian. Christian presuppositions are the only way to *think*. The alternative is not thought, but meaninglessness.

tian then asks the unbeliever to accept the Christian presuppositions, also "for the sake of argument." If the inquirer wishes, he may attempt to reduce the Christian position to absurdity. But we trust that he cannot do that. Thus, indirectly, we display the necessity of adopting Christian presuppositions as our ultimate standard of truth, and we communicate God's demand that the inquirer adopt those presuppositions in all his thought. But we present that demand subtly, in a way that continues, rather than terminates, the discussion.

APOLOGETIC METHOD

Presuppositionalist apologetics focuses on the above biblical teachings and draws various conclusions in regard to apologetic method:[16]

1. The goal of apologetics is to evoke or strengthen faith, not merely to bring intellectual persuasion. Directed toward unbelievers, it is an aspect of evangelism; toward believers, it is training in godliness. It is possible to be intellectually persuaded of a theistic worldview, as were the Pharisees, without a real heart commitment to Jesus as Lord and Savior. Furthermore, everyone has the intellectual knowledge required for faith. The need of the unbeliever is not for more information, but for God's grace motivating a heart change. It may of course be necessary for the apologist to bring factual information to the inquirer in order to challenge him to rethink the data. But the apologist seeks above all to be a channel through whom God's Spirit can bring repentance (including intellectual repentance) and faith.

---

[16]Many apologists have been called presuppositionalists, such as Cornelius Van Til, Francis Schaeffer, Gordon H. Clark, Carl F. H. Henry, and Greg L. Bahnsen. Even Edward J. Carnell was called a "modified presuppositionalist." My own approach owes more to Van Til than to anyone else, but in this essay I will speak only for myself. I have interacted with Van Til's writings (both positively and negatively) in *Apologetics to the Glory of God* and in *Cornelius Van Til.*

I wish we could find a better term than *presuppositional* to describe this chapter's approach to apologetics. In the apologetic literature, writers regularly contrast "presupposition" with "evidence," so that to call a method "presuppositional" may imply that that method disparages evidence. That is certainly not my intention. Further, the term *presuppositional* doesn't express very well the distinctives of this approach. Any apologetic method worth its salt must discuss the presuppositions that Christians and non-Christians bring to the apologetic encounter, and many apologists do this who would not want to be described as presuppositionalists. Nevertheless, because the term has achieved wide currency, I will employ it here.

2. Apologists, therefore, must resist temptations to contentiousness or arrogance. They must avoid the feeling that they are entering into a contest to prove themselves to be righter or smarter than the inquirers with whom they deal. I believe that kind of pride is a besetting sin of many apologists, and we need to deal with it. First Peter 3:15–16 focuses, surprisingly, not on the brilliance, cogency, or eloquence of apologists, but on their character: they must answer unbelievers with "gentleness and respect, keeping a clear conscience." Peter here tells us that a consistent Christian life plays a major role in the work of apologetics. Christianity is not just an intellectual system, but a comprehensive way of life. Nothing is more persuasive than a concrete, consistent example of that way of life,[17] and nothing is more detrimental to our witness than when our life betrays our message by our failing to show the gentleness and love of Jesus.

3. Our apologetic should take special pains to present God as he really is: as the sovereign Lord of heaven and earth, who alone saves his people from their sins. As the Creator of all things and the one who directs the course of nature and history by his providence (Rom. 8:28; Eph. 1:11), God is the source of all meaning and rationality. Our argument should lead to such a God. So we should not mislead unbelievers into assuming that they can understand any fact adequately without confessing its relation to God. We should make plain that even our methods of knowledge, our standards of truth and falsity, our views of logic, and our scientific methods must be reconciled first of all with God's revelation.

4. As such, our argument should be *transcendental*. That is, it should present the biblical God, not merely as the conclusion to an argument, but as the one who makes argument possible. We should present him as the source of all meaningful communication, since he is the author of all order, truth, beauty, goodness, logical validity, and empirical fact.

5. We can reach this transcendental conclusion by many kinds of specific arguments, including many of the traditional ones.[18] The traditional cosmological argument, for example,

---

[17]Francis and Edith Schaeffer led many to Christ through their ministry at L'Abri in Switzerland. In my view, the power of their ministry was found in the combination of a thoughtful apologetic ("honest answers to honest questions") and a loving ministry of hospitality.

[18]Here my concept of transcendental argument differs somewhat from that of Van Til and other presuppositionalists. See my discussion in *Apologetics to the Glory*

argues that God must exist as the First Cause of all the causes in the world. That conclusion is biblical and true, and if it can be drawn from true premises and valid logic, it may contribute to the goal of a transcendental conclusion. Certainly if God is the author of all meaning, he is the author of causality. And if God is the author of causality, the cause of all causes, he is the cause of all meaning. Therefore, the causal argument yields a transcendental conclusion.

If the argument is to be sound, however, we must, of course, interpret causality in a way that is itself consistent with the God of the Bible, risking the charge of circularity that we discussed earlier. We should not suggest that the unbeliever can assume some secular philosophical concept of causality (like those of Aristotle, Hume, or Kant) and reason from that.[19] Causality itself is not a religiously neutral notion, providing a common ground between believing and unbelieving worldviews, from which Christian conclusions can be reached. No, without God there would be no causal order, nor any possibility of causal argument.

6. Negatively, we should not say things to the unbeliever that tend to reinforce his pretense to autonomy or neutrality. For example, the great eighteenth-century apologist Joseph Butler said, "Let reason be kept to: and if any part of the Scripture account of the redemption of the world by Christ can be shown to be really contrary to it, let the Scripture, in the name of God, be given up."[20] This statement (like Butler's writing in general) fails to distinguish between reasoning on Christian presuppositions and reasoning on non-Christian ones. Therefore, it gives the impression that one may use the principles of reason advocated by secular philosophy to judge the truth of Scripture. For Immanuel Kant, it was axiomatic that reason should never

---

of God, 69–88, and *Cornelius Van Til,* 241–97, 311–22. I think Van Til exaggerates the differences between his presuppositionalism and the approaches of the older apologetic tradition. In my view, presuppositionalism should not be seen as the *antithesis* of "classical" or "traditional" or "evidential" apologetics, but as a Christian epistemology that seeks to supplement, clarify, and sharpen the traditional approaches with biblical teachings that are at least sometimes overlooked, or even contradicted, in the tradition.

[19]David Hume, for example, taught that there was no necessary connection between cause and effect. On this basis, one cannot infer the nature of a first cause behind the universe.

[20]Joseph Butler, *Analogy of Religion* (Philadelphia: J. B. Lippincott, 1865), 245.

accept any conclusion on the basis of a religious revelation alone. Would Butler have been pleased to judge the Scriptures by reason so defined? Butler seeks to find common ground with his non-Christian readers, but in doing so he greatly misleads them. The same criticism applies to the following passage from Edward J. Carnell: "Bring on your revelations! Let them make peace with the law of contradiction and the facts of history and they will deserve a rational man's assent. A careful examination of the Bible reveals that it passes these stringent examinations *summa cum laude*."[21]

This statement too, though eloquent, is highly misleading. It fails to distinguish between rationality governed by biblical principle and rationality governed by the denial of God's revelation. Thus, it conveys the notion that the latter appropriately judges the truth of Scripture. Reasoning based on biblical presuppositions, of course, is a reliable guide to truth. God gave it to us for that purpose. But Carnell's and Butler's formulations leave the crucial issue ambiguous.

7. The actual arguments we use in an apologetic witness will vary considerably, depending on who we are talking to. Apologetics is "person variable."[22] We must ask where the inquirer is coming from, his educational level, previous philosophical commitments, interests, seriousness, specific questions, and so on. Our goal is not to persuade rational creatures in the abstract, but to persuade the person we are talking to, with God's help.

A traditional causal argument, for example, might be persuasive to one person but not to another. The argument may be perfectly valid and sound from a logical standpoint, but it may be too complex or abstract for the second person. Some people, finding no fault in it, may still reject it, because they are strongly disposed toward skepticism, and they figure that an argument that complex must have some flaws even if they cannot identify them.

Often, one can focus in on the specific concerns of the inquirer by pursuing a *negative* argument, or *reductio ad absurdum*. Here we ask the inquirer to explain his own worldview, epistemology, and/or theory of value, and then we try to show that his unbelieving premises lead to a denial of meaning itself.

---

[21]Edward J. Carnell, *An Introduction to Christian Apologetics* (Grand Rapids: Eerdmans, 1948), 178.

[22]See George Mavrodes, *Belief in God* (New York: Random House, 1970).

I do not agree with some of my presuppositionalist colleagues that the *reductio* is the *only* argument compatible with biblical teaching,[23] but I believe it is very useful. It focuses on the inquirer's specific form of unbelief, and it focuses the dialogue on the transcendental conclusion.

8. It is especially useful when we can show how the errors of non-Christian worldviews arise, not merely from logical mistakes or factual inaccuracy, but from religious rebellion. Certainly unbelievers do make factual and logical mistakes. We do too, and each party should be free to expose these in the other. But since our goal is conversion, not merely intellectual persuasion, it is important to show how unbelief itself is a systematic source of error. We have seen how all unbelieving positions lead to the dead ends of rationalism and irrationalism. These can be avoided only through intellectual repentance, through turning to the true God. Thus, we expose the true nature of unbelief, not as a neutral or unbiased attempt to account for experience, but as a flight from the God we all know. And so apologetics merges easily into evangelism.

SKETCH OF AN APOLOGETIC

Here I would like to give an example of what an argument following the above principles might look like. This is only one of many possible arguments, for apologetics, as we have seen, is person variable. And this argument is only a sketch; I cannot here present all the clarifications, disclaimers, subarguments, answers to objections, documentations, and so on that I would include in a longer formulation.[24] I am addressing college-level readers.

As we think about "where it all came from," many answers have been suggested, and these answers can be classified in many ways. But let me suggest as a fruitful approach dividing the possible answers into two: personal and impersonal. In our experience, we are familiar with persons, and we are familiar with impersonal things and forces, like rocks, the law of gravity, and so on. The significant question is, which of these is more fundamental? Are persons made by impersonal objects and

---

[23]See references in n. 16 above.

[24]For additional and more complete examples of presuppositional argument, see my *Apologetics to the Glory of God*.

forces, so that you and I are "nothing but" matter, motion, time, and chance?[25] Or are the impersonal forces created and employed by a person? Is the universe, then, fundamentally personal or fundamentally impersonal?

Of all the religions and philosophies of the world, only those influenced by the Bible are personalistic in this sense.[26] Polytheistic religions have personal gods, but these personal gods are not ultimate; they are finite, themselves subject to larger forces. Hinduism presents Brahma as a kind of absolute reality, but Brahma is not personal, nor is the Buddhist nothingness, or the Platonic forms, or the Hegelian absolute. Only in biblical religion is there a personal absolute, a being who is truly ultimate, but who also plans, speaks, thinks, acts in history, rejoices, grieves, loves, and judges.[27]

Thus, the issue before us is this: Does the biblical God exist, or is the universe the result of impersonal things and processes? If you are undecided but fair-minded, you should give each of these hypotheses an equal hearing. Certainly it is not obvious that the biblical God *doesn't* exist. How could anybody establish the nonexistence of God? Negatives are notoriously hard to prove. You would need omniscience to know that there is no God anywhere in the universe. And, of course, if you were omniscient, then you would be God, and the contrary would be proven.

Since it is impossible to prove the nonexistence of God, we should at least be willing to give the theistic hypothesis a fair hearing. But such a fair hearing is rare in our society. Among the mainstream intellectuals and opinion-makers, the personalistic option is laughed away or not even considered. Writers on ethics usually do not even consider the possibility that our behavior is subject to the commands of a divine lawgiver. Although many scientists are Christians, it is rare to see mainstream scientists admitting that God may have played a role in the natural his-

---

[25]I gratefully acknowledge Francis Schaeffer (in many of his writings) as the source of this fourfold analysis of impersonal reality.

[26]Some philosophical systems that have been called personalistic, such as those of Borden Bowne and Edgar S. Brightman, are not so on my definition, for in these systems God is finite and to that extent subordinate to other realities. In these systems, the personal is not truly ultimate.

[27]Of course Islam, Judaism, and various sects like the Jehovah's Witnesses also approximate biblical personalism, though I think inconsistently. But their personalism, such as it is, is due to the influence of Scripture.

tory of the universe.[28] There is a significant Christian influence among professional philosophers today, but most philosophers still develop their theories on the assumption that impersonal explanations are more satisfactory than personal ones, and that religious revelation is irrelevant to the work of understanding the universe—the same for sociologists, psychologists, novelists, filmmakers, economists, political scientists, educators, jurists, and so on. In the current intellectual climate, autonomy is the rule. Even if there is a God, and even if he has revealed himself, so goes the assumption, his revelation must be subject to our standards, rather than the other way around.[29]

Why do you suppose it is that today's society so universally *assumes* the impersonalist option even though it cannot be proved? Could that assumption illustrate the Bible's teaching that people voluntarily repress the knowledge of the true God because they don't *like* to worship him (Rom. 1:18, 28)? The assumption is not a rational one; perhaps it is wishful thinking. Or perhaps it is based on a kind of faith, religious in essence but opposed to Christian faith.

There are many possible benefits in considering the personalistic alternative. Belief in the biblical God yields clear moral standards, for example, something that our society desperately needs. It assures us that there is meaning and purpose in life. It shows us that love, wisdom, beauty, and truth are at the foundation of the universe, not the periphery. History exists to manifest and glorify the divine personality.

But does this God exist? At some level of our consciousness, we know that he does. We assume, for example, that the laws of logic and mathematics[30] are universally and necessarily

---

[28]Phillip Johnson makes important observations in this regard. See his *Reason in the Balance* (Downers Grove, Ill.: InterVarsity Press, 1995).

[29]As Johnson (ibid.) points out, the argument is often made that theistic personalism must be excluded from schools, courts, and other forums of public discourse, because it is a "religious" view. I will not address here the arguments about the so-called wall of separation between government and religion. However, (1) since impersonalism cannot be proved, it must confess that it too is based on faith of a sort; and (2) the quest for truth can only be hindered if serious alternatives are dismissed in this way. It is more important whether a position is true or false than whether it is religious or nonreligious. "Religious" is often a nasty name that people give to a viewpoint in order to keep it from being discussed.

[30]A similar argument could be made concerning the laws of nature. Compare the taped debate between the late Greg Bahnsen, presuppositional apologist, and Gordon Stein, defender of atheism. This and other Bahnsen tapes are available from Covenant Media Foundation, (870)-775-1170. Their web site is http://www.cmfnow.com.

true. 2+2 = 4 does not just happen to be true; it *must* be true. And it is not true only in our part of the universe, but in every part. Now there is nothing in matter, motion, time, and chance that accounts for such universal necessity. But a personal God, who himself is logical, will naturally create a world that reflects his own perfect thought. Our assumption about logic fits the personal model of the universe, not the impersonal.

We also normally consider the fundamental principles of morality to be universal and necessary. Some do argue for ethical relativism, the view that ethical values are mere feelings of disapproval conferred by evolution. But few if any of us actually believe that fundamental ethical principles are relative. We are enraged at unkindness, cruelty, and unfairness, especially when we are the objects of them. And we refuse to believe that our rage is just a feeling, like a taste for hamburgers. People who are cruel have done what they ought not to have done. They have violated objective rules that are everywhere in force. Even if they belong to a very different culture from our own and live at a great distance from us, we hold them responsible to these objective norms.[31]

The main opposition today to objective norms comes from what is called "postmodernism."[32] The name comes from the view that "modern" thinking must be overcome. "Modern" thinking assumes the competence and goodness of secularized reason, technology, and the institutions of Western civilization. In turn, this confidence presupposes that there is a single objective truth accessible to human reason through logical and scientific methods. Postmodernism, however, denies that there is any one set of rules (*grand récit*, "metanarrative") for finding truth. There is on this view a multitude of criteria held by different people, different groups, in different settings, that may or may not be consistent with one another. Indeed, there is not even an authoritative way of interpreting any piece of language. The author's intention is not authoritative, for the meaning of language is independent of any individual intention.

Postmodernists are open to various kinds of mystical or

---

[31]Objective ethical norms are necessary also for logic and science. Because if there is no absolute rule as to how I *ought* to reason, as to the *responsible* way of analyzing data, logic and science could not exist nor could any other field of human study.

[32]An excellent introduction to postmodernism is William Edgar, "No News Is Good News: Modernity, the Postmodern, and Apologetics," in *Westminster Theological Journal* 57 (1995): 359–82.

symbolic ways of understanding,[33] but they deny any sort of objective truth. In Van Til's terms, they emphasize the irrationalist pole of unbelief's rationalist-irrationalist dialectic.[34] The claim of objective truth, in their somewhat Marxian view, is an oppressive claim. It amounts to oppression: males dominating women, whites dominating blacks, Westerners dominating other cultures, rich dominating the poor.

Certainly the postmodernists are right to protest the proud claims of modernist rationality. And, as a presuppositionalist, I appreciate their observation that all claims to knowledge are governed by presuppositions, that nobody is simply "neutral." Postmodernists understand that things look differently depending on where you sit. Literature looks different to women than to men, to poor than to rich, and so on. And certainly they are right to say that claims to objective truth can be means of oppression.[35] But to reject objective truth entirely is quite impossible. Postmodernists inevitably exempt their own writings from this kind of criticism. Edgar points out that

> Christopher Norris has shown how a scholar like Stanley Fish, in his vehement attacks on theory as a mere justification for personal preference, perpetuates the illusion that he is somehow outside of the confines of that personal preference. . . . The most serious flaw in [Jean-François] Lyotard's presentation, however, is the deep-rooted contradiction between his claims to do away with metanarrative and his own program, which is suspiciously like a metanarrative of another kind.[36]

If postmodernists want to be consistent in denying objective truth,[37] they should abandon the attempt to persuade others of

---

[33]Postmodernists are more or less allied with the neo-Gnostic New Age spiritualities described in Peter Jones, *Spirit Wars* (Escondido, Calif.: Main Entry, 1997). His discussions there are worth noting.

[34]But of course they are rationalistic in the dogmatism by which they assert their view. The rationalist pole in our society is emphasized by the naturalistic scientism discussed by Johnson in the work cited above. That naturalistic scientism is, however, irrationalist, in that it has no rational basis for its dogmatism.

[35]Some applications postmodernists are not inclined to make: dogmatism about women's rights is oppressive to unborn children; dogmatism about evolution is oppressive to Christians; dogmatism about the "separation of church and state" oppresses public school students who are trying to find truth.

[36]Edgar, "No News Is Good News," 379. He cites Christopher Norris, *What's Wrong With Postmodernism?* (Baltimore: Johns Hopkins University Press, 1990), chap. 2.

[37]But what would "consistency" mean if objectivity is excluded?

the truth of their position. What could that "truth" be if it is not objective truth? But if they want to set forth their position as objectively true, then their viewpoint must be substantially revised. We shall, therefore, set postmodernism aside and assume, as most everyone does, the objectivity of logical and moral norms.

What could be the basis of objective moral norms? Again, nothing in matter, motion, time, or chance can generate moral criteria. Many philosophers have pointed out that ethical values cannot be deduced from valueless facts: "is" does not imply "ought." What other source can there be? Here we should remember how we learned morality: usually from our parents, teachers, and others in society. Like other obligations, ethical obligation is an obligation to persons. Absolute obligations, therefore, can only be obligations to an absolute person. Just as only a person can generate logical and physical laws that are universal and necessary, so only a person can generate absolute and general moral obligations.

The above is not exactly a proof of God's existence; it is rather an analysis of how we usually think, the assumptions we actually make in our thought and life. To my mind, these assumptions show that we actually know God and don't need proof at all. How do we know God? Through the natural world, which is his creation, and through our own self-consciousness, since we are the image of God. Traditional proofs from causality, purpose, self-consciousness, and so on try to spell out in logical terms how we can move from the data of experience to the conclusion of God. These have their value, but the knowledge of God exists whether we can formulate these logical moves or not.

This God we know. Is he the God of the Bible? Well, if God is a person, we would expect him to reveal himself personally—that is, in language—as well as in nature. And as I indicated earlier, biblical religion is the only fully personalistic faith, so if there is a verbal revelation from God, the Bible would certainly be the leading candidate at the outset of our quest.

Further, the Bible makes historical claims that we may verify historically. We must not, of course, adopt principles of historiography like those of Hume and Kant that make it impossible to verify any supernatural event. If there is a personal God, then supernatural events are possible, and it is possible for that God to reveal them to us. Our principles of historical research must be theistic principles however much that methodology gives the appearance of circularity.[38]

We cannot here try to vindicate the historicity of the whole Bible. Many other authors have contributed to this work.[39] But central to this effort is the consideration of Jesus. He appears in history doing great signs and wonders and making enormous claims for himself. Make no mistake: Scripture does not claim merely that Jesus was a wise teacher, as Socrates and the Buddha, nor merely a prophet, as Mohammed. In line with Jesus' own claims, the New Testament identifies him with God himself (John 1:1–14; 5:16–27; Col. 1:15–20; 2:9; Heb. 1:1–14;[40] and many other passages).

Jesus, God the Son, came to earth to die in our place, to die the death that we deserve because of sin (Rom. 3:23; 6:23). Over many centuries, prophets foretold that he would come for this purpose (see, e.g., Gen. 3:15; Ps. 22; Isa. 7:14; 9:6–7; 52:13–53:12; Dan. 7:13–14; 9:25–27; Micah 5:2; Zech. 9:9; 12:10; 13:1).[41] He did die, by crucifixion; but it was impossible for death to hold him. He rose from the dead, demonstrating that his claims were true and that God the Father accepted his sacrifice for sin. With him, then, all who belong to him were raised to newness of life, their sins forgiven, in eternal fellowship with God.

The apostles, the earliest Christian preachers, proclaimed boldly that Jesus had risen from the dead. Is this message true? Many have examined the evidences for the resurrection and found them quite overwhelming.[42] Both Jesus' disciples and his

---

[38]See discussion of circularity earlier in this article.

[39]Here I am happy to salute the evidentialist tradition and to recommend the writings of Craig, Gerstner, McDowell, Moreland, Montgomery, Sproul, and many others. I only wish they were more explicitly theistic in their methodology.

[40]Here and many other places in the New Testament, writers quote Old Testament passages that speak of God and apply them to Christ.

[41]This list of passages contains striking references to the coming Messiah. But even more striking to me is the structure of Old Testament narrative, which prepares Israel to interpret its needs and God's character in ways that point inevitably to Christ. See *Apologetics to the Glory of God*, 136–40, and the remarkable book by Edmund P. Clowney, *The Unfolding Mystery: Discovering Christ in the Old Testament* (Phillipsburg, N.J.: Presbyterian and Reformed, 1991).

[42]Again here the evidentialist literature is useful. See, e.g., William Lane Craig, *Apologetics: An Introduction* (Chicago: Moody Press, 1984), 167–206; and his *Knowing the Truth About the Resurrection* (Ann Arbor, Mich.: Servant Books, 1988); Gary Habermas and Antony Flew, *Did Jesus Rise from the Dead? The Resurrection Debate* (a debate between a Christian and an atheist), ed. Terry L. Miethe (San Francisco: Harper and Row, 1987); Josh McDowell, *Evidence That Demands a Verdict* (San Bernardino, Calif.: Here's Life, 1979), 179–263.

opponents agreed that his tomb was empty. His opponents maintained that the disciples stole the body, but that notion is very implausible. The disciples would not likely have endured persecution and death for a lie. Many claimed to have seen Jesus after his death; the apostle Paul lists five such appearances in 1 Corinthians 15:3–7, one of them to five hundred people at once. So when Paul was writing, many eyewitnesses were still alive to confirm the truth of this message. The notion that all these appearances were really hallucinations does not bear scrutiny. Hallucinations do not remain constant among many different people in many different settings. Is the resurrection legendary? The time frame is too short for a legend to develop, especially during the lifetimes of people who claimed to be eyewitnesses.

Your full assurance of the truth of the resurrection will come only as you read for yourself. Christians believe that the Holy Spirit accompanies the Bible to bring supernatural persuasion. There are many details, a "ring" of authenticity,[43] that are hard to describe in arguments.[44] At best, the arguments only bear witness to the credibility of the biblical text itself.[45]

As you read, you will learn that you cannot remain the same after receiving this teaching. The gospel calls for a response. God calls you to repent of your sin, to turn away from it, and trust in Jesus as the sufficient sacrifice for sin (John 1:12; 3:16; Acts 2:38–39; Rom. 3:21–25; 6:23). He calls you to worship, honor, and obey Jesus as Lord (Phil. 2:9–11). He calls you to join yourself to a sound church by baptism (Acts 2:38, 42–47) and there to hear God's Word and worship Jesus with other believers (1 Cor. 14), observing the Lord's Supper with them (1 Cor. 11:23–32). He asks you to help bear the burdens of other Christians in the church (Gal. 6:2). That is the life of faith. If in this way you believe in Jesus, you know that you have eternal life (1 John 5:11–12). We do not earn eternal life by our good works (Eph. 2:8–10; Titus 3:5), but a genuine faith will prove itself by obedience to the Lord (James 2:14–26).

---

[43]E.g., the earliest witnesses to the resurrection were women. A fabricated story would not likely have included that detail, because the Jews did not consider women fit to testify in court.

[44]Recall our earlier distinction between evidence and argument.

[45]Paul's *main* argument for the resurrection of Jesus in 1 Corinthians 15 is that the resurrection is part of the apostolic preaching, part of the divine Word revelation. Therefore, we cannot deny it without calling the whole biblical gospel in question. See esp. vv. 1–2, 12–19.

Our Lord demands and deserves our absolute obedience in every area of our lives (1 Cor. 10:31; Col. 3:17), including our thought and reasoning (2 Cor. 10:5). In all of our studies, as well as in our life's endeavors, we are to think in obedience to God's revelation in Scripture. Like Abraham Kuyper, we should seek to bring everything human under the dominion of Jesus. We should seek a biblical philosophy, science, education, art, theology, politics, and economics. In none of these areas may we be content with the fashionable secular modes of thinking; we must constantly challenge them. We may never try to remain neutral between the wisdom of God and the wisdom of the world.

So we come full circle. If you have been persuaded of the argument and have become a Christian, you should also be a presuppositionalist.

A CLASSICAL
APOLOGIST'S RESPONSE

William Lane Craig

John Frame thinks of presuppositionalism as a version of Reformed epistemology, indeed, one that makes "a more profound use of Reformed convictions" than does Plantinga's version (p. 215, n. 11). I should be very interested to know what Kelly Clark makes of that claim! For my part, I think that presuppositionalism is, to borrow Plantinga's phraseology,[1] a "groping, implicit, inchoate" expression of the view articulated with such clarity by Plantinga under the name of "Reformed epistemology."

The central insight of presuppositionalism is that theological rationalism is a false doctrine. We are not dependent on argument and evidence in order to believe rationally in God or even to know that he exists. Frame and I agree that "The Spirit creates faith in the heart, . . . and that faith may or may not arise through an argumentative process" (p. 215).

Where presuppositionalism muddies the waters is in its apologetic methodology. As commonly understood, presuppositionalism is guilty of a logical howler: it commits the informal fallacy of *petitio principii,* or begging the question, for it advocates presupposing the truth of Christian theism in order to prove Christian theism. Frame himself says that we are "forced to say, 'God exists (presupposition), therefore God exists (conclusion),'" even though such reasoning is "clearly circular"

---

[1]Alvin Plantinga, "Self-Profile," in *Alvin Plantinga,* ed. James E. Tomberlin and Peter van Inwagen, Profiles 5 (Dordrecht: D. Reidel, 1985), 61.

(p. 217). It is difficult to imagine how anyone could with a straight face think to show theism to be true by reasoning, "God exists. Therefore, God exists." Nor is this said from the standpoint of unbelief. A Christian theist himself will deny that question-begging arguments prove anything.

If this were all presuppositionalism had to offer as an apologetic, it would be so ludicrous that no one would have taken it seriously. But at the heart of presuppositionalism lies an argument, often not clearly understood or articulated, which is very powerful. This is an epistemological transcendental argument. A transcendental argument, as Kant used the term, is an argument for a reality based on that reality's being the very conditions even of the denial of that reality. Thus, Kant argued for the existence of the categories of the understanding on the basis of their being the preconditions of all intelligible experience, including the denial that there are categories. Frame explicitly endorses such an argument, stating that our apologetic "should present the biblical God, not merely as the conclusion to an argument, but as the one who makes argument possible" (p. 220). Unfortunately, Frame fails to develop for us such an argument. Instead, he confuses transcendental reasoning with what medievals called *demonstratio quia*, proof that proceeds from consequence to ground.[2] The cosmological and moral arguments adduced by Frame are of this type, rather than being transcendental arguments. He approaches a transcendental argument most closely in a footnote to a quite different sort of argument when he says, "there is a sense in which all of the unbeliever's *thinking* is Christian. Christian presuppositions are the only way to *think*. The alternative is not thought, but meaninglessness" (p. 218, n. 15). Unfortunately, the insight is not developed. What is perhaps the most astonishing feature of Frame's essay is that when he comes to presenting his "Sketch of an Apologetic," he completely abandons presuppositionalism, flouts his own stricture that "our argument should be transcendental," and launches into a straight evidentialist apologetic that would delight the heart of any theological rationalist! Only when he comes to Christian evidences does he make a pretense of presupposing God's existence; but by that point he has, like the classical apologist, already given arguments for the truth of theism. Thus, Frame's apologetic turns out to involve no transcendental argument at all!

---

[2]Thomas Aquinas, *Summa theologiae* 1a.2.2.

By contrast, Plantinga's epistemology can be seen as an extended transcendental theistic argument. In volume 1 of his trilogy on warrant, Plantinga shows how all other accounts of what constitutes knowledge fail.[3] Then in volume 2 he develops his own explicitly theistic account of warrant.[4] Warrant accrues to a belief when it is formed by cognitive faculties functioning properly. What does it mean for cognitive faculties to function properly?—To function as God designed them to. On a theistic metaphysic, our cognitive faculties are constructed by their Creator according to a design plan aimed at producing true beliefs. Thus, the existence of God is a precondition of knowledge itself. Plantinga writes:

> Suppose . . . you are convinced (as most of us are) that there really is such a thing as warrant and really are (for natural organisms) such things as proper function, damage, design, dysfunction, and all the rest. . . . then if you also think there is no naturalistic analysis of these notions, what you have is a powerful argument against naturalism. Given the plausible alternatives, what you have, more specifically, is a powerful theistic argument.[5]

The nontheist who thinks that he is warranted in his nonbelief thus unwittingly presupposes the existence of God in his very denial of God, for warrant involves proper functioning, and proper functioning entails theism. Moreover, when the theist attempts to argue for the existence of God, he presupposes God's existence in that he assumes that his premises are warranted. This is not a vicious sort of circularity, but rather the inherent nature of a transcendental argument.

In addition Plantinga also provides an argument to show that naturalism is self-defeating, so that it cannot be rationally affirmed.[6] For according to naturalism, our cognitive faculties are aimed at survival, not truth. Thus, we can have no confidence in the truth of their deliverances—including the conclusion that naturalism is true! Thus, the very conclusion that naturalism is true is rationally undermined if naturalism is true.

---

[3]Alvin Plantinga, *Warrant: The Current Debate* (New York: Oxford University Press, 1993).

[4]Alvin Plantinga, *Warrant and Proper Function* (New York: Oxford University Press, 1993).

[5]Ibid., 214.

[6]Ibid., chap. 12.

Both of these arguments are philosophically sophisticated, careful articulations of themes that are rung in presuppositionalism, but with an uncertain sound. They are arguments that would be endorsed by any classical apologist and need to be differentiated from the confused claims of presuppositionalists about the inevitability of circular reasoning, the need to presuppose Christian theism in one's apologetic, and so on. Van Til, for all his insights, was not a philosopher, and it has fallen to another to discern the true shape of the argument in the cloud of confusion. The Reformed tradition needs to realize what a treasure it has in Alvin Plantinga and to appropriate his insights. People came from the utmost parts of the earth to hear the wisdom of Van Til, and behold, a greater than Van Til is here.

AN EVIDENTIALIST'S RESPONSE

Gary R. Habermas

John Frame's chapter is easy to read, gracious, and reverential. Who could object to his very first sentence? Apologetics is more than argument. In a real world of sentient beings, many of whom are hurting, we cannot be satisfied to appeal to reason as if this comprised the sole responsibility of thinking Christians.

POSITIVE CONTRIBUTIONS OF PRESUPPOSITIONAL APOLOGETICS

The major apologetic methodologies share numerous perspectives. A number of these are apparent in Frame's essay, which generally follows the Van Tillian approach. The reminder to glorify God in all our apologetics was certainly timely. Further, the apologetic task is to be carried out without pride, arrogance, or contentiousness. Our personal systems are not as important as honoring our Lord and serving others.

We do not act in our own power—saving grace and faith are not ours to dispense. The overall goal of the apologetic endeavor is to minister to others, both believers and unbelievers, keeping in mind their personal needs. Our approaches are person relative, and individual responses are necessary.

To be sure, Frame's brand of presuppositionalism majors on "negative" apologetics. His critique of postmodernists, keying on some of their self-contradictions is an example (pp. 213–14, 226–28). Both the Christian and the non-Christian should view their worldviews against the other paradigms, giving each "an equal hearing" (p. 224).

In this pursuit, evidences of all sorts may be employed. Frame makes several improvements over the Van Tillian model. He accepts data wherever it is found. This includes avenues such as the laws of logic, math, and morality, as well as investigations of nature and history. These may lead us to the traditional arguments for God's existence or historical investigations of the resurrection of Jesus, including critiques of naturalistic theories. Even extrabiblical data are useful, Frame admits, as long as they are used consistently with Scripture.[1]

Throughout, making a point of central importance to his system, Frame rightly attacks the notion of neutrality. No one can view a topic apart from a particular viewpoint. It is impossible to lay one's beliefs aside and study the pure evidence without respect to a particular outlook. As Frame states elsewhere, both Christians and non-Christians are "equally biased and equally prejudiced."[2]

Yet Frame is more open than Van Til to dialoguing with unbelievers too. Truth serves as our point of contact, and the evaluation of worldviews may come on several fronts, such as cause, purpose, and history.[3] Frame even allows and supports the notion of probability, suggesting that the word "deserves to be rehabilitated in Reformed apologetics. . . . we ought to admit that many of our arguments are only probable."[4]

Overall, there is little question that Frame has moved Van Tillian apologetics closer to its traditional cousins.[5] Recognizing the methodological similarities, he states:

---

[1]See John M. Frame, *Apologetics to the Glory of God: An Introduction* (Phillipsburg, N.J.: Presbyterian and Reformed, 1994), 60. Besides extrabiblical material, Frame says far more positive things about the use of evidence than did Van Til, such as complimenting the traditional arguments for God's existence (Frame, *Apologetics to the Glory of God*, 71, 85–86, and chap. 4).

[2]John M. Frame, *The Doctrine of the Knowledge of God* (Phillipsburg, N.J.: Presbyterian and Reformed, 1987), 126.

[3]Frame, *Apologetics to the Glory of God*, 82–85, 119; cf. idem, *Doctrine of the Knowledge of God*, 368.

[4]See Frame, *Apologetics to the Glory of God*, 86; cf. 78–82, including his comments that his own arguments are sometimes less than certain (pp. 90, 121). In *Doctrine of the Knowledge of God* (pp. 135–36) Frame notes that, along with Joseph Butler, sometimes we need to "accept the most probable possibility" (p. 136). Although he is critical of what he calls Butler's neutral approach to data, we note the differences between Frame and Van Til, for whom Butler was a chief "whipping boy." See Cornelius Van Til, *Christian-Theistic Evidences* (Phillipsburg, N.J.: Presbyterian and Reformed, 1978), 19–27.

[5]Frame, *Apologetics to the Glory of God*, 87.

Yet these strictures leave a wide scope for creativity, for using different methods, different starting points, depending on the area to be discussed, the gifts of the apologist and the felt needs of the non-Christian. Scripture itself is wonderfully rich in the methods it uses to lead us to repentance and faith. It is a shame, indeed, that modern apologetics has fallen so largely into stereotyped patterns.[6]

As an example of this stance, Frame affirms, "We must grant the claim of the evidentialists that the truth is found through the publicly observable events of nature and history."[7]

In these areas, I embrace many of Frame's thoughts, some of which he shares with other apologetic systems. On the surface, at least, this involves a fair amount of agreement between contrasting outlooks. A closer inspection will reveal some differences.

SOME CHALLENGES TO FRAME'S PRESUPPOSITIONALISM

My problems with Frame's analysis of the apologetic task generally involve places where he still holds earlier forms of presuppositional methodology. I will address a few of these problematic areas of concern.

Presuppositionalism and Christian Evidences

Frame acknowledges that Scripture frequently encourages the use of evidences, and so does he, noting their value in arguing for the truth of Christian theism. He regularly tells us, for example, that traditional apologists present strong cases for Christianity, complimenting many authors, including William Lane Craig and me, for arguments concerning God's existence, Scripture, and the resurrection of Jesus.[8] Still, these compliments are sometimes accompanied by little "jabs."[9]

---

[6]John M. Frame, "Epistemological Perspectives and Evangelical Apologetics," *Bulletin of the Evangelical Philosophical Society* 7 (1984), 7.

[7]Ibid.

[8]Other examples can be found in *Doctrine of the Knowledge of God*, 353–54, 379; and *Apologetics to the Glory of God*, 60, 71, 85–86, 145–47.

[9]Certainly Van Til is better known for this tactic. He categorized non-Reformed apologists as either Roman Catholic, Arminian, or even as less consis-

Yet, in spite of the acknowledged importance of Christian evidences, there appears to be extreme reluctance on the part of Frame and other Van Tillians to produce their own detailed, evidential arguments in favor of Christianity. While they often commend the biblical use of evidences (although variously nuanced), they almost always avoid providing careful accounts of their own reasons, explaining that they are not the ones to do this (p. 229).[10] This is indeed curious. What it appears to reveal may be even more interesting.

For more than twenty years, one long-standing criticism of Van Tillians is that, in spite of brief comments here and there and a few actual (but brief) exceptions, their method has been to eschew Christian evidences. Defenders protest that this is a misreading of Van Til,[11] and I have agreed with them on many occasions. But I suspect that this school of apologetics is the victim

---

tent Calvinists! All but those of his express conviction were viewed as presenting nonbiblical responses. See Cornelius Van Til, *The Defense of the Faith* (Phillipsburg: Presbyterian and Reformed, 1980), chap. 5, esp. pp. 90, 94, 96. While I know that Frame is definitely not mean-spirited about this, his present essay contains a couple of statements like these, which left me wondering. The comment that his variety of presuppositionalism is in some way more Reformed than adherents of Reformed epistemology (p. 215, n. 11) reminded me of Van Til. Also, how certain writers he mentions should have been "more explicitly theistic in their methodology" (p. 229, n. 39) escapes me.

[10]For some examples, see Van Til, *Defense of the Faith*, 199; Thom Notaro, *Van Til and the Use of Evidence* (Phillipsburg: Presbyterian and Reformed, 1980), 19–20. Frame comments that he is also not the one to provide the evidences, at least not in *Doctrine of the Knowledge of God* (p. 352). Even in the section on the Van Tillian's favorite argument for God's existence (the transcendental argument), Frame never delineates the details of the argument itself (*Apologetics to the Glory of God*, 69–75). Stranger still is that the job was recently performed in much detail by an evidentialist! See Stephen E. Parrish, *God and Necessity: A Defense of Classical Theism* (Lanham, Md.: University Press of America, 1997). Or, when addressing the epistemological, teleological, and cosmological arguments, Frame has a tendency to talk *about* them rather than to develop each case (*Apologetics to the Glory of God*, 102–14). Then, too, when discussing historical evidence for Jesus' resurrection in a chapter that is subtitled "Proving the Gospel," Frame begins what is only a two-page discussion of the resurrection by telling his readers that "I shall not add much to the voluminous literature showing the credibility of the biblical witness to this great event" (*Apologetics to the Glory of God*, 145). It should be carefully noted that I am not saying that Frame is incapable of developing the evidences himself. Rather, my point is that, although he says they are crucially important, neither he nor other Van Tillians provide careful treatments of Christian evidences.

[11]Probably the best example here is Notaro, *Van Til and the Use of Evidence*, chap. 1.

of its own repeated emphasis on other matters; the sheer majority of their comments outweigh the few exceptions.[12]

Interestingly, in an essay that influenced Frame's own treatment, George Mavrodes asks why Reformed thinkers so frequently devalue positive evidences. He decides: "Maybe it represents a deep ambivalence in Reformed thought, a tendency to oscillate."[13] It may be that certain theological commitments have caused the equivocation. Whatever the reason, Frame himself admits the anomaly: "Unfortunately, there has been very little actual analysis of evidence in the Van Tillian presuppositionalist school of apologetics."[14]

I think we can go further here. Frame truly differs from his mentor in his frequent and sincere references to the importance of Christian evidences, generally complimenting the nonpresuppositionalists who engage in careful arguments. Yet his approach still avoids developing these evidences from the perspective of his own system. So my question concerns the extent to which his brand of presuppositionalism represents a complete, distinctive apologetic strategy. It has done a good job of arguing negatively against those who would criticize Christian theism. But where is the other, indispensable side of apologetics—the positive confirmation?

In fact, maybe Van Tillian presuppositionalism is not that committed to the task of actually providing evidences. If it was

---

[12]Frame might respond that evidentialists have already done the job, so it doesn't have to be repeated (cf. p. 229). Once he seems to complain that there are already too many evidential treatments of the resurrection (*Apologetics to the Glory of God*, 145, n. 31). But I would make a few brief responses. (1) Since we have seen that presuppositionalists often complain that evidentialists do the job the wrong way (p. 229, n. 39, is just one example), this simply makes me wonder why they don't produce evidential treatments from their own vantage point. (2) Since evidentialists also frequently indulge (even extensively so) in negative apologetics against Christianity's critics, why doesn't this similarly stop the presuppositionalists from multiplying their own negative critiques? (3) If the presuppositionalists need to "borrow" from the evidentialists at this point, this sort of response would, once again, support my contention that the former is not a complete apologetic method.

[13]George Mavrodes, "Jerusalem and Athens," in *Faith and Rationality: Reason and Belief in God*, ed. Alvin Plantinga and Nicholas Wolterstorff (Notre Dame, Ind.: University of Notre Dame Press, 1983), 197–98.

[14]Afterward Frame adds: "I hope this gap in the Reformed apologetic literature will soon be filled, though I cannot fill it, at least not here and now" (Frame, *Doctrine of the Knowledge of God*, 352). But if Frame, who is perhaps the acknowledged pacesetter in the Van Tillian school of apologetics, does not take the lead here, who will do so? We have already seen that Van Til didn't accept the challenge either.

viewed as the important enterprise that Frame contends it is, then why haven't we seen these efforts from like-minded researchers over the last few decades? And if evidentialists and classical apologists don't do the full job that presuppositionalists wish they had, why wouldn't the latter be careful to craft their own treatments? But based on their own responses, we must conclude that evidences are not really of major importance to them. To be honest, their near absence screams to us that this pursuit is actually far down their list.

This, in turn, shows that presuppositionalism is only an incomplete apologetic system. I would even say that it fails in the most important aspect—providing positive reasons to believe. We want to do far more than show that our critics are wrong. We want to show that Christian theism is true! But especially when presuppositionalists affirm the need for evidences but then fail to produce their own treatments, they have skirted a major responsibility according to their own standards.[15] So this position is probably better described, not as a distinct apologetic method, but as a theological outlook on apologetics.

Interestingly enough, Frame again seems to admit something similar. Perhaps sensing how much movement has taken place since Van Til, he acknowledges that his tradition is now almost indistinguishable from traditional apologetic methods. He surprisingly states, "It may no longer be possible to distinguish presuppositional apologetics from traditional apologetics merely by externals—by the form of the argument, the explicit claim of certainty or probability, etc." Then he provides an honest appraisal: "Perhaps presuppositionalism is more of an attitude of the heart, a spiritual condition, than an easily describable, empirical phenomenon."[16] I agree.

The Problem of Circularity

Frame includes a treatment of circularity when he discusses the presuppositional framework, presumably because he is so frequently questioned on this subject. He responds by arguing that all philosophical systems are unavoidably circular (pp. 210, 216–17), regularly differentiating between narrow and broad

---

[15]It is the presuppositionalist who most wants to turn his opponent's argument around against him. But here it is the presuppositionalist who fails to follow up on his own explicit claims, leaving out the major building block of Christian evidences.

[16]Frame, *Apologetics to the Glory of God*, 87.

circularity (or some similar distinction) in order to explain how presuppositionalism is not viciously circular.[17] He acknowledges that one is justified in using a circular argument at only one point: "for the ultimate criterion of the system."[18]

Van Tillians seem to have a notion that all presuppositions except the most circular ones are on the same level. Since no one can be neutral, we must all begin with some sort of prior notions. Given such a stance, they can basically begin with the truth of Christian theism in at least some form. But somehow Frame proceeds from here to Scripture, as if this entire body of truth is justified by the need for a starting point.

Here Frame commits the informal logical fallacy of *false analogy*. He argues that rationalists must accept reason as an ultimate starting point, just as empiricists assume sense experience, and so on. So the Christian may begin with Scripture as a legitimate starting point.[19] But these are not analogous bases. While the rationalist uses reason and the empiricist uses sense experience as tools from which to construct their systems, Frame assumes both the *tool* of special revelation and the *system* of Scripture, from which he develops his Christian theism. In other words, he assumes the reality of God's existence, his personal interaction with humans, plus a specific product: Scripture. Does Frame not realize that, in the name of everyone needing a presupposition, he has imported an entire worldview when the others have only asked for tools?[20]

But these presuppositions are not all created equal! Frame allows rationalists and empiricists their methodological "hook," while he demands the hook, line, and sinker for Christianity! While the others still need to figure out how far their initial

---

[17]See also Frame, *Doctrine of the Knowledge of God*, 130–33; idem, *Apologetics to the Glory of God*, 9–14.

[18]Frame, *Doctrine of the Knowledge of God*, 130.

[19]Frame, *Apologetics to the Glory of God*, 10; *Doctrine of the Knowledge of God*, 130.

[20]Frame may respond that the starting point for rationalists and empiricists is more than simply tools. It is true that they build on this basis, but they do not require an entire edifice—both a foundation and a whole system of facts—to be in place before they even begin! To my knowledge, there are no similar analogies from major philosophical traditions. None require anywhere near what Frame does–especially the assumption of an inerrant text simply filled with data from an eternal source! In my opinion, there is simply no way to compare the extent of the Van Tillian presupposition with any other philosophical requirements. Lumping his presupposition with the others is quite convenient, but it is in this sense that I say that his argument presents a false analogy.

assumption will get them, Frame's kit came ready-made—he's all set to go fishing!

Contemporary apologists usually agree that no one can pursue evidence in a neutral manner, due to many sorts of biases and prejudices that color our thinking.[21] But it does not follow that we are all Van Tillian presuppositionalists. In fact, I think that Frame still argues circularly (in the sense of another informal logical fallacy).

Let's take a closer look at this specific case. Frame argues for the inspiration of Scripture, beginning with, "The Bible is the Word of God because it says so."[22] Two statements are involved here: (1) The Bible is the Word of God. (2) The Bible says it is the Word of God. Both are true. However, the Bible is not the Word of God *because* it says so. As an argument, this is a viciously circular statement. The problem is that Frame confuses truth itself with an argument for truth. In brief, while the two initial statements are true, one is not true because the other one says that it is so. He is right in his allegiance but mistaken in his grounds for the allegiance.

Frame acknowledges that there are "some serious disadvantages" with the "narrow" argument. In fact, "an unbeliever will likely dismiss it out of hand."[23] When someone questions

---

[21]I think that this is true across the contemporary apologetic spectrum. See Gary R. Habermas, "Philosophy of History, Historical Relativism and History as Evidence," in *Evangelical Apologetics*, ed. Michael Bauman, David W. Hall, and Robert C. Newman (Camp Hill: Christian Publications, 1996), 93; cf. my discussion of brute facts in chap. 2, "Evidential Apologetics" (pp. 94–95).

[22]Frame, *Apologetics to the Glory of God*, 14, cf. p. 136.

[23]Perhaps there is still another angle from which to view the problem here, beyond the untenable nature of Frame's first step as an apologetic argument. Studies in psychology of religion indicate that persons generally come to God for reasons other than intellectual ones. If they gain a scholarly interest in their faith, it usually comes later, after conversion. It is probably accurate to say that most Christians come to trust Scripture as the Word of God before they ever experience questions, doubts, or study the field of apologetics. So perhaps Frame should simply cast his first stage in a manner something like this: most Christians regularly do trust Scripture based on a childlike faith, usually apart from evidences. It is the ultimate standard of truth. But if they move on to intellectual matters, say, attempting to answer an unbeliever's questions, this is the point at which they move to the second, apologetic level. Couldn't that be a sufficient explanation of Christian belief at both stages? In brief, believers recognize that Scripture is true and that what it says about itself is also true, due to the witness of the Holy Spirit. But this is not apologetics. So we might distinguish between the two stages by referring to what believers hold (step 1) and why they hold it (step 2). The latter is the domain of apologetics. (For details, see Gary R.

this first sense of circularity, Frame very quickly jumps to the second, "broad" argument, which employs evidences from archaeology and history to show that the Bible is true. Thus, when the Muslim argues that the Koran is his presupposition, Frame addresses weaknesses in Islam.[24]

This is an intriguing move by Frame. Since he thinks that the narrow argument is a good one, why doesn't he stick with it solely by maintaining that the Muslim doesn't recognize it because of sin, without proceeding to Christian evidences? Or does Frame suspect that his narrow argument really is too circular but doesn't want to say so? Or, from a different angle, could it be that he doesn't want to face the same charge from a presuppositional Muslim with regard to the Koran, knowing that the issue could never be decided unless someone moved away from their narrow "argument"? Does Frame realize that, in such a case, apologetics is not being done at all, with both sides merely stating their beliefs against the other?

Since challenges especially from unbelievers cause Frame to move so quickly and directly to broad arguments to bolster the claim that Scripture is the Word of God, why doesn't he just go there immediately,[25] skipping his initial, though implausible (viciously circular),[26] move? This question exposes another problem, to which we will turn next.

Habermas, "The Personal Testimony of the Holy Spirit to the Believer and Christian Apologetics," *Journal of Christian Apologetics* 1, no. 1 [Summer 1997], 56–62.) Most believers already accept Scripture as God's Word when they defend it, so they are not necessarily judging it by another standard. One wonders why Frame would object here, in that he seems to speak similarly (pp. 209–10, 217–18). This may be one way to eliminate the first, viciously circular step, since it is not a viable part of the apologetic menu anyway.

[24]Frame, *Apologetics to the Glory of God*, 14. Again, we notice the first critique we raised above. Even after introducing the broad form of circularity, which utilizes evidences for Scripture, Frame still prefers to confront the Muslim with inconsistencies in his own position instead of offering any positive evidences for Christianity (*Doctrine of the Knowledge of God*, 130–33).

[25]Once (*Doctrine of the Knowledge of God*, 131) Frame moves so quickly past the narrow argument that, after only two brief sentences of definition, he immediately tells the reader that they can "broaden the circle." It is almost as if he identifies the initial stage out of duty, desiring to move on as soon as possible.

[26]This is not a derogatory reference. I emphasize that Frame's argument is "viciously circular" but not because I am trying to repeatedly "pound" on his method. He freely calls all of his arguments circular but denies that they are viciously so (p. 210). Thus, I must distinguish my use of the term by disagreeing with him in holding that his approach is circular precisely in the sense that he denies.

Testing Scripture

In agreement with a traditional emphasis in presuppositional thought, Frame is clear that we must keep the first, narrow argument for inspiration because not to do so would reveal that we are judging Scripture by another, more ultimate, standard (pp. 218–19). Rather, loyalty to God demands that we accept his Word instead of seeking to justify our own explanations, no matter how much sense they make or don't seem to make. As Frame asserts, "In the final analysis we must believe Scripture on its own say-so."[27]

Since we have rejected Frame's initial stage as an argument,[28] must the broad process of compiling evidences for the truth of Scripture now require us to judge the text by a more ultimate standard?[29] What if, far from judging Scripture, this evidential method was actually taught in Scripture? Then it would seem that Frame's entire approach would have to be seriously amended.

However, this is precisely what we find when we examine Scripture. Over and over again, with the help of several checks and balances, we are told to test God's revelation to us. To be reminded of just a few of these, potential prophets are to be tested according to their own predictions (Deut. 18:21–22).[30] More than once, God gives a similar test to other gods—let them predict the future and bring it to pass so that we may see and know that they are gods (Isa. 41:21–24; 44:7). God passed his own test (Isa. 41:25–29; 42:9; 44:24–28; 46:10; 48:5, 14). Perhaps

---

[27]Frame, *Apologetics to the Glory of God*, 14; cf. idem, *Doctrine of the Knowledge of God*, 130.

[28]Again, I have explained how the belief may be retained as a Christian conviction.

[29]It needs to be remembered that Frame seems to think that the "broad" step is less circular than the "narrow" one and "tends to hold the unbeliever's attention longer and to be more persuasive." Yet Frame thinks that it is still a circular move, and it can only be made after (or perhaps along with) the initial step. At any rate, it cannot be made by ignoring the first argument (Frame, *Apologetics to the Glory of God*, 14; cf. *Doctrine of the Knowledge of God*, 131).

[30]While it may be objected that this rule was only for the purpose of discovering false prophets, the initial context is that of the true prophet (Deut. 18:15–19). So the text would still require that all of them be checked, including the ones sent by God. More directly, how could they even discover the false prophet unless all of them were tested? Even noticing that what was predicted did come to pass would still fulfill this test.

most interesting for our purposes is that Israel was called to be his witness of these mighty historical acts of confirmation (Isa. 44:6–8; 52:6).[31] God could have simply sent his listeners to his Word, but he apparently did not think that these challenges to look at history were improper references to an authority above his written revelation.[32]

Miracles also served as such a test. While seeking an incredible heavenly sign, Elijah announced, "The god who answers by fire—he is God." The people were challenged to view an awesome miracle as God's vindication of his prophet and message (1 Kings 18:20–45). Centuries later, Jesus performed miracles on the spot to show John the Baptist that he was the Messiah (Luke 7:18–23). Both Peter (Acts 2:22–24) and Paul (Acts 16:30–31) proclaimed that Jesus' resurrection was the validation of Jesus' teachings.

These are just a few texts where both believers and unbelievers were told to examine history to ascertain God's truth. Audiences were regularly encouraged to use their minds and their eyes. They were witnesses. But there is no hint that these evidential challenges displeased God by suggesting ultimate standards being applied to his revelation. Indeed, God often made the challenge himself. Thus, it is not apparent why evidential attempts that reject Frame's first argument,[33] thereby suggesting that verifying Scripture be done on other grounds, should automatically be questioned for utilizing other standards.

---

[31]In the middle of a number of comments concerning how "Jehovah presents himself ... as the all-wise Sovereign of history," Gleason Archer notes that God "points to the testimony of fulfilled predictions" while "the Jewish nation stands as witness, furnishing verification to all the world that only Jehovah is God...." ("Isaiah" in Charles F. Pfeiffer and Everett F. Harrison, *The Wycliffe Bible Commentary* [Nashville: The Southwestern Co., 1962], 640).

[32]Frame could counter that this testing is due to the fact that revelation was not yet complete. But this would miss the point. Since God allows and even commands such testing of his own revelation even while it is still in progress, why is applying the same logic to the finished product automatically prohibited?

[33]It is very clear that Frame accepts evidences like these and will probably appear to acknowledge these and other biblical texts. But for some reason he insists that evidential methods misuse them by applying another standard to Scripture and by (somehow) not being "more explicitly theistic" (p. 229, n. 39). I have questioned his critiques, insisting that these texts allow us not only to skip his first step as an apologetic, but to go straight to verification without disobeying God. In brief, Frame has seemingly imputed apologetic standards to God that God does not require.

SUMMARY AND CONCLUSION

John Frame's version of presuppositionalism presents a number of strong points that should be welcomed by apologists. Yet it also includes several problematic areas, some of which I addressed here.

I argued, first, that while Frame regularly acknowledges the importance of developing evidences for Christian theism, even within a presuppositional system, he develops no historical arguments, for example. He even admits this to be the case with Van Tillians as a whole. But an apologetic strategy should be systematic, surely not omitting perhaps its chief objective: to argue for the truthfulness of Christianity. Thus, Frame's approach fails its own directive and is better considered a theological outlook on apologetics rather than a distinct apologetic approach.

Second, all presuppositions are not created equal, yet Frame assumes more truth on behalf of Christianity than is allowed for other systems. Still, his first stage of argumentation for Scripture is viciously circular and is better considered as a Christian conviction than as an apologetic argument, for it is incapacitated in the latter role.

Third, presuppositionalism has long charged that evidential treatments subject Scripture to a more ultimate standard. Yet it seems clear that God not only allows, but actually challenges, his people to examine and witness evidential manifestations that confirm his revealed truth. These God-given tests do not usurp his authority in the process.

While these and other, lesser issues remain,[34] my critiques do not eliminate many of Frame's excellent insights. But I think

---

[34]An example is the way in which Frame distinguishes between negative (or defensive) and positive (or offensive) apologetics, defining the latter with very little reference to evidences, but as "bringing criticisms against non-Christian ideas" (p. 215; cf. Frame, *Doctrine of the Knowledge of God*, 348–60, esp. 359; idem, *Apologetics to the Glory of God*, 75–77). This is indeed a peculiar approach that almost seems to ignore evidences from the very outset. Mavrodes, in a section on the same subject, makes the much more natural distinction that negative apologetics "consists of refuting and rebutting arguments against the faith," while positive apologetics presents arguments *in favor of* Christianity (Mavrodes, "Jerusalem and Athens," 197). Again we see the presuppositional avoidance of evidences.

Another issue is Frame's failure to distinguish between the types and extent of presuppositions. For example, he doesn't seem to realize that a nonpresuppositionalist can still reject epistemic neutrality (cf. pp. 222–23 with his *Doctrine of the Knowledge of God*, pp. 87, 354, 376). I have argued in my initial essay and elsewhere that evidentialists actually agree that there are no brute, uninterpreted historical facts.

that the larger problems are very difficult to overcome and disqualify his position as a separate apologetic system.

My critiques are offered in the spirit of collegiality, realizing that John Frame has certainly done much to further the cause of Christ. He exemplifies the intent of the apostle Peter, who tells us to offer our arguments "with gentleness and respect" (1 Peter 3:15).[35] May the desire to do all to God's glory be the cry of each one of us.

---

[35]For another example, see John Frame's kindly comments throughout his article, "Van Til and the Ligonier Apologetic," *Westminster Theological Journal* 47, no. 2 (Fall 1985), 297–98.

A CUMULATIVE CASE
APOLOGIST'S RESPONSE

Paul D. Feinberg

THE BIBLE AND EPISTEMOLOGY

John Frame begins his discussion of presuppositional apologetics with a section called "Biblical Epistemology." He says that the Bible has a great deal to say about epistemology and then goes on to cite a number of biblical texts in support of this claim. I would not want to dispute the fact that the Bible does have much to say about epistemology, but I think one has to be very careful about what is meant by this. The Bible has many things to say that must be taken into account in the development of an epistemology. It teaches that we can know a variety of things, including the fact that there is an external world. From this biblical teaching, we would have to reject any epistemology that taught complete skepticism.

However, I think Kelly James Clark is right in saying that there is no single true, biblical epistemology. The teaching of Scripture is compatible with a number of epistemological approaches. The way Clark puts it is that the biblical data *underdetermines* any epistemological theory (see chapter 5, "Reformed Epistemology Apologetics," p. 275). Another way of putting it is that the Bible has certain things to say to the epistemologist, but it is not an epistemology book. Because a variety of epistemologies are compatible with the teaching of the Bible, a variety of apologetic approaches will have legitimacy.

FAITH

Frame asks where faith comes from. He says that the question is ambiguous and may be understood in at least two ways. First, it may be asking what is the *cause* of faith. The answer is that God causes faith in an individual. That answer is correct, but it is too cryptic. We may ask a further question: How does God cause faith? The answer to that question is that he causes faith in a variety of ways. In at least some cases, the Holy Spirit uses evidence as a means to bring about faith in an individual who becomes a believer. If this is so, then an evidentialist approach is not contrary to the view that God causes one to have faith. Christian evidences may function in bringing one to faith, not simply to confirm one's faith.

Second, Frame thinks that the question may be asking what is the *rational basis* of faith. Throughout my responses I have spoken about my answer to this question. For some the rational basis of their faith is the inner witness of the Holy Spirit. Others may base their faith on some evidence like that for the resurrection. I agree with Frame that where there is evidence and there is the true witness of the Holy Spirit, that witness is in keeping with reality and truth. The Holy Spirit, who is called the Spirit of truth, does not lead people into error.

THE EFFECTS OF SIN

Frame goes on to point out that sin is an impediment to the apprehension of truth. Because we are sinners, we are not in a position of neutrality toward truth about God and our helpless state. Knowing the truth, then, is not simply a matter of the facts or the evidence; it is a matter of the will. There is in the unbeliever an unwillingness to accept the truth. I am in agreement with Frame so far, but there is a question that I do not see a clear answer to in his chapter: Is an unbeliever ever able to come to true knowledge about anything in general and about God in particular? At one point Frame says, "Both [believer and unbeliever] commit sin, and both grasp the truth in some measure." But at the same time he also thinks that "the differences [between believers and unbelievers] are too substantial to be described as mere differences in degree" (p. 214). I too believe that sin has effected the cognitive equipment of the human race and that we are in rebellion against God's truth. However, I think that human beings (including unbelievers) are capable of knowing things, even truth about God. If I am wrong about this, evidence will be useless even as a means in the hands of the Holy Spirit to bring about regeneration. If I am right, evidence may be an instrument in the Holy Spirit's hand at least in some cases.

An objection to what I have just said is that my view comes at the expense of the total sovereignty of God over all areas of human life. It sets up an autonomous reason over some areas of life. I take this criticism very seriously. I do not in the end, however, think that it is correct. I think that the ability of the unregenerate to arrive at some truth is a matter of God's grace as well—his common grace.

Frame sees value in apologetics for both believers and unbelievers. The value lies in three areas: the rational confirmation of the faith, replies to criticisms, and critically evaluating non-Christian ideas. A cumulative case apologist would agree that apologetics is valuable in these areas but would add a fourth area. Some evidence for Christian theism might be used by the Holy Spirit to challenge the unbeliever's view of the world and to point that person to faith in Christ. Frame seems to disagree with this, because it is impossible for the Christian to ask a nonbeliever to believe in Christ on Christian presuppositions. Again, he says that "the unbeliever cannot think according to Christian presuppositions" (p. 217). I do not understand why this is so. I can think about things from the presuppositions of an unbeliever, and I think that unbelievers can think about things from the standpoint of a Christian. Frame seems to recognize this as he says, "God made them to think with the Christian-theistic worldview as their presupposition" (p. 218). And in a footnote he says, "Again, I am referring here to the unbeliever's *dominant* presuppositions. As I said before, unbelievers often think Christianly in spite of themselves" (p. 217, n. 13). If the latter statements are true, it is possible to put on the Christian spectacles and see the world in a new way, a way the Holy Spirit can use in the conversion of the unbeliever.

COMMON GROUND

Frame's reticence in using evidence with unbelievers may be that he thinks it requires that we find some common ground, and this requires that we leave our biblical presuppositions and claim to be neutral. Doing this would be to indulge in a lie. I do not see, however, why this is an accurate appraisal of what occurs when we give apologetic arguments. Neither of us feign neutrality, nor do I grant to the inquirers a position on an intellectual throne or the right to wait until they have all their questions answered to their satisfaction.

TWO BENEFITS

A presuppositional apologetic is most successful in two areas. First, I think that it reminds us that all arguments have presuppositions. In arguing about conflicting worldviews, it is helpful to uncover these presuppositions and to discuss and debate them. The presuppositions behind any position will affect the way evidence is understood. Thus, one way to challenge unbelievers' thinking is to show some of the consequences of holding certain presuppositions and by pointing out data that conflicts or is in opposition with their belief systems.

A second strength of the presuppositional approach is that it demonstrates that direct "proofs" are not the only proofs. Frame holds that

> our argument should be *transcendental*. That is, it should present the biblical God, not merely as the conclusion to an argument, but as the one who makes argument possible. We should present him as the source of all meaningful communication, since he is the author of all order, truth, beauty, goodness, logical validity, and empirical fact (p. 220).

Such a proof is *indirect* or *transcendental*. Some have understood presuppositional apologetics as a transcendental or indirect argument for God and Christianity. Such arguments are Kantian at least in spirit and can offer another useful tool for the apologist. The argument is that without God these aspects of human experience would be impossible.

Frame does not always talk about arguing transcendentally for God and Christianity. Sometimes he speaks as though there is a certain circularity in the defense of the faith. He says that we are to *presuppose* the truth of Christianity in all our thinking. This also means that the truth of Christianity is assured before any argument is offered. We are also to presuppose that God's Word is true, assuring the conclusion at the beginning of the argument. Frame thinks that such reasoning is circular but not viciously circular. Twice he offers a diagram of a chain in support of the idea that the reasoning is linear and not circular.

There is an alternative way of looking at this that avoids Frame's problem. First, something needs to be said about rationality. It is rooted or grounded in God himself. It is not as if it is external to God, limiting him in some way. Furthermore, rationality is not entirely different for the believer and the unbeliever. For instance, both believers and unbelievers think using the law of noncontradiction. It is not as if the believer has one set of logical rules and the unbeliever has another entirely different set of logical rules. These rules of thought are a common ground between believers and unbelievers. This does not mean that there is agreement on all areas of human experience. As a matter of fact, we know there is not. Disagreement exists over whether there is a God and whether God has revealed himself in the person of Jesus Christ. But because there is some agreement on the rules of thought and other areas of common human experience, we do not simply have to presuppose the truth of Christianity. We can present evidence and debate its meaning.

A similar course of action is open on the Bible. I do not have to presuppose that it is true in order to show that it is true. Evidence supports its truth. That evidence includes what the Bible has to say about itself, as well as a variety of other lines of argument. At least some important part of that evidence is open to empirical testing so that the argument is not circular.[1] It is not necessary to presuppose the Bible's truth.

This does not mean that I must go through the proof every time I appeal to the Bible in support of some claim. For example, in the teaching of theology, I set out the evidence for the truth of the Bible at the beginning of our theology sequence. After that, I simply cite verses in support of the sinfulness of man, the deity of Christ, the necessity of salvation, and the coming of Christ. If, however, I were challenged on the accuracy or authenticity of a text, I could appeal to the argument that I gave in the beginning of the sequence.

---

[1]See Paul D. Feinberg, "The Meaning of Inerrancy," in *Inerrancy,* ed. Norman L. Geisler (Grand Rapids: Zondervan, 1980), 267–304; idem, "Bible, Inerrancy and Infallibility of," in *Evangelical Dictionary of Theology*, ed. Walter Elwell (Grand Rapids: Baker, 1984), 142–45, for the development of an argument that is evidential and not circular.

An objection to this approach might be that it leaves open the possibility that the Bible might not be true or that Christianity might not be the best explanation for the world we live in. Or that to enter into an argument you at least have to take a position of neutrality toward the conclusion, and that this is a deceit. Therefore, you must presuppose the conclusion and defend your method against the charge of circularity.

I have three things to say in response to this objection. First, I do not see how debating an issue requires that a position of neutrality is necessary. People argue over issues all the time while they are very committed to a view. No deceit is needed. All that is necessary is that one face the evidence and treat it fairly. Not everyone will be convinced by the evidence for Christianity or the truth of Bible. That is the work of the Holy Spirit, and one is simply using arguments as a tool in the hand of the Spirit of God.

Second, why should Christians be afraid of the evidence for their faith? Christianity is not a system of belief in which you are required to check your brain at the door. Someone like C. S. Lewis said that he was carried into the kingdom kicking and screaming by the evidence for the deity of Christ.[2] Alternative explanations will be posed for the Christian understanding of events. We see in the empty tomb a resurrection, while unbelievers think that the body of Jesus was stolen. But which is the more likely story when all of the evidence is examined and the Holy Spirit does his work?

Third, I think that behind this objection is a fear that the whole structure of reality might collapse if we don't presuppose the faith in our arguments, or that it at least totters until the apologist for Christianity wins the debate. None of this is the case. The debate is an epistemological one. The structure of reality remains in place whether the apologist wins or the antagonist refuses to accept the evidence. Refusal to accept the evidence only leaves one without the truth. In all too many cases this refusal is a matter of the will, as Frame has reminded us.

---

[2]C. S. Lewis, *Mere Christianity* (New York, Macmillan, 1960), bk. 2.

A REFORMED EPISTEMOLOGIST'S RESPONSE

Kelly James Clark

John Frame's essay is the best version of presuppositionalism I have read. Although I have read some of the published writings of Cornelius Van Til, presuppositionalism's founding father, I have always found him baffling. Either I don't understand what he is saying, or if I do understand it, what he says seems obviously false (or to entail obvious falsehoods) or, at best, arguably true (but seldom argued for). I am puzzled by the steady stream of his followers that has poured out of Westminster Seminary. Nonetheless, Frame has put presuppositionalism in a favorable and defensible light. I wonder, however, just how much of classical presuppositionalism remains in his views. Yet, I think some of the confusions of the master are in the pupil, so I will try to clarify some matters of concern. Before we turn to the confusions, let us consider some positive ways that Frame distances himself from other presuppositionalists.

THE DIFFERENCES BETWEEN FRAME AND OTHER PRESUPPOSITIONALISTS

Unlike some presuppositionalists, Frame believes that argument can play a positive role in coming to faith.[1] Unlike evidentialists, however, Frame is keenly aware of the limits of arguments

---

[1] If unbelievers can't know anything, how can arguments be used to persuade them of the truth of the Christian faith? There is, after all, no point of neutrality, according to Frame, between believer and unbeliever.

and the influence of our presuppositions on our believings. On this latter point, Frame and I are firmly in agreement.

Frame roots his epistemological commitments in Scripture and finds there support for the view that we can offer proof for our beliefs. Presuppositionalists have tended to believe themselves to be *the* biblical and Christian apologists (arrogantly so, in my estimation, when they call other apologetical approaches anti-Christian), but Frame is more generous in his assessments of other apologetic approaches.[2] I am dubious, however, of finding any ultimate or coercive support for epistemology in Scripture. The Hebrews were not theoretical thinkers—wisdom was for them profoundly practical. To say that "the fear of the Lord is the beginning of wisdom" is not to make a claim about proper procedure in physics, packaging, or the culinary arts. It is a claim about practical wisdom—how to live one's (moral and spiritual) life. The very idea of a biblical epistemology seems to me as misguided as the idea of a biblical meteorology.

Frame offers more by way of argument for his positions than most presuppositionalists. I have listened to the tapes (which Frame commends) of the debate between Gregory Bahnsen, presuppositional apologist, and Gordon Stein, defender of atheism. Quite frankly, I found Bahnsen's arguments precious thin and his approach wearisome—he simply repeated over and over that unbelievers have no grounds for reason and then offered the briefest defense of his view that only Christian theism provides grounds for reason. Van Til, I'm afraid, had a similar awkward tendency to prefer assertion over argument. Perhaps the presuppositionalists are right when they claim that only Christian theism can provide any grounds for reason, meaning, and the natural sciences. But making the case that this is so requires an enormous amount of research, thought, and argument. A paragraph or two scarcely suffice. We shall see if Frame succeeds on this score.

DO NON-CHRISTIANS KNOW ANYTHING?

Van Til's epistemological claims seem clearly to imply that non-Christians cannot know anything.[3] This has caused some

---

[2]See p. 229, n. 39. I think his generosity is all the more remarkable given the vitriol of the criticism of presuppositionalism offered by some of these thinkers.

[3]Van Til and his followers often claim that Van Til never claims this. The problem is that the conclusion—that unbelievers cannot know anything—follows fairly

embarrassment for his followers because it looks like it is obviously false. Surely even the most benighted unbelievers know that they aren't the only people who exist in the world, what their own names are, and what they ate for breakfast. The reason unbelievers can't know anything, according to presuppositionalists, is that the presuppositions upon which their knowledge is based are all wrong—they believe on the basis of autonomous human reason and not on the basis of the God who is reason. The rotting foundation affects the beliefs that are based on it. Presuppositionalists allege that there are also contradictions among the beliefs of unbelievers that undermine any justification that these and, it seems, all their beliefs could have.[4]

Frame himself claims to distance himself from this extravagant version of presuppositionalism. He contends, for example, that even unbelievers have conscious knowledge of God, that Pharisees had many true ideas, and that believer and unbeliever alike grasp truth. But he asks, "What is the difference, then, between believer and unbeliever?" (p. 213). A portion of his answer concerns the moral differences, but the primary thrust of his answer addresses epistemological differences. And here, I think, Frame makes statements that imply that unbelievers *cannot know anything* (even though they *believe* some truths). Before discussing Frame's view, I will provide a brief analysis of knowledge.

Philosophers standardly define knowledge as *justified true belief*. First, in order for someone to know something, they must believe it.[5] Second, the belief in question must be true; we cannot know things that are false. And third, knowledge requires that our beliefs be justified or warranted: justification separates knowledge from mere true opinion. What constitutes justification is controversial and beyond the scope of this essay; nonetheless, I shall make some cursory remarks on it as it pertains to Frame's discussion.

---

simply from their analysis of knowledge and the disparaging remarks they make about the unbeliever's lack of justification due to faulty reasoning.

[4]The problem of believing contradictions creates a problem for believers as well as unbelievers. I believe that we all have justified but inconsistent beliefs. Some of our beliefs are directly contradictory and others are probabilistically inconsistent. Thus, if consistency is a requirement of knowledge, no one—believer or unbeliever—knows anything at all. Omniscience, therefore, becomes a condition of knowledge.

[5]The beliefs need not be occurrent (i.e., present to immediate consciousness).

Frame suggests that humans are justified (rational) when their reasoning images God's reasoning. He contends that God's rationality is the rational basis for human faith, which is the rational basis for human reasoning. What justifies beliefs for human beings, therefore, seems to be faith in the Christian God. Lacking that faith, one cannot be rational and, hence, one cannot be justified in any of one's beliefs. The nontheist may hold many true opinions but cannot have knowledge—autonomous human reason is not sufficient to justify beliefs. Indeed, Frame makes the astonishing claim that "unbelievers are often more brilliant than believers, using their reason in the service of falsehood" (p. 214, n. 9). Newton (who was a theist but not a Christian), Einstein (who was not a theist or at least not a theist in any orthodox sense), and Watson and Crick (both nontheists) have made some of the most brilliant contributions to human knowledge. Was their brilliance merely a tool in the service of falsehood? Would their discoveries have been different or more rational if they had been Christian theists? Newton, Einstein, Watson, and Crick constitute a reductio of the presuppositionalist claim that unbelievers cannot know anything.

Presuppositionalists, in general, seem to assume that, lacking explicit knowledge of God, we cannot know things. Indeed, opposing apologetic approaches are considered defective because they work with a notion of rationality that excludes God.[6] But many Christian apologists believe that even for the atheist to know something, her cognitive faculties must have been designed by God; even for the atheist the *ontological fact* of God's existence is necessary for knowledge (but not the *epistemological awareness* of God). It does not follow that atheists must be aware of God's existence or submit to God's authority in order to know things. Although they deny the existence of God, their other cognitive faculties were nonetheless designed by God to produce true beliefs. So the atheist can know that the sky is blue, that 2 + 2 = 4, and that she had porridge for breakfast, even if she does not believe that God exists; her perceptual, arithmetical, and memory faculties can still function properly in the appropriate circumstances. Likewise, her digestive faculties can function properly even if she is unaware that they are designed by God.[7]

---

[6]See Frame, p. 229, n. 39, and the discussion surrounding it.

[7]I am drawing on an argument I made in "Plantinga vs. Oliphint: And the Winner Is . . . ," *Calvin Theological Journal* 33, no. 1 (April 1998): 160–69.

This is not a merely theoretical dispute between Frame and me. It has practical consequences, which, according to presuppositionalism, is where our beliefs are ultimately tested. If unbelievers don't know anything, how could we possibly communicate with them? How could we argue with them or reduce their presuppositions to absurdity? A minimal condition of dialogue is that the parties involved know (roughly) the meanings of the words that each other uses. Barring that, there can be no communication. Since some of our terms are referential, this occasionally requires understanding the (successful) connection between word and world. So, a presupposition, to borrow the term, of dialogue is common language that assumes some common knowledge. If there is a total noetic and linguistic *antithesis*[8] between believer and unbeliever, then all of our utterances to one another amount to little more than "ugh." Since we can, and often do, successfully dialogue with unbelievers, unbelievers know a great many things.

I think Frame understands this but has not yet sufficiently distanced himself from Van Til's rhetoric. Some of Van Til's language is downright misleading, and Frame would be better off simply discarding it and stating a clear view of rationality that captures our intuition that unbelievers know things.

ON KNOWING WHEN TO ARGUE

Philosophers are wont to argue—to defend, to challenge, to criticize, to refute. This is the peculiar virtue of philosophy that, as Frame rightly reminds us, is quick to turn into a vice. But we do, at least qua philosophers, need to argue for our positions, and this is our service to the Christianity community.

As I mentioned in the second section, presuppositionalists are often long on assertion and short on argument. This lacunae in Van Til's written work should have been filled up by his followers. Instead, as I mentioned in my comment on the Bahnsen debate, it has remained sadly unfilled. Perhaps presuppositionalists are right—reason can't be established on the basis of nothing but matter, motion, time, and chance—but we need an argument for this. Perhaps only Christian theism can establish reason—again we need an argument. Merely asserting these

---

[8]Although Frame has not used this presuppositionalist buzz word, the concept is present in his arguments.

claims over and over, perhaps more loudly and more forcefully, is not sufficient. I often feel like presuppositionalists are trying to gain by theft what should be obtained by honest toil.

Frame does offer an outline of an argument in his apologetic sketch. He divides worldviews into the personal and the impersonal, with only the "religions of the book" on the personal side.[9] He claims that there is nothing in matter, motion, time, and chance to account for the necessity of, say, the laws of logic. Here I would like to see an argument: a presentation of materialist defenses of logic and a careful refutation. What does Quine, perhaps the greatest American philosopher of the twentieth century, say about the status of logic? What about Wittgenstein, Quine's British equal? How do nontheist philosophers of mathematics understand the nature of numbers and arithmetical truth? There is hard and careful work to be done here and, to my knowledge, it simply hasn't been done by any presuppositionalists. We certainly don't get any sense from Frame as to how this might be done.

Alvin Plantinga has offered a complex, powerful, and intriguing refutation of reason given the assumptions of naturalism and evolution.[10] His argument has received a great deal of criticism and comment. Any proper defense of the view that naturalism cannot support reason requires consideration of all the objections (and probably a few that haven't been thought of yet). These sorts of philosophical undertakings have been ignored, by and large, by presuppositionalists. Perhaps it is fitting and proper, in some contexts, to ignore the details of these complicated arguments, but the leading thinkers of apologetic approaches cannot ignore these details.

I wish to make two more points about Frame's argument. First, not all of the "impersonal" options are the same—not all of them assume that all that ultimately exists is matter, motion, time, and chance. Plato and Hegel, for example, deny that matter is all there is. Some Buddhists and some philosophical idealists deny the existence of matter altogether. Polytheists of certain stripes deny that chance exists. In "refuting" the impersonalist option, Frame's remarks leave these views untouched. Can we account for reason if reality is ultimately nonmaterial and gov-

---

[9]I shall not dispute him on this point, but I think it's false.

[10]Alvin Plantinga, *Warrant and Proper Function* (New York: Oxford University Press, 1993), 194–237.

erned by fate? I don't really know, but any adequate refutation of the so-called impersonalist options must consider all of the options case by case. Again, this vastly complicates the apologetic project. So be it. But, again, as far as I know, it hasn't been attempted by the presuppositionalists.[11]

The second point is that given that all three "religions of the book" can account for reason, Frame puts a heavy burden of proof on the historical evidence for the incarnation and resurrection in order to demonstrate the rational preference of Christianity over Judaism and Islam. Unfortunately, Frame fails to heed his own comments about the nonneutrality of reason and seems to suggest that the evidence is compelling to the sufficiently open-minded.[12]

IN DEFENSE OF REASON

Frame makes many disparaging remarks about "autonomous human reason" as the standard of truth. I don't know of any philosophers who have suggested that reason is the *standard* of truth. A great many philosophers, however, have suggested that reason is the best human tool for *figuring out* the truth. And, if reason is sufficiently broadly defined, it does seem to be the best human tool for discovering the truth. Let us define reason in terms of all of a human being's truth-aimed cognitive faculties—reasoning, inductive, perceptual, aural, memory, and so on. We can include among the deliverances of reason all of our properly basic or foundational beliefs—beliefs in the past, in an external world, and so on. Of course, some philosophers have mistakenly restricted reason to reasoning, drawing inferences from obviously true propositions. But the follies of this view have been unmasked. Reasoning is sterile without the evidential input of all of our cognitive faculties. Here I (under)stand; I can do no other.

Thus construed, is autonomous human reasoning a bad thing? Again, I think we need to remind ourselves that Frame and I both believe that our cognitive faculties are designed by God. We also both believe in the noetic effects of sin—that our cognitive faculties are distorted primarily toward ends that

---

[11]Frame likewise asserts (without much argument) that unbelievers have no foundation for significant philosophical issues such as causation, ethics, the meaning of life, and the sciences (see pp. 220–24).

[12]Frame goes so far as to suggest that the evidence for the resurrection is as cogent as the evidence for Wellington's defeat of Napoleon.

enhance a person's self-interest. We depart, I believe, on where we draw the limits of the noetic effects of sin. I am inclined to believe that our beliefs are most likely to be distorted when they pertain to the fundamentally human—such as theology, morality, and psychology—and see the distorting effects lessened in other domains—as in the sciences, architecture, and culinary arts. I also don't believe that the noetic effects of sin have destroyed our moral or spiritual senses; we can come to some moral and spiritual truths unaided by the Holy Spirit.

Let us return to our question: Is autonomous human reasoning a bad thing? If it's a bad thing, it is all the worse for us, because it is all we have. Although people often oppose revelation to reason and suggest that revelation is superior, there can be, in the end, no real opposition. Here is the problem: Each person must decide (tacitly or explicitly) that a purported revelation *is* revelation. Each person must decide that what is being said in some particular holy writ *is* the voice of God. Each person must decide *what* is being said and then what it *means*. And each person must decide what it *means today* that God said something a long time ago. At every level, human reason is operative.

Unless the Holy Spirit totally overwhelms a person, human reason (of the autonomous variety) is still operative. We can seek to bring our minds into conformity with God's will, but we have to decide which God and what is his will. We decide. "To claim neutrality is to claim that *I* am the one who ultimately decides what is true or false" (p. 218). But surely I *am* the one who decides what is true or false. Who else could do that for me? Of course, our deciding does not *make* something true or false; that is not my point. My point is that each of us must make decisions using our best judgment about what is true and false. I don't see any other way around it. We have no other faculty than reason (in the broad sense) to come to our best judgment of which god to follow (or not) and what it means to follow that god.

I suspect that some presuppositionalists believe that Scripture is so clear that submission to God's truths does not involve any imposition of human reason. But the tremendous diversity of Christian interpretations of Scripture suggests otherwise. Every take on Scripture is *interpretation*—and interpretation is a function (at least partly) of "autonomous" human reason. We may damn reason in some of its restrictive forms, but it is the best (and only tool) that intellectually free human beings have to discover the truth.

CONCLUSION

What Frame and I write about how to do apologetics probably does not differ very much. It is on the *whys*, not the *hows*, that we differ. But the whys have a big implication for the hows. The consequences of Frame's presuppositionalist views would make apologetics impossible. That seems good reason to me to reject his presuppositionalist presuppositions.

Chapter Five

REFORMED EPISTEMOLOGY
APOLOGETICS

Kelly James Clark

REFORMED EPISTEMOLOGY APOLOGETICS

Kelly James Clark

Suppose a stranger—let's call him David—sends you a note that declares your wife is cheating on you. No pictures are included, no dates or times, no names. Just the assertion of your wife's unfaithfulness. You already have had fifteen good and, so far as you know, faithful years with your wife. Her behavior has not changed dramatically in the past few years. Except for David's allegation, you have no reason to believe there has been a breach in the relationship. What should you do? Confront her with what you take to be the truth, straight from David's letter? Hire a detective to follow her for a week and hope against hope the letter is a hoax? Or do you simply remain secure in the trust that you have built up all those years?

Suppose, even worse, that your son Clifford comes home after taking his first philosophy course in college. He persuades you of the truth of the so-called problem of other minds. How do you know that other minds and, therefore, other people exist? How do you know that people are not simply cleverly constructed robots with excellent makeup jobs? How do you know that behind the person facade lies a person—someone with thoughts, desires, and feelings? You can't experience another person's feelings; you can't see another person's thoughts (even if you cut off the top of his head and peer into his brain); and even President Clinton can't really feel another person's pain. Yet thoughts, desires, and feelings are all essential to being a person. So you can't tell from the outside or just by looking, so to speak, if someone is a person. I can know that *I* am a person because I experience my own thoughts, feelings, and desires. But I can't know, because I don't have any access to your inner experience, if you, or anyone else, is a person.

Since you can't know if anyone else is a person, you rightly infer that you can't know if your wife is a person. Unsure that your wife is a person, how do you treat her? Do you hire a philosophical detective to search the philosophical literature for a proof that people-like things really are people? Do you avoid cuddling in the meantime, given your aversion to snuggling with machines? Or do you simply trust your deep-seated conviction that, in spite of the lack of evidence, your wife is a person and deserves to be treated as such?

Two final "supposes." Suppose that you come to believe that there is a God because your parents taught you from the cradle up that God exists. Or suppose that you are on a retreat or on the top of a mountain and have a sense of being loved by God or that God created the universe. You begin to believe in God, not because you are persuaded by the argument from design—you are simply taken with belief in God. You just find yourself believing, what you had heretofore denied, that God exists. Now you have come across the writings of David Hume and W. K. Clifford, who insist that you base all of your beliefs on evidence. Hume raises a further point: your belief in an all-loving, omnipotent God is inconsistent with the evil that exists in the world. Given the fact of evil, God cannot exist. To meet this demand for evidence, do you become a temporary agnostic and begin perusing the texts of Aquinas, Augustine, and Paley for a good proof of God's existence? Do you give up belief in God because you see Hume's point and can't see how God and evil could be reconciled? Or do you remain steady in your trust in God in spite of the lack of evidence and even in the face of counterevidence?

My suppose-this and suppose-that stories are intended to raise the problem of the relationship of our important beliefs to evidence (and counterevidence). Since the Enlightenment, there has been a demand to expose all of our beliefs to the searching criticism of reason. If a belief is unsupported by the evidence, it is irrational to believe it. It is the position of Reformed epistemology (likely the position that Calvin held) that belief in God, like belief in other persons, does not require the support of evidence or argument in order for it to be rational. This view has been defended by some of the world's most prominent philosophers, including Alvin Plantinga, leader of the recent revival in Christian philosophy. Plantinga was Reformed epistemology's first contemporary defender, and his home institution, Calvin College, supported the research of other prominent philosophers in its development, including Nicholas Wolterstorff, William Alston, and George Mavrodes.[1] The firstfruit of their labors was the jointly published *Faith and Rationality*,[2] which in turn produced an entire industry of defenses of religious belief. Important and influential works were published on religious experience, revelation, Christian belief, epistemology, and the problem of evil. The renaissance of Christian philosophy owes a great debt to the intellectual power and fertility of Reformed epistemology.

The claim that belief in God is rational without the support of evidence or argument is startling for many an atheist or theist. Most atheist intellectuals feel comfort in their disbelief in God because they judge that there is little or no evidence for God's existence. Many theistic thinkers, however, in particular Roman Catholics and some recent Protestant evangelicals, insist that belief in God requires evidence and that such a demand should and can be met. So the claim that a person does not need evidence in order to rationally believe in God runs against the grain for atheist thinkers and has raised the ire of many theists. In spite of the vitriolic response to Reformed epistemology, I believe it is eminently defensible. In order to defend it, let us examine its critique of the Enlightenment demand for evidence.

THE DEMAND FOR EVIDENCE

W. K. Clifford, in an oft-cited article, claims that it is wrong, always and everywhere, for anyone to believe anything on insufficient evidence. Such a strong claim makes one speculate on Clifford's childhood: one imagines young W. K. constantly pestering his parents with "Why? Why? Why? . . ." It is this childish attitude toward inquiry and the risks that belief requires that leads William James to chastise Clifford as an *enfant terrible*. But, rather than disparage his character, let's examine the deficiencies of his claim that everything must be believed only on the basis of suf-

---

[1]This story is retold in Kelly James Clark, *Philosophers Who Believe* (Downers Grove, Ill.: InterVarsity Press, 1993), 7–16.

[2]Alvin Plantinga and Nicholas Wolterstorff, *Faith and Rationality* (Notre Dame, Ind.: University of Notre Dame Press, 1983).

ficient evidence (relevance: If everything must be based on sufficient evidence, so must belief in God).

The first problem with Clifford's universal demand for evidence is that it cannot meet its own demand. Clifford offers two fetching examples (a ship owner knowingly sends an unseaworthy ship to sea, and in the first example, it sinks, and in the second example, it makes the trip) in support of his claim. The examples powerfully demonstrate that in cases like these, rational belief requires evidence. No one would disagree: some beliefs require evidence for their rational acceptability. But *all* beliefs in *every* circumstance? That's an exceedingly strong claim to make and, it turns out, one that cannot be based on evidence.

Consider what someone like Clifford might allow us to take for evidence—beliefs that we acquire through sensory experience and beliefs that are self-evident like logic and mathematics. On the next rainy day, make a list of all of your experiential beliefs: the sky is blue, grass is green, most trees are taller than most grasshoppers, slugs leave a slimy trail. . . . Now add to this list all of your logical and mathematical beliefs: $2 + 2 = 4$, every proposition is either true or false, all of the even numbers that I know of are the sum of two prime numbers, in Euclidean geometry the interior angles of triangles equal 180°. From these propositions, try to deduce the conclusion that it is wrong, always and everywhere, for anyone to believe anything on insufficient evidence. None of the propositions that are allowed as evidence have anything at all to do with the conclusion. So Clifford's universal demand for evidence cannot satisfy its own standard! Therefore, by Clifford's own criterion, it must be irrational. More likely, however, the demand is simply false, and it is easy to see why.

We, finite beings that we are, simply cannot meet such a demand. Consider all of the beliefs that you currently hold. How many of those have met Clifford's strict demand for evidence? Clifford intends for all of us, like a scientist in a laboratory, to test all of our beliefs all of the time. Could your beliefs survive Clifford's test? Think of how many of your beliefs, even scientific ones, are acquired *just because someone told you*. Not having been to Paraguay, I only have testimonial evidence that Paraguay is a country in South America. For all I know, all of the mapmakers have conspired to delude us about the existence of Paraguay (and even South America!). And, since I have been to relatively few countries around the world, I must believe in the existence of most countries (and that other people inhabit them and speak in *that* language) without support of evidence. I believe that e = mc² and that matter is made up of tiny particles, not because of experiments in a chemistry or physics lab (for all of my experiments failed), but because my science teachers told me so. Most of the beliefs that I have acquired are based on my trust in my teachers and not on careful consideration of what Clifford would consider adequate evidence. And in this busy day and age, I don't really have the time to live up to Clifford's demand for evidence! Even if we had the leisure to test all of our beliefs, we could not meet the demand. Since we cannot meet that demand, we cannot be obligated to do so.

The demand for evidence simply cannot be met in a large number of cases with the cognitive equipment we possess. No one, as mentioned above, has ever been able to prove the existence of other persons. No one has ever been able to prove that we were not created five minutes ago with our memories intact. No one has been able to prove the reality of the past or that, in the future, the sun will rise. This list could go on and on. There is a limit to the things that human beings can prove. A great deal of what we believe is based on faith, not on evidence or arguments.

I use the term "faith" here, but I think it is misleading. I don't mean to oppose faith to knowledge in these instances. For surely we know that the earth is more than five minutes old and that the sun will rise tomorrow (except perhaps in cloudy Grand Rapids) and that Paul converted to Christianity (and lots of other truths about the past), et cetera, et cetera, et cetera. In these cases, we know lots of things, but we cannot prove them. We have to trust or rely on the cognitive faculties that produce these beliefs. We rely on our memory to produce memory beliefs (I remember having coffee with my breakfast this morning). We rely on an inductive faculty to produce beliefs about the veracity of natural laws (if I let go of this book, it will fall to the ground). We rely on our cognitive faculties when we believe that there are other persons, there is a past, there is a world independent of our mind, or what other people tell us. We can't help but trust our cognitive faculties.

It is easy to see why. Suppose we were required to offer evidence or arguments for all of our beliefs. If we offer statements 1–4 as evidence for 5, we would have to offer arguments to support 1–4. And then we would have to offer arguments in support of the arguments that are used to support 1–4. And then we would need arguments. . . . You get the point. Reasoning must start somewhere. There have to be some truths that we can just accept and reason from. Why not start with belief in God?

WITHOUT EVIDENCE OR ARGUMENT

We have been outfitted with cognitive faculties that produce beliefs that we can reason from. The kinds of beliefs that we do and must reason to is a small subset of the kinds of beliefs that we do and must accept without the aid of a proof. That's the long and short of the human believing condition. We, in most cases, must rely on our God-given intellectual equipment to produce beliefs, without evidence or argument, in the appropriate circumstances. Is it reasonable to believe that God has created us with a cognitive faculty that produces belief in God without evidence or argument?

There are at least three reasons to believe that it is proper or rational for a person to accept belief in God without the need for an argument. First, there are very few people who have access to or the ability to assess most theistic arguments. It is hard to imagine, therefore, that the demand for evidence would be a requirement of reason. My grandmother, a paradigm of the nonphilosophical believer, would cackle if I informed her that her belief in God was irrational because she was unable to understand Aquinas's second Way or to refute Hume's version of the argument from evil. The demand for evidence is an imperialistic attempt to make philosophers out of people who have no need to become philosophers. It is curious that very few philosophers (like most ordinary folk) have come to belief in God on the basis of theistic arguments. I commissioned and published a collection of spiritual autobiographies from prominent Christian philosophers just to see if philosophers were any different from my grandmother on this count.[3] They weren't.

Second, it seems that God has given us an awareness of himself that is not dependent on theistic arguments. It is hard to imagine that God would make rational belief as difficult as those who demand evidence contend. I encourage anyone who thinks that evidence is required for rational belief in God to study very carefully the theistic arguments, their refutations and counter-refutations, and their increasing subtlety yet decreasing charm. Adequate assessment of these arguments would require a

---

[3]See Clark, *Philosophers Who Believe.*

lengthy and tortuous tour through the history of philosophy and may require the honing of one's logical and metaphysical skills beyond the capacity of most of us. Why put that sort of barrier between us and God? John Calvin believed that God has provided us with a sense of the divine. He writes:

> "There is within the human mind, and indeed by natural instinct, an awareness of divinity." This we take to be beyond controversy. To prevent anyone from taking refuge in the pretense of ignorance, God himself has implanted in all men a certain understanding of his divine majesty. Ever renewing its memory, he repeatedly sheds fresh drops.... Indeed, the perversity of the impious, who though they struggle furiously are unable to extricate themselves from the fear of God, is abundant testimony that this conviction, namely that there is some God, is naturally inborn in all, and is fixed deep within, as it were in the very marrow. From this we conclude that it is not a doctrine that must first be learned in school, but one of which each of us is master from his mother's womb and which nature itself permits no one to forget.

Calvin contends that people are accountable to God for their unbelief not because they have failed to submit to a convincing theistic proof, but because they have suppressed the truth that God has implanted within their minds. It is natural to suppose that if God created us with cognitive faculties that by and large reliably produce beliefs without the need for evidence, he would likewise provide us with a cognitive faculty that produces belief in him without the need for evidence.

Third, belief in God is more like belief in a person than belief in a scientific theory. Consider the examples that started this essay. Somehow the scientific approach—doubt first, consider all of the available evidence, and believe later—seems woefully inadequate or inappropriate to personal relations. What seems manifestly reasonable for physicists in their laboratory is desperately deficient in human relations. Human relations demand trust, commitment, and faith. If belief in God is more like belief in other persons than belief in atoms, then the trust that is appropriate to persons will be appropriate to God. We cannot and should not arbitrarily insist that the scientific method is appropriate to every kind of human practice. The fastidious scientist who cannot leave the demand for evidence in her laboratory will find herself cut off from relationships that she could otherwise reasonably maintain—with friends, family, and even God.

WITH OR WITHOUT EVIDENCE

I haven't said that belief in God could not or, in some cases, should not be based on evidence or argument. Indeed, I am inclined to think that the theistic arguments do provide some noncoercive evidence of God's existence. By noncoercive I mean that the theistic arguments aren't of such power and illumination that they should be expected to persuade all rational creatures. Rational people could rationally reject the theistic proofs. Rational people—and this is a fact with which we must live—rationally disagree. Nonetheless, I believe that someone could rationally believe in God on the basis of theistic arguments, but no one needs to do so.

I also believe, like Calvin, that the natural knowledge of himself that God has implanted within us has been overlaid by sin. Part of the redemptive process will require the removal of the effects of sin on our minds. Attention to theistic arguments might do that. Also, some of the barriers to religious belief—such as the problem of evil or the alleged threat of science to religion—may need to be removed before one can see the light that has been shining within all along.

But the scales can fall from the mind's eye in a wide variety of means: on a mountaintop, while listening to a sermon, through a humbling experience, or by reading *The Chronicles of Narnia*. The list goes on, yet a certain common feature should be noticed (and not the fact that few people have ever acquired belief in God as a result of the study of theistic proofs). The primary obstacle to belief in God seems to be more moral than intellectual. On the mountains one may feel one's smallness in relation to the grandness of his or her surroundings. A sermon may convict one of sin. The loss of a job or a divorce may reveal one's unjustified pride. And *The Chronicles of Narnia* may awaken the dormant faith of a child. In all of these cases, the scales slide off the mind's eye when the overweening self is dethroned (not to mix too many metaphors!). Humility, not proofs, seems more appropriate to the realization of belief in God.

My approach to belief in God has been rather descriptive. I believe that we need to pay a lot more attention to how actual people actually acquire beliefs. The psychology of believing may tell us a lot about our cognitive equipment. The lessons learned from observing people and their beliefs support the position that I have defended: rational people may rationally believe in God without evidence or argument.

REFORMED EPISTEMOLOGY AND THE BIBLE

What is the biblical or theological basis for Reformed epistemology? Not much, I'm afraid, but I believe that Scripture woefully underdetermines most any philosophical position. By "underdetermines" I mean that there is not sufficient inescapable evidence to lead us invariably to one conclusion over another; the data do not determine a particular conclusion. There is some data, but the data are consistent with a wide variety of differing theories. Is God inside or outside of time, simple or complex? Does God suffer, or is he impassible? Can God change the past? These, and countless other positions, affirmed by one group of Christians and just as enthusiastically rejected by others, are simply not sufficiently well-supported by scriptural evidence to make a universally coercive case for them. Likewise, a coercive case from Scripture cannot be made for one's apologetic approach; there is simply not enough unambiguous evidence from Scripture to support evidentialism, presuppositionalism, or Reformed epistemology as *the* biblical view.

Here is some of the evidence. The first sort of evidence seems to favor evidentialism: Yahweh calls the Hebrews to reason with him (Isa. 1:18), the apostle Paul claims that the Creator can be known through his creation (Rom. 1:20), and Peter tells us to be ready to give a reasoned account of the hope that is within us (1 Peter 3:15). Of course, in context, these verses do not necessarily imply that it is irrational for anyone to believe in God without first considering the evidence. The reasoning in Isaiah has nothing to do with initial belief in God, the verse from Romans could mean that knowledge of God is either inferentially derived from or immediately produced by the creation, and the reasoned account of Peter may simply be, "I once was blind but now I see."

On the other hand, Scripture itself simply starts with God: "In the beginning God created the heavens and the earth" (Gen. 1:1). Never, within Scripture itself, is there an attempt to prove the existence of God; if proving God's existence were demanded of all believers, one might expect to find at least one of the believers in the Bible discussing theistic arguments. On the other hand, Scripture is rife with attempts to demonstrate that Yahweh is God (and not, for example, Baal). On the other hand, Paul and Peter's admonitions do not settle whether or not knowledge of God is produced immediately or through inference. Is Paul claiming that when one sees a beautiful sunset from the top of a mountain and is taken with the awesome grandeur of it all, that one is overwhelmed with belief in God? Or is Paul claiming that in such a circumstance one reasons like this: Here is the apparent handiwork of a really terrific creator; it is reasonable to argue from apparent handiwork to real handiwork; therefore, it is likely that a divine handiworker exists. So, maybe Romans 1:20 supports a kind of argument from design. On the other hand, Paul himself never employs the kind of apologetics that a contemporary evidentialist defends (his philosophical arguments in Acts 17 are more accommodations to Greek culture than philosophical arguments, more declaration than inference). On the other hand....

There are so many other hands, I cringe when people claim that their apologetic approach is *the* biblical approach. Anyone can find some support for his or her position in Scripture. So let a thousand apologetical flowers bloom!

The reason that Scripture underdetermines any contemporary apologetic approach seems clear. The Bible was written during a time when virtually everyone assumed the existence of some god or another. The Bible does try to make a case that Yahweh is God, and the New Testament tries to make a case that he has revealed himself uniquely in the Christ (in both instances, the biblical writers refer to the kinds of beliefs that people in their culture might find appealing). But everywhere the existence of a god is assumed. That we should directly import that approach into our contemporary context seems ill-advised. In our culture, a great many people do not believe in the existence of a god. How those people might be best approached, therefore, will require a great deal of human ingenuity and not merely reflection on how it was done in biblical times. Since so much has been left to human ingenuity and since Scripture both underdetermines one's apologetic and was written to and for another culture, there will be many Christian apologetics and not merely one. What Christian virtue requires in dealing with one another's views is charity, intellectual respect, fairness, and humility.

POSTMODERNISM[4]

I shall, skipping lightly over the history of modern philosophy, define postmodernism against the backdrop of modern philosophy. The early modern world was in intellectual turmoil awaiting a rational decision procedure by a Descartes, a Locke, or a Kant. In science, politics, and religion, revolutions were rife and the time ripe for a method of rational discernment.

Although it is impossible to set a precise *modus operandi* for modern philosophy, there are some shared concerns among its key players. Foremost among these concerns was the quest for both certainty and rational consensus. Descartes writes: "I will follow the same path I took yesterday, putting aside everything which admits of the least doubt, as if I had discovered it to be absolutely false. I will go forward until I know something certain—or, if nothing else, until I at least know for certain that nothing is certain." If the foundations are certain and the principles of inference are truth- and certainty-preserving, then the resultant beliefs must also be certain.

Locke was likewise devoted to certainty: "I should only show . . . how men, barely by the use of their natural faculties, may attain to all the knowledge they have, without the help of any innate impressions, and may arrive at certainty, without any such original notions or principles." And Kant writes: "As regards the *form* of our enquiry, *certainty* and *clearness* are two essential requirements, rightly to be extracted from anyone who ventures upon so delicate an undertaking. As to *certainty*, I have prescribed to myself the maxim, that in this kind of investigation it is in no wise permissible to hold *opinions*." The problems with the Cartesian project have been well documented and I shan't recount them.[5]

---

[4]This section is conceptually difficult and unduly compressed. But it is beyond the scope of this essay to develop it in any more detail. Feel free to skip to the next section if you like.

[5]The Cartesian, Lockean, and Kantian foundations proved insufficient for justifying significant beliefs; that is, there are beliefs we surely know that are reduced to mere belief or faith on their accounts. Descartes and his followers were trying to make epistemological gold out of base metals. Belief in other minds, the past, an enduring self, just to mention a few, could not be justified on Cartesian assumptions. Given that we know that there are other persons, that we have a self that persists through time, and that the world has a substantial past, Cartesian foundationalism must be wrong.

A second pervasive assumption of the Cartesian project is *internalism*.[6] The central contention of internalism is that the justifying conditions of a belief are somehow internal to the believing agent; whatever it is that justifies belief, and here the accounts vary widely, is something to which the believer has internal access. Justification is a property of beliefs that can be seen and understood simply by careful examination of one's own set of beliefs. If one's set of foundational beliefs has the requisite justificational properties, it is a simple matter of careful attention to belief construction to determine if higher-level beliefs have similar properties; if one's higher-level beliefs fail to have the right sort of luster, they ought to be discarded. What makes internalism attractive is that it places the justification of our beliefs within our own intellectual purview. I simply need to check my foundational beliefs, the inferences that I've made, and the resultant beliefs to see if my beliefs are justified. Beliefs wear their justification on their sleeves, so to speak, according to internalism. So, according to internalism, the entire responsibility for one's believings belongs to oneself.

I take the Cartesian project as the defining ideal of the modern period; so the postmodern period we are in now should be understood as post-Cartesian. Gone, I believe, are the prospects both for rational certainty and consensus (at least on matters of fundamental human concern). Likewise, I believe that hopes for internalism are illusory. We don't have direct access to all of the conditions that justify our beliefs. Here's the rub. If internalism is a failure, we don't have access to the conditions necessary for the judgment of whether or not these conditions have been satisfied. Whether or not we are justified in our beliefs may not be simply up to us (even assuming we are very attentive believers).

Plantinga argues that modern foundationalism has misunderstood the nature of justification.[7] Modern foundationalism is based on an unattainable quest for certainty and is unduly internalist. Plantinga calls the special property that turns true belief into knowledge "warrant." A belief B has warrant for one if and only if B is produced by one's properly functioning cognitive faculties in circumstances to which those faculties are designed to

---

[6]Although internalism is a difficult term, I shall describe some common characteristics that are agreed upon by all, or nearly all, of its adherents.

[7]Alvin Plantinga, *Warrant: The Current Debate* (New York: Oxford University Press, 1993); and idem, *Warrant and Proper Function* (New York: Oxford University Press, 1993).

apply; in addition those faculties must be designed for the purpose of producing true beliefs. So, for instance, my belief that *there is a computer screen in front of me* is warranted if it is produced by my properly functioning perceptual faculties (and not by weariness or dreaming) and if no one is tricking me say, by having removed my computer and replaced it with an exact painting of my computer (they have messed up my cognitive environment); and surely my perceptual faculties have been designed (by God) for the purpose of producing true beliefs. I have stated this succinctly, roughly, partially, and without nuance.

Note briefly the portions of Plantinga's definition that are not within one's immediate or direct purview—whether or not one's faculties are functioning properly, whether or not one's faculties are designed by God, whether or not one's faculties are designed for the production of true beliefs, whether or not one is using one's faculties in the environment intended for their use (one might be seeing a mirage and taking it for real). We cannot acquire warrant, according to this theory, simply by attending to our beliefs. According to Plantinga, warranted belief or knowledge is not entirely up to us. It depends crucially upon whether or not conditions neither under our direct rational purview nor our conscious control are satisfied. Justification is by faith, not by works. Warrant, to be more precise, is not solely due to efforts on our part.

POSTMODERN APOLOGETICS

How might a Reformed epistemologist defend her faith in our postmodern world? Here I shall primarily speak of belief in God, belief in an omnipotent, omniscient, wholly good creator of the universe. I do not have a well worked out strategy for defending Christian belief, although I suspect that the strategy I suggest can be extended to Christian belief.[8] Indeed, because of the intrinsic difficulties of Christian belief, I am dubious of any evidentialist approach (see my response to the evidentialists in chapter 2).

According to the theory of warrant developed above, a person has a warranted belief in God if her belief in God is produced

---

[8]For a well-developed Reformed defense of Christian belief, see Alvin Plantinga, *Warranted Christian Belief* (New York: Oxford University Press, 1999).

by her properly functioning cognitive faculties in circumstances to which those faculties are designed to apply. I have mentioned above that it appears that we do have a faculty that produces belief in God in us in appropriate circumstances. This faculty, more often than not, produces belief in God *immediately* without the support of a theistic argument. This does not mean that belief in God is not grounded in experience or that it cannot be based on such an argument. But if we do have such a cognitive faculty and it produces belief in God in the appropriate circumstances, then belief in God is warranted if it is not based on an argument.

One good apologetic strategy, therefore, is to encourage unbelievers to put themselves in situations where people are typically taken with belief in God: on a mountain, for example, or at the sea, where we see God's majesty and creative power.[9] We are far more likely to encounter the Creator if we attend to his creation. Now I am not suggesting that a person in such a circumstance is (tacitly?) processing the argument from design. She is not saying to herself, "The world appears designed. If something appears to be designed, it is likely designed. Therefore, the world in all likelihood has a designer." Her judgment that God is creator more than likely wells up within her, ineluctably, perhaps surprisingly. She is taken with belief in God.

A variety of circumstances are appropriate to evoking or awaking belief in God, for example, the birth of one's child, watching the sunset on the mountains or the ocean, examining the beauty of a flower, noting that we are "fearfully and wonderfully made," or walking through the woods in a time of quiet reflection. These situations often occasion belief in God because in these circumstances we come into contact with the Creator and belief in God is quickened, enlivened, or made apparent. The scales fall from our eyes as we see that we are standing on holy ground.

We move from circumstances that are full of wonder to circumstances that are full of terror. Death often awakens a dormant sense of the divine. As we face our own end (which most of us repress, pretending with all our might that we are immortal), we recognize that we are finite, impotent, mere creature. The illusion that we are gods dissolves, and we recognize our true

---

[9]I think Pascal's wager is intended to persuade people that it is worth attending to one's immortality and that given the stakes it is worth taking the effort to see if God exists or not.

impoverished self. Our humiliation in the face of the immense cosmos and the eternity of time, which ignore and eradicate our feeble accomplishments, permits us to recognize our dependence.[10]

If apologetics is helping someone to see or experience God, then one part of apologetics will be assisting people in the removal of barriers to belief. We can help some of the scales fall. This is often called "negative apologetics"—the attempt to remove intellectual obstacles to faith. Here, in our day and age, the primary issues are the problem of evil, science and religion, and the hermeneutics of suspicion.

By the latter, I mean the hermeneutical critiques of religious belief offered by Marx, Nietzsche, and Freud. They peer into the dark underbelly of belief and find ignoble motives. In displaying these motives—the desire for power, the need for a father figure, the fear of death, the justification of one's socio-economic stature—they seek to undermine religious belief. I believe that the hermeneutics of suspicion provides a much needed corrective to our natural tendency toward spiritual pride,[11] but nonetheless, people still need to be shown that this secular trinity has not proven that God does not exist or that it is irrational to believe in God.

The apparent threat of science to religion seems to have recently intensified. Richard Dawkins, whose new appointment at Oxford seems to have carried with it the charge to critique religious faith, has stated that Charles Darwin made it possible to be an intellectually fulfilled atheist.[12] Concerning evolution, Daniel Dennett contends that those who doubt that evolutionary theory explains the origin of species are inexcusably ignorant and suggests that such people should be locked up.[13] There are at least three options for the thinking Christian apologist. One option is to resist evolutionary theory,[14] another is to remain agnostic about

---

[10]I develop this in my *When Faith Is Not Enough* (Grand Rapids: Eerdmans, 1997), pt. 2.

[11]For a fascinating and challenging defense of the spiritual benefits of studying Marx, Freud, and Nietzsche, see Merold Westphal, *Suspicion and Faith* (New York: Fordham University Press, 1998). Thinking Christians skip this book at their peril.

[12]Richard Dawkins, *The Blind Watchmaker* (New York: Norton, 1987).

[13]One hopes that Dennett was just exaggerating. At any rate, he makes these statements in *Darwin's Dangerous Idea* (New York: Penguin Books, 1995), 47, 519.

[14]Recent critics of evolutionary theory include Michael Denton, *Evolution: A Theory in Crisis* (Bethesda, Md.: Adler and Adler, 1986); Michael Behe, *Darwin's Black Box* (New York: Touchstone, 1996); and Philip Johnson, *Darwin on Trial* (Downers Grove, Ill.: InterVarsity Press, 1991).

the truth of evolutionary theory,[15] and yet another is to embrace it.[16] The latter option is often difficult for conservative Christians because it seems to remove God from the creative process entirely; God is rendered superfluous. But Christians have progressively embraced the notion that the manner in which God acts might be explained naturalistically. We might thank God for the rain yet recognize that its antecedent causes are various high and low pressure systems. God might use the sun to cause the corn to grow. Neither the corn nor the rain require God as their immediate causes, yet God may nonetheless be their ultimate cause. The same may be true of the origin of species.

The problem of evil is the most formidable and apparently intractable obstacle to belief in God, and it is easy to see why. It is difficult to imagine that God could exist given the various kinds and amounts of evils that exist in the world today. While Plantinga has refuted the charge that God and evil are logically inconsistent,[17] there still seems to be too much evil for God to exist. The experiences that engender unbelief range from the global—seeing thousands die in an earthquake—to the local and personal—the tragic suffering and death of a (one's) child. When it comes to explaining evil, Christians are often tempted by the trivial, the trite, and the superficial. The goods that are appealed to in explaining the suffering often redound to the benefit of others (and perhaps to God) but not to the sufferer herself. Even if the child's death brought his father to believe in God, we still haven't adequately explained the tragedy with respect to the child. Even if a poor country learns from the earthquake how to build stronger houses, we still haven't fully explained how God could permit the suffering of the people involved. Not just any good that comes about because of some evil is an adequate explanation of that evil. We shouldn't underestimate the suffering of the world, and we shouldn't glibly explain it away. "The world's more full of weepin'"—Yeats' haunting refrain—"than we can understand."

I can only suggest that Christian apologists do their homework. A great deal of recent thought has gone into the problem of evil. It is useful, I believe, to venture outside our comfortable

---

[15]For an excellent introduction to bad arguments on both sides of the issue, see Del Ratzsch, *The Battle of Beginnings* (Downers Grove, Ill.: InterVarsity Press, 1996).

[16]For a Christian defense of evolutionary theory, see Howard Van Til, *The Fourth Day* (Grand Rapids: Eerdmans, 1986).

[17]Alvin Plantinga, *God, Freedom and Evil* (Grand Rapids: Eerdmans, 1977), 7–64.

sphere of belief—to hear challenges in their full weight and to learn how other theistic traditions address the problem of evil. I have found the Jewish tradition especially insightful on both counts; Jews have faced unspeakable evil, and many have come out with a deeper, more reflective faith. The book of Job teaches us that one thing is certain: We are more likely to go wrong than right in our theodicies. Intellectual humility is called for in the face of horrific evil.

Again, nothing that I have said precludes the use of arguments in apologetics. I think we do best, however, when we are aware of and admit to the limits of argument. There simply is not a belief-neutral, obvious set of beliefs upon which to base theistic arguments. That is, premises in theistic proofs are often not obvious (even though, at first glance, they might seem to be). In addition, premises in theistic proofs are often acceptable only to those who either already believe or aren't ardently opposed to religious belief. These caveats are true not only of theistic arguments, but of most arguments concerning matters of fundamental human concern.

I won't rehearse the theistic arguments or their criticisms, because the evidentialists in this collection already have done so. I have, however, discussed and defended some of the arguments as have other Reformed epistemologists.[18] One thing seems clear: People need to be disposed to accept the premises of the so-called proofs.[19] We are attempting to prove something to someone, and that someone has been encultured to accept certain things and to reject others.

When I lectured recently about reason and belief in God in Ukraine, I learned firsthand the barriers to effective rational dialogue with people whose institutionally enforced atheism began shortly after birth. How does one persuade a convinced materialist that morality requires God or that the universe depends on God for its existence? What beliefs do we share in common to which either of us could appeal to persuade the other of the truth of theism or materialism?[20] I recently observed one of my colleagues trying to persuade Chinese students of the moral need

---

[18]See Kelly James Clark, *Return to Reason* (Grand Rapids: Eerdmans, 1990), chap. 1; and Plantinga, *God, Freedom and Evil*, 85–112.

[19]I say proofs "so called." In *Return to Reason*, I defend person-relative proofs. For purposes of this essay, we will understand proofs as "reasons to believe."

[20]I left hoping that God would take the circumstances of their atheism into account. Here, it seems to me, the Soviet social engineers severely distorted their

for atonement—of the need to bridge the gap between our feeble moral capacities and the severe moral demand.[21] These students had been taught, as have most Chinese people, that humans are by nature good, and they resisted my colleague's efforts to persuade them of original sin. The indifference to religion among the Chinese is not attributable to perniciousness. How do you persuade such people of their need for a savior?

We could provide example upon example to demonstrate that a successful proof is not simply a matter of presenting true premises. In matters of fundamental human concern, truth is not obvious. Christian apologists often wave theistic arguments around as if the truth were obvious and the proofs simple. But these sorts of fundamental truths are neither obvious nor simple (witness that apparently rational people around the world disagree about nearly every matter of fundamental human concern). I have seldom seen a debate between, say, a Democrat and a Republican in which the Democrats in the audience did not declare a victory for the Democrat (or the Republicans for the Republican).[22] This is a debate among people who share a common commitment to democracy. What about a debate between a Marxist and a capitalist? How does the capitalist persuade the Marxist that people have a natural right to property? Is it really so obvious that people have a natural right to property? If so, why did nearly everyone fail to recognize this "obvious truth" until the time of John Locke?

My point is not to make people skeptics. Rather, it is my intention to demonstrate the obvious truth that rational people rationally disagree. What people start with determines what people will end up with. What people reason *from* determines the kinds of inferences that it is rationally permissible for them to accept. There is no belief-neutral, obvious foundation of beliefs to which to appeal in arguing for the existence of God. The starting point for our beliefs is our socio-cultural upbringing. Our beliefs are situated in a specific historical context. Should you embark on the reason-giving project, you need to recognize this and try your best to find some common beliefs to appeal to.

---

cognitive environment. I also hoped that the young people, who had not been so thoroughly inculcated in atheism, might find opportunity to come to know God.

[21]See his book, John Hare, *The Moral Gap* (New York: Oxford University Press, 1997).

[22]The exceptions prove the rule. If there is a consensus, one of the debaters had to have been a dismal failure to persuade even the faithful of their deficiencies.

CONCLUSION

It is often claimed that Reformed epistemology endorses belief in God without proof or evidence; there is a sense in which that claim is true, but it is surely an exaggeration. I have argued that one can reasonably believe in God on the basis of an argument. But those who believe without an argument may still have a basis, or grounds. The basis of some people's belief in God is the experience of God. The circumstances described above provide the occasion of a legitimate encounter with God. So belief in God can be based on reason or on the evidence of religious experience. But experience of God need not be the basis of a warranted belief in God. One's properly functioning cognitive faculties can produce belief in God in the appropriate circumstances with or without argument, evidence, or religious experience.[23]

---

[23]Portions of this essay were published previously. I have drawn from "Plantinga vs. Oliphint: And the Winner Is ...," *Calvin Theological Journal* 33, no. 1 (April 1998): 160–69; and "How Real People Believe," *Modern Reformation* 7, no. 1 (January/February 1998): 23–26. These essays are used with permission.

A CLASSICAL
APOLOGIST'S RESPONSE

William Lane Craig

Kelly Clark's so-called Reformed epistemology apologetics has much in common with the approach I have defended (see chapter 1, "Classical Apologetics"). I agree with his central theses that "belief in God ... does not require the support of evidence or argument in order for it to be rational" (p. 267), and that "the theistic arguments do provide some noncoercive evidence of God's existence" (p. 273).

I shall, however, highlight some different nuances with respect to each thesis. With respect to the first, I am very skeptical that any *sensus divinitatis* exists. Clark offers three reasons why we as Christians[1] should believe that humans have a cognitive faculty that produces in us belief in God. But none of these reasons goes to show that belief in God is grounded in a natural instinct or inborn awareness of the human mind rather than in the witness of the Holy Spirit. I know of no scriptural warrant for such a *sensus divinitatis* (John 1:9 would be an exegetical stretch), whereas there is wide biblical support for a *testimonium*

---

[1]His arguments certainly would not be helpful in persuading a non-Christian. The first reason would be dismissed, since if the Christian God does not exist, there is no reason to think belief in his existence should be widespread. The second reason—that God has given us an awareness of himself that is not dependent on theistic arguments—is a good reason (one to which I appeal), but unfortunately this is not the argument Clark goes on to develop, which is that God would not make rational belief so difficult as evidentialism implies. The third reason assumes that there is such a personal being as God to be known—which is precisely the question.

Spiritu sancti internum. In the absence of any scriptural support for such an inner instinct, I do not know how one could justify its existence, since the witness and work of the Holy Spirit serve to explain any phenomenon of religious experience that one might think to explain by the *sensus divinitatis.*

Is this difference significant? I think that it is. The witness of the Spirit is a matter of religious experience. It furnishes us with assurance of our salvation and our adoption of God's children. In his important study *Baptism in the Holy Spirit*, New Testament scholar James D. G. Dunn explains:

> The one thing which makes a man a Christian is the gift of the Spirit. Men can have been for a long time in Jesus' company, can have made profession of faith and been baptized in the name of the Lord Jesus, can be wholly 'clean' and acceptable to God, can even be 'disciples,' and *yet not be Christians* because they lack and until they receive the Holy Spirit.[2]

Dunn goes on to emphasize that the gift of the Spirit was *"fact of experience"* for the early Christians.[3] Thus, the witness of the Spirit is an experiential reality.

On Clark's account, however, despite initial appearances, it seems that the *sensus divinitatis* is not a matter of religious experience. This becomes evident from the last sentence of Clark's essay: "One's properly functioning cognitive faculties can produce belief in God in the appropriate circumstances with or without argument, evidence, or religious experience" (p. 284). The *sensus divinitatis* is thus not a matter of religious experience. One may just find oneself with a belief in God produced by some belief-forming mechanism without any experience of God at all. Since Clark rejects internalism, we seem to have no way of knowing that we are justified in holding this belief. Clark's view seems to be that we are in fact justified in believing that God exists, but that we may be as ignorant of this fact as we are of the number of boulders on the surface of the moon. His externalism thus seems to rob us of any assurance of knowing the truth of the Christian faith. One's belief in God may be as fully warranted as possible, and yet one be utterly oblivious of this fact. If asked whether one's belief is warranted, one may have to confess that

---

[2]James D. G. Dunn, *Baptism in the Holy Spirit* (London: SCM Press, 1970), 93 (Dunn's emphasis).

[3]Ibid., 225.

he doesn't know. Indeed, one could be filled with doubt and gnawing uncertainty about this belief. But this seems a far cry from the full assurance of which Paul and John speak in reference to the testimony of the Spirit. Belief in God is not the result of some secret faculty functioning silently within, but of the testimony of God himself to our soul. We must, if we are to be faithful to the New Testament, be internalists at least to the degree that one who experiences the witness of the Spirit knows that he is experiencing God's working in his heart. It is for this reason that I call the Spirit's witness "self-authenticating."

As for the thesis concerning theistic argumentation, Clark has unfortunately little to say about apologetics per se. When he speaks of "good apologetic strategy" (p. 279), what he is really talking about is *evangelistic* strategy. Apologetics is that branch of Christian theology that seeks to give a rational defense of Christian truth claims. Clark's suggestions for bringing someone to belief in God have little to do with this task. Doubtless this is because he construes apologetics to be "helping someone to see or experience God" (p. 280). This idiosyncratic definition is justified neither by etymology nor by use; it is, in fact, a definition of evangelism, not apologetics. What Clark really seems to be saying is that apologetics plays a minor role in evangelism.

I agree with Clark that few people are directly converted through the presentation of apologetic arguments. It's hard to convince a person to change his mind. But winning even one C. S. Lewis is surely worth the effort. And would we be more effective if we eschewed all argument and simply told people to attend to the *sensus divinitatis?* Would the Chinese students have converted to Christianity had John Hare not engaged them in argument but simply told them that the noetic effects of sin had clouded their judgment and was preventing them from seeing the truth of his position? I doubt it. Having just returned from a conference on religious epistemology in Beijing with Clark, I think that I can confidently say that my evidential approach was as well-received by the Chinese philosophers as was his Reformed epistemology. In fact, following the conference, I spoke to several hundred students at two other Chinese universities, describing the evidence from contemporary cosmology for the existence of a Creator and Designer of the universe, and found them captivated by the subject and eager to hear more.

Successful evangelism involves not only harvesting, but sowing and watering, too. We must never think that because a nonbeliever remained unconvinced by our case that our apologetic has failed. For one encounter is not the end of the story. Just this week I received an encouraging letter from Gary Simpson, the director of Campus Crusade at the University of Calgary, where I had participated in a debate on the existence of God. Gary reported:

> We've seen two more people come to Christ as a result of the groundwork of the debate you did with J. J. MacIntosh. . . . the moderator of that debate whom you met with for about an hour and a half that day is now the U. of C. student body president. He told me this week that we need to do a debate on Jesus is God. . . . He is now a theist. I've been able to maintain a good friendship with him. . . . He's come a long way![4]

Apologetics may be but one aspect of God's providential work in drawing people to himself. What we have said by way of argument may help to make the unbeliever more disposed to see God when he does watch the sun set over the ocean or take a walk through the forest.

Moreover, even if people tend to end up where they start, we must not forget that where they start may well be partially the result of argument and evidence. As a boy I believed that God existed because when I looked up at the stars at night I thought that it all had to come from somewhere. I had never heard of the cosmological argument, but that was my reasoning all the same. I suspect that many people have reasoned to themselves that God exists in ways that are rudimentary forms of the traditional theistic proofs. By the same token, many nonbelievers are where they are because as adolescents they reached the conclusion that the evidence does not support God's existence. The fact that people tend not to change their beliefs gives all the more urgency to the task of sharing simple but sound reasons to believe with young children and adolescents while they are still open to change.

Finally, what has been overlooked in all this is the leavening effect apologetics has on our culture. Even if few are converted directly through apologetic arguments, still such arguments help to

---

[4]Gary Simpson to William Lane Craig, September 10, 1998.

shape an intellectual milieu in which the gospel can still be heard as a credible alternative. In North America, Christianity is still a live option for most people. By contrast, in Europe, where I and my wife lived and ministered for thirteen years, the culture is so post-Christian and so secularized that it is difficult for Christianity even to get a hearing. European students on the campuses at which I spoke were sometimes so skeptical that they thought I was literally an imposter—no one espousing faith in Christ could really be a professor with two European doctorates!

What is called for in such a situation is not an abandonment of apologetics—there are already plenty of theologians at European universities telling people that belief in God is not based on argument and evidence, and they are universally ignored—but rather a renaissance of apologetics aimed at rolling back the Enlightenment and restoring a cultural milieu wherein the gospel can be heard afresh. Barring a miracle, it seems already too late for Europe. But in China and the former Soviet Union, the disillusionment with atheistic Marxism affords a door of opportunity for a cultural change in those nations. And in North America, as it slips into what Alastair MacIntyre has called "the New Dark Ages," it is still not too late to reverse the tide. J. G. Machen's admonition in "Christianity and Culture" remains as relevant today as ever:

> We may preach with all the fervor of a reformer, and yet succeed only in winning a straggler here and there, if we permit the whole collective thought of the nation or of the world to be controlled by ideas which, by the resistless force of logic, prevent Christianity from being regarded as anything more than a harmless delusion. What is today a matter of academic speculation begins tomorrow to move armies and pull down empires. In that second stage, it has gone too far to be combated; the time to stop it was when it was still a matter of impassionate debate. So as Christians we should try to mold the thought of the world in such a way as to make the acceptance of Christianity something more than a logical absurdity.[5]

A robust natural theology and display of Christian evidences can help to foster an intellectual climate in which belief in Christ, even if not based on argument, is a living option for thinking people.

---

[5]J. Gresham Machen, "Christianity and Culture," *Princeton Theological Review* 11 (1913): 7.

A final word of concern: ideas can have undesired cultural consequences. The warm Pietism of eighteenth-century Germany found its issue in F. D. E. Schleiermacher and the liberal theology of the next generation. In the same way, if out of deference to the "postmodern mentality" we abandon natural theology and Christian evidences and tell people to attend to the inner divine sense as they watch the sun set over the mountains or on the ocean, then I fear that what we shall reap in the next generation is a whirlwind of religious relativism and pluralism, according to which each community has its own properly basic beliefs and own standards of belief assessment, and none is capable of showing its beliefs or standards to be correct. This is emphatically *not* the position of Reformed epistemology; but it is terrifyingly easy to see how, in the absence of a vigorous emphasis on natural theology and Christian evidences, Reformed epistemology can give birth to such deformed progeny. This is a warning to the church.

AN EVIDENTIALIST'S RESPONSE

Gary R. Habermas

The contribution by Kelly Clark is intriguing in that comparatively few readers have probably encountered this approach to Christian apologetics. Yet it is challenging, interested in implementing philosophy into real life, and is refreshing in several ways.

POSITIVE CONTRIBUTIONS
OF REFORMED EPISTEMOLOGY

While reading Clark's essay, I enjoyed a number of his emphases. Clark embraced an intriguing combination of Alvin Plantinga's Reidian foundationalism with existential interests in the traditions of Sören Kierkegaard and Blaise Pascal.

Clark judges that epistemic evidentialism needs to be abandoned in favor of a less restricted, more defensible system of acquiring knowledge (pp. 268–71). Delineating between knowledge and proof, rational persons can believe in God without evidence, since this is a "properly basic," justified belief.[1]

Still, Clark espouses the use of evidences regarding God's existence (pp. 273–74, 281, 283). These are noncoercive, person-relative arguments that are helpful for some, though not all.[2] Further, like other methodologies, Clark encourages the use of negative apologetics, such as his critiques of skepticism, relativism, and pluralism (pp. 280–83).[3]

---

[1]For further details, see Kelly James Clark, *Return to Reason* (Grand Rapids: Eerdmans, 1990), 97, 125–51.

[2]Cf. Clark, *Return to Reason*, 34, 42–46, 53–54. See also Kelly James Clark, *When Faith Is Not Enough* (Grand Rapids: Eerdmans, 1997), 33–35, cf. 91.

[3]Clark, *When Faith Is Not Enough*, 103–4.

Clark's existential side is manifest in several ways. His apologetic strategy of exposing unbelievers to "situations where people are typically taken with belief in God" (p. 279) is reminiscent of Pascal's suggestions of jolting non-Christians with the terror of death, the vastness of the universe, or the despair of unfulfilled longings.[4] Clark explains that Kierkegaard and other existentialists were the chief inspiration for his volume *When Faith Is Not Enough*.[5] His treatments of death, suffering, and despair provide insights into his integrative approach, as do his interests in personhood, doubt, developmental theory, and other aspects of the psychology of religion.[6] In each of these subjects, Clark provides wisdom, insight, and a perspective that differs from most evangelical treatments. His challenges are worthy of consideration. Along the way, Clark models both epistemic and methodological humility.[7] He also encourages apologetic variety in both systems and arguments (pp. 274–75).

I agree with Clark at each of these points. Scripture does not exclusively teach any particular variety of apologetic method, and I think Paul's efforts, for instance, point in the direction of proclaiming truth by using a variety of approaches (1 Cor. 9:21–23). As Clark proclaims, "So let a thousand apologetical flowers bloom!" (p. 275).

SOME CHALLENGES TO CLARK'S REFORMED APOLOGETICS

Kelly Clark has provided his own challenges to practitioners of the other, more familiar apologetic strategies. Yet his apologetic methodology needs to answer some questions of its own.

Epistemic Evidentialism and Reformed Epistemology

Certainly a central tenet of the Reformed epistemology platform is its critique of epistemic evidentialism. More often than not, this evaluation is linked to its perceived connection with clas-

---

[4]See Blaise Pascal, *Pensées: Thoughts on Religion and Other Subjects*, trans. William Trotter (New York: Washington Square Press, 1965), nos. 72, 194, 233.

[5]Clark, *When Faith Is Not Enough*, xi–xii.

[6]Ibid. 47–51; 73–92, 101–2; 140–58; 181–90; Clark, *Return to Reason*, 55–56, 82–89; 113–18.

[7]Other examples are found in Clark, *When Faith Is Not Enough*, 104, 189–90.

sic foundationalism.[8] Plantinga states, "I have argued that the evidentialist objection to theistic belief is rooted in classical foundationalism."[9] Apparently in agreement, Clark maintains that "the evidentialist contention that the theist *must* have adequate evidence for rational belief in God is grounded in the classical foundationalist conception."[10]

A few comments are in order here. Although I agree that epistemic evidentialism, so defined, is flawed, especially as a religious epistemology, this does not mean that it is proper to link it so closely to classical foundationalism that both are eliminated. Such definitions are unnecessary, perhaps even consisting of "straw men," forced conceptions. Other approaches, such as that of Anthony Kenny, incorporate broader conceptions of classical foundationalism, hence escaping the force of the Reformed critique.[11] Some appropriate basis for faith needs to exist, although perhaps not only of the self-evident, sensory, or incorrigible varieties, as often required by classical foundationalists.

Let's look at this critique from another angle. Plantinga defends the view that "it is entirely right, rational, reasonable, and proper to believe in God *without any evidence or argument at all*."[12] Yet Plantinga takes great pains to contend "that the Reformed epistemologist is not a fideist at all."[13] Clark also defends this method against those who would charge it with fideism, reminding his readers that Plantinga affirms many theistic arguments but thinks that they are unnecessary.[14]

---

[8]In addition to those below, others have critiqued these areas. See Stephen J. Wykstra, "Toward a Sensible Evidentialism: On the Notion of 'Needing Evidence,'" in *Philosophy of Religion: Selected Readings*, ed. William L. Rowe and William J. Wainwright, 3d ed. (Fort Worth, Tex.: Harcourt Brace, 1998), 481–91; Philip Quinn, "In Search of the Foundations of Theism," *Faith and Philosophy* 2 no. 4 (Oct. 1985): 468–86.

[9]Alvin Plantinga, "Reason and Belief in God," in *Faith and Rationality: Reason and Belief in God*, ed. Alvin Plantinga and Nicholas Wolterstorff (Notre Dame, Ind.: University of Notre Dame Press, 1983), 90. Plantinga comments similarly throughout (pp. 17, 47–48, 62).

[10]Clark, *Return to Reason*, 135–36 (his emphasis). Not far behind is the Reformed epistemic critique of internalism (pp. 277–78), a view that has been defended vigorously as well. But this subject is too vast to detain us in an evaluation of apologetic methodology.

[11]Anthony Kenny, *What Is Faith? Essays in the Philosophy of Religion* (New York: Oxford University Press, 1992), chaps. 2–3, esp. pp. 24–32.

[12]Plantinga, "Reason and Belief in God," 17 (my emphasis).

[13]Ibid., 90; cf. pp. 87–90.

[14]Clark, *Return to Reason*, 154–57.

I think this is a quandary for Reformed epistemologists. They stand between the Scylla of avoiding arguments and evidence in order to justify their system, and the Charybdis of fideism. Plantinga's Reformed epistemology is not fideistic. But this is because it employs thoughtful arguments of various sorts. Even the concept of God's existence as properly basic can be and is argued. Granted, they do not seek evidence in the same way internalists do, because they are often externalists. While their arguments may look different, they are nonetheless arguments. They should admit that, just as they present a different variety of foundationalism,[15] so they support a different form of epistemic evidentialism.[16]

Why shouldn't they admit this, contrary to Plantinga's statement above? In short, since they are not fideists, they seem to employ some variety of epistemic evidentialism.[17]

Proper Basicality and Christian Theology

We have seen that the heart of the Reformed epistemologist's apologetic strategy is the contention that belief in God is properly basic, and persons can be rational in this belief without having to garner evidence for their position. But this contention has been criticized, even severely so, by many scholars.[18] Since there is not room here to summarize the dissension, I will con-

---

[15]Ibid., 141.

[16]Norman Kretzmann levels a similar charge, but much more forcefully (Norman Kretzmann, "Evidence Against Anti-Evidentialism," *Our Knowledge of God: Essays on Natural and Philosophical Theology*, ed. Kelly James Clark [Dordrecht: Kluwer Academic, 1992], 17–38). He complains that Plantinga gives "the evidentialist canon an unnatural interpretation" (p. 17). Arguing that evidentialism does not stand or fall with foundationalism, Kretzmann states: "Evidentialism is logically, psychologically, and, no doubt, historically prior to any such system; it is a truistic, pre-theoretic, typically implicit canon of rationality itself. . . . Foundationalism is rooted in evidentialism" (p. 22). Further, even Plantinga's properly basic beliefs "must present credentials. . . . Evidence by any other name is still subject to the evidentialist canon" (p. 30). Therefore, "Plantinga's theism 'without evidence' is *not* without evidence" (p. 31, his emphasis). Kretzmann concludes: "The 'evidentialist challenge' has *not* been 'challenged and overcome'. . . . The evidentialist challenge hasn't even been challenged" (p. 32).

[17]See Kretzmann, 38, n. 49.

[18]One notable example is Mark S. McLeod, *Rationality and Theistic Belief: An Essay on Reformed Epistemology* (Ithaca, N.Y.: Cornell University Press, 1993), esp. 113–54.

tent myself with simply raising a few issues that are more relevant within the parameters of apologetic methodology.

While I think that Reformed epistemology does better in the area of determining a starting point for religious knowledge,[19] I think there is less warrant for belief in God's existence being placed among those properly basic truths. It even seems that this belief stands out from the rest as of a different kind, in spite of their analogy of other minds.[20] While it is an intriguing subject and definitely needs to be pursued, it is not clear to me how we move from the need for some properly basic beliefs to "God exists" being one of them.[21]

Further, when Clark examines the traditional arguments for the existence of God, he points out what he calls a "crucial problem"—we can't get from them to the God of Scripture.[22] I ask similarly—even if it could be determined that belief in God is properly basic, how do we know that this is the God of Christian theism? Could it be that the Muslim or the theistic Hindu might enthusiastically agree that his belief in god is properly basic? Clark could respond that his properly basic belief is simply the belief in the *Christian* God. But this would not be in accord with the experience of the non-Christians. Clark may say that he could care less what they believe. But now I think that we would be coming close to begging the question. I don't know how we can solve these pithy issues from *within the parameters* of properly basic truths without reference to apologetic arguments.[23]

But since Clark thinks that theistic argumentation has a serious problem because it would "prove precious little," therefore yielding "little of religious significance,"[24] of what theological value is the Reformed epistemologist's perspective, unless it is able to answer the same issue of which view of God we are

---

[19]E.g., Clark, *Return to Reason*, 138.

[20]See Clark's list, ibid., 141.

[21]I mentioned earlier that the witness of the Holy Spirit might be helpful here, but it is not clear that the witness falls into the parameters of properly basic truth. For instance, Bill Craig seems to argue that it is known by a separate process, besides exhibiting other differences, such as immediacy and not being subject to defeaters. (See chap. 1, "Classical Apologetics," pp. 32–33.)

[22]Clark, *Return to Reason*, 26, 44.

[23]Once again, even if one did refer to the witness of the Holy Spirit at this point, I still think this, by itself, will not answer the question. It quickly becomes a question for apologetics. (See my response to Craig in chap. 1, "Classical Apologetics," pp. 61–63.)

[24]Clark, *Return to Reason*, 26.

addressing? Shouldn't Clark also conclude that his position falls prey to his own criticism—that even if we know that belief in God is properly basic, it still provides too little of theological significance, such as God's identity, worship, and obedience?[25] A prerequisite for examining a system's apologetic methodology is that we know that it has the theological credentials of a specifically Christian system!

Reformed Epistemology and the Use of Positive Evidences

But Reformed epistemologists have another problem here. How would Clark move to Christianity from within his own methodology? At least evidentialists and classical apologists would go beyond theistic argumentation in order to employ detailed historical arguments. Clark could respond the same way he does concerning the theistic arguments—that he is entirely open to the use of historical apologetic in a noncoercive, person-relative context. But he does not make any detailed historical moves.

Clark does encourage negative apologetics, and his colleagues have done an excellent job arguing that crucial Christian doctrines can be defended against objections.[26] But where is his positive defense? I am reminded of George Mavrodes's thoughts on this subject, while commenting on Reformed epistemology: "Why are Reformed thinkers skeptical of the value of positive apologetics? . . . Maybe it represents a deep ambivalence in Reformed thought, a tendency to oscillate between holding that belief in God is backed by plenty of evidence and holding that it involves no evidence whatsoever."[27]

Unlike John Frame's Van Tillian apologetic, Clark arguably has a noncircular case for belief in the existence of God as prop-

---

[25]In ibid. (p. 26), Clark also lists worship as another missing element in the theistic arguments. Plantinga has provided an excellent defense of exclusivism, arguing that it is not morally or epistemically deficient, and that something similar is inevitable. (See "A Defense of Religious Exclusivism," in Louis P. Pojman, ed., *Philosophy of Religion: An Anthology*, 3d ed. [Belmont, Calif.: Wadsworth, 1998], 517–30.) But this still does not give Clark what he needs. Even if some sort of exclusivism were simply granted, we are by no means able to derive the needed sort of theological significance from the Reformed epistemic position alone.

[26]Thomas Morris, *The Logic of God Incarnate* (Ithaca, N.Y.: Cornell University Press, 1986).

[27]George Mavrodes, "Jerusalem and Athens Revisited," in *Faith and Rationality*, ed. Plantinga and Wolterstorff, 198.

erly basic. But like Frame, there seems to be a paucity of arguments specifically in favor of Christian theism. Clark could respond, as Frame does, by referring the reader to evidentialist arguments of this nature (cf. p. 282). But such a response would be problematic. Since Clark often complains about the way evangelical apologists argue,[28] he should develop Christian evidences from his own perspective. Further, he pursues negative apologetics in spite of the evidentialists' efforts in this area,[29] so why not pursue the positive as well? Last, if he needs to refer to the evidential development of evidences, his method is incomplete in this area.[30]

With regard to apologetic methodology, then, Clark develops in some detail a strategy for belief in God. Unquestionably, Reformed epistemologists have particularly excelled in many areas like this one and in defending Christian theology against its detractors. I don't think any comparable movement has gone as far in arguing fruitfully that many of Christianity's central doctrines are rational. I, for one, want them to continue to develop their massive efforts, which are riding on an incredible wave of momentum.

My concern at this point, however, is that the efforts of Reformed epistemologists have not, to my knowledge, moved very far in the direction of actually establishing the truth of Christian theism. Beyond showing the rationality of Christian doctrines, can we argue equally well that Christianity is also true? Although he thinks a system can be worked out, perhaps Clark realizes this problem: "I do not have a well worked out strategy for defending Christian belief" (p. 278). Maybe there is a sense in which these scholars think the positive move cannot be made well. Or maybe some of them are not very interested in this step. In any case, I think Mavrodes is right about the ambivalent status of positive apologetics in Reformed thought. But without it, I wonder how Reformed epistemologists establish Christian theism in terms of their apologetic methodology.

---

[28]See also Clark, *Return to Reason,* 46–53.

[29]For examples, see Clark, *Return to Reason,* 68–81; idem, *When Faith Is Not Enough,* 103–5.

[30]Clark could argue that his own discipline (philosophy) is not as conducive to the evidential enterprise. But philosophers have long contributed to the notion of historical evidence, for example. Besides, that Reformed epistemology as a whole has produced so little in this area tends to suggest that it is perhaps not a major concern, illustrating my point of incompleteness.

Intervention in Doubt and Suffering

Kelly Clark and I share a mutual interest in the subjects of religious doubt, existential suffering, and the meaning of life.[31] We even share a profound head-on experience with death that helped shape our perspectives.

I would characterize Clark's volume *When Faith Is Not Enough* as a generally existential approach to these topics.[32] I have long held a special respect for existential insights in counseling. Specializing on the deepest questions of life and the anxiety they cause, the advice is often profoundly personal. No approach is better at framing the appropriate questions.[33] And so I resonated with Clark when he addressed areas like faith as a journey, God's answer to Job, and ministering individually to those who suffer.[34]

Yet, just as more than one apologetic strategy can be found in Scripture, so it offers much broader perspectives than the existential and interpersonal counseling models. Similarly, a wider range of intervention strategies is needed today. Clark might agree, but his own approach needs to be broadened. A major method, both in Scripture[35] and in current psychotherapy,[36] is the growing family of approaches known as cognitive or cognitive-behavioral techniques. In the most general terms, the main idea is that how we think governs how we feel and act. In recent studies, these procedures work especially well for the sort of existential and emotional struggles we are discussing here.

---

[31]My two volumes on this topic are *The Thomas Factor: Using Your Doubts to Draw Closer to God* (Nashville: Broadman and Holman, 1999) and *Dealing with Doubt* (Chicago: Moody Press, 1990). My own interests range from some of the most theoretical areas in the philosophy of psychology to the painful struggles of religious doubters.

[32]Not only is Clark's *When Faith Is Not Enough* chiefly concerned with the topics of doubt, death, the meaning of life, and discovering an authentic faith, but his chief "inspiration" for the volume is the work of Kierkegaard and other existentialists (x–xii). But further, his approach is one that is, above all, personal and concerned with life's great questions.

[33]For an excellent overview, see Rollo May and Irvin Yalom, "Existential Psychotherapies," *Current Psychotherapies,* ed. Raymond J. Corsini and Danny Wedding, 4th ed. (Itasca, Ill.: Peacock, 1989), 362–402.

[34]See Clark, *When Faith Is Not Enough,* 67–68, 73–92, 189–90.

[35]For just a few instances, see Pss. 42:5–6, 11; 43:5; Lam. 3:19–26; James 4:7–10; 1 Peter 5:7–9. Perhaps the best example is Phil. 4:6–9.

[36]See Albert Ellis, "Rational-Emotive Therapy," in *Current Psychotherapies,* ed. Corsini and Wedding, 196–238; and Aaron T. Beck and Marjorie E. Weishaar, "Cognitive Therapy," in *Current Psychotherapies,* ed. Corsini and Wedding, 284–320.

This does not mean that sufferers need the recitation of either apologetic evidences or philosophical hypothesizing. In dealing with the existential aspects of evil, those who are suffering do not want to hear abstract theories. In fact, very seldom do such approaches calm their embattled emotions. This mental aspect of their pain needs to be addressed. So Clark is right when he says, "We can, like Christ, however, suffer with that person."[37]

There is also a cognitive dimension that is exceptionally effective in healing. It should include empathy, but it goes far beyond it to specific patterns of thinking that deal with the things we tell ourselves. After all, we do wish those who are suffering to get some relief. And in literally dozens of empirical outcome studies, cognitive therapies have proven time and time again that they usually work at least as well, if not even better than, medication in treating emotional distress. Further, there is far less relapse when a cognitive healing pattern is employed.[38] Far from cold, hard, laboratory data that are unconnected with the real world of existential heartache, I emphasize that these outcome studies were done with the same sort of sufferers with whom we are concerned. These are real cases of suffering and grief.

Perhaps best of all, then, cognitive methods are exceptionally practical. Application to topics like doubt and grief can and must be shared by the counselees themselves.[39] Existential techniques may well ask the best questions; cognitive approaches seem to provide the most relief. Both can be used, even together, but the latter seems to promote more healing.

In a section entitled "My Grief Observed," Clark narrates the touching story of his father's unexpected death, just two days before a Thanksgiving visit, leading to the most profound unbelief in his life.[40] Even here, he and I share a close encounter with death.

In 1995, Debbie, my wife and best friend of almost twenty-three years, was very unexpectedly diagnosed with stomach cancer. She died just four short months later—at home, with our four

---

[37]Clark, *Return to Reason*, 88. On the emotional aspect of doubt, see pp. 85–89; and idem, *When Faith Is Not Enough*, 9, 97, 102.

[38]For the results of many of these studies, see Beck and Weishaar, "Cognitive Therapy," 291, 316; Paul M. Salkovskis, ed., *Frontiers of Cognitive Therapy* (New York: Guilford, 1996), esp. chaps. 14–16, 19; Jan Scott, "Cognitive Therapy of Affective Disorders: A Review," *Journal of Affective Disorders* 37, no. 1 (March 1996): 1–11.

[39]Habermas, *Thomas Factor*, chaps. 4–10; idem, *Dealing with Doubt*, chap. 4.

[40]Clark, *When Faith Is Not Enough*, 47–50.

children and a few relatives. We had watched her closely as she slowly wasted away, her digestive system ravaged by the disease. The day she died was her forty-fifth without food. There is just no way to briefly describe all the conflicting emotions. I was left to help the children through their pain and agony, not to mention my own. All I will say here is that, while existential elements were surely both present and unspeakably special, it was the cognitive truths that helped all of us the most.[41]

Yes, we should take the time to suffer with hurting persons just as Christ did. More than one counseling strategy may be very helpful too. But Christ also healed those who suffered. While his skills are not ours, we must at least work in that direction. Wherever possible, we should both share and then move on toward healing.

SUMMARY AND CONCLUSION

Clark's Reformed epistemology presents a challenging approach, roughly in the presuppositional tradition, though it includes a number of improvements. Yet I still think that problems remain before it can be considered a complete apologetic method.

First, after exaggerating the definition of epistemic evidentialism and its relation to classic foundationalism, Reformed epistemologists frequently denounce both. But since they do provide a foundation of their own, thereby avoiding the charge of fideism, they should also specify the sense in which they accept some sort of evidentialist underpinnings. By the very way they argue, they support the notion that faith needs an adequate basis.

Second, Reformed epistemologists' belief in God as properly basic opens Reformed epistemology to an array of criticisms. Even if established, this concept determines far too little of theological significance about the nature of this theism. Which theism is true, and do we have a being to be worshiped? Before we even move on to discuss apologetic methodology, we need other specifically Christian credentials as a basis: What are we defending?

Third, the absence of detailed positive (especially historical) evidences for Christian theism in Clark's approach makes me wonder how we can know that Christian theism is actually true.

---

[41]Her story is told in Gary R. Habermas, *Forever Loved: A Personal Account of Grief and Resurrection* (Joplin, Mo.: College Press, 1997). Both Clark (*When Faith Is Not Enough*, 73–92) and I (chap. 9, "Job and Me") include discussions of Job's dilemma.

The seeming antipathy toward these positive evidences in Reformed apologetics, even in a noncoercive, person-relative context, makes me wonder how they fulfill a crucial component of apologetic methodology—arguing in favor of Christianity.

Fourth, like apologetic methodology, various counseling strategies should be employed when ministering to those who suffer emotional quandaries regarding their faith. While definitely making use of existential approaches, we need to add cognitive components, chiefly because of their exceptional promise for significant amounts of relief and even healing.

Other issues also remain. Clark needs a detailed investigation of the role of the Holy Spirit's testimony. Since believers can know of their salvation apart from evidences, this would seem to be a fruitful avenue for him to pursue. I also think that he makes too many concessions, such as his comments on evolution (pp. 280–81) and especially evil. Evil makes it "difficult to imagine that God could exist." Or, in spite of Plantinga's excellent work here, "there still seems to be too much evil for God to exist" (p. 281). I didn't find this sort of tenor in his books, so perhaps I have misread him.

While Kelly Clark's methodology is much different from mine in various respects, I also deeply appreciate his efforts and perspective. His "intellectual humility" (p. 282) is evident throughout. I think he has much to offer us.

A CUMULATIVE CASE
APOLOGIST'S RESPONSE

Paul D. Feinberg

The scholarly world and evangelical thought owes a great deal to Reformed epistemology. Over the past twenty-five years, work done by philosophers identifying themselves with this movement have been responsible in large part for a renaissance of Christian philosophy or the philosophy of religion. They have defended Christianity as well as clarified our understanding of many important theological issues. Kelly James Clark is correct in pointing out our debt to them.

At the heart of their defense of belief in God is a rejection of the demand for evidence in support of that belief. They have argued that the evidentialist's challenge to belief in God is both recent and wrong. In their literature there are two ways in which this claim may be understood, a stronger and a weaker way. The stronger version is that belief in God *must* be properly basic or without evidence. If belief in God is based on evidence like that of natural theology, it is misformed. I find this stronger form troublesome for reasons that will be given in the course of my discussion of Reformed epistemology.

The weaker version of Reformed epistemology is the view that for some people belief in God may be properly basic or without evidence. For them that belief is not misformed or irrational. From what Clark says, he is defending the weaker version of this approach. He asks whether evidence is needed to support all beliefs everywhere and concludes that the answer is no. I agree with Clark on this point. For example, there are many very devout and simple Christians who have an unshakable faith in God, but who could not give you arguments or evidence for God's existence or the truth of Christianity. To argue that they were not within their epistemic rights to hold such a belief, or that that belief was in some way epistemically deficient, is wrong.

Clark uses a number of arguments to defend the right to believe without evidence. He argues that those who demand evidence in order for a belief to be rational cannot even give evidence to support that demand. That is, the demand fails its own criterion for rationality. However, there is a very simple way around problems like this. One may distinguish between rules governing a system and the system itself. The latter must meet the rules, while the former do not. An example that is often given of this point is drawn from mathematics. The axioms and postulates in geometry do not have to meet the same requirements of proof that theorems do. Thus, one might argue that the evidentialist principle is a rule of epistemology or belief. Of course, there is a consequence associated with making this move. It is that one is under no obligation to accept that rule or principle.

I find more convincing the arguments that there must be beliefs that we accept without evidence since we have neither the time nor the cognitive equipment to find evidence for every belief. We must, Clark argues, accept some beliefs because we accept the authorities from whom we have learned them or because they are the result of proper belief-producing equipment. For instance, I must believe my sense perceptions unless I have some reason to doubt their accuracy, like the room being dark or my going color-blind. Justification for beliefs must stop somewhere.

Yet Clark has said that some, not all, beliefs can be properly basic. So why should belief in God be rational without evidence? He gives three reasons (see pp. 349–51). The first is that most people do not have access to, or the intellectual ability to evaluate, the theistic proofs. Anyone who has read the literature on the proofs realizes how sophisticated their statement can be. Sometimes one wonders whether philosophers even understand them. But I wonder what we would say if there was no one who understood theistic proofs or could give evidence for God's existence. Would we still be within our rights to believe in God? The second reason is found in the fact that God has given us some immediate, direct awareness of himself. On a matter as important as his existence, God has not left humanity in a state of neutrality on that question. A third reason that belief in God may be rational without evidence is that "[it] is more like belief in a person than belief in a scientific theory" (p. 272). I am not sure of the entire force of this reason. Clark says that the scientific approach is "inadequate" or "inappropriate" for personal relations. We are not required to doubt first, examine the evidence available, and then believe. Personal relations require trust, commitment, and faith. This is surely true. Sometimes, however, the distinction between personal and scientific knowledge is taken to mean that propositional knowledge about persons is impossible, and this can lead to a depreciation of the Scriptures. I do not think that either Clark or I hold this position.

When Clark talks about evidence, he seems to equate that with the theistic proofs. He thinks that they can be used as evidence for belief in God. He says that they do "provide some noncoercive evidence of God's existence" (p. 273). This is in keeping with the view of most Christian philosophers about those arguments. I do not think, however, that these arguments are the only evidence for God's existence and the truth of Christianity. The Holy Spirit uses a variety of ways and evidence to convince people and bring them to faith. I would agree that we ought to pay greater attention to how real people actually acquire belief in God.

I said earlier that I thought that Clark defends the weaker version of Reformed epistemology. He does not hold that one *must* believe in God apart from evidence. This is supported by Clark's view that Reformed epistemology is not the only approach that has a biblical or theological basis. I am in agreement that the Bible's data on apologetic methodology is compatible with a variety of approaches. There is not just one biblical way to defend God's existence and Christianity. The effectiveness of a method may change over time since cultures are dynamic and change over time. Moreover, cultures at any specific time in history differ. An apologetic that is very effective where Western ways of thinking prevail may be quite ineffective where Eastern thought patterns rule. I would agree heartily with Clark when he says, "Anyone can find some support for his or her position in Scripture. So let a thousand apologetical flowers bloom!" (p. 275). The discussion in this book is not, as I see it, about faithfulness to the teaching of Scripture. Scripture "underdetermines" any apologetic methodology. Let Clark be heard, "What Christian virtue requires in dealing with one another's views is charity, intellectual respect, fairness, and humility" (p. 275).

Coming from the Reformed tradition, Clark's caution that we must be aware of the limitations of arguments is not surprising. Arguments alone, no matter how well constructed and defended, will not produce faith. That is the work of the Holy Spirit. Not only do arguments not produce faith, but they are not the basis of the certainty in the heart and mind of the believer. Much of Western epistemology has been engaged in a quest for certainty. Today most epistemologists believe that such a quest is misguided. What is required for a belief to be justified and count as knowledge is proper warrant. Because we are sinners, our cognitive faculties have been effected. Therefore, at least a part of that warrant is given to the knowing subject by the Holy Spirit.

It is common in Reformed epistemology to distinguish between "negative" and "positive" apologetics. Negative apologetics is the attempt to answer objections to the truth and rationality of Christianity. The objective is to show either that the objections are wrong or that at least they do not constitute a final reason for rejecting the faith. Having answered the criticisms, believers are within their epistemic rights (or are not irrational) in continuing to believe in God and Christianity.

Positive apologetics goes beyond negative apologetics in that it attempts to show that unbelievers should accept Christianity's truth claims. There is not only the attempt to answer attacks on Christian theism, but also to show that there is evidence that supports Christianity in a way that rational agents should become Christians. Reformed apologists find less of a place for positive apologetics. They are not entirely opposed to this approach, but commonly they think that most people do not become convinced of Christianity because of arguments. Thus, Clark will say that we ought to study how actual people do come to belief in God. As a matter of fact, some think that "evidentialist" apologetics really takes its impetus from John Locke. Prior to him, negative apologetics was all that was practiced. He undertook the development of Christian evidences to establish the intellectual respectability of Christian faith and to quiet the "enthusiasts" who questioned it.[1] What Locke took to be a

---

[1]See Nicholas Wolterstorff, "Can Belief in God Be Rational If It Has No Foundations?" in *Faith and Rationality: Reason and Belief in God*, ed. Alvin Plantinga and Nicholas Wolterstorff (Notre Dame, Ind.: University of Notre Dame Press, 1983), 177–78.

strength of his approach was in fact a disaster, as it played into the hands of those who believed in the evidentialist challenge—a belief is irrational if it lacks sufficient evidence. Those who based belief on evidence did not realize that the dominant view would become the view that belief in God could not meet the evidentialist challenge.

While it is true that atheism was not widely held until the modern period, I think that the defense of the faith by positive evidence predates Locke. One can see an evidentialist approach in the New Testament. When the two women came to the empty tomb on Easter Sunday, they were told to come and see the place where the Lord lay (Matt. 28:6). John's gospel is developed around signs to show that Jesus was the Son of God (e.g., John 2:11; 4:54). Furthermore, Luke-Acts has a clear apologetic purpose. Thus, there is at least some biblical support for an evidentialist approach to apologetics in the New Testament. Moreover, the very earliest church fathers were called the "Apologists." Positive apologetics, then, is not the child of John Locke.[2]

---

[2]See F. F. Bruce, *Defense of the Gospel in the New Testament* (Grand Rapids: Eerdmans, 1959).

A PRESUPPOSITIONALIST'S RESPONSE

John M. Frame

I am very grateful to Alvin Plantinga, Kelly James Clark, and others for developing and arguing the thesis that it can be rational to believe in God (and in other things) without argument. I think their case for this thesis is quite cogent, and I agree with it entirely.[1] To prevent confusion, however, I would add a qualification: Warranted belief does not need to be based on argument, but it does need to be based on fact, on reality.[2] I take it this is what the Reformed epistemologists mean when they say that warranted belief without argument is not groundless.

A REDUCED CLAIM

But to say that unargued theism can be a rational belief is to say very little compared to the traditional claims of apologetics. Consider the different claims apologists over the centuries have made for the epistemic status of their conclusions: necessary truth (Anselm), demonstration (Aquinas, William Craig),

---

[1]My review of Alvin Plantinga and Nicholas Wolterstorff, eds., *Faith and Rationality* (Notre Dame, Ind.: University of Notre Dame Press, 1983), can be found as appendix 1 (pp. 382–400) in my *Doctrine of the Knowledge of God* (Phillipsburg, N.J.: Presbyterian and Reformed, 1987). That review supplements my remarks here.

[2]And therefore it should be based on evidence in one sense. "Evidence" may be distinguished from "argument" as the objective data on which arguments are based, or it may refer to some aspect of the arguments themselves. In the former sense, but not the latter, it seems to me that belief must be based on evidence.

high probability (Joseph Butler), the best explanation (Gary Habermas, Paul Feinberg), rational believability (Clark). I list these in roughly descending order of strength. Rational believability is about the weakest claim that could be made for Christian theism. It merely says that one can believe in Christian theism without being irrational, at least until one is exposed to evidence and arguments on the other side. I grant, of course, that Clark may want to defend a stronger claim with regard to some of the apologetic arguments he does not discuss here in detail. But in my view, a robust faith in Christian theism will certainly claim more than that one can be rational in so believing. In my own view, even Anselm's claim is too weak. Our claim should be that the Christian theistic revelation is the very criterion of truth, the most certain thing we know.[3]

DEFEASIBILITY

We can see more easily the weakness of the rational belief claim if we note that, as Plantinga and others have indicated, we may sometimes be rational in believing things that aren't true. Usually, a five-year-old child is rational in believing what his parents tell him about, say, the Vietnam War. The child has no other way of gaining knowledge about that war, and his cognitive faculties may be functioning quite properly. Nevertheless, the parents' teaching may be false.

So in Plantinga's view, and I think in Clark's as well, when we rationally believe in God without argument, we should at the same time admit that our belief could be false. On their view, it is rational to believe in God without argument, but such belief is defeasible: it can and should be overturned when there is sufficient evidence to the contrary.

But surely Christian faith is not defeasible in this sense.[4] It is sure, certain.[5] We are not merely *permitted* to believe in God until we are persuaded otherwise; rather, we are *obligated* to believe

---

[3]See chap. 4, "Presuppositional Apologetics," for my defense of this position.

[4]I like the comments by Craig in chapter 1, "Classical Apologetics," about how faith should persist even in the presence of alleged "defeaters."

[5]I am somewhat disturbed that Clark seems to speak approvingly of the postmodern view that "Gone . . . are the prospects both for rational certainty and consensus (at least on matters of fundamental human concern)" (p. 277). He is right, I think, on the prospects for consensus, until Christ returns. But we should not dismiss so quickly the possibility of rational certainty.

in him. Even more, as I indicated in chapter 4, "Presuppositional Apologetics," Scripture implies that our faith governs our reason; it serves as the believer's ultimate criterion of truth and falsity. Examples: (1) Abraham believed God's promise even though the empirical evidence available to him seemed to point the other way (Rom. 4:18–22), and he was right to do so. (2) For us to accept the authority of Scripture is to confess that we are obliged to believe what it teaches and to accept those teachings as the criteria for evaluating all other teachings.

So Christian faith must be something more than a belief we are rational in holding. We must ask not only what we are rationally permitted to believe, as do the Reformed epistemologists.[6] We must ask what we are obligated to believe: What are those beliefs that God requires of us? And what are those beliefs that should govern the acceptance and rejection of other beliefs?

Clark's essay is not very helpful in these areas. I can imagine some potential directions he might take in attempting to define and justify epistemic categories stronger than rational believability. He might derive them from the testimony of the Holy Spirit, as have some other contributors to this volume, or from the authority of the Word of God, as I have tried to do, or from some combination of these.[7] Or he might want to appeal to some particular kind of evidence and thus become more of an evidentialist. But I gather that he doesn't believe that any evidence has that stronger kind of credibility.

More likely, he would build on the suggestions in his present essay, urging inquirers to put themselves in places where their epistemic equipment is likely to produce belief in God. But what situations would give rise to beliefs that transcend evidential defeasibility?

THE BIBLE AND EPISTEMOLOGY

To investigate any of these possibilities, I think that Clark will have to do some more Bible study. For it is in Scripture that we learn about the testimony of the Holy Spirit, the nature of the Word of God, and the role of natural revelation. It is in Scripture,

---

[6]As I mentioned in chap. 4, "Presuppositional Apologetics," I find it a bit awkward to refer to Plantinga and Clark as "Reformed epistemologists" in distinction from my own position. I continue to think that I am at least as Reformed as they are.

[7]Such recourse to Word and Spirit would make more credible Clark's claim to have a Reformed epistemology.

if anywhere, that we are likely to discover a source of nondefeasible religious knowledge.

I was rather disappointed at Clark's treatment of the role of the Bible in determining apologetic principles. I grant that Scripture "underdetermines" many philosophical questions (p. 275), including some that Clark mentions, and I also grant that the apologetic situation we face today is significantly different from the situation that existed in Bible times. But can any serious reader of Scripture doubt that God's Word plays a determinative role in the human knowledge of God? That the testimony of the Holy Spirit is essential? That there is an antithesis between godly wisdom and the wisdom of the world? That the fear of the Lord is in some sense the beginning of knowledge? Certainly Scripture leaves many questions unanswered and to that extent leaves room for a plurality of approaches. But it also answers some important questions, as I tried to show in my essay. Indeed, in my view, it answers enough questions to warrant the essentials of presuppositionalism.

When Clark says that "anyone can find some support for his or her position in Scripture" (p. 275), he sounds much too much like the village atheist who says, "You can make the Bible teach anything." When I hear people talking like this, whether they be village atheists or philosophical apologists, I am inclined to think that they haven't tried hard enough to find out what the Bible says.

SOME COMMENDATIONS, WITH QUALIFICATIONS

Nevertheless, there is much in Clark's essay that I find refreshing and edifying. When he says that "reasoning must start somewhere. There have to be some truths that we can just accept and reason from. Why not start with belief in God?" (pp. 270–71), I rejoice. This is a mighty first step toward a presuppositional understanding. But if this divine starting point is the sovereign Lord of Scripture, it will not be enough to say that belief in him is independent of argument; rather, we must allow him to establish the very standards that govern argument. I'm not sure that Clark understands all that is involved in accepting God as an epistemic starting point.

I also like Clark's emphasis that belief in God, like belief in other persons, demands "trust, commitment, and faith" (p. 272). Apologists typically try to avoid making their case depend on faith, because faith is what they are arguing for. They don't want to argue in a circle, nor do they want to be reproached as "fideists." But Scripture tells us that faith is essential (Heb. 11:6).

And I'm thankful for Clark's emphasis on the multitude of situations that can evoke belief in God, with and without arguments. Indeed, "humility, not proofs, seems more appropriate to the realization of belief in God" (p. 273), particularly, as Clark later adds, in the face of the problem of evil.

I also agree that "the theistic arguments aren't of such power and illumination that they should be expected to persuade all rational creatures" (p. 273). Not only logical difficulties, but as Clark points out, cultural differences as well, make it difficult to find premises acceptable to everyone.[8] I would insist, however, that the *facts* of God's creation[9] (including his Word, his world, and ourselves as his image) do have the power to persuade all. Indeed, Paul tells us that they do persuade all, but that apart from grace people renounce their persuasion, suppressing the knowledge of God that they have (Rom. 1:20–21). The clarity by which God reveals himself leaves unbelievers without excuse.

And of course this presuppositionalist resonates warmly to Clark when he says:

> What people start with determines what they will end up with. What people reason *from* determines the kinds of inferences that it is rationally permissible for them to accept. There is no belief-neutral, obvious foundation of beliefs to which to appeal in arguing for the existence of God (p. 283).

But then he disappoints: "The starting point for our beliefs is our socio-cultural upbringing" (p. 283). Only that?[10] Not our religious convictions? After all, he did say earlier that God is a kind of starting point. Doesn't the Bible say anything about the starting points of both believers and unbelievers, particularly that they stem ultimately, not from culture, but from belief or unbelief in the true God?

---

[8]Compare my discussions of "common ground" with Craig, Habermas, and Feinberg.

[9]And therefore "evidence" in the *objective* sense; see n. 2 above.

[10]Is Clark, after all, among those postmodernists for whom socio-cultural background is all-determining? I confess to some concern that his discussion of postmodernism is entirely affirmative. Is there nothing in this movement that Christian apologists should challenge?

And does the Christian faith have nothing to say about what kinds of inferences we ought to accept? If a mere socio-cultural background can generate such norms, why should we not expect the mighty Lord of heaven and earth to do so? For Christians, our socio-cultural background is far less important in governing our lives than our covenant with the almighty God, who tells us to do all things to his glory (1 Cor. 10:31). Can all things possibly exclude reasoning?

I see Clark making some progress toward the presuppositional kingdom, but he is not quite there. Nevertheless, he has much to say of interest, enlightenment, and encouragement to presuppositionalists. That is to be expected since, after all, presuppositionalists too are Reformed epistemologists.

Chapter Six

CLOSING REMARKS

A CLASSICAL APOLOGIST'S CLOSING REMARKS

William Lane Craig

AD FRAME

I am happy to say that John Frame and I do not seem to have any substantive disagreements. A comment is in order, however, concerning the role of God's Word in apologetic methodology. Frame begins by arguing that the testimony of the Holy Spirit is virtually always to God's Word. He concludes this section of his paper by complaining that I assign "no distinct role to Scripture" in my religious epistemology (p. 76).

Frame has made a leap here; for, as he himself acknowledges, we cannot make a simplistic equation between God's Word and Scripture. When Paul reminded his Thessalonian converts of the Word of God that he preached, he was referring to "the apostolic message," the gospel proclaimed by the apostles (p. 74). When one tries to show Christianity to be true, one is arguing for the truth of the gospel. So even if one does not quote Scripture, the Word of God is not missing at all, for one is defending the truth of that Word. Similarly, when one knows by the inner witness of the Holy Spirit that Christianity is true, what one knows is that the gospel is true. It is God's Word that one knows to be true, even if one has never seen the Bible.[1]

---

[1]Moreover, the Scripture's authority is derivative in character. Were the Scriptures not inspired by the Holy Spirit, they would be merely the words of human authors, having no more authority than other ancient religious texts. Thus, Scripture's authority ultimately derives from God himself.

But one knows even more: Through the Spirit's witness, one is aware of one's own participation in that salvation proclaimed in the Word of God. The Spirit does not simply bear witness to some general, third-person promise, such as "Everyone who calls on the name of the Lord will be saved" (Rom. 10:13), but to the truth that "I am a child of God." In virtue of the first-person perspective expressed in this truth, I could not know it through the Spirit's witness to Scripture or even to the message of the gospel alone. Rather, what Paul says is that God's Spirit bears witness *with our spirit* that *we* are children of God. The witness of the Spirit is thus intensely personal. The Spirit's witness is thus to truth, the truth not only of the gospel, but also of my participation in its promises.

Notice that if we restricted the Spirit's witness to the Scriptures, we should have to say that believers who have not yet heard or read the Scriptures (perhaps due to lack of translations) have no experience of the witness of the Spirit. But even believers without the Scriptures surely do know on the basis of the Spirit's witness that they are God's children. I therefore appeal to the witness of the Holy Spirit himself rather than Scripture in explaining how it is that we *know* Christianity is true. Furthermore, it would be circular reasoning if we were to try to *show* that the gospel is true on the basis of the Scriptures, since the Scriptures are a written expression of the gospel. Thus, while one can use the Scriptures as historical documentary evidence, one cannot, without begging the question, use them as God's Word to argue for the truth of God's Word. That is why Scripture as God's Word does not play a greater, distinct role in my religious epistemology.[2]

How do we decide which arguments are worth believing? We see whether they follow the pattern of valid inference forms, are informally valid, and have true premises that are more plausible than their contradictories. Frame thinks that the causal premise of the cosmological argument is true only if God exists. Deny God, and you deny the truth of the causal premise. Here we see a confusion between ontology and epistemology. Of course, if—*per impossible*—God did not exist, neither the causal premise nor any other premise would be true. There would be nothing. But that does not imply that the *kalam* argument is

---

[2]This is obviously not to say that the Scriptures do not play a central role in *evangelism*, for since they are God's inspired Word, he speaks powerfully to people through them. Therefore, in sharing the gospel, we should liberally quote from the Bible.

question-begging—that one's reason for believing the causal premise is that one believes in the existence of God.

AD HABERMAS

Gary Habermas and I seem to agree on virtually everything! Still, he is exercised to distinguish his position from mine by portraying classical apologetics as entailing the claim that Christian evidences necessarily presuppose independent theistic arguments. He presents me with the following dilemma (p. 60): I can either accept what my classical apologetics colleagues say about their methodology or else repudiate my own statements that Christian evidences can of themselves constitute grounds for accepting theism. No sleep lost over this choice! Although some contemporary thinkers represent classical apologetics as committed to the disputed claim, I see no reason to agree with such characterizations. The classical apologists themselves employed both natural theology and Christian evidences in support of Christian theism, but I am unaware of any who maintained that Christian evidences are nugatory in the absence of natural theology or that such evidences would not in themselves lend any support to theism.[3] I wonder if Habermas is aware of any statements from classical apologists expressing such a view.

But if arguments from miracles can constitute evidence for theism, why employ arguments of natural theology? Simply because one's case will be so much stronger if one does! Why not offer cosmological, teleological, moral, and other arguments for God's existence if these are sound? It would be foolish to prefer a weaker case when a stronger, fuller case is there for the having. Moreover, natural theology actually strengthens the argument from miracles itself. Letting G = God's existence, M = some putatively miraculous event, and B = our background information, the theistic argument from miracles contends that

$$Pr(G/B\&M) > Pr(G/B).$$

But as philosopher of science John Earman points out,[4] this implies that

$$Pr(M/B\&G) > Pr(M/B).$$

---

[3] I speak, of course, of apologists in the modern era, since pre-modern apologists like Aquinas did not even have the historical method and so were dependent solely upon natural theology.

[4] John Earman, "Bayes, Hume, and Miracles," *Faith and Philosophy* 10, no. 3 (1993): 303.

Therefore, if one has independent arguments for God, the probability of the miracle's occurrence is greater than it is in the absence of those arguments. The miracle is more likely to have occurred if one has first shown theism to be true. This conclusion is logically implied by Habermas's own method. Thus, natural theology not only strengthens one's case overall, but it makes the argument from miracles itself stronger.[5]

What the classical apologists saw is that once you have demonstrated via natural theology the existence of God, there remains for Christian evidences a much more important role to play than simply reinforcing theism. For they serve to show, as Samuel Clarke put it, the "interposition of God in the world" in attestation to Jesus' claims and teaching.[6] Therefore, it is only reasonable to employ them in this role.

So much concerning *showing* Christianity to be true; what about *knowing* Christianity to be true? Habermas wonders why I spend so much time on this subject. I do so simply because it has been the key differentiating issue between traditional evidentialists and presuppositionalists in the past! The knowing/showing distinction is an attempt to prove that the presuppositionalists were right about knowing and the evidentialists about showing. What we are seeing in the present volume is a remarkable convergence of views, which is cause for rejoicing.

Habermas is ambivalent about the knowledge imparted by the Holy Spirit. He appears to be inconsistent in agreeing that "the witness imparts knowledge to the believer," but then backing away and construing the witness "primarily in terms of assurance and conviction" (p. 62). For one can have assurance and conviction of falsehoods (think of Joseph Smith or Jim Jones). If all the Spirit gives us is assurance, then he does not after all "impart knowledge to the believer."

Habermas presses the objection based on false claims to the Spirit's witness, but his development of the objection is not clear to me. At first it sounds as though Habermas thinks that the

---

[5]If one eschews a Bayesian approach and adopts instead the method of inference to the best explanation, then natural theology will strengthen the argument from miracles by making it less *ad hoc*. For given theistic arguments, one already knows that God exists.

[6]Samuel Clarke, *A Discourse Concerning the Unchangeable Obligations of Natural Religion and the Truth and Certainty of the Christian Revelation* (London: W. Botham, 1706), 359.

problem concerns the claimed exclusivity of the experience of the Spirit's witness by Christians. Non-Christians want to claim that they have experienced it, too. Certainly; but, as I explained, the Christian can be confident that any claim to the Spirit's witness on behalf of a doctrine incompatible with truths attested by the Spirit's witness or implied thereby is a spurious claim, resting on either a nonveridical experience or a misinterpreted experience. That is what John means when he enjoins us to "test the spirits" (1 John 4:1–3). Habermas then says, however, that the problem does not concern our knowing Christianity to be true, but our showing it to be true. I do not see the problem. I maintained that in showing an adherent of some non-Christian religion that Christianity is true, we should present him with arguments and evidence—and hope that the Holy Spirit will crack his false confidence.

AD FEINBERG

Paul Feinberg claims to offer a "one-step" apologetic (p. 67); but it is important to see that he is using this expression in a completely different way from Habermas. Habermas claims that one may prove Christian theism to be true via Christian evidences alone, without natural theology. It is evident that Feinberg, however, does not agree with this claim; on the contrary, he insists on the necessity of a cumulative case; evidences alone will not do the trick. Look at his procedure when discussing the so-called external witness of the Holy Spirit: "First, there are the *theistic arguments*" (p. 160), "The second element [is] ... *religious experience*" (p. 161), "A third external element ... is the *moral law*," (p. 163), "Finally, the external case ... includes *revelation*" (p. 165). This is classical apologetics! Even if all these steps are taken simultaneously, there are still relations of logical priority among them.

With respect to knowing Christianity to be true via the self-authenticating witness of the Spirit, Feinberg's misgivings are, I think, based on misunderstandings. First, as I indicated in my response to his essay, Feinberg construes the internal witness of the Spirit far too broadly. In the believer's life it is fundamentally the assurance of salvation (Rom. 8:16). Hence, it is a mistake to apply it to cases of assurance of healing or direction, as Feinberg does. God has not chosen to provide assurance in such matters. Second, a belief's being properly basic should not be interpreted to mean that the belief does not presuppose other knowledge. My memory belief that I had eggs for breakfast presupposes my beliefs that chickens lay eggs, that I woke up this morning, that the sun rises early in the day, and so on. But my basic belief is not inferred from these other beliefs. Similarly, belief in one's innocence remains properly basic even if it presupposes other knowledge. Again, the fact that one can imagine scenarios in which a basic belief in one's innocence is defeated is no refutation of the claim that in the scenario envisioned by Plantinga that basic belief is an intrinsic defeater of the defeaters brought against it. Similarly, the witness of the Holy Spirit is an intrinsic defeater of all defeaters brought against it.

We should not conclude that the believer and unbeliever have a different epistemic status before God. For there is also a witness of the Holy Spirit directed specifically to unbelievers (John 15:26–27; cf. 16:8). The unbeliever has no excuse before God for not heeding this witness. Would Feinberg say that for some unbelievers the rational thing to do is to refuse the Spirit's witness? I find that difficult to square with the New Testament.

AD CLARK

As might be expected, the principal divergence between Kelly Clark's views and mine comes with respect to the task of showing Christianity to be true. In his response to Habermas, Clark at most endorses what has been called "negative," or, as I prefer, defensive apologetics, while I endorse as well "positive" or offensive apologetics (yes, I see the unfortunate pun here!). Clark believes that the most that apologetics can achieve is defeating the ostensible defeaters brought against Christian truth claims; on balance it cannot, however, provide any preponderance of warrant for those claims (cf. pp. 143–44).

Clark is not unwilling to endorse as sound certain arguments of natural theology. But he thinks that on balance such arguments do not serve to tip the scales of probability in favor of theism. Why not? He argues that even a successful deductive argument like the *kalam* cosmological argument does not prove that God, properly speaking, exists. The *kalam* argument shows only that a Personal Creator of the universe exists, but it does not show that this Creator is omnipotent, omniscient, or wholly good. In order to arrive at a full-fledged theism, we must therefore have recourse to other theistic arguments and build a cumulative case for theism. In Clark's eyes, however, there are two problems with such a cumulative case approach. (1) He is unsure whether there even is such a cumulative case to be built. I have defended the *kalam* cosmological argument, but where are my defenses of the teleological or moral or ontological arguments? Unless we have such a case before us, we cannot justifiably claim that theism is warranted by the evidence. (2) The probabilities involved in a cumulative case are either inscrutable or nonexistent. The best we can do is make a considered judgment as to which way the evidence points. But our judgments are to a great degree conditioned by our epistemic situation in the world, the historical, cultural, and social nexus in which we live. Therefore, we may think that we have shown theism to be true, but we cannot tell if we ourselves are not making skewed judgments due to our conditioning.

What can be said in response to these allegations? It is certainly true that the *kalam* argument does not prove that the Creator is omniscient or morally good. But need it prove that the Creator has these attributes in order for us justifiably to call the Creator "God"? Notice that in order to prove that something exists, it is not necessary to prove that an entity possess all the essential attributes of that thing; otherwise, we should be left with complete skepticism.[7] We must work with definitions of things that include only a few of their key properties that serve to set them apart from other things. With respect to God, the property *being the Creator of the universe ex nihilo* will seem sufficient to many people to distinguish a being possessing it as God.[8] The question remaining would then be whether we have reason to think that God, so understood, is omnipotent, omniscient, or wholly good.

In any case, even if one insists on using a fuller definition of "God," I have said from the start that I am quite happy to admit that the *kalam* argument does not prove the existence of God, so construed, but simply of a Personal Creator of the uni-

---

[7]E.g., one of the essential properties of Kelly Clark is that he is created by God. Thus, in order to show that Kelly Clark exists, we should first have to show that God exists, which Clark thinks cannot be done. Should we therefore be skeptical about Clark's existence?

[8]This is the definition accepted in the famous BBC debate between Frederick Copleston and Bertrand Russell (Bertrand Russell and F. C. Copleston, "A Debate on the Existence of God," in *The Existence of God*, ed. John Hick, Problems of Philosophy Series [New York: Macmillan, 1964], 167).

verse, and the argument can proceed from there.[9] Has this Creator remained distant and aloof from the world that he has made, or has he revealed himself more fully to humankind that we might know him more completely? Here one moves to the claims of Jesus of Nazareth to be the unique personal revelation of such a Creator. It will then be the Christian evidentialist's turn to take over the oars from the natural theologian.

What, then, about Clark's problem (1), that it is not clear that a cumulative case for theism exists? As we have seen, that all depends on how you define "God." In any case, I think a good number of theistic arguments in addition to the *kalam* argument are successful and serve to round out the nature of the being we have agreed to call "God." I have elsewhere defended the moral and teleological arguments, which give us God's moral perfection and supreme intelligence.[10] As for omnipotence, this very concept is notoriously difficult even to define, and a being with the power to create the entire universe out of nothing not only meets the biblical requirements for being almighty, but the consensus of church theologians has also been that *ex nihilo* creation is a power belonging to God alone. Thus, I think that a good cumulative case for theism is on the table.

As for Clark's problem (2), we may agree that the probabilities involved in a cumulative case are difficult to determine and compare. Paul Draper, who to all appearances is a sincere agnostic philosopher, recently remarked to me that the reason he is agnostic is because he simply finds it impossible to assess the comparative probabilities involved in the problem of evil, the *kalam* cosmological argument, and so forth. My heart went out to him in his perplexity, but his agnosticism did not prompt me to think that the case for theism was therefore inconclusive.

---

[9]It is noteworthy that even so bare-boned a conception of God as the Personal Creator of the universe *ex nihilo* already narrows the field of world religions down to the Judeo-Christian tradition.

[10]William Lane Craig, "The Teleological Argument and the Anthropic Principle," in *The Logic of Rational Theism*, ed. William L. Craig and M. McLeod, Problems in Contemporary Philosophy 24 (Lewiston, N.Y.: Edwin Mellen, 1990), 127–53; idem, "The Indispensability of Theological Meta-Ethical Foundations for Morality," *Foundations* 5, no. 2 (1997): 9–12. If the teleological argument is faulted as still falling short of omniscience, I should commend to the reader Quentin Smith's fine development of the conceptualist argument for God's existence, which does yield divine omniscience (Quentin Smith, "The Conceptualist Argument for God's Existence," *Faith and Philosophy* 11, no. 1 [1994]: 38–49). Smith's argument needs to be supplemented with a case against Platonic realism.

Why?—because I have read Draper's objections to the *kalam* argument and found them to be based on misconceptions,[11] and I have read his argument from evil and found it to be based on a mistaken construction of the probabilities involved.[12] Until Clark shows us specifically which probabilities are inscrutable or nonexistent, what reason do we have to call the case for theism into question?

Clark's remark about the probabilities' being inscrutable or nonexistent leads me to think that he is employing Bayes' Theorem to calculate the probability of theism, and—as we saw in my application of that theorem to the resurrection hypothesis (see my response to Habermas, pp. 125–27)—sometimes values cannot be assigned with confidence to the relevant probabilities,

---

[11]See Paul Draper, "A Critique of the *Kalam* Cosmological Argument," in *Philosophy of Religion*, 3d ed., ed. Louis P. Pojman (New York: Wadsworth, 1998), 42–47. Draper agrees that the absurdities I bring forth to illustrate the impossibility of the existence of an actual infinite require us to abandon one of an inconsistent triad of propositions: (1) A set has more members than any of its proper subsets. (2) If the members of two sets can be placed in a one-to-one correspondence, then neither set has more members than the other. (3) There are actually infinite sets. But he asks why we should reject the proposition that there are actually infinite sets. The answer, apart from cavils about Draper's formulation of the propositions, is that the absurdities remain unrelieved so long as one retains this proposition (e.g., Hilbert's Hotel). Draper also thinks the argument equivocates on "begins to exist." Not so; the univocal sense is "x begins to exist" = def. "x exists at t and there is no time prior to t at which x exists." Draper says that if t is a first moment of time, then the universe does not need a cause because it has always existed. Here Draper is the one guilty of equivocation. If "always" means "at every time there is," then it is not true that something that always exists need not have a cause, for if past time is finite, that thing began to exist and so needs a cause. A cause is not needed only if "always" means "permanently; without beginning or end." But in this sense it is false that the universe always exists.

[12]See Paul Draper, "Evolution and the Problem of Evil," in *Philosophy of Religion*, ed. Pojman, 219–30, esp. p. 229. Draper's argument hinges crucially on the claim that evolution (E) is more probable on naturalism (N) than on theism (T): Pr $(E/N) \gg Pr(E/T)$. The justification he gives for this is that given naturalism, evolution is the only way to account for sentient life, whereas given theism, any number of options are open to God. This is confused. I should say that $Pr(E/N)$ is next to nothing; given naturalism not only sentient life, but any life at all, is incomprehensibly improbable, not to mention the fine-tuning of the initial state of the universe. Thus, $Pr(E/T)$ is vastly greater. What Draper's argument at best justifies is $Pr(E/N\&S) > Pr(E/T\&S)$, where S = the existence of sentient life. That is to say, given our existence, evolution is more likely if naturalism rather than theism is true. But this probability does not allow Draper's argument to work. I also disagree with his assignments of value to other probabilities at play in the argument.

so that a Bayesian approach is not helpful. In that case, we must, as Clark says, make a considered judgment about the evidence. But the reader needs to understand that such a process is not arbitrary; rather, inference to the best explanation will be guided by criteria like a hypothesis' explanatory scope, explanatory power, plausibility, accordance with accepted beliefs, and so forth.

Clark is correct, of course, that all of us are epistemically conditioned, which will affect how we assess the evidence. But so what? Such a consideration cannot be used to support historical relativism, for then the belief in historical relativism is itself a mere product of one's socio-historical situation! Clark comes close to making self-refuting statements when he asserts, "We can provide reasons or evidence that, *for all we can tell*, support our beliefs. But we can't tell if *we* are sufficiently informed or if *our* cognitive faculties are working properly (or, on the other hand, if the nontheist's are working properly)" (p. 88). How can Clark know that "we can't tell if we are sufficiently informed" if we can't tell if we are sufficiently informed? Such skepticism about the workings of one's cognitive faculties is self-defeating, since the skepticism is the result of the working of those faculties (cf. Plantinga's transcendental argument[13]). Because it is self-undermining, this sort of skeptical relativism cannot be rationally affirmed.

Besides, since this sort of epistemic conditioning affects everything in general, it affects nothing in particular—for example, Christian theistic belief. We just have to proceed as normal, doing our best to construct sound and persuasive arguments. What we should not do is wallow in a relativistic bog.

Fortunately, Clark himself draws back from historical relativism. His conclusion is a modest one: that we should listen to the arguments of our interlocutors, since we might be wrong and since we may thereby discover common ground to which we can appeal (p. 89). This conclusion is incontestable—if by "being wrong" Clark means that our apologetic might be wrong (not that Christianity might be wrong, since we agree that it is not based on argument, but on God's own witness). Ironically, modesty in our conclusions is not only epistemologically required, but it will actually make our arguments more persuasive. And I agree that we should appeal to commonly accepted

---

[13]See my response to Frame above.

facts. Thus, Clark's conclusions are much less radical than what his argument might have led one to expect. He presents no insuperable obstacle to natural theology.

What, then, of Christian evidences? Clark claims that the probability of the resurrection hypothesis relative to the background information alone (Pr[R/B]) is fantastically low, such that the resurrection hypothesis is "wildly implausible" when considered apart from specific evidence (p. 141; cf. pp. 139–40). Furthermore, "Inference to wildly implausible best explanations requires a lot of evidence. Indeed, the evidence must preponderate sufficiently to swamp our initial skepticism of the implausible hypothesis in question" (p. 141). But in the absence of a prior commitment to theism historical evidences cannot hope to overcome the initial improbability of the resurrection hypothesis. Even given the conclusions of natural theology, "It is not clear to me that reason can establish enough about God to permit the evidence of the resurrection to overcome the vast implausibility (the scandal) of the incarnation and the resurrection" (p. 143).

The reader needs to appreciate that this objection is just Hume's old argument against the identification of miracles in new dress. Its repackaging, however, does not remove its fallaciousness. Consider Clark's claim that establishing a wildly implausible claim requires a lot of evidence. This claim is erroneous. Stimulated by Hume's original argument against miracles, there arose a discussion among probability theorists stretching from Condorcet to John Stuart Mill over what evidence is required in order to establish the occurrence of highly improbable events.[14] It was soon realized that if one simply weighed the probability of the event against the reliability of the witness, then we should be led into denying the occurrence of events, which, though highly improbable, we reasonably know to have occurred.[15]

[14]For an account, see S. L. Zabell, "The Probabilistic Analysis of Testimony," *Journal of Statistical Planning and Inference* 20, no. 3 (1988): 327–54.

[15]E.g., if on the morning news you hear reported that the pick in last night's lottery was 7492871, this is a report of an extraordinarily improbable event, perhaps one out of several million, and even if the morning news' accuracy is known to be 99.99 percent, the improbability of the event reported will swamp the probability of the witness's reliability so that we should never believe such reports. Clark's claim would have us require a lot of evidence in favor of the morning news' reliability, enough to counterbalance the improbability of the winning pick, in order to believe the report, which is absurd.

Theorists saw that what also needs to be considered is the probability that if the reported event has not occurred, then the witness's testimony is just as it is. Mill wrote:

> To know whether a coincidence does or does not require more evidence to render it credible than an ordinary event, we must refer, in every instance, to first principles, and estimate afresh what is the probability that the given testimony would have been delivered in that instance, supposing the fact which it asserts not to be true.[16]

This realization has been embodied in Bayes' Theorem, which requires, in order to show that a miracle M has probably occurred on the basis of specific evidence E and our background information B, that

$$Pr(M/B\&E) > Pr(\neg M/B\&E).$$

Even this needs some finessing, however, as we have seen. We need not show that the probability of the resurrection on the evidence and background information is greater than the probability of no resurrection on the same evidence and information. Rather, what we must show is that the probability of the resurrection is greater than any of its alternatives. That is why, in my response to Habermas, I turned to the so-called odds form of Bayes' Theorem to assess the comparative probabilities of the resurrection hypothesis R and any alternative hypothesis A_n:

$$\frac{Pr(R/B\&E)}{Pr(A_n/B\&E)} = \frac{Pr(R/B)}{Pr(A_n/B)} \times \frac{Pr(E/B\&R)}{Pr(E/B\&A_n)}$$

This implies that the resurrection hypothesis will be probable just in case

$$Pr(R/B) \times Pr(E/B\&R) > Pr(A_n/B) \times Pr(E/B\&A_n).$$

Clark's claim is the same as Cavin's, namely, that (R/B) is so wildly improbable that the values assigned to the other probabilities in question cannot overcome it.[17] I, however, call into

---

[16]J. S. Mill, *A System of Logic*, 2 vols. (London: 1843), bk. 3, ch. 25, sec. 6, cited in Zabell, 331. Thus, to return to our example in the previous note, the probability that the morning news would announce the pick as 7492871 if some other number had been chosen is sufficiently remote that it is rational to believe such testimony to the wildly improbable event in question.

[17]Clark also takes a halfhearted stab at showing that $Pr(E/B\&A_n)$ may not be so low. But I think that nonspecialists simply do not appreciate that the central facts

question Clark's claim that $Pr(R/B) \ll 0.5$. What reasons does Clark give for thinking (R/B) to be wildly improbable? His first reason, a theological one, is based on a misinterpretation. He says that the incarnation is "folly to the Greeks and a stumbling block to the Jews" (p. 142), that is to say, it is rationally and religiously offensive. But when Paul wrote those words, he was talking about the *cross*, not the incarnation and resurrection (1 Cor. 1:23).[18] Clark has misunderstood the scandal.

His second reason, a philosophical one, is also untenable. He seems to construe the improbability of (R/B) in terms of *frequency:* "Incarnations and resurrections, not being as plentiful as raspberries, require a great deal of evidence to support their rational belief" (p. 143). Again, "Isn't our uniform experience, after all, that dead people stay dead?" (p. 142). Clark seems to think that the resurrection of Jesus is improbable because such events are so rare. But as Earman has pointed out, the frequency model of probability simply will not work in this context. For trying to ground all the terms in Bayes' Theorem in objective frequencies would, he observes, disqualify the probabilification of many of the theoretical hypotheses of the advanced sciences.[19] In the case of $Pr(M/B)$ the guidance for assigning probability "cannot take the simple-minded form" of using the value of the frequency of M-type events in past experience; that frequency may be flatly zero (as in proton decay), but it would be unwise to therefore set $Pr(M/B) = 0$.[20]

In short, I do not think Clark has any good reason for thinking $Pr(R/B) \ll 0.5$. To be sure, the incarnation and res-

---

which, I believe, inductively imply the resurrection of Jesus are agreed upon by the majority of New Testament critics today. I know this sounds unbelievable, but it is true. That is the strength of Habermas's "minimalist evidence." The problem lies not in the evidence, but in philosophical presuppositions. It is their reluctance to posit a nature miracle or to infer supernatural causes of mundane effects that precludes most critics' inferring the resurrection hypothesis as the best explanation.

[18]In a Greco-Roman culture that was replete with a colorful assortment of divine men, incarnations, and heroic divinizations, an incarnation was not offensive to reason. What was offensive was "Christ crucified," to Corinthian Greeks who sought spiritual enlightenment via knowledge and to Jews who entertained no such notion that Messiah should suffer the humiliation of being executed as a common criminal.

[19]Earman, "Bayes, Hume, and Miracles," 303. E.g., scientists are investing long hours and millions of dollars hoping for an observation of an event of proton decay, though such an event has never been observed.

[20]Ibid., 301.

urrection of Jesus are wondrous and awe-inspiring, but I know of no good reason to think them intrinsically improbable.[21]

Finally, what about Clark's claim that natural theology does not provide sufficient information about God to overcome the improbability of (R/B)? Letting G = God's existence, I explained in my response to Habermas that

$$Pr(R/B) = Pr(R/B\&G) \times Pr(G/B).$$

I think that natural theology establishes $Pr(G/B) \gg 0.5$. The question raised by Clark is, in effect, whether it also helps us to determine $Pr(R/B\&G)$. The difficulty here is that we are dealing with a free agent (the Creator of the universe), and how do we know what he would do with respect to raising Jesus? I should say here, however, that if the moral argument goes through as well as the *kalam* cosmological argument, then we do have enough information to surmise that $Pr(R/G\&B)$ is not low. For, as the Creator of the universe, God has the power to raise Jesus, and as the locus and source of all goodness, it is not unlikely that God would act redemptively in the world. Thus, it cannot be said that the resurrection hypothesis is improbable relative to God's existence and our background information.[22] Thus, if we allow that the moral argument as well as the *kalam* argument succeeds, we have enough information for the evidentialist's case to proceed.

In conclusion, my own experience in evangelism suggests that argument and evidence can do much more than merely defeat the defeaters brought against Christian faith.[23] We can present a positive case that God can use to help those whose hearts he has prepared come to faith in Christ. For example, I recently flew up to Chicago at the invitation of Willow Creek Community Church to take part in an evangelistic outreach. Christian believers were to invite their nonbelieving friends who had intellectual problems with the Christian faith. The goal was to get

[21]It has been alleged that the incarnation is logically incoherent. But see to the contrary Thomas V. Morris, *The Logic of God Incarnate* (Ithaca, N.Y.: Cornell University Press, 1986).

[22]This serves to underscore the ineptness of the frequency interpretation of the relevant probabilities. For God may have chosen the resurrection as the means of vindicating his Son *precisely because* of its being such a striking overreach of nature's powers and, hence, naturally impossible and therefore rare.

[23]I want to note that Steve Evans, *The Historical Christ and the Jesus of Faith* (Oxford: Clarendon, 1996), 283–84, agrees with me here.

folks to join "seeker small groups," where their questions could be discussed. Lee Strobel, at that time one of the ministers at Willow Creek, told me that around 80 percent of those who join such groups become Christians. About 600 people filled the tables throughout the ballroom, and Lee gave me fifteen minutes to summarize the historical case for Jesus' resurrection. He then pumped me with tough questions for another quarter hour and then invited people to discuss the issues around each table. After the discussion each table was then given a chance to put one question to me. The entire evening was stimulating and dynamic, and when the comment cards were collected, 116 people indicated that they wanted to join a seeker small group! It was a wonderful illustration of how apologetics done within the framework of a loving community can be a means by which people can be drawn to Christ. I appreciate Clark's endorsement of negative apologetics, but it seems to me that we can go further in arguing positively for Christianity's truth and that people will respond when this is done well.

AN EVIDENTIAL APOLOGIST'S
CLOSING REMARKS

Gary R. Habermas

The major goal of an apologetic strategy is to defend and support the Christian message in terms of particular issues and interests. While this is not synonymous with securing the agreement of other experts, such would be a nice side benefit. Of the four responses to my initial essay, I was quite gratified to note that only a single reaction was very critical of my central tenets. Not only did the replies by Bill Craig, John Frame, and Paul Feinberg not raise a single major issue, but they were largely complimentary, often augmenting my own comments. By this I mean that, even if these three colleagues' concerns were justified, my approach would still not be compromised at any crucial points. Given the nature of this volume to locate problems in apologetic systems, this was very satisfying. Further, none of the four replies questioned any details of the factual argument based on the resurrection of Jesus, which formed the major emphasis of my initial essay.

AD CLARK

The chief reaction to my perspective was by Kelly Clark. Accordingly, my response here will be directed mainly to him. Space limitations require that everything I say be exceptionally brief. The insightful reader will hopefully be able to see the direction I am heading and make additional inferences.

Clark repeatedly makes three main responses to my evidentialist method. (1) He charges that a historical apologetic suffers from not having initial theistic grounds, hence proving "little or nothing" (p. 138). (2) There is an extreme antecedent improbability against the incarnation of Jesus, his miracles, and so on, making the unlikelihood "vastly more difficult" than the reality of "ghosts, UFOs, and magic" (p. 142). Because of this improbability of events like the resurrection, no plausible naturalistic theory is even needed. (3) Unbelievers can reject the Christian message without being irrational. In fact, it may even be "more rational" to do so (p. 140). Thus, apologists ought not take the hard line that all reasonable people should become Christians. I will respond to each charge, as well as pursuing some additional critiques of Clark's position. It is my contention that he has misconstrued the subject at every point.

Historical Apologetics

Appearing at the outset to agree with classical apologists, Clark rejects historical arguments for Christianity unless the first step of God's existence has been established. But this is quite misleading, since, in describing Bill Craig's view, Clark still states his doubt as to whether Craig can move from God to miracles: "the vast implausibility (the scandal) of the incarnation and the resurrection" is still too large to overcome (p. 143). Later, Clark is even more direct: "Both Craig's and Habermas's evidential approaches cannot show the truth of Christian belief" (p. 143).

Clark's stance is problematic for more than one reason. Initially, why even require theistic arguments to precede the use of historical evidences unless the former will then be helpful in the overall argument? Then why reject the approach once his condition is fulfilled and we move on to the case for Christianity? Perhaps Clark thinks that we need to use different evidences. But this would oppose his overall lack of evidential interest. As I said in my initial critique, he avoids positive evidences that would specifically support Christian theism at almost every opportunity.

Actually, there is another significant problem here. Clark repeatedly blames Van Tillian presuppositionalists like John Frame in that they are "often long on assertion and short on argument" (cf. his response to Frame, p. 259). Yet, while asserting that historical arguments are insufficient, Clark fails to provide even a single critique of my approach. He never even attempts to argue against the historical particulars.

True, Clark most likely does not do so because of his next argument that Jesus' incarnation and miracles are so antecedently improbable. But if this is his point, the first critique collapses into the second. In short, it is worth noting before moving on that he has made no specific response to the historical arguments themselves, but they cannot be dismissed by his mere assertions alone.

Antecedent Improbability

Is the very center of Christianity—the incarnation and resurrection of Jesus—so incredibly improbable from the outset that this unlikelihood nullifies all historical arguments, even if God's existence is probable? Can these doctrines properly be compared to the arrival of an extraterrestrial, as in Clark's extended parable? Is it really the case that the Christian scenario is "vastly more difficult to believe in than ghosts, UFOs, and magic"? This is Clark's central theme.

Clark's scenario has several serious problems, three of which I will briefly mention here. First, the calculation of antecedent probabilities (in whatever direction), including how much evidence is sufficient to overcome certain presuppositions (usually of unstated strength), simply exposes an abundance of confusing beliefs.[1] But there is absolutely no objective way to

---

[1]E.g., note the way Clark introduces "the multiplication axiom" (although he doesn't tell the reader there is more than one variety) into his extraterrestrial story (p. 140). The impression, especially for those unfamiliar with probability calculus, is that the entire process of figuring antecedent probabilities is also straightforward, just like the formula he provides in his endnote. But this is decidedly incorrect. First, the axiom itself is a simple, straightforward formula in which the probabilities are determinable, such as rolling two sixes on the dice or pulling two diamonds from a deck of cards on consecutive attempts. It can never be applied precisely to the likelihood of philosophical truth or historical events. (Of course Clark is aware of this, but I am speaking to readers who might wrongly think that his comments about probability calculus also apply to antecedent probabilities.) Second, Clark never tells us why he uses the "multiplication axiom" in the first place, even where it is applicable. I have argued at length that apologetics should be construed in a disjunctive rather than a conjunctive manner. Apologists could use the following, more helpful formula (sometimes called the General Addition Rule): $P(A \text{ or } B \text{ or } C) = PA + PB + PC - P(AB) - P(AC) - P(BC) + P(ABC)$. A simpler way to do the same calculus is by computing the probability of nonoccurrence: $PA = 1 - P(\text{non-A})$. At any rate, Clark's presentation is more problematic, still without coming any closer to solving the problem of antecedent probability. For details on the approach I have suggested and its limitations, see Gary R. Habermas, "Probability Calculus, Proof and Christian Apologetics," *The Simon Greenleaf Review of Law and Religion*, vol. 8 (1988–89), 57–88.

compute such figures. The question has more to do with one's overall outlook on reality than on any evaluation of data.

More pointedly, noting the "radically different interpretations" of probability, Keith Parsons objects that "it is hard to see how meaningful probabilities are to be assigned" to either atheism or theism. And even though Parsons is an atheist, he still concludes: "We have absolutely no empirical basis for assigning probabilities to ultimate facts."[2] If, like Clark, antecedent improbability is our primary critique of Christian evidences, preventing us from viewing the relevant facts, it would appear that we have an uphill battle to even get the notion on the table in a manner agreed to by everyone—an almost impossible prerequisite, indeed. But without this agreement, Clark's approach would easily break down into head shaking and choruses of "no way."

Second, mounting antecedent improbabilities betrays both an *a priori* bias against the evidence for supernatural occurrences, as well as a circular argument. Why should it be assumed that miracles face insurmountable evidential obstacles? How do we know that there is an insufficient background basis to recognize and interpret them? Why shouldn't God's existence be exceptionally relevant here? In a theistic universe, couldn't he decide to perform an event regardless of the prior probabilities? In fact, why couldn't the resurrection be the single, best-evidenced miracle precisely because God wanted to particularly verify Jesus' unique person and message?

We will never know the answer to these and other questions until we study all the evidence. In brief, Clark's objection from antecedent probability is not self-confirming: it doesn't stand on its own say-so. But neither does it allow the evidence to speak for itself.

Steve Parrish explains a further problem this way: "*If one knew atheism were true,* then one would be completely justified in assigning miracles a very low order of antecedent probability. However, the possibility of miracles cannot be summarily rejected when using them as evidence to decide between some variety of theism and atheism, as that would be begging the question."[3] Parrish continues: "If there are two or more hypothe-

---

[2]Keith Parsons, "Is There a Case for Christian Theism?" in J. P. Moreland and Kai Nielson, *Does God Exist? The Great Debate* (Nashville: Thomas Nelson, 1990), 179–82.

[3]Stephen E. Parrish, *God and Necessity: A Defense of Classical Theism* (Lanham, Md.: University Press of America, 1997), 156 (my emphasis).

ses which all explain some data equally well, the truth of one of the hypotheses cannot be assumed and then used to demonstrate the truth of that particular hypothesis. Yet this is exactly what their argument against miracles does."[4]

Why should Clark speak as if miracles are so improbable? Parrish answers that many philosophers, consciously or otherwise, assume that a naturalistic worldview, with its corresponding probability structure, represents "the neutral or objective viewpoint." From this angle, "no amount of evidence would ever be enough to justify" the belief in miracles.[5] Parrish appears to describe precisely Clark's position, including this same bias.[6] It is certainly puzzling why Clark feels the need to take this outlook.

Third, the evidentialist can also grant that, even given a sense of the antecedent *unlikelihood* of miracles (instead of their practical impossibility), the challenge can *still* be met. The resurrection of Jesus is the chief example purporting a high level of evidence in the presence of both strong background and interpretive data.[7]

This is especially noticeable in Clark's failure to either critique my resurrection apologetic or offer a naturalistic theory. He says repeatedly that one need not even offer an alternative hypothesis. He apparently thinks that this event is so incredibly improbable that he doesn't even need to explain the historical facts. This would be a strange reaction. Perhaps he is just not able to devise a hypothesis that makes sense of all the known historical facts. Such is the challenge of the resurrection.

For these reasons, then, Clark's chief basis for rejecting an evidentialist argument fails. He opts for the arbitrary and questionable territory of antecedent probability when the move itself is not objectively supported. Further, he rejects the evidence for miracles in an *a priori* manner, begging the entire question by

---

[4]Ibid.

[5]Ibid., 156–57.

[6]Echoing Parrish's sentiments, and in spite of his earlier words, Parsons comes very close to Clark's position on the unlikelihood of miracles, saying that "*any* alternative scenario, no matter how improbable" is preferred to a miracle (p. 192, Parson's emphasis). Remarkably, Parsons also makes it clear more than once that he is viewing the issue from an atheistic angle, adding that theists have a different viewpoint (p. 191). Sadly, from my perspective, Parsons would probably appreciate Clark's position as that of a theist who agrees with him in so many aspects of this discussion.

[7]On the evidence, background, and interpretive information supporting the resurrection of Jesus, see my responses to Bill Craig and John Frame below, pp. 56–67 and 236–48.

embracing what is essentially an antisupernatural position before any investigation. Finally, the evidence he fails to allow could be precisely what is needed to defeat the prior unlikelihood of miracles.

Hard and Soft Apologetics

Clark's final issue concerns the strength of the apologetic enterprise. He holds that unbelievers can *rationally* reject Christianity. In fact, it is "more rational" to reject implausible theses (p. 140), and the Christian message is about as difficult to accept rationally as anything can be (p. 142).[8] Therefore, believers ought to reject the hard line that all reasonable people ought to become Christians, and be satisfied that they hold a rational position.

In one sense, Clark's point is entirely moot. Obviously, our opinions do not change the actual evidence or its limitations. It is possible both to overemphasize and to underemphasize each. If evidentialists like Bill Craig and I are right, Christianity is not only defensible, it can also be shown to be true. If Clark is right, Christianity is still rational, though we are unable to argue strongly that it is true or to refute naturalism.

Yet it just seems that Clark's position does not go far enough. As Parsons forcefully argues:

> If . . . theists want to claim no more than that they are within their epistemic rights in believing in God, atheists should not bother to belabor the point. After all, [this] in no way indicates that atheists are one whit less rational in not believing in God. . . . If someone claims no more for their position . . . the appropriate response is apathy rather than hostility.[9]

It does seem to me that we want to say more than this. But neither Craig, Clark, Frame, Feinberg, nor myself claims that Christianity is irrational or false. We also agree that many will hear our case and not become believers, usually owing to volitional and other presuppositional factors. It is true that there are differences between us, but ultimately, this last charge does nothing to change the arguments themselves.

---

[8]I always find myself wondering if the apostle Paul would agree to the rationality of the unbeliever's position, given passages like Romans 1!

[9]Parsons, "Is There a Case for Christian Theism?" 178–79.

Emotions, Cognition, and Our Presuppositions

My last point of critique returns to a topic I raised in my initial response to Clark. I mentioned the need to augment his existential counseling strategy with cognitive insights. Now I will suggest that this idea be extended to Clark's overall apologetic strategy. He responds to Craig, "Our believings are inextricably entwined with our passions, emotions, and will." He realizes, too, the potential danger here: "Of course our passions and emotions can both prevent us from attending to and being persuaded by the argumentation" (p. 85).

If I am right that the most common form of doubt is emotional, then Clark's last warning ought to be taken very seriously. He describes how doubt often begins: "more likely, we are just overwhelmed with our own personal experience . . ." (see his response to Craig, p. 83). Clark and I have both been stung severely by this variety of uncertainty. Clark's most "profound sense of unbelief" came after the sudden death of his father.[10] He has just given us a few more hints. Only Clark knows, but perhaps his deepest questions about the evidence may not be derived from the evidence itself, but from his feelings about the evidence.

The specialty of cognitive methodology is stripping away certain presuppositions that are untrue, unhelpful, and even harmful, especially those of an emotional or volitional nature.[11] In the briefest of terms, I think we should ascertain which of our beliefs are firmly rooted in the data and which ones are our own private outlook on the data.[12] Clark repeatedly warns us about the influence of our own presuppositions, yet he misses the force of his own words. Within limits, we can battle back against the "passions and emotions" that, as Clark says, can persuade us against good arguments.

---

[10]Kelly James Clark, *When Faith Is Not Enough* (Grand Rapids: Eerdmans, 1997), 48.

[11]Gary R. Habermas and Gary Sibcy II, "Religious Uncertainty and Negative Emotionality: A New Instrument for Measuring Religious Doubt," forthcoming. See also, Gary R. Habermas, *The Thomas Factor: Using Your Doubts to Draw Closer to God* (Nashville: Broadman and Holman, 1999), chaps. 4–10. See especially the sources listed in footnotes 36 and 38 in my earlier response to Clark.

[12]I am hardly picking on Clark here, as if he were alone in these struggles. I will be the first to admit that I passed through the deep waters of doubt for well over ten years. Consistent with the vast majority of cases, most of my uncertainty was also emotional in nature.

AD CRAIG

As noted, Craig has very little to say of a critical nature. He certainly doesn't question any of my major tenets, which is gratifying. I will still clarify briefly two issues: the nature of evidentialism and the use of Bayes' Theorem.

Craig charges that if the chief emphasis of evidentialism is that historical evidences can justify Christian theism, then it is not a very distinctive method, and he would include himself among the evidentialists (p. 122). But the reason Craig doesn't find much distinction here is that he does not take the classical position of the classical apologist! As I indicate in my first response to him, he *is* an evidentialist, just as he admits![13] But such is not the case with other classical apologists like Geisler, Sproul, and Gerstner, who clearly reject the evidentialist argument.[14] I will not repeat my previous criticism here. From the "other" classical perspective, evidentialism does have a distinguishing feature.[15] I need not take this issue further—it is a matter between them.

Here is my chief point on this matter. The one-step argument is the major tenet of evidentialism, proceeding naturally

---

[13]For a fair portion of his response to me, Craig continues to note several aspects of appreciation for the evidentialist method. E.g., he comments that the evidentialist "pushes back" from historical events like the resurrection appearances to God's action, just as the natural theologian "pushes back" from the Big Bang to God's creation (p. 123). I have called the former the retrospective argument from miracles to God. (See my essay in chapter 2, "Evidential Apologetics," plus my volume *The Resurrection of Jesus: An Apologetic* [Grand Rapids: Baker, 1980; Lanham, Md.: University Press of America, 1984], chaps. 2–3.) In another instance, Craig agrees with me against Clark that antecedent probability is not the issue here at all, since even agnostics must be "equally agnostic" about the possibilities before they look at the data (p. 125).

[14]And they would reject Craig's version, too, to the extent that he also thinks that we can make the move from the resurrection to the God of Christian theism (as I outlined in my first response to Craig). For the typical classical argument that such a move is circular, see R. C. Sproul, John Gerstner, and Arthur Lindsley, *Classical Apologetics: A Rational Defense of the Christian Faith and a Critique of Presuppositional Apologetics* (Grand Rapids: Zondervan, 1984), 146–47, 276; Norman Geisler, *Christian Apologetics* (Grand Rapids: Baker, 1976), 95–96, 147. I will respond briefly to this charge in the next section on John Frame's apologetic.

[15]I will mention that the working definition given to me by the editor of this volume before this project even began also indicated that historical argumentation to Christian theism ("one step") was the primary contribution of the evidentialist apologetic position.

from its historical emphasis. But it is not an integral part of the classical view, which is not as historically oriented, and generally even denounces the move. So in the rare case that a classical apologist (like Craig) admits it, *it still flows from evidentialist methodology and is thus a concession to it!* Classical apologists may allow it, but it is in no way integral to their system. So I think it is clear that Craig has moved toward evidentialism by admitting its main tenet. Yet, sometimes it seems that Craig is simply charging that his argument plus mine is stronger than mine alone!

Concerning Bayes' Theorem and the need for items like background information for the resurrection, the evidentialist has several options. The most obvious is to take the route that I did in my initial essay and elsewhere,[16] linking the resurrection to Jesus' life and claims, both concerning himself and his Father. If Craig thinks the one-step approach is a weaker argument, as shown by Bayes' Theorem, then why does he so frequently state and pursue with such gusto the resurrection-to-God argument? His own writings surely attest to his agreement with me, thereby undermining the force of his objection from Bayes' Theorem.[17]

Another intriguing direction I often use on college campuses is to move from highly evidenced instances of near death experiences, as a limited case for minimal life after death, on to the resurrection.[18] The point here is not to argue that near-death experiences are of the same metaphysical nature as Jesus' resurrection, but precisely to provide the sort of relevant background support that "breaks the ice" for those who are slow to accept supernatural claims. Finally, as I mentioned in both my initial essay and my response to Craig, evidentialists frequently move from God's existence to the resurrection. Even the possibility of

---

[16]For my most detailed account, see my *The Resurrection of Jesus: An Apologetic*, chaps. 2–5.

[17]Craig should not object, since he has regularly emphasized the importance of many of the same details. See his volumes *Assessing the New Testament Evidence for the Historicity of the Resurrection of Jesus* (Lewiston, N.Y.: Edwin Mellen, 1989), 419–20; *The Historical Argument for the Resurrection of Jesus During the Deist Controversy* (Lewiston, N.Y.: Edwin Mellen, 1985), 499–501; *The Son Rises: The Historical Evidence for the Resurrection of Jesus* (Chicago: Moody Press, 1981), 137–43.

[18]Gary R. Habermas and J. P. Moreland, *Beyond Death: Exploring the Evidence for Immortality* (Wheaton, Ill.: Crossway, 1998), chaps. 7–9; Gary R. Habermas, "Near Death Experiences and the Evidence—A Review Essay," *Christian Scholar's Review* 26, no. 1 (Fall 1996): 78–85.

God can be sufficient.[19] These moves are helpful in some instances, like the one here.[20] I think that Jesus' life and claims, near-death experiences, and God's existence provide exceptionally fruitful background areas for such discussions.[21]

In sum, I would hardly object to Craig's comments on providing appropriate background information for historical evidences. I have frequently developed this case precisely for the reason that the resurrection is not a brute fact—it needs a context, as I have said many times in my initial essay and elsewhere. Neither do I shun theistic arguments. They fit nicely into certain situations. I don't think I have ever known an evidentialist to oppose them, either. We do argue, however, that it is not necessary to begin with that route. Further, historical evidences are not only a legitimate avenue of argument for Christian theism, but, on many occasions, they may be the best way to proceed.

AD FRAME

While Frame raises a few more issues than Craig, I had to look hard to find any actual critiques. Frame is more inclined to provide compliments punctuated with very brief complaints (usually less than a sentence each), or comments on other topics. As with Craig, I note that he did not challenge any of my primary points.

Frame's chief complaints involve the following: the biblical nature of my remarks, epistemic common ground, the relation between historical evidences and God, critical agreement, and my answer to skepticism. I will respond briefly to each.

Frame thinks that Craig and I[22] do not link our views care-

---

[19]I list this option in *The Resurrection of Jesus: An Apologetic*, 49–60, 72–75.

[20]So when Craig responds to me that natural theology could provide helpful information in a case for Christian theism (pp. 127–28), I do not disagree. Once again, as in my earlier response to him, there are two primary differences between evidentialists and classical apologists: the former don't think the first step is *necessary*, and "Evidentialists just want to argue the second, historical, step as well" (p. 61, n. 13).

[21]Areas like these three also help provide what Clark demands, since they show that the plausibility of the resurrection is much higher than he allows. For a positive evaluation of how the background evidence for miracles alone might both disprove Hume's approach and also argue for the probability of theism, see Rodney D. Holder, "Hume on Miracles: Bayesian Interpretation, Multiple Testimony, and the Existence of God," *British Journal for the Philosophy of Science* 49 (1998): 49–65.

[22]On Frame's question about the difference between my method and Craig's (p. 134), see my response to Craig in chapter 1 as well as above.

fully enough to Scripture. But it is very difficult to know exactly what he means. On the Holy Spirit, I simply disagree that the primary object of the witness is the Bible, although the witness comes through the text.[23] Frame even admits the possibility of my position (see his response to Craig, pp. 76–77). Do I fail to use enough Scripture in my response? Surely he doesn't refer to the number of texts I use; a count will show that I included more than he does! Again I'm puzzled.[24]

On epistemic common ground, this concept does not require total agreement between unbeliever and believer. Of course the former has major disagreements with the latter. Evidentialists just think there are areas where there is enough commonality that meaningful discussion may still ensue. Sure we should expect "some startling shifts" of position, but since Frame allows for at least tentative agreement with the unbeliever, I don't see why this subject is an issue. Our differences with the unbeliever may affect our delivery, and so believers need to be persistent, but this doesn't change the message we communicate. I suspect that Frame and I agree in more places than we disagree here.

Frame asserts some agreement that the resurrection proves God's existence but says that the historical argument assumes a theistic context. Although he doesn't say this, I will briefly address the further point that a historical argument for theism is circular unless God is first shown to exist.[25] This charge is false.

1. We can discuss the issue as a hypothetical scenario, taking a two-paradigm approach: What do naturalism and Christian theism predict about God, the laws of nature, the resurrection, life after death, and so on? What data do we have? This strategy does not assume any worldview but discusses which one best accounts for what we know.

2. The resurrection argument can be cast in the same logical form as the classical theistic arguments, perhaps as a species

---

[23]I try to carefully spell out my view on this particular issue in Gary R. Habermas, "The Personal Testimony of the Holy Spirit to the Believer and Christian Apologetics," *Journal of Christian Apologetics* 1, no. 1 (Summer 1997): 55–57.

[24]In one form or another, Frame makes similar comments to each of the other contributors in this volume. I do not at all question his sincerity, but it seems apparent from several recurring comments that he thinks no other position is as biblical as his. I guess in one sense this is only natural. But I seldom understand his specific concern.

[25]I noted earlier that many classical apologists agree (excluding Craig), and Clark might have some slight inclination here, although he does not specifically say so.

of inductive teleological argument. As such, it is not necessarily circular, just as they are not.

3. As I mentioned above in my response to Craig, there is sufficient background and interpretive data, as well as the evidence itself, to provide a meaningful scenario for Jesus' resurrection. The convergence of these evidential strands can be accomplished in a noncircular manner.[26]

One smaller matter deserves comment simply due to the number of times Frame brings it up. He states that Craig and I "overestimate" the extent of critical agreement on "the general reliability" of Scripture accounts (p. 132). He adds that "it is possible for this scholarly spectrum to be wrong" (p. 135), so "we should not proceed casually on the assumption that 'everybody will agree' on this or that" (p. 136).

Several brief rejoinders are necessary. I simply disagree with Frame on the subject of the resurrection: although there are exceptions, the general tenor of critical interaction is stronger than he apparently realizes. This is especially the case with 1 Corinthians 15:3–8. Further, of course the critics can be wrong! That's why I explicitly said in my initial essay (chapter 2): "Not only may the critics themselves be mistaken, but the intellectual climate may change" (p. 100). So why repeat my own words back to me as if I had never said them? I even add the additional condition that this critical mood may change. And I do not proceed on the casual assumption that "everybody will agree." I very carefully say that this principle is secondary to being well-evidenced.

Frame also misunderstands my minimal facts approach. I do not assume critical agreement on the "general reliability" of the resurrection accounts. My argument for the resurrection, to the contrary, is built on an approach that bypasses such reliability in favor of a case-by-case study, as I argue in chapter 2.

As long as we are careful, I still think that using the critics' own methodology against them is a worthwhile tool. But why should presuppositionalists disagree? Their chief methodological move is to do the same. Frame should be supporting me here!

---

[26]I outlined 1 and 3 in my initial essay (see "Confirmation of Jesus' Claims" [pp. 116–20]). For specific details on all three options, see Habermas, *The Resurrection of Jesus: An Apologetic*, chaps. 1–5. See also R. Douglas Geivett, "The Evidential Value of Miracles," in *In Defense of Miracles: A Comprehensive Case for God's Action in History*, eds. R. Douglas Geivett and Gary R. Habermas (Downers Grove, Ill.: InterVarsity Press, 1997), 178–95.

Finally, while acknowledging that my resurrection argument is very strong and completely convincing to him and perhaps others (including some unbelievers), Frame asks how I would respond to a "more modest" form of skepticism that says the Christian message is just too incredible to believe (p. 137, no. 6).

Reminiscent of Clark's position on antecedent improbability, I would work through responses like the three I addressed to him above. I think background information like the examples I gave in my response to Craig (above) would show that the Christian message is not too incredible, but fits nicely with what we know about Jesus and the universe. After finding any "rub," I would ask for *direct* objections to my data.[27] Apart from a criticism that we needed to address further, I would add that this skeptical position does not disprove the apologetic; it only chooses not to believe it. Of course, no one has ever claimed that everyone we talk to will be converted. After all, even Jesus didn't have those results! But this does not discredit the strength of the evidence.

AD FEINBERG

Not only does Feinberg not mention any critiques of my initial essay, but almost his entire response is occupied by noting six major areas where he agrees with my methodology. In particular, he appreciated my development of a one-step historical argument for Christian theism. This was also gratifying.

In my first response to Feinberg, I mentioned several times that I thought his argument was best considered as a species of evidentialism. In his opening paragraph, he confirmed this identification, calling his method "an extension or modification of what is called the evidentialist approach" (p. 129).

Without repeating the chief critique I developed briefly in my initial response (pp. 184–93), I note that Feinberg still prefers an apologetic that builds on the trustworthiness of Scripture. But a *prima facie* case for the Bible does not allow us to guarantee everything in it. Of course, supernatural claims will be the first to be questioned by critics, just as we would challenge the same sorts of claims in other traditions. Thus, arguing from a generally trustworthy text is not the best way to proceed here. Not

---

[27]I would respond similarly to Frame's rewording of Hume, stated in the same context (pp. 136–37).

only does it fail to produce solid and specific confirmation for the resurrection,[28] but it keeps us from responding sufficiently to supernatural reports like those by Tacitus and Suetonius.

Feinberg approvingly cites John Warwick Montgomery's approach here, but there is perhaps no better example of the problems I am pointing out. Montgomery likes to use a six-step apologetic that moves from the general trustworthiness of Scripture, to Jesus' claims to be God, to Jesus' resurrection, to inspiration.[29]

But a general case for the reliability of Scripture cannot bear the burden of the next five steps. Since trustworthiness does not guarantee every single truth between the covers of a volume, we would have to go to other evidences to make sure that the additional steps are warranted. Further, we have definitely not hereby provided the best arguments for Jesus' deity and resurrection, which can be done far more assuredly on the basis of specific texts and arguments. Finally, if we are not careful, a modified form of Montgomery's argument might come close to vindicating the supernatural claims of generally trustworthy writings like those of Tacitus, Suetonius, or someone else. In brief, while the trustworthiness argument is certainly helpful in some instances, resting the very heart of the Christian gospel on it is not one of them!

Feinberg compliments my minimal facts argument but adds that "miracles will still be problematic" on these grounds (p. 131). But this is to confuse a *historical* argument with a *philosophical* one, since the minimal facts alone cannot be used to show God's actions; additional criteria beyond these facts are required to ascertain a miracle.[30] After all, there are no brute facts. Further, as Feinberg correctly says just a paragraph earlier,

---

[28]If it is argued that the trustworthiness approach could incorporate these specific arguments, I would just point out that it would then no longer be a general strategy, especially since these amendments need to be added in other places too. Further, if it must borrow from the minimal facts approach at these crucial points, then this would simply justify my charge that these specific steps are necessary in order to properly support the case.

[29]John Warwick Montgomery, *Where Is History Going?* (Grand Rapids: Zondervan, 1969), 35, 179; John Warwick Montgomery, *The Shape of the Past: A Christian Response to Secular Philosophies of History* (Minneapolis: Bethany Fellowship, 1975), 138–39.

[30]The minimal facts show, for instance, that the resurrection occurred, but it must then be linked to God. See my treatment of this is the "Confirmation of Jesus' Claims" in my main essay, as well as in my *The Resurrection of Jesus: An Apologetic*, esp. chaps. 2–3.

critics too often dismiss miracles, not because of the lack of data, but because they are prejudiced against them (pp. 130–31). Additionally, we must remember that even if critics reject our conclusion, this doesn't mean that our apologetic wasn't accurate. It is still a matter of the will. The minimal facts approach begins the process on the strongest grounds.

Finally, Feinberg asks if I am open to an extension of my evidential approach, using other, cumulative elements as one-step arguments to Christian theism. As I have said repeatedly, evidentialists are eclectic in their methodology. While not all arguments are necessarily equal, we do have the potential of multiple starting points for apologetics.

CONCLUSION

While Kelly Clark thinks that some arguments for God are useful with certain persons, he steadfastly refuses to provide the next step: detailed positive evidences for Christian theism. Besides this almost total absence, he also ignores virtually any careful interaction with the particulars of evidence provided by others. What we get is *proclamations* against the evidence. He declares that his view is true without careful argumentative support, then criticizes the use of evidence without specifically engaging the technicalities. But, just as he said to Frame (pp. 259–60), we need more than his confident assertions.

In reading Clark, it seems that he is talking more *about* evidences than getting his hands dirty with the details. Maybe this is precisely what he means by his comment concerning our "passions and emotions" that can make us slant good arguments, in that they "can both prevent us from attending to and being persuaded" by them (Clark to Craig, p. 85). But for all Clark's comments about overconfident apologists who need to do their homework, he frequently refuses to engage in careful evaluations of the evidential details or to provide positive arguments for his own system.

I have no major problems with Bill Craig. I simply welcome him back to the evidentialist fold! His seeming perplexity at how to critique evidentialism shows both the strength of the latter and the extent of his agreement with it.

I still think that John Frame has serious quandaries within his system, and that it is not a distinctive apologetic method. Freely admitting that his approach is circular (if not worse), along with providing too little of a positive apologetic, he also creates an inadequate method. But I will not repeat what I have said, especially in my initial response to him.

I also have no major disagreements with Paul Feinberg beyond my questions concerning where and how we use arguments from the general trustworthiness of Scripture. But working out these and other issues among evidentialists is more a matter of degree than kind.

These colleagues are my friends. One thing I think this volume has shown is that contributions to Christian apologetics can come from various angles and from differing systems. May we labor together to give joint testimony to our great God.

A CUMULATIVE CASE APOLOGIST'S CLOSING REMARKS

Paul D. Feinberg

The purpose of this response is to clarify certain issues that either I did not make clear enough or that were not understood correctly, and to offer my response to matters on which I differ with the other contributors to this discussion.

GENERAL REMARKS

The Goal of Apologetic Method

The place to begin is with Kelly James Clark's question as to whether I think the goal of apologetics is the establishment of the truth or rationality of belief or the persuasion of the unbeliever. It should be clear that I think that it is the persuasion of the unbeliever. This does not mean that I think that the truth or rationality of belief are unimportant. I think that the truth and rationality of belief in God and the Christian view of the world are fundamental, but they are not enough. Any argument offered for Christianity must be sound; that is, it must be true and reasonable. However, an argument may be sound but may not convince unbelievers. It is for this reason that I hold that to talk of proof in any meaningful sense one must be speaking of a demonstrably sound argument. Contrary to Clark's claim, however, I do not think that there is just one reasonable conclusion that a person can reach in light of the evidence. My claim is that the Christian interpretation is the best explanation of all the evidence, not the only reasonable one.

Thus, one who offers a cumulative case argument is seeking to convince the unbeliever that Christianity is true or rational because it makes the best sense or is the most adequate explanation of a number of elements of our common human experience.

The Nature of the Cumulative Case Argument

The move to what I have called a cumulative case approach follows from the belief that the apologist seeks to convince unbelievers of Christianity, and that proof in the aforementioned sense will not be possible because arguments that make such claims will have premises that will be rejected by those they are intended to convert. A cumulative case argument is a broad-based argument involving many elements formulated as an informal argument. It is broad based in the sense that it includes arguments for God's existence, religious experience, and God's revelation in the Scripture—to name of few of the elements—rather than relying on a single kind of argument. It is informal in the sense the arguments are set in a domain that is different from philosophical argumentation. This does not mean that deductive and inductive reasoning are prohibited, but that they are not used in a formal sense. When William Craig argues that cumulative case arguments are an example of inductive reasoning, he is right, but that is not the point that I am making. Such reasoning is informal, like that used in the setting out of a legal brief. I agree with much of what Craig says about theistic arguments. Where I think we disagree is on how they are to be used. He wants to use them as "probabilistically sound theistic proofs," whereas I think it is more prudent to include them in an argument that requires explanation for the existence of the universe and its orderliness among other things.

A further feature of informal reasoning as I have described it is that it requires one's opponent to offer explanations that are at least as good as mine. It is true that unbelievers will continue to reject some key element in my case. For instance, they may well argue that behavioral change I attribute to God and conversion is explainable on psychological or sociological grounds. It is no longer enough, however, to show that there is some possible alternative explanation. It must be shown that that explanation is at least as good or better than the one I offer. Those who criticize my approach because it will not lead to a demonstrable argument are correct. However, it is no longer enough to simply refuse a move in my argument. One must offer an alternative move and show that this move is as reasonable or better than mine.

Also true is that some of the elements that are a part of the Christian's cumulative case may also be a part of another's, say Muslim's, cumulative case. A Muslim might include theistic arguments, religious experience, and the Koran as part of such a case. Thus, we can imagine a variety of cumulative cases for a variety of religious beliefs. This is why there must be some tests for truth. It is also a further reason why the test of comprehensiveness is an important one. That is, the adequacy of a system of belief must be judged in terms of how comprehensively it explains all the aspects of our experience. For instance, it is easy to see how atheism might claim to have a better explanation for the existence of evil than does theism. No God exists to restrain or eliminate evil. However, that is not the only aspect of experience that needs explanation, and Christian theism has an answer as well to the existence of evil in the doctrine of the fall.

The use of the ten-leaky-buckets objection may be misleading. It has to do with the objection that the combination of ten bad or defective arguments can't be combined and make a good argument. There are cases where this objection is a good one, but the cumulative case argument that I have presented is not one of them. The reasons are that the context of argumentation is changed from formal to informal, and that the elements stand or fall as a whole. The case for Christianity is not a demonstrably sound proof. It is an argument that endeavors to show that the Christian view of the world is reasonable. Moreover, while many find arguments for God's existence less than compelling, now there are other elements that must be explained as well. It is in this last sense that there is a variety of elements that reinforce one another. One element does not necessarily grow out of or even depend on another. The preponderance of the evidence drawn from these elements points toward the truth of Christianity. The certitude or confidence that the believer has in the truth of Christianity is *added* or *given* by the Holy Spirit.

More than once I have been criticized in these pages for not doing much in the way of developing arguments. The reason for this is twofold. First, this is a book on apologetic methodology, not apologetics per se. Second, a cumulative case approach, because of its eclectic nature, is able to incorporate arguments from other approaches. Craig's work on theistic arguments and the resurrection are most helpful. Gary Habermas's development of the historical proof for the resurrection would be a part of the cumulative case. Clark's understanding of epistemology and rationality, as well as John Frame's claim that the presuppositions of a system of belief must be examined, would all form a part of the approach to apologetic methodology that I am proposing.

Postmodernism

I am in pretty substantial agreement with Craig that we should not overestimate the importance of postmodernism. It is taken with greater seriousness in different parts of the world and in different disciplines. In Europe it has greater credibility than in the United States. In history and literature its influence is greater than in philosophy. One doubts that it will survive long since it is so nihilistic. Having said that, however, I do think that postmodernism is self-referentially incoherent, to use Craig's terminology, or prevented from being true since it denies that there is truth in Frame's way of stating the criticism. My purpose for stating that it fails the test of livability is that I sought to evaluate it within the method of doing apologetics that I set out. There is no test called self-referential incoherency, but there was one that requires that one not contradict in practice what one defends in theory. The fact that a postmodernist might be willing to live with that contradiction is neither here nor there. The contradiction shows that there is a problem with that belief system.

I now turn to more miscellaneous responses to some of the other contributors. These are short comments on criticisms to the cumulative case.

AD FRAME

John Frame thinks that I ought to have included Scripture among my tests for truth. I see a need to distinguish between the methods and tests for truth in apologetics and systematic theology. To make Scripture a test for truth in apologetics is to argue circularly. I find this to be a problem. Once one has established the Christian worldview, Scripture becomes a test for the truth of the systematic theology that is developed from it.

AD CRAIG

William Craig criticizes my use of the witness of the Spirit in describing a cumulative case approach. He says that the witness of the Spirit is never used in Scripture for an external witness. This may be true, but theologians and apologists use terms that are not even found in the Scripture like *trinity* or *hypostatic union*. I do not claim that this is the way the term *witness of the Spirit* is used in the Bible or in Reformed theology, just that it is an idea around which a cumulative case can be developed. Nevertheless, nothing hangs on this, and one can choose to eliminate it without harm to my approach.

AD HABERMAS

Finally, Gary Habermas expresses concern over the way I use Scripture or develop the argument for it. He points out that a book that is generally reliable need not be accepted at every point. If this is so, then why should the unbeliever accept what the Bible has to say about itself or about the deity of Christ? This is an important issue, and I have three responses. First, in my response to Habermas's statement of his approach to apologetics, I said that I thought his development of a minimal-facts apologetics method was something that I found helpful. Thus, I am not in very great disagreement with him. Second, I am less concerned about my use of the Scripture than he is, because I would not establish the general reliability of Scripture only on evidence internal to it. I think that the reliability of the Bible rests on the fact that evidence external to it corroborates what it claims. Third, given my approach to the reliability of the Scriptures, it will not be enough to reject a miracle story simply because one does not believe that miracles happen. There must be something in the story itself that makes it unbelievable or false.

A PRESUPPOSITIONAL APOLOGIST'S CLOSING REMARKS

John M. Frame

First, I shall reply to some of the criticisms made by my colleagues. Then I shall make some concluding comments on our discussion.

AD CLARK

Is There a Biblical Epistemology?

Kelly James Clark and Paul Feinberg are not persuaded by my view that Scripture teaches the outlines of an epistemology. I will respond to Clark, who argues the point at greater length. As in his main essay (chapter 5, "Reformed Epistemology Apologetics"), Clark says he is "dubious . . . of finding any ultimate or coercive support for epistemology in Scripture" (p. 256). But in my main essay (chapter 4, "Presuppositional Apologetics"), I presented biblical support for several significant epistemological principles, and Clark has not interacted with any of my exegesis. Rather than attack the specifics of my biblical epistemology, he brings against it only one very general consideration: "The Hebrews were not theoretical thinkers—wisdom was for them profoundly practical." It was practical, he says, in teaching them "how to live one's (moral and spiritual) life" (p. 256). Thus, in Clark's view, biblical wisdom is moral and spiritual but not epistemological.

I grant that wisdom in Scripture is practical, moral, and spiritual. But I think it would be very difficult to show from the

Bible a sharp distinction between, say, theory and practice, or between the realm of ethics-spirituality and the realm of knowledge, and then to show that wisdom is exclusively limited to one side of that divide. Certainly, Clark has not shown any such distinction to exist.[1] To the contrary, consider (1) the fear of the Lord is not only the beginning of wisdom (Ps. 111:10), but also of knowledge (Prov. 1:7).[2] (2) Solomon, the Old Testament paradigm of wisdom, not only wrote proverbs, but also described animal and plant life in detail (1 Kings 4:33–34). So his wisdom was not only moral and spiritual, but also botanical and biological. (3) God's own wisdom (described, for example, in Ps. 104, and in God's wisdom contest with Job in Job 38–42) does not consist only of moral or spiritual matters, but includes also the ingenuity by which he created the world and governs the course of nature. (4) The wisdom of Christ (1 Cor. 1:30) is something that transforms and governs the whole of life. It gives us a new "mind" (1 Cor. 2:16) and calls us to bring every thought captive to Christ (2 Cor. 10:5). So it is not limited to some narrowly defined "moral" or "spiritual" realm. (5) Even apart from the doctrine of wisdom, Scripture has much to say about how we gain knowledge: the doctrine of revelation, the Word of God, the Holy Spirit. None of these factors in our knowledge of God is limited to the moral and spiritual realms.

Do Non-Christians Know Anything?

Also on epistemology: Clark[3] thinks that I implicitly deny that non-Christians can know anything, because I say that true beliefs are justified by their imaging God's beliefs. This is a correct statement of my view of the justification of beliefs. But Clark goes on to add that according to me, "What justifies beliefs for human beings, therefore, seems to be faith in the Christian God" (p. 258). That is not my view.

---

[1]This is the sort of distinction people make when they try to limit the inerrancy of Scripture only to "religious" truth rather than to anything relevant to history or science. In all these cases, the distinction in my view is insupportable.

[2]Of course, I grant that *knowledge* in Scripture is not merely theoretical. But propositional, factual knowledge is part of it. I attempt to sort out some of these issues in my theological epistemology, *Doctrine of the Knowledge of God* (Phillipsburg, N.J.: Presbyterian and Reformed, 1987).

[3]Feinberg presents the same objection. I think my response here to Clark will deal with Feinberg's concern as well.

Non-Christians do have knowledge, indeed knowledge of God, but not by saving faith.[4] Romans 1:18–21 indicates, rather, that they know God from natural revelation. Beliefs derived from natural revelation image God's thought and are thereby justified beliefs, that is, knowledge. Of course, the passage also teaches that the unbeliever represses this true knowledge, so the situation is mixed—true knowledge plus the lies by which that knowledge is repressed.[5]

I agree with Clark that some of Van Til's expressions can be understood as teaching that unbelievers have no knowledge, but Van Til's overall view of this matter is the same as mine.[6]

I will not apologize for my statement that brilliant unbelievers use their reason in the service of falsehood. As a Calvinist, I believe that Genesis 6:5; 8:21; Isaiah 64:6; Romans 3:9–18; 8:5–8; and other passages teach the total depravity of the human race, namely that, apart from Christ, we are all servants of Satan's lies. I also believe that by his common grace God enables unbelievers to accomplish good things for society.[7] These doctrines are part of the Reformed confession, and those who profess Reformed epistemology should take them seriously.

---

[4]One can say that *for Christians* faith justifies knowledge, because their faith in the Scriptures governs the use of their natural knowledge.

[5]See the more detailed account of Romans 1 in chap. 4, "Presuppositional Apologetics" (p. 211).

[6]On the rather difficult question of *antithesis*, see my *Cornelius Van Til: An Analysis of His Thought* (Phillipsburg, N.J.: Presbyterian and Reformed, 1995), 187–213, 215–30. I disagree with some of Van Til's formulations, but I still know of no thinker who is more insightful and helpful to the work of developing a biblical apologetic. I must take strong exception to Craig's rather thoughtless (I presume) comment that "Van Til, for all his insights, was not a philosopher." Van Til studied philosophy at Calvin College under W. Harry Jellema, a widely admired teacher of philosophy who later taught both Alvin Plantinga and Nicholas Wolterstorff. Van Til earned his Ph.D. in philosophy from Princeton University, writing his dissertation under A. A. Bowman, comparing the Idealist absolute with the biblical doctrine of God. He had a very thorough knowledge of the history of philosophy, though he did not focus much on Anglo-American language analysis. In my estimation he made more and greater contributions toward Christian philosophy and theology than to apologetics narrowly defined. Of the twenty-nine chapters of my *Cornelius Van Til*, only two deal with his apologetic argument as such. The rest deal with Van Til's philosophical, epistemological, theological, and historical ideas. This balance of topics, I think, reflects the nature of Van Til's thought and the relative importance of his contributions in the different areas.

[7]See ibid., 187–213, 215–30.

Are Presuppositional Arguments Adequate?

Clark says that presuppositional apologetic arguments, including mine, are not sufficient to establish the truth of Christian theism. He wishes that in my comments on logic, for example, I had dealt with Quine and Wittgenstein; and, like Craig, he compares my performance unfavorably with that of Alvin Plantinga's remarkable *Warrant* trilogy. If I had thought the editor of this volume wanted me to write a treatise comparable to Plantinga's, but in only forty manuscript pages, there is not much chance that I would have participated in this symposium. Judged by these standards, I don't think any of the essays in this book, including Clark's, come anywhere near to passing muster.

I do agree with Clark that there is much more work to be done. More thorough and rigorous volumes and articles should be produced. This kind of apologetic work is rare, I think, not only because few of us can equal Plantinga's astuteness, but also because most apologetic writing is directed to ministerial students, to Christian lay people, and/or to inquirers of "average intelligence." Few in these groups are trained well enough in philosophy to benefit from, or even to understand, the kind of argument Clark wants to see. That, of course, is not to excuse the lack of this sort of literature. We need to write on both the popular and the academic levels.

Nevertheless, I think the argument of my initial essay (chapter 4, "Presuppositional Apologetics") has more value than Clark attributes to it. I do think that there is an intuitive plausibility in the argument that only an absolute, personal being can justify objective moral obligation and a universal rational order. In this book (and in my book *Apologetics to the Glory of God*)[8] I have focused on this type of argument, though I recognize that there are additional objections to be answered and alternatives to be considered,[9] because I think that this datum has a kind of

---

[8] *Apologetics to the Glory of God: An Introduction* (Phillipsburg, N.J.: Presbyterian and Reformed, 1994).

[9] Contrary to Clark, however, I do think that my argument has something to say to nonmaterialistic philosophies and religions. Everyone (including Plato and Hegel) who rejects an absolute-personal ground of the universe affirms chance as an ultimate. For the opposite of chance is not determinism (deterministic systems may themselves originate in chance), but personal design and governance. But chance cannot account for morality, knowledge, and universal order. Van Til shows the deep affinity between the seeming opposites, Hegelian idealism and pragmatism, in his "God and the Absolute," in *Christianity and Idealism* (Philadelphia: Presbyterian and Reformed, 1955).

transparency. It doesn't persuade everybody; but I think its persuasive power is somewhat simpler to grasp than in the case of, say, Craig's *kalam* argument or a complicated system of evidences or a cumulative case. The apostle Paul says that God is "clearly" known from the creation (Rom. 1:19–20). Reproducing that clarity in some measure is apologetically desirable, so I think that there is value in arguments that are relatively simple and transparent. Of course, no argument is so transparently cogent that nobody will object to it.

AD HABERMAS

Circularity and Autonomy

Craig, Feinberg, and Habermas have accused my argument of vicious circularity. I have replied to this objection in this volume and elsewhere, but Craig makes no reference to any of these replies, so I really don't know what more to say to him on the subject. Feinberg refers to my replies but drops the discussion there, suggesting that I should avoid the problem altogether by becoming more evidential. Perhaps his and Craig's concerns are to some extent the same as those of Habermas.

Habermas does discuss some of my responses to the circularity objection. He does not discuss the point I made in my major paper of this volume, namely, that in one sense the presuppositional argument is linear rather than circular (God's rationality → human faith → human reasoning). I consider that point something of a refinement in my own position and of the presuppositional position generally, and I am disappointed that those who were concerned about circularity did not interact with it. Nor does Habermas consider my point that argument for an ultimate standard of truth, whether Christian or non-Christian, must necessarily be circular in one sense.

Nevertheless, I will discuss the issues Habermas raises. He says:

Frame commits the informal logical fallacy of *false analogy*. He argues that rationalists must accept reason as an ultimate starting point, just as empiricists assume sense experience, and so on. So the Christian may begin with Scripture as a legitimate starting point. But these are not analogous bases. While the rationalist uses reason and the empiricist uses sense experience as tools from which to construct their systems, Frame assumes both the *tool* of special revelation and the *system* of Scripture. . . . Does Frame not realize that, in the name of everyone needing a presupposition, he has imported an entire worldview when the others have only asked for tools? (p. 242)

I disagree here with Habermas's understanding of rationalism and empiricism.[10] Historically, philosophical rationalists have not merely presupposed the use of human reason as a "tool." If they had done only this, Christians should have no quarrel with the role of reason in their thought. Rather, these thinkers have presupposed autonomous[11] human reason as the ultimate criterion of truth and falsity;[12] similarly for empiricism. Christians, on the contrary, presuppose God's Word as the ultimate standard of truth.

Habermas thinks there is an asymmetry between presupposing Scripture and presupposing autonomous reason, because Scripture is a great big book full of content, and autonomous reason is merely a simple human faculty, with minimal or no specific content. But (1) considered merely as rival standards of truth, the two are entirely parallel and opposed. It is irrelevant, even if it is true, to say that the Christian standard has more

---

[10]And also that of Clark, who says that philosophers have favored reason only as a tool, not as a standard of truth.

[11]I should remind the reader of how I define this term. Autonomous reasoning is reasoning that rejects the authority of God's revelation in favor of some other ultimate norm. Clark may be using a different definition when he says of autonomous reasoning that "if it's a bad thing, it is all the worse for us, because it is all we have" (p. 262). At least I hope he's using a different definition, although he hasn't told us what that definition is. On my definition his statement is clearly wrong from a Christian point of view. Autonomous reasoning is not the only alternative for human thought, for we are surrounded by God's clear revelation of himself (Rom. 1:18–21). Transcending such autonomy is both our obligation and our privilege.

[12]This is the obvious meaning of the passage from Joseph Butler I quoted in chap. 4, "Presuppositional Apologetics," where he said that if anything in Scripture is found to be contrary to reason, Scripture should be given up. (For less obvious meanings of the statement, see my *Cornelius Van Til,* 269–83.) With these words, Butler was merely echoing similar statements of the Deists against whom he wrote his *Analogy of Religion.* So I don't agree with Clark's view that few if any philosophers have made this claim. Further, when a thinker rejects God's Word as the ultimate standard of truth, he necessarily adopts another standard, and the only other plausible standard is the autonomous human mind. So, whether they say so explicitly or not, I believe that those who reject the ultimate authority of divine revelation have *ipso facto* adopted human reason (whether understood in rationalist, empiricist, or some other terms) as the ultimate standard of truth.

content than the rationalist standard. The point is simply that these are two standards that contradict one another. (2) Rationalists historically have not thought of reason as devoid of content. Indeed, they have had a tendency to equate "reason" with the full metaphysical and epistemological content of their philosophical systems. (3) Autonomous reason does indeed have content; in fact, it entails a worldview antagonistic to Christianity. For if reason rightly proceeds autonomously, then there is no one with the authority to command our beliefs and methods of thought. In other words, if autonomous reason is legitimate, the biblical God does not exist.

Habermas also objects to my statement that "the Bible is the Word of God because it says so," a statement that I did not make in my major paper in this volume, but in *Apologetics to the Glory of God*. In that book I did not present this statement as an apologetic argument directed to unbelievers. Rather, I presented it as what I called a "narrowly circular" argument and urged readers to avoid such arguments in practical apologetic situations. In apologetic encounters, I urged them, rather, to use "broadly circular" arguments: arguments that include evidence, logical syllogisms, and so on. These arguments are just as circular as the narrowly circular ones in the sense in which I have admitted circularity: they argue for an ultimate standard of truth by appealing to that very standard. But they are less obviously circular and therefore more persuasive to those who do not understand the rationale for the kind of circularity I espouse.

I agree with Habermas, therefore, that the narrowly circular argument is not an apologetic argument in a serious sense. In *Apologetics to the Glory of God* I mentioned it mainly by way of contrast to those arguments that I believed to have real apologetic value. Habermas, however, evidently thinks also that there is no truth at all in the narrowly circular argument. He says that of the two statements, (1) The Bible is the Word of God, and (2) the Bible says it is the Word of God, that both are true, but (1) is not true *because* of (2). I respectfully disagree. Let us formulate the argument a bit more formally:

Premise 1: Whatever the Bible says is true.
Premise 2: The Bible says it is the Word of God.
Conclusion: Therefore, the Bible is the Word of God.

Both premises are true from an evangelical viewpoint, and they do imply the conclusion validly. So the conclusion is true *because* the two premises are true. We believe that the Bible is the Word of God because it says that it is the Word of God (granted premise 1, which is also an evangelical truism). Moreover, for Christians, the argument expresses an important truth: As our supreme standard, Scripture is self-attesting. There is nothing higher than God's Word by which God's Word may be validated.

Testing Scripture

Habermas asks, however, "Must the broad process of compiling evidences for the truth of Scripture now require us to judge the text by a more ultimate standard? What if, far from judging Scripture, this evidential method was actually taught in Scripture?" (p. 245). He believes it is indeed taught in Scripture, and he cites some texts to that effect—tests of prophets by verification of their prophecies, attestation by miracles, and so on. I entirely agree that there are provisions in Scripture for testing God's Word empirically and rationally.

But now what follows? As I read Habermas's two questions, he expects a negative answer to the first. In his view, in other words, testing Scripture by standards endorsed by Scripture does not involve judging Scripture by a higher standard. He believes, in other words, that such testing does not violate Scripture's right to attest itself. He is right. This procedure is what I would call a "broadly circular argument," an argument in which Scripture is verified by Scripture's own standards. How is it, then, that once we grant the legitimacy of such tests, "Frame's entire approach would have to be seriously amended" (p. 245)? I have never opposed the process of verifying Scripture by scriptural standards. Indeed, that is the heart and soul of my apologetic method.

Is Presuppositionalism a Complete Apologetic System?

The above discussion and my comments to follow indicate that (contrary to Van Til) I see considerable common ground between presuppositional apologetics and the other schools of thought represented in this volume. I gladly join with Habermas in testing Scripture by scriptural criteria, and I do not automatically reject theistic proofs and Christian evidences as nontranscendental. Habermas and Craig, along with some of my fellow presuppositionalists, think that for these and other reasons I am not a pure presuppositionalist. Or, to put the issue in another way: presuppositionalism as I formulate it is not clearly distinct from the other methodologies.

Habermas gives another reason as well for thinking that presuppositionalism is not a complete and distinctive methodology. He says that presuppositionalists have been unwilling to develop thorough treatments of Christian evidences from a distinctively presuppositional point of view but have either ignored evidences or relied on writers of other schools of thought. As he points out, I too have acknowledged that weakness in the presuppositional literature. I would hope to remedy that sometime, unless a fellow presuppositionalist beats me to it.[13] In the meantime, I am happy to recommend writings of Habermas, Craig, and others in these areas. In my books and in this volume, I have indicated in general terms how a presuppositional account of Christian evidences should differ from traditional accounts. Thus, I don't think it is urgent to produce a presuppositionalist volume of Christian evidences, though it would certainly be desirable.

Even from this book, it should be evident to readers that presuppositionalists have a somewhat different slant on the use of evidence, some differences in epistemology and in emphasis. Are these distinctives enough to make presuppositionalism a "complete apologetic system" distinct from the others? I'm not sure. Habermas's quotations of me indicate some of the ambivalence that I feel about that question. In any case, to me that question is not terribly important. If presuppositionalism is not a "complete apologetic system," so what? Whatever the case may be, presuppositionalism has in the past and will continue to stress biblical principles that others are not stressing nearly enough. That is what is important to me.

Through much of the twentieth century, American evangelical apologists have been battling one another vigorously over apologetic method. I have participated in those battles to some extent, as in this volume, but I am not happy about this sort of division in the evangelical community. Scripture abhors factionalism (1 Cor. 1–3), and I believe that the denominational and theological divisions among Christians do not please God.[14]

---

[13]I do have some ideas for a book along these lines. However, like many evangelical seminary teachers, I am something of a theological generalist, and I therefore must give attention to other fields as well, in dogmatics, ethics, modern culture, and so on. So further writing in apologetics will have to wait a while.

[14]I have argued this position in *Evangelical Reunion* (Grand Rapids: Baker, 1991), now out of print.

Therefore, my inclination both in apologetics and theology has been to try to bring warring parties closer together. I look for formulations that ease the differences somewhat, that grant and celebrate the insights gained by members of factions other than my own. It would be wrong merely to paper over differences, to make two positions appear closer than they really are. But if there are legitimate ways of showing that the differences between apologetic schools are not as great as previously thought, I am delighted. As Christians, our motivation should not be to preserve our traditional polemics at all cost,[15] but rather to seek, on the one hand, truth and, on the other, the unity of the body of Christ.

AD CRAIG

William Craig says that I have confused transcendental argument (an argument showing that the biblical God is the one who makes argument possible) with *"demonstratio quia*, proof that proceeds from consequence to ground" (p. 233), and that, except perhaps for one footnote, my sketch of an apologetic is not transcendental at all.

There is some debate among presuppositionalists on this subject. Greg Bahnsen[16] maintained Craig's view, namely, that transcendental argument is sharply distinguished from all other argument and should never be confused with traditional theistic proofs and evidences. My position, on the contrary,[17] claims that transcendental arguments may and usually must incorporate arguments of other sorts.

How can you prove the transcendental conclusion that the Christian God makes argument possible? In Plantinga's argument, which Craig commends as properly transcendental, the proof is that our noetic faculties can produce warranted beliefs

---

[15]I think that in most every Christian group there are some who react negatively to any formulation that blunts the traditional polemics of that group against its rivals, whether or not that formulation is scripturally promising. Again, my view is opposite to this. If we can find formulations that are genuinely scriptural, that don't compromise the truth, but nevertheless bring the factions closer together, I rejoice to acknowledge them.

[16]In *Van Til's Apologetic: Readings and Analysis* (Phillipsburg, N.J.: Presbyterian and Reformed, 1998), esp. 496–529.

[17]In my *Apologetics to the Glory of God*, 69–77; and *Cornelius Van Til*, 311–22. Bahnsen's arguments in the Stein debate mentioned in chap. 4 above are certainly no more "purely transcendental" than those in my article.

only on the condition that God has designed them to do that. But why should we not construe this argument as an argument from consequence (the existence of warranted beliefs) to ground (God's design)? Why should we not read this as a traditional teleological argument from the epistemic realm?

Indeed, many traditional types of arguments can be steps toward a transcendental conclusion. For example, if Craig's *kalam* cosmological argument (an argument he probably would not describe as transcendental) is sound, it implies that the world cannot exist unless God has begun the process. So nothing can exist (including rationality, science, argument, meaning) unless God is the first cause of the world.

Thus, I don't see the deep chasm between transcendental arguments and other sorts of arguments that Craig insists upon. I think apologetics needs to have a transcendental *direction* or *goal:* we should be concerned to show that God is the condition of all meaning, and our epistemology should be consistent with that conclusion. But that conclusion cannot be reached in a single, simple syllogism. A transcendental argument normally, perhaps always, requires many subarguments, and some of these may be traditional theistic proofs or Christian evidences.

AD FEINBERG

I have dealt with some of Feinberg's objections in the above sections. Beyond these, he does not say anything that I need to address at length, but there are some specific points and questions to which I should respond:

1. How does God "cause" faith? First, by regeneration (John 3:3, 5), a supernatural act of the Spirit. Second, through the preaching of his Word (Rom. 10:17), which, to be sure, often includes the presentation of evidence and argument. I have never denied the value of evidence and argument; I have only said that they should be presented on the basis of a Christian worldview and epistemology, so that the argumentation may be, in fact, a presentation of the Word.

2. As I said in response to Clark, I do think that the unregenerate have some true knowledge, and I am quite willing, as Feinberg, to attribute this fact to God's common grace.[18]

---

[18]See the discussion of the unbeliever's knowledge in my *Cornelius Van Til*, 187–213, and of common grace in the same, 215–30.

3. Feinberg thinks I might disagree with his suggestion that "some evidence for Christian theism might be used by the Holy Spirit to challenge the unbeliever's view of the world and to point that person to faith in Christ" (p. 251). I do not disagree with that; this is part of what I call "offensive" apologetics. Certainly the unbeliever's presuppositions are a barrier to his or her knowledge of the truth; but they cannot shut out the truth entirely. Thus, I have no "reticence in using evidence with unbelievers" (p. 251, see [1] above).

4. I am glad that Feinberg does not "feign neutrality." But some traditional apologists have done so (recall the quotes in my essay from Butler and Carnell). And if Feinberg wants to eschew neutrality, it continues to bother me that he, like Clark, resists the concept of a biblical epistemology. If we are not to be neutral, certainly we must hear what God says to us in this area, along with all the others.

5. I agree with Feinberg that there are propositions on which Christians and non-Christians can agree, even with regard to reason, logic, knowledge. But those are true because the Christian God has made them so, and the unbeliever accepts them on the basis of what Van Til called "borrowed capital": involuntarily, he is reasoning as a Christian. His own presuppositions do not justify any truth claims at all. In this sense, it is, contrary to Feinberg, "*necessary* to presuppose the Bible's truth." If, like Feinberg, we want to avoid neutrality, this is the stance we must take.

6. Debating the truth of Christianity does not presuppose neutrality, and I never said it did. Neutrality appears, not in the decision to debate, but in the way one debates.

7. A presuppositional approach is not grounded in a fear[19] of presenting evidences, as Feinberg suggests. It presents evidences enthusiastically, knowing that the evidences all point to God. Nor is it grounded in a "fear that the whole structure of reality might collapse if we don't presuppose . . ." (p. 254). Nonsense. The structure of reality depends on God, not on our presupposing him. As Feinberg says, "Refusal to accept the evidence only leaves one without the truth" (p. 254). I would say the same thing about a refusal to accept Christian presuppositions.

---

[19]There is no more reason for saying that presuppositionalism arises out of fear, than for saying that nonpresuppositionalism arises from a fear of losing academic respectability. But come on, now! We can do better than to speculate on one another's emotional motivations.

CONCLUSION

In the course of developing arguments for the truth of Christianity, apologists have often sought to persuade the intellectual establishment that Christianity is intellectually respectable. To do this, they have often invoked the respected secular philosophies of the day. The church fathers and early medieval apologists appealed to Plato. Aquinas and his successors invoked Aristotle as well. More recently, apologetics has been patterned after the thinking of Descartes, Locke, Kant, Hegel, Reid, Kierkegaard, Wittgenstein, Whitehead, modern scientists, and many others.

We can learn from secular thinkers, certainly. But there are dangers along this path. Accommodation of Christianity to secular thought, even by those with good apologetic-evangelistic motives, has been a fruitful source of heresy. We need to remind ourselves that there is an *antithesis* (sorry for the buzzword) between the wisdom of the world and the wisdom of God (1 Cor. 1–3), that much of what the world considers wise, God considers foolish, and vice versa. We need to be more radically critical of our philosophical and other secular sources, and to get into the habit of using Scripture as our standard of criticism.

This is the most important issue for me in the discussion of apologetic method. I could wish the whole debate over methodology would just go away, with all its partisanship and divisiveness. But I am willing to fight over one thing, and that is the principle of *sola scriptura*, the principle that only God, speaking in Scripture, has supreme authority over the human heart and mind. I have written a number of articles about that principle recently, and I am convinced that evangelicals need to be reminded of it in many areas, such as worship, the use of confessions, and the critique of culture.[20] Inerrantist evangelicals do not actually find fault with Scripture. But in some areas, I note them placing Scripture second to various secular theories of aesthetics, politics, psychology, science, and culture. This danger exists in apologetics too, as it has existed since the apologetics of the church's early centuries.

---

[20]See my *Contemporary Worship Music: A Biblical Defense* (Phillipsburg, N.J.: Presbyterian and Reformed, 1997), esp. appendix 2. The appendix was also published in *Westminster Theological Journal* 59, no. 2 (Fall 1997): 269–318, with replies by Richard Muller and David Wells and a fuller response from me. This article is the most urgent message I have to bring to my fellow evangelicals.

Whatever may be said for or against presuppositionalism, the main motivation of it is to be scriptural, whatever may be the cost to its academic respectability. Indeed, I am inclined to say that the most fundamental point of presuppositionalism is the application of *sola scriptura* to apologetics. If all apologists come to take that principle seriously, however the other methodological questions come out, I will believe that the presuppositional movement has accomplished its purpose.

A REFORMED EPISTEMOLOGIST'S CLOSING REMARKS

Kelly James Clark

I was shocked to discover that my esteemed fellow contributors disagreed with the claims in my essay. I was sure that they would simply read my careful, clear, and cogent arguments and say, "Amen." End of debate. I guess I was wrong!

I should say at the outset that in my main essay (chapter 5, "Reformed Epistemology Apologetics") I chose to present those distinctives of Reformed epistemology that would clearly set it apart from its alternatives. Perhaps this is the main point of emphasis: *Being rational is not identical with having reasons.* Supplying evidence often leaves people with the impression that there is a requirement for people to understand and assent to theistic proofs or evidence of the resurrection before they can be rational in holding their Christian beliefs. I did not want to perpetuate that impression.

I also focused on distinctives because I suspected that there would be a great deal of agreement concerning, for example, the utility of theistic arguments and the dismantling of the problem of evil. But if we all roughly agreed, the reader would have been disappointed. That would have been like paying to see a boxing match in which the boxers occasionally remark on the other's fine footwork but neither lands any blows. In my essay and responses, I tried to land some blows (and, now I see, to produce a target for my opponents). But I believe—like my opponents—that theistic arguments are useful in apologetics (but not necessary for rational belief). Let me make some general responses and then take each essay individually.

GENERAL REMARKS

Reformed epistemologists have carefully studied theistic arguments and found them wanting (at least as coercive or demonstrative proofs). They have recognized that there seems to be, among those who accept, say, theistic arguments, an eagerness to confirm what one already believes; likewise, among atheist scholars there seems a reluctance to accede to premises that, at first glance, seem obvious (but which entail the distasteful conclusion that there is a God). A suspicion arises: Theistic proofs and Christian evidences support what the Christian evidentialist wishes, with all her heart, to believe (and vice versa for the nontheist). Lucky (or providential) for her that all of the evidence comes out—forcefully, clearly, and unambiguously—on her side. The suspicion ripens: The heart guides, for better or for worse, the assessment of the evidence (on both sides of the debate).

Here I will restate some of the major claims made in my essay: Reason is not neutral. It does not stand dispassionately, without prejudice (prejudgment), overlooking the evidence; it is not bias-free (at least on matters of fundamental human concern). Believing, very often, is seeing. Reason is situated, located, embodied in this person at this time and in this place. It is moved by our biases to attend to this sort of evidence and to ignore that sort of evidence. It values this experience and discounts that one.

Now of course we must attend to some and ignore other pieces of evidence; we must value or discount evidence. We, in this busy day, do not have the time to do otherwise. Plus—being psycho-socio-historico–conditioned creatures—we cannot do otherwise. Here's the problem once again: We can't attain *the view from nowhere* to check our beliefs against the facts (independent of our beliefs). Let me offer a simple example with our perceptual beliefs. Consider the pine tree that you seem to be perceiving now (this works best if you actually look at a pine tree). Now suppose you want to prove that there is a material object, independent of your beliefs, that resembles your perception of the pine tree. To do so, you would have to remove yourself from your body, perceive (without prejudice) *both* the pine tree *and* your perception of the pine tree, and then see if they are similar. But we are stuck both within ourselves and the world as it presents itself to us; we cannot stand outside ourselves to compare our beliefs to the reality we suppose they tell us about.

We simply cannot get the view from nowhere—not with respect to trees and surely not with respect to gods. We are finite, believing creatures with all that attends that fact.

All of my opponents in this debate believe they can, with their arguments, secure the view from nowhere. That is, they believe they can transcend finite human limitations without terribly much trouble and grasp the divine reality. Craig and Feinberg are the most modest in their claims, but I think they claim too much. Frame is the least modest in his claims, and he surely claims too much. We simply cannot, this side of the grave, obtain religious certainty. Now I will consider my opponents' objections one at a time.

AD FEINBERG

Paul Feinberg seems to agree with or concede most of the major claims in my essay. Perhaps this is because Reformed epistemology is well suited to a cumulative case approach. Whatever problems he does raise are stated more strongly by the other respondents, so I will address them in the sections below.

AD CRAIG

Truth be told, I will say it again, I could have written much of what William Craig has written. Since Reformed epistemology is often maligned and misunderstood by evidentialists, I chose to defend it as thoroughly as possible, leaving the apologetical case for the evidentialists. As I said in my essay, I think that there are decent arguments for the existence of God. I and other Reformed epistemologists have defended such arguments, and I think Craig's version of the cosmological argument is one of the most interesting.[1] Since I was sure that Craig and others would present such arguments in this collection, I ignored them in my essay. Of course, I caution the reader concerning the limitations of such arguments and warn of the influence of our prior commitments in the acceptance of the crucial premises in such arguments. I did say, however, that theistic arguments and the like are part and parcel of apologetics. Enough said on that.

---

[1]See my *Return to Reason* (Grand Rapids: Eerdmans, 1990), Alvin Plantinga, *God, Freedom and Evil* (Grand Rapids: Eerdmans, 1974); see also Plantinga's "Belief in God," in Kelly James Clark, ed., *Readings in the Philosophy of Religion* (Peterborough, Ontario: Broadview Press, 2000), where he offers nearly two dozen theistic arguments.

My essay focused primarily on belief in God, not belief in Jesus. The claims I make about the *sensus divinitatus* refer to belief in a divinity, which seems nearly universal and requires some accounting whether based on Scripture or not. I don't mean to suggest that the *sensus divinitatus* operates in place of the testimony of the Holy Spirit in supporting *Christian belief.* I agree with virtually everything that Craig says about the testimony of the Holy Spirit.

I don't think my externalist views rob anyone of their assurance of knowing the truth of the Christian faith. Externalism may deprive us of intellectual certainty but not knowledge. In addition, the epistemological commitment to externalism says nothing about the witness of the Holy Spirit (who can provide assurance of faith). But this is different from intellectual certainty and does not necessitate epistemological internalism.[2]

I agree with Craig's defense of apologetics, at least to some degree. I have long admired Craig's faithful ministry of apologetics. He has sacrificed a great deal to spread the gospel where it has been banished (either by law or by indifference). I have only done a little of that, but when faced with the prospect of defending religious belief in strange lands, I have used similar apologetic strategies. When I lectured in many universities in Ukraine and Great Britain in 1995–96, I offered my own versions of a moral argument and the argument from design. I left those countries thinking that my arguments had little effect on fifty-year-olds (some of whom, in Ukraine at least, had been steeped in Marxism from the cradle) but felt that they had some, not insignificant, effect on the students in the audience. I have offered similar arguments at universities in China and in secular universities in America. I wholeheartedly agree with Craig that a reasoned defense of the faith is the best apologetic strategy in such circumstances.

Thus, there is probably very little practical difference between Craig and me when it comes to apologetics. Nevertheless, I will mention some possible differences.[3] Reformed epistemologists might be more forthcoming about the limitations of natural theology (which I addressed in my responses to Craig and

---

[2] I don't hold to externalism willy-nilly. I hold to it because of the nearly proven failure of the alternative.

[3] Readers can decide for themselves whether or not these differences are significant.

Habermas). Reformed epistemologists might be considerably less sanguine about the prospects for success concerning the kinds of historical arguments that Craig and Habermas offer. And Reformed epistemologists, believing that the Holy Spirit needs to warm the heart of the unbeliever, might spend more time removing obstacles to belief than trying to create belief.[4] Such obstacles might include the problem of human suffering, science and religion, Marxist and Freudian critiques of belief in God, and so on. I qualify each of these claims with "might" for there is no single view of apologetics endorsed by Reformed epistemologists.

AD HABERMAS

I loved Gary Habermas's section on the positive contributions of Reformed epistemology; but it went downhill from there! He had his chance to say, "Amen," and missed it! Sigh.

Habermas suggests that my only critique of evidentialism is that it is rooted in the defective classical foundationalism. The historical roots of evidentialism are, as Plantinga has well argued, classical foundationalism. So the self-refutation of classical foundationalism will surely lead to the reasonable rejection of evidentialism in so far as it is rooted in classical foundationalism. Of course, there are evidentialists who are not classical foundationalists, so this criticism will not affect their views. Granted. But historically, at least since the Enlightenment, the evidentialist objection to belief in God is surely rooted in something like classical foundationalism. Uncovering those damaged roots should slay *those* forms of evidentialism.

My primary attack on evidentialisms of all kinds is my defense of Reidian epistemology. Belief, for human beings at least, begins with trust, not with doubt. We must simply accept most beliefs—those beliefs delivered to us by our properly functioning cognitive faculties—unless we have adequate reason to cease accepting those beliefs. Our epistemology, I argued, must fit our cognitive capacities. The evidentialist demand, in most cases, is a demand that simply cannot be met. And if we cannot meet it, we are not obliged to meet it. I had neither the time nor space to critique every form of evidentialism, but the two primary critiques I offered were not aimed, as Habermas suggests, only at "straw men."

---

[4]I don't mean to imply that Craig or Habermas claim to be trying to create belief.

Habermas's own evidentialist claim, that "some appropriate basis for faith needs to exist" (p. 293), still seems extravagant to me. Exist for what? He doesn't say. For the rational acceptability of belief in God? Again, such a requirement would turn ordinary believers and most philosophers into philosophers of religion. I can't imagine God putting such an obstacle between himself and the people with whom he wishes to be in relationship.

Contrary to Habermas's claim, Reformed epistemology is neither "a different variety of foundationalism" nor of epistemic evidentialism (p. 294). Just because arguments are required to defend Reformed epistemology, it does not follow that any believers are required, on pain of irrationality, to understand and assent to these arguments.[5] Indeed, if Reformed epistemology is correct, people could have been rational in their beliefs in God without anyone ever arguing in favor of Reformed epistemology.

Rather than answering my charge that theistic proofs prove little about God, Habermas claims that Reformed epistemology also justifies little about God. This is a form of the *tu quoque* fallacy.[6] I don't see why the *sensus divinitatus* could not produce different beliefs in different people depending on their socio-cultural-historico background. Indeed, our experiences are filtered through our background beliefs. Thus, one might expect different pictures of the divine from people of different cultures.[7] But it does not follow that some people, for whatever reason God ordains, don't have pictures of the divine that are closer to the truth than others. Although theistic proofs are afflicted with the problem of justifying too little, if successful, Habermas's project would justify a lot. Unfortunately, I have given what I believe are compelling reasons for thinking that his project cannot succeed.

The problem of competing hypotheses is an intractable problem, however, for theistic proofs. For example, suppose you come home and find all of the nuts removed from your house. A window is slightly ajar, and a screen has fallen on the ground beneath the window. At least two hypotheses present themselves:

---

[5]Habermas makes what is called a "levels confusion" in epistemology.

[6]Literally, "you too." Or you think my position has flaw *x*; your position has flaw *x* as well. It is often referred to, more colloquially, as the "So's yo mama" fallacy.

[7]To see the effect of one's socio-cultural-historico background on one's Christian beliefs, one should examine the portraits of Jesus from diverse cultures. Another phenomena, if veridical, that shows the effect of one's socio-cultural-historico background on one's religious beliefs is near-death experiences. The experiences of the "divine" vary dramatically depending upon one's culture.

(1) The local family of squirrels found their way into your house and removed the nuts; (2) the nut-loving Kevin found his way into your house and removed the nuts. Since the evidence is equally compatible with either (1) or (2), you have no reason to prefer one hypothesis over the other (even if [2] is true). An analogous problem holds for theistic arguments: The existence and design of the universe are thoroughly explicable by a tremendous variety of competing hypotheses. An omnipotent, omniscient, perfectly good creator may be the right explanation of the data, but based on the data alone, there is no reason to prefer that hypothesis to any of the others (for example, an almost omnipotent, almost omniscient, pretty good Creator).

The *sensus divinitatus,* however, may make one aware of the truth independent of the ambiguous evidence. If so, it has a decided advantage, at least with respect to Habermas's *tu quoque* charge, over evidentialism.

I am reluctant to criticize Habermas's defense of cognitive-emotive therapy because his poignant example concerns his wife's untimely death. But since it raises a significant issue, I will make some brief remarks. After reading this section of Habermas's essay, I kept waiting for the answer to human suffering. During his cognitive psychotherapy, which answers did he find satisfying? What was the *cognitive* part of the therapy? But, in his essay, no answer was offered. If he had provided an answer to the question, "Why did your wife and family suffer?" I would probably have expressed my incredulity.[8] Although I think some general comments may be made about God and human suffering, I am skeptical of any explanation of any particular instance of human suffering. We simply don't know the mind of God in any specific case (nor could we, Job suggests). The generic explanations are, I think, too coolly rational and emotionally distant to help anyone through her suffering. So, not knowing the answers, the best I can do is sit beside her in her mourning seat.

AD FRAME

Whenever I read presuppositionalists I almost always think, "Saying it's so doesn't make it so." Saying that Christianity is

---

[8] I don't know what other sorts of questions might be relevant in such circumstances. Habermas's historical apologetic would not be appropriate—it would be, at best, the right answer to the wrong question. I can only suppose that the person who suffers wishes, with all his or her heart, to know "why?"

the criterion of truth (whatever that could mean), that Christian belief is the most certain thing we know, that Christian faith is not defeasible, and that Scripture supports these views, does not make it so. There are few apologetic approaches that are so long on assured proclamation and so short on argument.

Presuppositionalists pride themselves on finding their view (and their view alone) supported by Scripture. Indeed, Frame patronizingly suggests that I need to do more Bible study. Let me suggest the same for him. He claims, for example, that the Bible clearly teaches that there is an antithesis between godly wisdom and the wisdom of the world. However, the term *antithesis* never occurs in the Bible. I am likewise not aware that the Bible ever uses any synonymous terms or even any similar terms that mean just what the presuppositionalists mean when they use the term *antithesis*. What's more, most biblical terms are in Hebrew or Greek, which require translation; this moves us one step toward interpretation already. I also think a serious reader of Scripture can doubt that God's Word plays a determinative role in the human knowledge of God. Indeed, Scripture itself claims that people who have not heard of Scripture have knowledge of God (Rom. 1:18). The selective and tendentious reading of Scripture by those who claim to be most sensitive to Scripture is curious indeed.

Two areas where Christians in general and presuppositionalists in particular should pay more careful attention to Scripture are faith and certainty. Frame claims that faith is not defeasible (and, hence, is certain and indubitable) and offers Abraham as his example. But Abraham is surely not a good example. He laughed at God, slept with his maidservant, banished his son (Ishmael), and lied twice about his wife to protect himself (with the implication that Sarah slept with foreign kings). Read the life story of any of the so-called heroes of faith in Hebrews 11 and see if it supports Frame's claims. Read carefully through the lament Psalms and see if you come away with the belief that faithfulness implies certainty. Now here's where I suggest we pay attention to Scripture: Faith is a journey fraught with peril, risk, and uncertainty. We see through a glass darkly, and we see the goal from afar. Certainty is the goal or the ideal, not the beginning or the reality. We are not perfect (*ante mortem*) in practice, nor are we perfect (*ante mortem*) in belief. Scripture itself is painfully honest about doubt and the struggle of faith.[9]

---

[9]For a thorough discussion of faith and doubt, see my *When Faith Is Not Enough* (Grand Rapids: Eerdmans, 1997), part 1.

CONCLUSION

I will repeat where I agree with the evidentialists in this collection. The giving of arguments is useful and often necessary for apologetics. The kinds of arguments that one might offer are the very ones offered by Craig. These will not, of course, as both Craig and Habermas concede, bring people to faith in Jesus. They can, however, provide stepping stones to faith. Our hearts (passions, needs, and desires and aversions) play an epistemic role in the assessment of arguments and may need to be moved in ways suggested by, for example, Pascal, Edwards, and myself. The simple laying out of (true) premises is not sufficient cause, given our cognitive limitations, of belief or unbelief.

Now I will repeat the reason I offered little by way of theistic argument in my essay. I and other Reformed epistemologists are concerned to eliminate the unjust impression that belief in God requires evidence or argument. Belief in God may be perfectly rational without evidence or argument. If Reformed epistemology is right, ordinary believers and professional philosophers alike are not obliged by reason to spend their time shoring up their beliefs. Belief in God is perfectly proper, intellectually speaking, if produced immediately by our properly functioning cognitive faculties.

Finally, I think this achievement is a great one, considerably greater than Frame contends. The intellectual tide, at least since the time of the Enlightenment, was decisively turning toward agnosticism and atheism (in the West). The forces that moved that tide were the claims that evil made God's existence impossible or improbable and that the lack of evidence made belief in God irrational. By refuting the former and rejecting the evidentialist assumption of the latter, Reformed epistemologists have turned back that tide. By demonstrating the rationality of religious belief while not refuting atheism, intellectual space has been reopened for belief in God. It is certainly a major improvement on the intellectual state of religious belief of, say, fifty years ago. For that the Christian community should be grateful for the impressive work of Alvin Plantinga, Nicholas Wolterstorff, and William Alston; and I would like to thank them publically (I just did).

Perhaps demonstrating that Christian belief is at least as rational as its alternatives is the best that can be expected of apologetics. This could be explained in a variety of ways: God wishes us to freely choose him, not to be coerced by the evidence; faith is properly a matter of the will, not of the intellect; the work of faith in the heart of the believer is through the witness of the Holy Spirit. I wish Reformed epistemology and/or theistic arguments could do more than establish that belief in God is rationally permissible, but I'll settle for rational permissibility. That way I can know that my faith is not blind. I may be taking a leap in the dim, but it is not a leap in the dark. Leaping is still risky business, but in faith, I hope that God will make my landing soft.

CONCLUSION

Steven B. Cowan

In a book of this kind, readers will have to make their own assessment as to which of the contributors has made the better case. I will, in this conclusion, however, try to give the reader some assistance in this endeavor by outlining the areas of agreement and disagreement that have been expressed by the participants in this debate. Hopefully, this will not only help you, the reader, make your own decision regarding apologetic methodology, but will also provide a basis for further discussion of this topic among scholars.

AREAS OF AGREEMENT

1. The need for both positive and negative apologetics. Though the five contributing methodologists would give different weight to positive and negative apologetics, they all agree that apologists can and should not only defend Christianity against objections (negative apologetics), but also provide some positive reasons for Christian faith (positive apologetics). When such positive apologetics is appropriate, how it is to be done and what it is meant to accomplish will nevertheless be points of contention.

2. The value of theistic arguments and Christian evidences. There is general agreement that classical arguments for God's existence as well as historical arguments for the Christian faith are useful tools in apologetics. Of course, each participant would differently evaluate their degree of usefulness and would use them in different ways and for different reasons.

3. *The noetic effects of sin.* Again, the seriousness of sin's effect on the unbeliever's mind vis-à-vis apologetics would be variously evaluated by the five contributors. Yet there is basic agreement that sin does negatively affect the ability or willingness of unbelievers to accede to the conclusions of apologetic arguments even when those arguments are sound.

4. *The importance of the Holy Spirit in apologetics.* All the apologists are agreed that the work of the Holy Spirit is crucial if apologetics is to succeed in convincing unbelievers of the truth of Christianity. As even Gary Habermas, one of the least reformed of the contributors, says, "Human agency is not responsible for regeneration. Apart from God's influence, conversion will never take place" (p. 96). This means that apologetic arguments cannot by themselves bring a person to faith in Christ.

5. *The existence of common ground with unbelievers.* All five contributors, including presuppositionalist John Frame, admit that there is some epistemological common ground with unbelievers, such as sense perception and common modes of reasoning. Of course, there is no consensus over how far that common ground extends or how it is to be used in apologetics.

6. *A rejection of postmodern relativism.* The authors are unanimous in giving a negative critique of postmodern challenges to objective truth claims. Though some take the challenge of postmodernism more seriously than others, there is a consensus that its skeptical and relativistic outlook is self-defeating and/or unwarranted and does not pose an insuperable obstacle to doing apologetics (at least not apologetics as the particular contributor practices it!).

AREAS OF DISAGREEMENT

1. *What is the role of the Bible in apologetic methodology?* Bill Craig contended in his major article that the Bible supports the classical method of apologetics. John Frame is even more adamant that the Bible teaches not only the presuppositional method, but also that the Bible plays a normative role in religious epistemology. That is, the Bible teaches a particular epistemology, and the Bible "sets the rules for thinking and knowing" (p. 76). Our other contributors believe that the Bible is much more ambiguous with regard to epistemology and apologetic method so that, as far as Scripture is concerned, we could "let a thousand apologetical flowers bloom!" (see Clark, p. 275).

2. *How are we to classify apologetic methods?* As noted in the introduction, the issue of apologetic taxonomy is difficult, and not all of the contributors to this volume are agreed on how to delineate the various approaches. This comes out most clearly in the debate between Habermas and Craig over how to define classical apologetics. Habermas takes the lead of most recent classical apologists and sees the primary distinction between that school and his own turning on the question of whether natural theology must precede historical evidences. On this view, the classical apologist is one who answers that question affirmatively, while the evidentialist answers negatively. Craig, on the other hand, objects. As he sees it, a classical apologist can concede the plausibility of the "one-step" argument as long as he or she sees that argument as significantly weaker than the natural-theology-then-historical-evidences approach. He also challenges Habermas to find any examples of classical apologists of past eras who insisted on natural theology first as a logical necessity. Habermas responds that the one-step approach is the major tenet of evidentialism's historical emphasis. But it is not an integral part of the classical method. Thus, if the viability of the one-step argument is admitted, it is a concession to evidentialism and not vice-versa.

Additionally, Craig challenges Habermas's delineation of the evidential approach. Habermas allows that the evidential method can utilize the theistic arguments, but that these arguments are not necessary for making a complete case for Christianity. Craig, though, seems to understand the evidential method as rejecting natural theology and using only historical arguments. This is why he accuses Habermas of not holding a distinct methodology (the very thing of which Habermas accuses him!). It seems clear that there is work to be done in finding an agreeable way of classifying apologetic methods.[1]

---

[1]It appears to me that there may be a way out of this conundrum in the approach I have suggested in the introduction, namely, the criterion of argumentative strategy. On that criterion, Craig would be right (contra most of his classicalist colleagues) that a classical apologist can grant to the evidentialist the possibility of miracles-to-God arguments while holding that the true hallmark of classical apologetics is simply the view that the two-phase approach is the best argumentative strategy (given what Craig takes to be the weaknesses of the one-step approach). On the same criterion, Habermas could rebut Craig's charge that his (i.e., Habermas's) evidentialist method is not distinctive even while allowing that Craig is a classical apologist. Even though Habermas agrees on the usefulness of natural theology, he

3. *May one invoke the concept of miracle to explain an historical event without first establishing that God exists?* Related to the previous point is the question of whether one can legitimately claim that the supernatural activity of God is the best explanation for some (perhaps unusual) event if one has not previously proven God's existence via natural theology (or some other kind of philosophical argumentation). Craig, Habermas, and Feinberg would answer this question in the affirmative: One does not have to prove God's existence before invoking the notion of miracle. This answer is, in fact, central to Habermas's "one-step" approach. On the other hand, Clark and Frame would seem to say no: It is not possible to explain any event as the supernatural action of God unless one has first proven God's existence.

4. *How good are positive arguments in demonstrating the truth of Christianity?* As pointed out above, the five methodologists give disparate evaluations of the degree of usefulness of theistic arguments and Christian evidences. Though all of the contributors would say that such arguments cannot bring a person to saving faith in Christ, they differ over whether they ought to be persuasive in doing so. That is, there is a disagreement over whether or not a person who understands, say, the cosmological argument has sufficient reason to accept the argument's conclusion. Craig, Habermas, and Frame seem willing to argue that the objective case for Christianity is so strong that an unbeliever cognizant of that case has every reason to assent to the truth of Christianity and ought to do so.[2] Clark and Feinberg, on the

---

could argue against Craig and other classical apologists that the one-step argument is the best argumentative strategy and is the strongest argument for Christian theism. Or he could argue that evidentialism is just an eclectic approach that is not committed to either strategy as being better than the other. Habermas would have to back off of his claim, though, that anyone who merely grants the possibility of a miracles-to-God argument would count as an evidentialist. Even so, of course, Habermas could still say that Craig's allowance for the value of the one-step argument is a concession to evidentialism.

Assuming that this suggestion were followed, we could then borrow a line from Kelly Clark and call those classical apologists who insist that natural theology is a logically necessary prerequisite to historical evidences "hyper-classical apologists." Likewise, those who use historical evidences exclusively and eschew natural theology we could call "hyper-evidentialists." Of course, we might be able to find less pejorative terms for these last two views.

[2]This is not to say that any of these apologists believe that Christian apologetic arguments are *coercive* in any sense that prevents one from rejecting their conclusions. After all, people obviously do reject Christian arguments, and Craig, Haber-

other hand, claim that no positive argument for Christianity is that strong, and that an unbeliever may very well have good reason to reject them.

Another way of putting this point is that Craig, Habermas, and Frame would say that (in at least some cases) the only thing that keeps an informed unbeliever from acceding to the apologist's case is his or her own stubborn will. It is the influence of sin on the unregenerate mind and will that keeps the unbeliever from seeing the arguments for what they are. Clark and Feinberg would disagree by claiming that an unbeliever may also fail to give in to the apologist's arguments because the arguments themselves are defective or fall short of a compelling proof. In other words, even apart from the influence of sin, a person may fail to be persuaded by the apologist's arguments.

5. *Are all worldviews defended circularly?* John Frame stands alone among the contributors in advocating the view, typically held by presuppositionalists, that the case for Christianity is ultimately circular. This is not supposed to be a problem, though, because all such reasoning is ultimately circular. That is, every worldview or philosophy presupposes certain unprovable first principles or ultimate standards of truth that are intrinsic to that worldview. And, according to Frame, these principles are implicit in every reasoned defense of that worldview.

This belief in the circularity of all reasoning is what leads Frame to his conviction that there can be no "neutral" arguments or premises in apologetics, and therefore apologetic methodology must be presuppositional. The other contributors to this volume strongly disagree with this view, believing that apologetic arguments need not be circular as Frame contends; that Frame's belief that all arguments are circular is based on a confusion of ontology and epistemology. As Craig puts it, it is true, for example, that if God did not exist, then the causal principle would be false (because the truth and existence of anything is ontologically dependent on God's existence). But, according to Craig, it does not follow from this fact of reality that one's reason or justification for believing in the causal principle is that one believes in God's existence. One can know and believe in the causal principle without believing in God. Hence, it is not question-begging

___

mas, and Frame acknowledge that fact. The question, though, is this: In rejecting, say, the cosmological argument or the evidence for Jesus' resurrection, does the unbeliever have *any good reason* to do so?

to use the causal principle in an argument for God's existence. In any case, Craig and the others would argue that circular reasoning of any kind is fallacious—that it commits the fallacy of begging the question.

6. *Is the resurrection of Christ antecedently improbable?* Clark's case against Habermas's evidentialist method includes the charge that the resurrection is antecedently improbable. Clark extends this critique to Craig's historical arguments too. He says that Christian beliefs like the resurrection of Jesus are "vastly more difficult to believe in than ghosts, UFOs, and magic" (p. 142). And since these latter kinds of things are improbable, the resurrection of Christ is much more so. This antecedent improbability of the resurrection makes it difficult if not impossible to argue for the truth of Christianity on the basis of such miracle claims. The point here is that the resurrection is so improbable that we cannot even make a convincing case that it happened, much less show that it was a divinely caused miracle.[3]

Craig, Habermas, and Feinberg, however, would deny the antecedent improbability of the resurrection. They would say, among other things, that Clark's position actually begs the question in favor of naturalism. Or, put another way, one can assign the resurrection a low level of antecedent probability only if one implicitly assumes that naturalism is true.

As I close this volume, I think it is worthwhile to reflect on one more area in which the authors agree. Despite the differences just enumerated, all will agree with Bill Craig's comment that in the book we "are seeing . . . a remarkable convergence of views, which is cause for rejoicing" (p. 317). When I first encountered the question of apologetic methodology almost two decades ago, the debate was often heated and the various approaches starkly polarized. There could not have been, for example, any two systems of thought that seemed more diametrically opposed to each other than classical apologetics and presuppositionalism.

I think this volume, however, represents a growing consensus that the various apologetic methods are not as polarized as they once seemed. At least some disagreements have been

---

[3]Let the reader keep in mind here that Kelly Clark does believe that the resurrection happened and that it was a divine miracle! He is simply expressing a skepticism about being able to prove these things in apologetic arguments.

found to be based on misunderstandings, divergent definitions of terms, and the like. In other cases, apologetic methodologists of various schools have been willing to concede views that they once would have opposed. For instance, presuppositionalists like John Frame allow that the traditional theistic proofs are useful and persuasive arguments (Gordon Clark must be turning over in his grave!). Also, Bill Craig has granted to evidentialists like Habermas that miracles can be defended without presupposing God's existence, contrary to many earlier and contemporary classical apologists. Moreover, Craig's knowing-showing distinction is designed to grant to the presuppositionalist (and Reformed epistemologist) that we can know God exists without rational argument, while still maintaining that positive apologetics (showing that we know God exists) requires such argument. It appears as well that Habermas and Feinberg would agree that one may be within his epistemic rights to believe in God apart from evidence in the form of philosophical arguments. Thus, it may very well be that the various apologetic methods are not nearly so far apart as we once thought.

Let me be quick to add that there are still substantial differences, as we have seen above. Furthermore, not every current practitioner of these methodologies would agree on the points made in the previous paragraph. Some classical apologists will no doubt strongly disagree with Craig's admission of the legitimacy of miracles-to-God arguments. Some of John Frame's colleagues will think that he has abandoned the presuppositional ship. And a few evidentialists may balk at Habermas's and Feinberg's appeal to the internal testimony of the Holy Spirit, who may work "even apart from evidences" (see Habermas, p. 97). Only time will tell whether this volume does represent a remarkable convergence of views or only the idiosyncrasies of these particular apologists.

ABOUT THE CONTRIBUTORS

Kelly James Clark, professor of philosophy at Calvin College, earned his doctorate at the University of Notre Dame, where he studied with Alvin Plantinga, the most prominent defender of Reformed epistemology. Dr. Clark is author of numerous books and articles in the philosophy of religion and epistemology, including *When Faith Is Not Enough, Philosophers Who Believe,* and *Return to Reason.*

Steven B. Cowan is pastor of Immanuel Baptist Church in Fayetteville, Arkansas, and an adjunct professor at Ouachita Baptist University and Midwestern Baptist Theological Seminary. He earned his Ph.D. in philosophy from the University of Arkansas. Dr. Cowan has published several articles in the areas of philosophy of religion and theology.

William Lane Craig earned a doctorate in philosophy at the University of Birmingham, England, before taking a doctorate in theology from the Ludwig Maximiliens Universität-München, Germany. He is currently a research professor of philosophy at Talbot School of Theology. He has authored over a dozen books, including *The* Kalam *Cosmological Argument; Theism, Atheism, and Big Bang Cosmology;* and *Assessing the New Testament Evidence for the Resurrection of Jesus,* as well as nearly a hundred articles in professional journals of philosophy and theology.

Paul D. Feinberg is professor of biblical and systematic theology at Trinity Evangelical Divinity School. He holds a Th.D. in systematic theology from Dallas Theological Seminary, and is a Ph.D. candidate in philosophy at the University of Chicago. Dr. Feinberg is coauthor (with Norman Geisler) of *Introduction to*

Philosophy: A Christian Perspective and (with John Feinberg) of *Ethics for a Brave New World,* and has published numerous articles in philosophy and theology.

John M. Frame earned an A.B. in philosophy from Princeton University, a B.D. from Westminster Theological Seminary, and an M.Phil. in philosophical theology from Yale University. He has taught at Westminster Theological Seminary in Philadelphia and is currently professor of apologetics and systematic theology at Westminster Theological Seminary in California. Mr. Frame is the author of *The Doctrine of the Knowledge of God* and *Apologetics to the Glory of God,* and other books on epistemology, apologetics, ethics, church unity, and worship, along with many articles and reviews.

Gary R. Habermas is distinguished professor and chair of the Department of Philosophy and Theology at Liberty University, besides serving as visiting or adjunct professor at eleven other seminaries and graduate schools over the last two years. He has authored or coauthored twenty-one books—including *The Historical Jesus, Did Jesus Rise from the Dead? The Resurrection Debate* (with Antony Flew), and *Beyond Death: Exploring the Evidence for Immortality* (with J. P. Moreland)—plus more than one hundred articles. Dr. Habermas received his Ph.D. from Michigan State University and a D.D. from Emmanuel College, Oxford, England.

SCRIPTURE INDEX

PERSON INDEX

SUBJECT INDEX

More Counterpoints:

The **Counterpoints** series provides a forum for comparison and critique of different views—both Christian and non-Christian—on important theological issues.

Find Counterpoints *at your favorite Christian bookstore*

ZondervanPublishingHouse
Grand Rapids, Michigan 49530
http://www.zondervan.com

We want to hear from you. Please send your comments about
this book to us in care of the address below. Thank you.

ZondervanPublishingHouse
Grand Rapids, Michigan 49530
http://www.zondervan.com